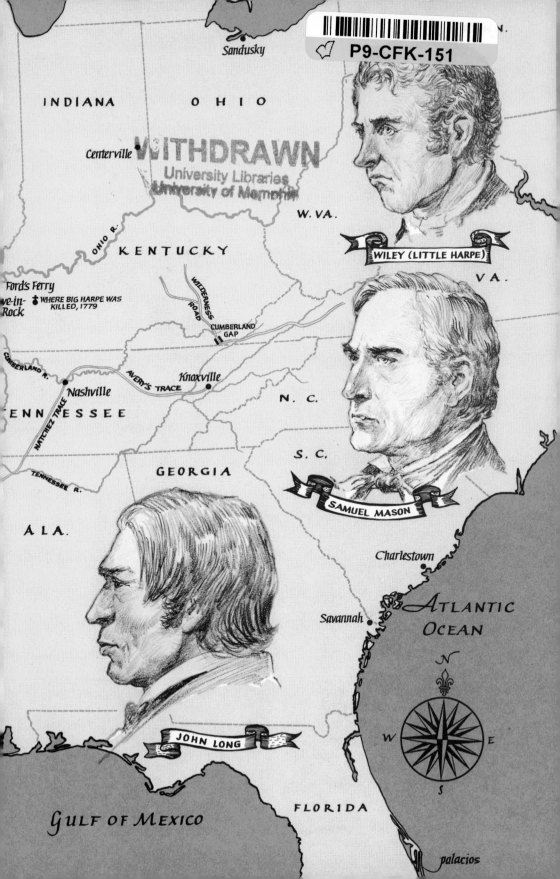

INDIANA

OHIO

Sandusky

Centerville

W. VA.

KENTUCKY

VA.

WILEY (LITTLE HARPE)

Ford's Ferry
ve-in-Rock
WHERE BIG HARPE WAS KILLED, 1779

OHIO R.

WILDERNESS ROAD

CUMBERLAND GAP

CUMBERLAND R.

AVERY'S TRACE

Knoxville

N. C.

Nashville

NATCHEZ TRACE

ENNESSEE

S. C.

SAMUEL MASON

TENNESSEE R.

GEORGIA

Charlestown

ALA.

ATLANTIC OCEAN

Savannah

N

JOHN LONG

W   E

S

FLORIDA

GULF OF MEXICO

palacios

SPAWN OF EVIL

PAUL I. WELLMAN

History

THE INDIAN WARS OF THE WEST
DEATH ON THE PRAIRIE
DEATH IN THE DESERT
THE TRAMPLING HERD
GLORY, GOD AND GOLD
A DYNASTY OF WESTERN OUTLAWS
SPAWN OF EVIL

Novels

BRONCHO APACHE
JUBAL TROOP
ANGEL WITH SPURS
THE BOWL OF BRASS
THE WALLS OF JERICHO
THE CHAIN
THE IRON MISTRESS
THE COMANCHEROS
THE FEMALE
JERICHO'S DAUGHTERS
RIDE THE RED EARTH
THE FIERY FLOWER
MAGNIFICENT DESTINY

Biography

STUART SYMINGTON

Reminiscence

PORTAGE BAY

For Younger Readers

GOLD IN CALIFORNIA
INDIAN WARS AND WARRIORS: EAST
INDIAN WARS AND WARRIORS: WEST
RACE TO THE GOLDEN SPIKE

SPAWN

OF

EVIL

The Invisible Empire of Soulless Men Which
For a Generation Held the Nation
In a Spell of Terror

PAUL I. WELLMAN

DRAWINGS BY LORENCE BJORKLUND

DOUBLEDAY & COMPANY, INC., GARDEN CITY, NEW YORK, 1964

To

MANLY WADE WELLMAN

whose writings have delighted countless readers,
and who, through a lifetime,
has been not only brother and friend to me,
but merriest of companions.

Contents

A Word to the Reader

A previous book of mine, *A Dynasty of Western Outlaws*, dealt with the succession of crime in the West, following the Civil War. This present work has to do with an earlier era, the notable outlaws and their histories and fate in the forested frontiers of the Mississippi and Ohio valleys, following the American Revolution and prior to the Civil War.

In every primitive society brutality is a frequent concomitant of crime, and those old frontiers were primitive in a way that far exceeded any condition of more recent date. Weapons were cruder. The long-barreled single-shot rifle, the tomahawk, and the hunting knife did the work later accomplished by the repeating rifle and the nimble six-shooter.

There were extremes of ignorance. In physical combat, without weapons, men gouged out each other's eyes, bit off ears or noses, broke bones or necks, and the onlookers made no interference, all this being accounted fair so long as neither fighter used a weapon.

Such was the background from which came the outlaws of the forest country. In many respects those malefactors were more evil and inhuman than the outlaws of the West. Jesse James, a "classic" bandit of the West, for example, might shoot and kill, in order to commit a robbery, save himself from capture, sometimes for revenge. But he spared women and children; and when he killed he did not horribly mangle the bodies of his victims as did the Harpes, Mason, Murrell and others of their ilk.

When the forest people at last managed to catch up with their outlaws after a reign of terror, it can perhaps be understood why the ends of those criminals were sometimes condign.

To the frontier, evil was evil. No tears were shed over a malefactor as a "victim of society." And so the people did not experience the depressing spectacle of sadistic sex murderers of little girls "rehabilitated" and released to commit further sex murders on little girls; of conscienceless killers pardoned for further conscienceless killings; of criminals of all types who *prefer* crime as a career, freed to continue their criminal activities. The frontier put a period to the depredations of such as these.

In the early part of the last century, and even later, a considerable literature existed concerning some of the criminal personages discussed in this book. Admittedly, however, in not a few cases documentary records of certain of their activities are so scanty that one must, where direct testimony fails, cite tradition.

But why not tradition? Those dreadful men assuredly lived, and wrought their terrible deeds. And the people knew of them and recounted them. They still in fact repeat those stories. John A. Murrell, for example, is today as frequently discussed and as much a part of the oral traditions of Arkansas as was, say, Robin Hood in Victorian England—though with less of romance accorded to him and far greater disapprobation.

Some traditions extant are remarkably correct when checked with known records. Others vary; but even those that cannot be checked give some account, based on the memory of the generations, of episodes which otherwise would be only gaps in the careers of those wild and ferocious men, providing also color and the peculiar flavor of the times.

In cases where written records do not agree, I have sought to arrive at the version which seems most logical and probable; and when I rely on tradition I have indicated it.

I must here acknowledge my debt of gratitude to my brother, Manly Wade Wellman, of Chapel Hill, North Carolina, who out of his good will and kindness, and his interest in and great knowledge of the era and territories involved—in which few can equal him—did for me many important researches.

My thanks also to Betty Wood Vedder, who assisted me in collating my research, and typed, proofread and saw the manuscript to completion with the interest and intelligence she has devoted to a dozen previous books of mine in which she has acted in the same invaluable capacity.

I must express my gratitude of Colonel Kenneth Croswell, U. S. Marine Corps (Ret.), and his wife Mrs. Daphne Croswell, who out of friendship and as a personal favor visited the Murrell country in Arkansas, where Colonel Croswell grew up as a boy, and there collected and brought me additional tales and traditions of the great outlaw to add to my already accumulated data.

Many others deserve well of me for their kindnesses in aiding me with valuable information. Among these I particularly wish to acknowledge my obligations to: W. M. Hackett, of Little Rock, Arkansas; Mrs. Margaret B. Hollinshead, of Nashville, Tennessee; Dr. Dan M. Robison, Tennessee State Librarian and Archivist; Dr. James W. Patton, Director of the Southern Historical Collection of the University of North Carolina; and the Library of the University of California at Los Angeles, which has unstintingly made available to me not only its own magnificent collections of printed and manuscript materials, but has furnished its facilities in obtaining rare books and journals from libraries and historical societies elsewhere. To all these my sincerest thanks.

PAUL I. WELLMAN
Los Angeles, California

I.   *The People of the Forest*

1.

The great enemy was the forest.

Seen from the top of some ridge it was like an almost limitless sea of treetops, stretching westward from the seaboard settlements for a thousand miles, its expanse broken only here and there by the course of some river wide and deep enough to cut a crooked gash through the foliage.

Monster brown trunks searched upward so thickly that in many places a man could scarcely pass between them; while the canopy of leaves high above was so dense that it shut out the sun, creating an everlasting green twilight below. Vines, underbrush and brambly growths interlaced and knitted those great columns; and to make the forest still more impassable, the ground was cumbered and criss-crossed by an enormous abatis of fallen trees in various stages of decay, and the rains or melted snows, trapped by humus and rotting leaves, formed swamps and morasses sometimes miles in extent.

One who sees the populous Middle States of America in this day, with all their cities, towns, industries, and farms, requires an effort of

imagination to picture that forest, the clearing of which in less than a
hundred years was one of the great human achievements of history.
But to those living on its verges it was very real: a haunted mystery,
dark as night and perilous.

Wild beasts and wild men ranged there. True, a few adventurers at
times entered the unknown, and *sometimes* came back: stark "long
hunters" chiefly, restless wanderers who disappeared for months, even
years at a time; free-lance rovers, gaunt with the everlasting struggle
to kill before they were killed.

Many were never again heard from. They died as a result of accidents, exposure, encounters with savage beasts or deadly reptiles, even
starvation. But most of those who did not come back fell in the attacks or ambuscades of the fiercely hostile Indians.

The best of those who adventured deep into the awesome forest
were honest men, like Dan Boone, who penetrated into the Kentucky
country as early as 1769, and survived all perils to blaze the first trail
across the mountains to the Blue Grass. But in that vast forest outlaws
also ran wild; men desperate and murderous; criminals by intent or
nature, who left the settlements conveniently ahead of vengeful justice, and struck upon the vein of savage life, enemies of all mankind.

Oppressive, threatening, dark and fearful was the forest.

2.

Land hunger possessed the people of the settlements on the Atlantic
seaboard. Trails were found into the wilderness: the Wilderness Road
pioneered by Boone; Zane's Trail into the Ohio country; Avery's Trail
into Tennessee, and others. Even before the American Revolution a
thin trickle of settlers—and by this is meant not mere adventurers but
families, including women and children—had begun to cross the mountains into the wilderness.

At best the trails were bridle paths, rough and dangerous. Women
and children clung to the backs of gaunt horses, their few scanty possessions on pack animals, guarded by rifle-toting men. Bridges were
non-existent, except for an occasional "raccoon bridge," consisting of a
tree which had fallen or was felled to lie across a stream, over which
a precarious way might be made.

A diary, kept by William Calk, who crossed the mountains by way
of Cumberland Gap, reveals the hardships and dangers of such a trek.
Without attempting to give dates of separate entries, a few excerpts
give the flavor of the whole:

. . . Snowed in the Eavening very hard and was very Coald . . .
wind Blowsz very hard and cold . . . a turable mountain that tired us
almost to death to git over it . . . Eanock Abram and I got lost
tuesday night and it a snowing and Should a lain in the mountains had
not I . . . fired guns and they heard them and caim in By the Report
. . . my hors got scard ran away threw Down the Saddel Bags and broke
open a walet of corn and lost a good Deal and made a turrabel flus-
tration amongst the Reast of the Horses . . . we loose Driver . . .
Comes a letter from Capt. Boone at caintuck of the indians doing mis-
chief and some turns back for fear of the indians but our Company goes
on . . . a Raney morning But we pack up and go on we come to Rich-
land Creek it is high we tote our packs over on a tree and swim our
horses over and there we meet another Companey going back . . .

So goes the diary, with its writer's inimitable spelling. The member
of the party named Driver, or a driver of the pack train (the journal
is not specific) who was lost—and for whom, presumably, a search was
made as in the case of Calk himself—is not again mentioned. Almost
certainly he died, perhaps at the hands of a lurking Indian.

Despite all discouragements and the desertion of some of its members this party "in number some 40 men and some neagros," eventually reached "Boon's foart" (Boonsborough, Kentucky).

No women were in this company. To take families required the
transportation of household goods, and for heavier burdens this meant
travel by water—the westward flowing rivers, natural but perilous
routes of travel. Another diary, that of Colonel Jack Donelson, gives a
vivid picture of the perilous adventures experienced by a flotilla of
flatboats and other craft, carrying families and household goods, which
floated down the Holston River, in eastern Tennessee, to the Tennessee, around the great bend of that river to the Ohio, and then by the
severe labor of rowing, up the Ohio to the Cumberland and again up
the Cumberland to their destination, the present site of Nashville,
Tennessee.

In the party when it started were one hundred and twenty women,
girls and children (another child was born on the trip) with forty men
to navigate the boats and guard them. The rest of the men of these
families had marched overland to prepare rude dwellings for their
arrival at the agreed destination. One of the passengers was a pretty,
flashing-eyed lass, Colonel Donelson's thirteen-year-old daughter, Ra-
chel, who one day would win a place in history as the wife of the
great Andrew Jackson.

The voyage began December 22, 1779. At first there were no serious
mishaps though it was bitter cold and the Holston River was full of
ice. We pick up the journal after five weeks of travel, when they were
on the Tennessee River late in February, 1780:

Sunday, the 27th Struck the Poor-valley . . . In much distress.

Monday, February 28th, 1780—got off the shoal after landing thirty persons to lighten our boat . . . lost sundry articles . . .

March 2nd—Rain and . . . Mr. Henry's boat being driven on a point of an island was sunk . . . Reuben Harrison went hunting and did not return.

They were by now in Cherokee country. Along the Tennessee River were villages of that hostile tribe: Chickamauga, Tuskegee, Running Water, Nickajack, Long Island, and Crow Town. Cherokee warriors were at that very time stealthily following the boats down the stream, and it must therefore be presumed that the unfortunate Reuben Harrison was killed by the Indians—the first casualty.

Tuesday 7th—Very windy . . . Smaller craft in danger . . . Wife of Ephraim Peyton delivered of a child.

Peyton, husband of the new mother, was one of the men who had gone ahead overland to make ready the beginnings of a home on the Cumberland. But though her husband was absent, the processes of life must go on, and the midwifery of sympathetic women on the boats helped Mrs. Peyton through her ordeal.

Almost at once—in fact the very next day after this birth—the party encountered its gravest danger, for the flotilla reached the stormy rapids of Muscle Shoals, which the awkward and unwieldy flatboats must attempt to run. In the midst of the difficult and dangerous navigation of the stream with its tossing waters, treacherous eddies, and sunken rocks, the party found it had to fight its way through Indian ambuscades, laid along this treacherous and perilous stretch of the river.

Wednesday 8th—Must regret the unfortunate death of young Mr. Payne [killed by an Indian] . . . and the more tragical misfortune of poor Stuart, his family and friends in the number of twenty-eight . . . Being diseased with small pox, it was agreed that he should keep [his boat] some distance to the rear; and he was warned each night when the encampment should take place by the sound of a hoarn. The Indians . . . killed and took prisoners the whole crew; their cries were distinctly heard.

Twenty-nine members of the company at one fell swoop! But in the massacre of the Stuart party, the Indians themselves may have suffered. By taking scalps from persons ill with smallpox, or carrying away prisoners infected with the disease, they perhaps introduced a deadly epidemic in their own village. At one time or another smallpox destroyed one-half of the entire Cherokee Nation.

The diary, as of the same date, March 8, continues:

We are now arrived at the Whirl or Suck [Muscle Shoals] . . .
John Cotton's . . . canoe was overturned and the little cargo lost . . .
the company concluded to assist him in recovering his property . . .
When the Indians . . . firing down . . . occasioned a precipitate retreat to the boats . . . We have now passed through the Whirl . . .
except the family of Jonathan Jennings, whose boat ran on a large rock
. . . where we were compelled to leave them [being carried out of
reach by the current] perhaps to be slaughtered.

The Jennings party was at once assailed by the Indians. On this
boat was Mrs. Peyton with her day-old babe. The boat crew defended
the stranded craft with their rifles, but in the hot little battle that ensued, Mrs. Peyton's tiny child was the first to be killed. Two of the
men, who landed to try to get the craft off the rocks, were captured,
and without question put to death. Another was drowned. The survivors managed to beat off their foes, save their boat, and eventually
rejoin the fleet.

There were further dangers and more brushes with the Indians.
Not until April 24, four months after the perilous cruise began, and
with thirty-four of its number lost on the way, did the company reach
its destination, "a few log Cabbins on a Cedar Bluff," near where
present-day Nashville stands.

3.

The social and economic dislocations caused by the Revolution
and its aftermath spurred migration. Settlements crude and extremely
primitive sprang up. The people of the forest who had come to this
new country after such adversities did not often return to civilization.
Cut off from the East by mountains and wilderness, it was not strange
that they grew to be almost a race apart. Seymour Dunbar gave one
of the best descriptions of them:

Their faces, brown from exposure to the elements, were singularly
set in expression and carried a sort of grimness. Nothing surprised them.
The happening of every event was discounted in advance. Its coming
was calmly awaited, and whatever action it demanded from them was
performed so quickly that it seemed rather to be by instinct than as the
result of thought or reason. Their eyes were the distinguishing feature
of their countenances. Clear, inscrutable and direct, the vision of man
or woman saw everything . . . and a single glance had the gathering
power of a fisherman's net and the analysis of a microscope . . . Somewhat above the average height, as men and women go, they were lean
and supple . . . Much walking and incessant labor had given them

great endurance. The strength of their rough hands could break bones.
Those who were weak died early, and many of the rest lived [only]
until they were killed in one way or another. They walked with a soft
and swinging stride, keeping themselves always well poised, for no man
ever knew whether his next move would be a leap to the right or to the
left, a dive behind a log, a dash ahead or a rush backward over the
path he had come . . . They were a nervous people in a certain sense,
yet they held themselves in such a grip that they seemed almost phleg-
matic. Nerves—or at least any indulgence in the state of mental excita-
bility which has become a modern disease—were not in harmony with
the surroundings. When a man or woman aimed a rifle the body that
upheld it was like a carved figure. And after the smoke floated away
there was no exultation to be seen; only the same outward calmness.[1]

Death—violent death—was an everyday occurrence, and accepted
as such, especially in the early days when the Indians were bad. W. H.
Bogart cited a striking illustration of this strangely fatalistic frame of
mind and its effect on the sensibilities of the people of the early
settlements:

An old lady who had been in the forts [in Kentucky] was describing
to Dr. Brown the scenes she had witnessed in those times of peril and
adventure; and, among other things, remarked that during the first
two years of her residence in Kentucky, the most comely sight she beheld, was seeing a young man dying in his bed a natural death. She had
been familiar with blood, and carnage and death, but in all these cases
the sufferers were the victims of the Indian tomahawk and scalping
knife; and that on an occasion when a young man was taken sick and
died, after the usual manner of nature, she said that the rest of the
women sat up all night, gazing upon him as an object of beauty.[2]

There were no schools. A boy did not read, but he learned the skills
of the frontier: how to use the axe, froe, hoe and plow; how to fight
Indians and hunt; alertness and self-reliance. At the age of twelve or
fourteen his father handed him a rifle of his own—and with that act he
was invested with the status of manhood, doing a man's work, taking
a man's responsibilities, and being assigned "his particular loophole to
defend."

Before she reached her teens a girl was mistress of the primitive
arts of a housewife: cooking, spinning and weaving, preserving meats
and fruits, sewing, caring for a family. Frequently a youth fifteen or
sixteen years old married a girl thirteen or fourteen, and such was
their training that they were fully capable in that simple society of

[1] From *A History of Travel in America*, by Seymour Dunbar, copyright 1915,
1943 by the Bobbs-Merrill Company, Inc., reprinted by special permission of the
publishers.

[2] W. H. Bogart, *Daniel Boone and the Hunters of Kentucky*.

setting up housekeeping, rearing a family and living in complete independence.

The settlers were unlettered and incredibly naïve. One man, asked
what he thought of the tariff, said "he had never seen one but believed it was bad for sheep." A candidate for Congress on the frontier
was defeated because in a campaign speech he mentioned the railroad, then being experimented on in England, and predicted that
"some day the cars will carry passengers at thirty miles an hour." His
auditors voted against him on the ground that either he was crazy, or
considered them fools, the consensus of opinion being that "a man
couldn't live a minute at such speed."

Communication was slow, sporadic, and often dangerous. Senator
Oliver H. Smith, a circuit lawyer in the early years, wrote in his
memoirs of the frontier:

> There was not a foot of turnpike road . . . plank roads had never
> been heard of; the girdled standing trees covered the cultivated fields;
> not a bridge . . . and traveling all done on horseback, the husband
> mounted before on the saddle, with from one to three of the youngest
> children in his arms—the wife, with a spread cover reaching the tail of
> the horse, sitting behind, with the balance of the children . . . in her
> lap; not a carriage or buggy in all the country.

All open lands, both north and south of the Ohio River, were soon
taken up, and those who thereafter wanted land must wrest it from
the forest. This entailed enormous labor, since trees had to be felled
by hand.

The most frequent practice was to "girdle" trees in a given patch
by cutting away the bark in a ring about the trunk, causing the tree to
die, so that some sunlight fell through its bare branches to the soil
below, which was planted.

But eventually trees, even if dead, must be cut down. Since there
was no way to remove the vast trunks—sometimes eight or ten feet in
diameter—they had to be burned where they lay before the ground
could be tilled. A constant haze of smoke in the air and a smell of
burning wood were characteristic of all new forest settlements.

It took a year or two to clear even a small patch. But meantime a
cabin was raised, rough furniture built, a stake-and-rider fence
erected, and life could begin.

4.

The forest people were hardy, reasonably truthful and honest, but
rough; and sometimes, especially when they were "in licker," they
were inclined to be violent. Fights were common, and singularly brutal

combats, called "rough and tumble," in which no rules obtained, were
a vogue of the times. Some modern writers find it hard to believe that
these frontier man-to-man combats were so ferocious, and had ventured the opinion that the ferocity has been exaggerated by legend.
But consider this law—and there were others similar to it in Virginia,
Indiana, Kentucky and elsewhere—which was promulgated in the
Northwest (Ohio) Territory in May, 1798, which reads in part as follows:

> Whosoever . . . shall voluntarily, maliciously, and on purpose, pull
> out or put out an eye while fighting or otherwise . . . shall be sen-
> tenced to undergo confinement in jail . . . and shall also pay a fine of
> not less than fifty dollars and not exceeding one thousand dollars, one
> fourth of which shall be for the use of the Territory, and three fourths
> . . . to the use of the party grieved, and for want of means of pay-
> ment, the offender shall be sold into service by the court . . . for any
> time not exceeding five years, the purchaser finding him food and rai-
> ment during the term.

The phraseology refers to the ugly frontier practice in fighting of
gouging out a human eye with a thumb, and the actual existence of
such a law removes that practice from the realm of legend; while the
severity of the penalty—the only instance I can find in frontier laws
where a white man could be sold into slavery—indicates the gravity
with which the matter was regarded.

In such a fight the object was to disable the opponent, no matter
how. Blows were struck, but this was no boxing match. The antagonists circled, hands ready to clutch and bear down the adversary.
Kicking in the crotch, groin, or belly, throttling, biting off of ears or
noses, breaking of backs or limbs, tearing out corners of mouths, and
eye gouging were all reckoned permissible.

We have eyewitness accounts of such brutalities. One, in the diary
of Major Eluries Beatty, who was in Louisville, Kentucky, in 1791,
describes one as follows:

> Saw the barbarous custom of gouging practiced between two of the
> lower class of people here; their unvaried way of fighting. When two
> men quarrel they never have any idea of striking, but immediately
> seize each other, and fall and twist each other, [thrusting] thumbs or
> fingers into the eye and push it from the socket until it falls on the
> cheeks, as one of those men experienced today, and was obliged to
> acknowledge himself beat, although he was on top of the other—but he,
> in his turn, had bit his adversary most abominably . . . It chilled my
> blood with horror to see this unmanly, cruel condition these two men
> were left in today from this manner of fighting, and no person, although
> a number stood by, ever attempted to prevent them from thus butch-

ering each other, but all was acknowledged fair play . . . One of these
. . . gougers, a perfect bully; all the country round stood in awe of
him, for he was so dextrous in these matters that he had, in his time,
taken out five eyes, bit off two or three noses and ears and spit them in
their faces.[3]

Fortunately, all quarrels did not reach the stage described in Major Beatty's diary. There have always been blusterers. One man,
charged with assault and battery, illumined a primitive court record
with the following statement:

"I told him he lied; he told me I lied. I spit in his face; he spit in
my face. I slapped him in the face; he slapped me in the face. I
kicked him; he kicked me. I tripped him up; he tripped me up. I
struck him and knocked him down; he got up and knocked me down.
I then got mad; he got mad. And we was just a-going to fight when
the saloon keeper got betwixt us."

In this case the squire[4] fined defendant and plaintiff one dollar
each, which under the circumstances seems fair.

Most of the forest people were fairly honest, but rascals always exist in any community, and there was some thievery. At first this was
confined to articles rather than cash. "Actual money was a thing of
fable . . . If any man by some strange chance came into possession of
those curious pieces of copper or silver, he hastened to swap them for
something of practical use."[5]

But in the absence of cash other forms of larceny were sometimes
practiced, the most serious being horse stealing. Horses were valuable
and could be transported easily, and primitive jurisprudence was especially severe against this form of crime. A usual penalty upon conviction was thirty-nine lashes on the bare back, given with a cowhide
whip that cut the skin to shreds. Sometimes imprisonment was added
(although frontier jails were too porous to hold for long any really
serious minded jailbreaker), or there might be a fine up to one thousand dollars, and branding with a "T" or an "HT" (Thief or Horse
Thief) with a red-hot iron on the ball of the thumb, or the back of the
hand, occasionally even on the forehead.

Sometimes cases were handled quite directly. Such an instance occurred in a court presided over by Judge Marston G. Clark, a cousin
of George Rogers Clark, a quaint figure "about six feet in his stock-

[3] Connelly and Coulter, *History of Kentucky.*

[4] On the frontier a justice of the peace was commonly called "Squire," as is still
the custom in some localities in the eastern states today.

[5] Seymour Dunbar, *A History of Travel in America.*

ings, of a very muscular appearance: wore a hunting shirt, leather
pants, moccasins and a fox-skin cap, with a long queue down his
back." The defendant before this magistrate was charged with horse
theft and employed a slick frontier lawyer, who interposed several
trivial objections:

Objection No. 1: The defendant was not properly named, his middle initial being omitted.

Judge Clark's ruling: "That makes no difference. I know the man
and that is sufficient."

Objection No. 2: No value was put on the horse in the indictment.

Ruling: "I know an Indian pony is worth ten dollars."

Objection No. 3: It was charged in the indictment that the animal
was a horse, when he was a gelding.

Ruling: "I consider a gelding a horse. Motion overruled."

The trial proceeded, the malefactor was found guilty and sentenced
to receive the customary thirty-nine lashes. At this the lawyer offered
still another objection:

"We move arrest of judgment, on the ground that it is not stated
in the indictment that the horse was stolen within the jurisdiction of
this court."

Judge Clark pondered this. At last he said, "That, I consider a more
serious objection. The court will take it under advisement until morning."

When he adjourned court, the judge held a brief conference with
the sheriff. At midnight the horse thief was taken from the jail, led far
out into the woods where his howls could not be heard, tied to a tree,
and given thirty-nine fearful lashes on his bare back. The following
morning Judge Clark directed the sheriff to bring the culprit once
more before the bench.

"I have considered your counsel's objection of yesterday," he said
with poker-faced gravity, "and have come to the conclusion that you
deserve a new trial. A second indictment will therefore be drawn and
you will be tried for a second time."

"No, your honor!" screamed the prisoner, leaping frantically to his
feet. "No, for heaven's sake! I don't want a new trial! I discharge my
lawyer and withdraw the motion!"

5.

After the Indians were suppressed, killed, or driven out, the people
began to produce surpluses—stone-ground flour, corn, livestock, hemp,
flax, tobacco, cured meats, furs, leather, and whiskey. A market for
these must be found, but to transport produce back to the East over

mountain trails and through forests was too costly and difficult to be practical.

There were, however, rivers flowing westward. The Wabash, Cumberland, Kentucky, Tennessee, and other streams emptied into the Ohio, which in turn flowed into the Mississippi, which took its course southward. And southward lay Natchez and New Orleans, ready to buy the produce of the interior for real money.

From 1787 on, a brisk river traffic began. It required from March to July or August for a crew with a boat-load of merchandise to reach the lower Mississippi markets, and strangely varied craft were employed in the long floating trip: huge and unwieldy arks, flatboats sometimes as much as sixty feet long, broadhorns named from the two big sweeps that projected like horns from each side, barges and even pirogues which were nothing but large canoes hollowed out of logs.

And with these sprang up a separate class on the frontier: the professional boatmen. Again we have Dunbar's description of a specimen:

> He was of the restless type that in every period of American development has done the unusual and dangerous thing just for the love of doing it; who has never been satisfied unless each new day brought some unexpected event; who was only happy when he could always keep moving. He was an epicure of excitement. Work no other man could do was his one luxury. In physical make-up the typical boatman was tall, thin and sinewy. His immobile face was tanned to a dark brown, and from above high cheekbones and a long nose two dull gray eyes gazed blankly. In his normal state he was silently waiting for something to happen, knowing quite well it certainly would. When the bomb of circumstance exploded, the human creature was on that dot of time transformed into a combination of rubber ball, wildcat and shrieking maniac, all controlled by instantaneous perception and exact calculation. After the tumult he subsided again into his listless lethargy of waiting, the monotony being endured by chewing tobacco and the marvelous accuracy with which he could propel a stream of its juice for any distance up to fifteen feet.
>
> The costume he wore was as picturesque as his personality and in essential features was so widely adopted as to be almost a uniform. It consisted of a bright red flannel shirt covered by a loose blue coat—called a jerkin—that reached only to his hips, and coarse brown trousers of linsey-woolsey. His head covering was a cap of untanned skin, often with the fur side out; the universal moccasins clad his feet, and from a leather belt hung his hunting knife and tobacco pouch. Still a third distinguishing feature of the professional flatboatman was his iridescent vocabulary.[6]

[6] From *A History of Travel in America,* by Seymour Dunbar, copyright 1915, 1943 by the Bobbs Merrill Company, Inc., reprinted by special permission of the publishers.

These men were all rough-and-tumble fighters, and they produced champions who wore a red feather as proof of their prowess, and ruffled it aboard the boat or in the streets of the settlements, daring anyone to challenge them.

They had to be skilled river men, for there were many perils they had to watch for and avoid. "Sawyers" were sunken trees in the river, lifting one end treacherously at brief periods to the surface under the influence of the current, to rip the bottom out of a boat. "Planters" were logs so solidly fixed in the bottom that they never moved, yet protruding an end at the surface like a spear waiting for an unwary victim. Whirlpools, submerged rocks and bars, and narrow, treacherous channels each offered separate dangers. Last, but not least, were the river pirates.

For the river traffic introduced a new era into the frontier, by converting goods into money, real money, to which the frontier very soon became acquainted and prized for its values. One frontiersman remarked, "a little circle of silver in the palm outweighs the hindquarters of a fat buck."

With the incentive of cash—and with it greed—came a new kind of crime.

A society so rough, so accustomed to all kinds of danger, might seem difficult to shock. But the deviltry introduced by the river pirates was different, a deviltry so vicious, cruel and bloodthirsty, that it eclipsed all other forms of terror and appalled even the callous frontiersmen.

II. *The Beginning of the Terror*

1.

In the fall of the year 1797 the body of a young man named Moses
Doss was found near a trail leading to the Cherokee Indian town of
Nickajack, in eastern Tennessee. He had been murdered and fright-
fully mutilated.

The Cherokees at the time were hostile to the white settlers, but
this murder, which in some respects surpassed the ferocity of the savages, was not committed by Indians. Moses Doss was killed and
mangled by a white man—a white man who was supposed to be his
friend.

The murderer's name was Micajah Harpe, and the motive appears
to have been jealousy. This might account for the way in which the
victim's body was mutilated; but it is impossible not to presuppose also
a dreadful and ghoulish insanity which made more fiendish the perpe-
tration of the horror.

Such a supposition is reasonable. The ghastly record of the two
Harpes, Micajah and Wiley, almost certainly indicates that at least
one of them was a homicidal maniac, and that both were of the most

bestial type. And if the Doss murder actually did have a motive, it is a rarity in the long series of barbarous butcheries that were to succeed it. A horrible blood lust seemed to actuate these two human fiends who were destined to leave a trail of death and terror, of which the Doss slaying was only the first act.

Who were the Harpes? A strange, baffling mystery surrounds them.

Not even the descriptions of them agree. For example, one description of Micajah—commonly called Big Harpe—says he had red hair, whereas he appears in fact to have had dark curly hair. Wiley—known as Little Harpe—was described as dark-haired, whereas he very certainly had red hair.

But allowing for such discrepancies we do have a picture of the two, so horrific as to arrest the imagination.

Big Harpe was "above the ordinary stature of man. His frame was bony and muscular, his breast broad, his limbs gigantic. His clothing was uncouth and shabby, his exterior weatherbeaten and dirty, indicating continual exposure to the elements."

He had a physical peculiarity: his head was "larger than ordinary," and his face had "a kind of ferocity that made it exceedingly repulsive." On that huge head he wore no covering most of the time and his thick coarse hair, uncombed and almost kinky, "gave evidence of long exposure to the rudest visitations of the sunbeam and the tempest." To complete the picture, the man's complexion was strangely unhealthy, with "a livid unnatural redness, resembling that of a dried and lifeless skin."

Little Harpe was as repellent as the other. His hair was "fox-red," and he "bore a hang-dog look of cunning and treachery." Somewhat smaller than Big Harpe, he was nevertheless capable of extraordinary activity; and though he often seemed to take a secondary place in some of the bloody scenes in which they participated, he was probably the more scheming and cunning of the two.

Both outlaws were armed—almost invariably armed—with rifle, knife, and tomahawk, the weapons of the frontier. And they knew the forest and mountain trails as few on the frontier knew them, from having long lived, hunted, and raided with the Cherokee Indians.

Where were they from, and who were their ancestors? Again there is mystery.

Usually they were regarded as brothers, and this the evidence seems to indicate they were; yet one early writer[1] asserted they were cousins, their fathers being two brothers who emigrated from Scotland to North Carolina, probably soon after the disastrous Highland uprising of 1745,

---

[1] T. Marshall Smith, *Legends of the War of Independence.*

with the resulting reign of terror created by "Butcher Cumberland" and his hangmen.

It is a commentary on the dogged Scottish loyalty to their sovereign, that those very Highlanders many of them stout supporters of the English ruler, who were driven from their homes under circumstances of injustice and frequent cruelty, remained among the strongest supporters of the British king during the American Revolution.

The two Harpes, like many others of their blood, were Tory in sympathy during the latter conflict. But their wild, lawless ferocity so set them apart, and their depredations created such hatreds that they had to flee from North Carolina. Seeking shelter among the Cherokee Indians who sided with the British during the war, they became the most notorious and dreaded outlaws of their time.

2.

To return to Moses Doss and his murder: the Harpes had two women at the time he was killed, with whom they were living and cohabiting. Micajah claimed both of them as his: but the evidence shows that he shared their favors with his brother Wiley.

Generally the two feminine consorts of the Harpes are spoken of as Betsey and Susan Roberts, sisters, brought from North Carolina. At the time of the Doss killing, Micajah was about twenty-six years old, his brother Wiley two years younger. Susan and Betsey were, at the best guess, twenty and eighteen years old respectively—mere girls but already accustomed to the brutal rigors of outlaw life.

They may have come with the Harpes willingly; or they may have been kidnaped. One source gives a circumstantial account of their abductions, naming Big Harpe and Moses Doss, aided by two Cherokee Indians, Antoka and Ochetta, as their captors. This story asserts that the girls were unwilling victims, but were forced "to endure the lustful dalliance of their bestial tormentors." The account is fanciful, not even naming the girls as Roberts, although giving their first names correctly, yet the author claims to have obtained their stories from the women themselves.[2]

I think this version is dubious, in view of the subsequent behavior of the women. But willing or no, if there was more than one "bestial tormentor," as is suggested, Moses Doss was not one of them.

It was for the very reason that Doss became interested in one or both of the girls—perhaps wishing to take his turn in enjoying their

[2] T. Marshall Smith, *Legends of the War of Independence.*

favors—that Big Harpe slew him. Strangely, Big Harpe's jealousy, exhibited toward Doss in this violent and bloody form, did not extend to Little Harpe. It is evident that the two outlaws took their pleasure with the girls interchangeably, as their whims dictated, without any resentment toward one another. In their curious subhuman minds was at least this one redeeming quality: they were loyal to each other, if to no other person in all the world.

The killing of Doss occurred a short time before "some Tennesseeans and Kentuckians under the command of Capt. A. Jackson, later President of the United States" attacked Nickajack, sacked the Cherokee town, and killed or put to flight its inhabitants in retaliation for Indian attacks on Nashville, and elsewhere. Since Nickajack was destroyed in December, 1794, we have that date as a sort of peg in this confused chronology.

The Harpes were not present at the village when it was attacked. T. Marshall Smith indicates that in some manner they learned of the coming of Andrew Jackson and his riflemen. They did not trouble to inform their hosts, the Cherokees, but stole off with their women and four Indians, and hid in a canebrake nine or ten miles away on the night that Jackson launched his thunderbolt attack on Nickajack.

When the border captain marched away with his men, having burned the village, the Harpes with their women and their Indian friends traveled by devious routes to a hiding place in the Cumberland Mountains, a place they were to use as a covert more than once. This hidden lair is described as "in western Virginia, near the Cumberland Gap."[3] That would place it in the extreme southwest part of Virginia, in the present Lee County, near where the Tennessee and Kentucky lines meet on the Virginia border. There the little band remained for almost two years, hunting, and varying the monotony of life with a little horse stealing from frontier settlements, abetted by their renegade Indian associates.

It was while they were in this lonely and squalid camp that one of the girls, Susan, the elder of the sisters, gave birth to a child. What was its name and sex we do not know, and it must have died soon, for there were no children with the party when, in the spring of 1797, they suddenly reappeared in Tennessee.

[3] Otto A. Rothert, *The Outlaws of Cave-in-Rock*.

3.

Until this time their names were unknown and their depredations had never been traced to them. The frontier in fact was quite unaware of the menace hanging over it. There soon was a fearful awakening.

The first man to see the Harpes—and identify them—was a minister "of the Wesleyan (Methodist) persuasion," named William Lambuth. He was young—twenty-three years old—and slight—five feet five inches and one hundred and nine pounds—but he was filled with evangelistic ambition and fervor. Youthful as he was, he had been sent from Baltimore by Rev. William McKendree, then the Methodist presiding elder of all the West, across the mountains to form a preaching circuit among the settlements in middle Tennessee and the Green River country of Kentucky.

The year was in the spring—April, 1797—and the leaves on the trees were just beginning to come freshly out. Along the trail the young minister jogged his horse, perhaps going over the points of his next sermon. Somewhere between the infant towns of Nashville and Knoxville, he suddenly was aroused from his abstraction, by a loud order to halt.

Two men, "white, but very black and ragged in attire and ferocious in countenance," and both armed with rifles, had stepped out on the path ahead of him. Behind them, Lambuth noted, stood two draggle-tail women, their garments rags or skins, their hair tangled and disarrayed, their faces dirty and sunburned and lacking any expression.

"Git down!" came the fierce order from the larger man. A menacing motion of a rifle reinforced the command. The young minister could only obey.

As the robbers advanced toward him every movement they made was so menacing and savage that he was thoroughly frightened. First they took possession of his horse and his small purse of money. What they might next have done can be easily conjectured—in view of their later incredibly ferocious acts—had it not been for a curious little diversion.

In the bosom of Lambuth's coat, as they searched him, the outlaws found a small Bible. Quickly the bigger villain of the two riffled through its pages—looking for paper bank notes which very commonly were carried hidden in such a place. No money was found, but on the flyleaf the robber saw written the name *William Lambuth*, and below it, *George Washington*.

Lambuth remarked later that the man must have had some schooling, for he could read the names; and also that he was of Scottish blood, for he "spoke with a broad Scotch accent." The second of the two names on the flyleaf seemed to interest the fellow most.

"Is that the general?" he presently asked.

"Yes," said Lambuth.

"Did ye ever see him?"

"Once, in Richmond."

The great, scowling villain looked again at the name. Then he snapped the Bible shut and made a strange statement: "That is a brave and good man, but a mighty rebel against the king."

It was Micajah Harpe who spoke; and by his words and accent he revealed both his Scottish and Tory backgrounds. Nevertheless, the name of George Washington seemed to impress him.

"Ye're a preacher?" he asked.

"I am," said Lambuth.

"Have ye ever traveled this country before?"

"No," replied the minister.

"Ye'll be needin' your horse to travel here," said the outlaw. Then, after a brief conference with his brother, he returned the horse, Bible, and even the money to Lambuth.

With that, herding their women like livestock before them, the wild men disappeared in the dense forest. As they reached the limit of his sight, one of them turned to Lambuth with a shout:

"We are the Harpes!"

In later years, after he learned the species of savage inhuman beasts he had that day encountered, the Rev. Mr. Lambuth was wont to use this episode in his sermons as arguing "the special protecting providence of God over his servants." He compared it, indeed, with the miraculous closing of the mouths of the lions which preserved Daniel when he was thrown into their den.

The comparison did not lack aptness. The episode is the only instance on record when the Harpes had a helpless individual in their power, in which they showed the slightest mercy toward him. From that day, every other person, regardless of age or sex, whom they met alone, was ruthlessly and brutally murdered. Between Daniel's lions and Lambuth's Harpes it is probable that the former were less pitiless, bloodthirsty, and bestial than the latter.

4.

We are the Harpes!
That wild yell, uttered for the first time, was to be their warwhoop,

a cry so sinister and terrifying that it had the power to rout armed men when the dreadful nature of the two human hyenas became generally known.

For the present, however, the name still lacked significance. It had as yet no long list of causeless crimes to lend it terror.

After the Lambuth encounter the two outlaws and their women traveled slowly eastward and presently arrived in the vicinity of the new town, Knoxville, Tennessee.

Knoxville, in 1797, was "just a pup" as the saying was. Within very recent memory it had been Fort White, a trading post on the Tennessee River, four miles or so downstream from the confluence of the Holston and French Broad rivers which flowing together created the larger watercourse. James Weir, who passed through it in 1798, was shocked by its cheerful lack of piety, as he disclosed in his diary:

> In the infant town of Knox the houses are irregular and interspersed. It was County Court day when I came. I saw men jesting, singing, swearing; women yelling from doorways; half naked Negroes playing on their "banjoes," while the crowd whooped and danced about them. Whiskey and peach brandy were cheap. The town was confused with a promiscuous throng of every denomination—blanket-clad Indians, leather-shirted woodsmen, gamblers, hard-eyed and vigilant. I stood aghast, my soul shrank back to hear the horrid oaths and the dreadful indignities offered to the Supreme Governor of the Universe . . . There was what I never did see before, viz., on Sunday, dancing, singing, and playing of cards, etc. . . . It was said by a gentleman of the neighborhood that "the Devil is grown so old that it renders him incapable of traveling and that he has taken up in Knoxville and there hopes to spend the remaining part of his days . . . as he believes he is among friends."[4]

In such a community the Harpes, in spite of their rude appearance and actions, passed almost unnoticed at first. And for the only time in their lives they seem to have made some shift to appear as honest citizens. About eight miles from the hamlet, on Beaver Creek, they found a small clearing. In it they put up a log cabin, and a pen for horses; and they even made some pretense at cultivation.

It was at this time that the fifth member of the band was added—a girl named Sally Rice, daughter of John Rice a backwoods preacher living about four miles north of the Harpe place. Wiley Harpe courted her almost formally, and presently bore her off to join the two Roberts sisters in the log hut on Beaver Creek. One would assume that Little Harpe and Sally went through some sort of marriage ceremony before

[4] *Tennessee, a Guide to the Volunteer State.*

her ministerial father, but there is no record of this. In any case, marriage, legal or otherwise, meant nothing to the Harpes.[5]

Before Sally Rice was introduced to the outlaw circle, the Roberts sisters, Susan and Betsey, were taken to bed by either of the wild brothers, as the whim moved them. When Sally joined the other two, she very quickly became like them, completely subservient; almost, it seems, living in a sort of trance or hypnotic state, so that she never dreamed of disobeying the Harpes. She was simply added to the "pool" of womenkind, and since she was the youngest and prettiest of the three, she no doubt underwent more than her share of the "lustful dalliances" of her two masters.

The role of "honest citizens" could not long be maintained by the Harpes. Every market day they went to Knoxville, often taking horses to sell, or pork and mutton, ready butchered, for disposal. With the money they made from these transactions, they frequently got drunk and sometimes engaged in fights; and what they did not spend on liquor they gambled away.

In one of those town fights Wiley Harpe was slashed on the chest by a man named John Bowman. It was not a serious wound—a trivial cut, really, which quickly healed and which Little Harpe soon forgot. But the scar it left was destined to play a decisive part in his final doom.

As already mentioned the Harpes sometimes sold pork or mutton in Knoxville; also horses. When neighbors in the Beaver Creek district began to complain that they were missing hogs and sheep, suspicion turned on the Harpes, whose shiftlessness was so evident that their possession of animals the meat of which they took to market seemed difficult to explain.

John Miller, a Knoxville merchant, who had bought meat from the Harpes, became convinced that they were hog thieves, and said so, and further "suspected that their dishonesty and meanness had no limit." Others shared this opinion of the outlandish pair.

One night, shortly after, arsonists set fire to some houses and stables near Knoxville. The destruction appeared wanton, and no motive could be ascribed for it, so it was "attributed to downright rascality."

It is probable that the Harpes were guilty of this crime. Some of those whose property was thus destroyed, including John Miller, had spoken too openly of their suspicions, so that this could be an act of

---

[5] With regard to their married state, it is to be noted that later on, when the Harpes were tried for one of their murders, the three women—and it must have been on their own statements—were designated as "spinsters" (unmarried), though two of them gave their surnames as Harpe.

retribution. Yet it is also quite in keeping with their reckless and irresponsible characters that they deliberately set the buildings aflame as a malignant sport.

Their final act was a piece of horse larceny too close to home. Stolen animals had frequently been sold in Knoxville by the Harpes, one of them later identified as having come from as far away as Georgia. The outlaw brothers are believed to have worked with renegade Cherokee Indians—perhaps the very four with whom they conspired at the Nickajack village. Thus far, however, no inquiry had been made, since the horses all came from distant places and owners had not appeared to identify and claim them.

But one day Edward Tiel, a farmer living near Knoxville, appeared in the town and reported that he had "lost several of his best horses." Tiel, moreover, had ideas concerning who might be the horse thieves. With a hastily gathered posse of his friends, he rode straight to the Harpe cabin on Beaver Creek.

The place was empty—completely deserted. Evidently the Harpes had been, in some manner, forewarned. But it was also evident that horses had recently been tied to trees about the cabin, and held in the log pen: not one or two, but several.

At once Tiel and his posse discovered a trail—a child could have followed it, for there was no attempt to conceal it—and rode in pursuit. They crossed the Clinch River, and followed the track up toward the Cumberland Mountains.

Suddenly they saw the Harpes, driving Tiel's stolen animals before them up one of the mountain trails.

The thieves made no effort to resist or escape when the posse galloped up and surrounded them. They stared rather blankly at their captors, and surrendered almost meekly, hardly seeming to realize the gravity of their situation.

It was as if an odd dementia affected them. Insanity takes many forms. One form is characterized by a persecution complex which the Harpes were to display frequently. This type is at times excited, at other times emotionless to the extent almost of stupor. When its tendency is homicidal it is extremely dangerous. Again and again in the future the Harpes were to show, as on this occasion, symptoms of dull stupidity—followed by periods of frightful and murderous activity.

With their prisoners and the stolen horses the Tiel party turned back toward Knoxville. But now the apathy which seemed to affect the Harpes departed. They, of course, knew the heavy penalty for horse theft—thirty-nine lashes with a cowhide whip on the bare back, and possible branding and imprisonment also.

Those thirty-nine lashes were never endured by the brothers. So willingly did they seem to go along with their captors that Tiel and the others grew careless in watching them.

The party had returned to within a few miles of Knoxville when suddenly the Harpes, cunning as wild beasts, saw their chance. Without any apparent signal or communication between themselves, they both burst away, and together leaped into the thickest part of the forest.

So quickly did they dive into covert that there was not time to send even one shot winging after them. There was no following them in the tangle: they could lose any pursuer in that wilderness. No horse could be forced through the heavy growth, and on foot not a man in Tiel's party could have come near overtaking, much less finding and overpowering the outlaws. Cursing their own lack of alertness the members of the posse returned to Knoxville without the prisoners, though with the stolen horses.

5.

The Harpes were on the loose again, but at that time they had not yet built up the dreadful reputation as wanton murderers that later made them so notorious. There probably was a feeling of "good riddance" in Knoxville; and it was the common belief that with such a scare the outlandish brothers would not soon dare show themselves in the vicinity. The supposition was wrong. It was impossible then, or later, ever to predict the erratic movements of the outlaws; and the Harpes had some unfinished business in the neighborhood.

On the bank of the Holston River, five or six miles above Knoxville, stood a tavern operated by a man named Hughes and his wife. Robert M. Coates, in his fine book *The Outlaw Years,* has description of this place, which I have not been able to discover elsewhere. It dealt, according to Coates, in a variety of goods and also served meals. Whiskey, "such as will sink tallow; thus was the proof determined," was sold through a lattice by the proprietor.

It had been a hangout for the Harpes, and had a bad name, "a rowdy groggery." On the evening after the escape of the outlaws from Tiel, Hughes had as customers in the tavern his wife's two brothers named Metcalfe, and a man named Johnson.

We do not know Johnson's first name, or whence he came. But evidently he had been intimate with the Harpes, and perhaps was the informant who set Tiel's posse on their trail. On this evening he was sitting in the groggery, hobnobbing with the Metcalfe brothers and drinking whiskey, when the two wild men burst into the place.

Instantly a furious struggle took place in the half-dark tavern. Furniture was overturned, there were heavy blows, a wild appeal for mercy came from Johnson and a cry for help, and it was over. The Harpes were gone as suddenly as they came, and with them had gone Johnson.

Two days later his body was found. It displayed evidences of ghoulish brutalities which had been visited on him by the Harpes, and also an "invention" by them: a method, no less, of disposing of the body, which was destined to chill the blood of people for a generation because of its use, not only by these human hyenas, but by other murderers who imitated them.

The Harpes had ripped open the body of their victim, performed the revolting act of pulling out his intestines, and filled the cavity with stones, so that it would sink and stay down in the river. In this instance, however, the corpse for some reason must have turned in such a manner as to lose part of its "ballast." It floated to the surface in an eddy of the Holston River and so was discovered.

That ghastly and gruesome process of getting rid of a dead body, the device of madmen, was destined to be used later by others who were not crazed but were cold-blooded as reptiles: Mason, certainly; probably Hare; most particularly Murrell. It became in fact a sort of horrid trademark of that class of criminal murderers known in their day as "land pirates" or "river pirates."

But meantime the Harpes were gone. As completely as if they had taken flight like vampires, they disappeared.

After the body of Johnson was found, "regulators" visited Hughes's tavern. They were met by the bland proprietor and his brothers-in-law, who stated with truth that the Harpes committed the deed. So unsavory were their reputations that all three were arrested and lodged in the Knoxville jail. For lack of evidence they were acquitted when they came to trial, and the Metcalfes, as soon as they were released, lost no time in fleeing from the country.

But Hughes was too sure of himself. As if nothing out-of-the-way had occurred, he reopened his groggery.

It was too blatant. The "regulators" called on him again. This time Hughes was tied to a tree and the cowhide cut his bare back to bloody shreds. Then he was forced to watch while they tore down his building and destroyed his wares. After that he was given a warning of a nature so grim that with his wife he at once left "for parts unknown," as the chronicle puts it.

III. *The Charnel Trail*

1.

What of the women of the Harpes?

They were not with their masters when Tiel's force captured the outlaws. They had been sent on ahead; walking, in spite of the fact that by this time, early in December, 1798, all three were pregnant, Susan for the second time. They seem to have had one horse, an old bag of bones, which carried their few miserable belongings as baggage.

It was some fifty miles to the old rendezvous, the lonely camp in the Cumberlands at the corner of Virginia, where the two Roberts girls stayed before, and where Susan's first child was born and died.

Meantime the Harpes themselves, who were disarmed when they were arrested by Tiel, somehow obtained new weapons. Presumably they did so in their raid on Hughes' tavern, when they carried off Johnson and later murdered him, although there is no direct testimony on this important fact. The tavern, so far as I can discover, was the only place they entered prior to their disappearance into the mountains. Yet when they next were seen both carried rifles and knives, and Little Harpe, at least, had a tomahawk as well. As soon as they rejoined their women, hardly pausing to rest, they headed back toward the settlements, this time into Kentucky, following the Wilderness Road.

But now they had changed evilly. The murder and evisceration of Johnson seemed to release completely the eerie madness in their natures. From this date onward they "lived like man-eating animals" and had "a cannibal lust for blood."

Nor were they long in finding their first victim. A few miles from the Cumberland Pass, where the Wilderness Road crossed the Cumberland River, they overtook a lone traveler named Peyton. He was a peddler, one of that wandering breed of humble traders who, with a small stock of articles, such as needles, spools of thread, pans and pots, cutlery, and other household utensils capable of being carried in the saddlebags or on a pack horse, traveled from place to place, selling what they could. This particular peddler did not even own a pack horse, only the sorry nag he rode.

He was poor and harmless, but that did not deter the Harpes. A meaning glance between them, one fell behind him a step, there was a blow when he least suspected it, and Peyton was dead. Having murdered him, they "took his horse and some of his goods." They did not even bother to take everything. Profit always was a secondary consideration to them; the killing of the man was the important thing.

Leaving the body of poor Peyton covered with a few branches from the trees beside the road, the Harpes went on, their crazed mission— *of man hunting*—now fully crystallized.

Primitive Kentucky was as if especially designed for their ghastly purpose. There were no public conveyances. Travel was by horseback or on foot. Here and there small villages existed, but the Harpes invariably camped outside of these, although they and their three women sometimes ate at public houses. Between the hamlets, human habitations were few and far apart. So wild was the country, and so densely forested, that communications were infrequent and residents hardly knew the people who might be living in the next valley. As for strangers who might chance to pass through, no account or track was ever kept of them.

Because of the obvious dangers, travelers usually went in company, and solitary wayfarers often asked to accompany larger groups, while the invitation to "join up" quite generally was forthcoming in a most hospitable manner. This last custom played perfectly into the plans of the murdering Harpes.

Their next victim, after Peyton, must have been Stephen Langford, because his murder came next on the route they followed. It is true that early accounts listed Bates and Paca ahead of him; and it is also possible that they preceded him to doom. One of the evidences of the madness of the Harpes was the illogic of their movements. They acted solely on impulse, like souls demented. They might, for example, travel some distance on a given route, and then double back on their trail for no apparent reason, as they were known to do more than once in their subsequent career.

In this case, however, such a backtrack as would have been required for the murder of Langford after the two just mentioned, would have been almost impossible for the Harpes to accomplish in the time that elapsed.

Langford, a young Virginian, had crossed Cumberland Gap on his way to some destination in Kentucky, and stopped overnight at a tavern operated by John Farris, which stood beside the Rockcastle River, not far from present Mount Vernon, Kentucky. The stretch of trail before him, leading to Crab Orchard, was extremely wild, and was in fact called "the Wilderness" as indicating that it surpassed even the rest of the wilderness of that day in danger and difficulty.

After a night at the Farris tavern, Langford was eating breakfast on the morning of December 12, when two men and three women came up, "their appearance denoting poverty, with but little regard to cleanness." They had "two very indifferent horses, with some bags slung across them," but were themselves on foot, even the three pregnant women.

They were the Harpes.

"Squalid and miserable, they seemed objects of pity, rather than of fear, and their ferocious glances were attributed more to hunger than to guilty passion."[1]

For a time they stood about uneasily, saying nothing, but looking hungrily at the victuals on the table. When Farris, the landlord, inquired if they wanted breakfast, they shook their heads, and one of them volunteered that they did not have the money to pay for it.

At that Stephen Langford was moved with pity, invited them to eat at his expense, and watched them while they "ate voraciously." Then he called for the bill and paid it, in doing so showing a handful of silver coins—and thus unwittingly signing his own death warrant.

[1] Judge James Hall, *Letters from the West*, quoted by Rothert.

2.

Langford had intended to ride through the wild stretch ahead alone; but the arrival of this party, dirty and disreputable as it appeared, gave him promise of company and, as he supposed, greater safety on his journey.

No man could have been more tragically mistaken. When later the Harpes and their women emerged from "the Wilderness" at Crab Orchard, the young Virginian was not with them. His horse, however, was—although it was not at the time identified as his property.

Still traveling westward from Crab Orchard, a day or so afterward, at their slow pace, the Harpes were overtaken by two young men from Maryland. Their names were Bates, about thirty years old, and Paca, a few years younger. Both were mounted on fine horses, and both carried good rifles—enough to arouse the cupidity of the two outlaws.

There was a short colloquy with the newcomers. The Marylanders mentioned that they were heading for Logan's Station, a point on the road to Harrodsburg. At this the Harpes asked to travel in company with them to Logan's.

What ensued is known only through the story told by Susan, the oldest of the three Harpe women, when she was under arrest later in Russellville, Kentucky.

According to Susan's account, it began to rain, and the party waited for several hours, taking shelter under the thick foliage of a grove of trees. By the time travel could be resumed it was so late that the prospect of reaching Logan's Station, or any other habitation, before nightfall seemed remote. The Marylanders remarked that they would have to camp.

At that glances, and a whispered word or two, were exchanged by the Harpes. Then Big Harpe spoke up, assuring Bates and Paca that night travel in that section of Kentucky was dangerous "because of renegade Indians." He urged that the whole party remain together for safety, and to this the Marylanders agreed.

Night was approaching and Logan's was still many miles distant. They reached an open glade and Bates proposed that they make camp there. But Big Harpe objected. A mile or so farther on, he said, he remembered a place where not only was there water, but good grass for the horses.

The sun had set and it was growing dark as the party approached this new destination. Silently the Harpes fell behind the Marylanders,

Big Harpe back of Bates and Little Harpe back of Paca. The three
women trudged along eight or ten yards in the rear.

Suddenly, as if at a signal, both Harpes raised their rifles and fired.
The Marylanders pitched forward, out of their saddles, to the ground.

The startled horses had to be seized by the bridles and held. By
this time it was too dark to see clearly, so one of the Harpes lit a light
with a flint and steel. Bates was examined, and proved to be dead.
Paca, however, not yet dead but unable to speak, was struggling to
rise. Little Harpe finished him by splitting his head with a tomahawk.

Now they rifled the pockets of their victims, finding some gold and
silver money, and "a large quantity of continental paper" which at
that time was practically worthless. After this they stripped the
clothes from the two bodies. Big Harpe discarded his own tattered
garments and dressed in those of Bates, who was a large man; while
Little Harpe donned the clothing of Paca, who was smaller. "Each
of them, after that appeared in tolerable decent trim for woodsmen,"
and Big Harpe, "putting on a less turbid and threatening countenance," asked Susan, "if she did not think he looked like a handsome
gentleman."[2]

When they had preened themselves for awhile, like savages gloating over new adornments, the outlaws carried the two corpses into
the woods and concealed them. They now had five horses (including
those of Peyton and Langford) making a mount for each of the party.
Going on to a place somewhat farther along the trail they camped
for the night beside a small creek, cooked and ate their supper, and
slept as if their consciences were wholly clear—the three women as
well as the two bloody men.

One wonders about those women. Did they shrink at the sight of
the violent murders and the corpse robbings that followed them? Did
any of them turn sick or protest at these horrors?

From any evidence available they did not. Even Sally Rice, still in
her teens and a comparatively new addition to the Harpes' little
harem, seems to have looked on while men were butchered before
her eyes, without a shudder. It was not that the women were as ferocious as their masters. They simply were so completely dominated by
the fiends who possessed them that they did not dream of behaving
any other way than that all was entirely right, natural, and proper.
Perhaps they were becoming so calloused that such sights no longer
had the power to stimulate horror in them.

[2] T. Marshall Smith, *Legends of the War of Independence.*

3.

The Harpes had now committed four treacherous and brutal murders in a few short days on this one march. Thus far they had exhibited a curious mixture of caution and the absence of it, cold calculation and sudden impulse. But though they made some shift to hide the evidences of their crimes, one of their victims was shortly discovered.

It was not the body of Peyton, nor those of the two Maryland men, which first came to light. Those murders were not found out for some weeks after. But a curious circumstance brought about the discovery of the corpse of Langford.

On December 14, 1789, just two days after he was killed, a party of drovers with a herd of cattle was heading east toward Virginia on the Wilderness Road. Suddenly their cattle left the road, rushed down into a gully in the woods, and began bellowing and pawing as cattle do when they smell blood.

The drovers, hearing the "blood bellow," followed and saw a dead man. He was lying behind a log, covered over with brush and leaves, and only the smell of his blood had betrayed him to the cattle. That he had been murdered was evident. One account says that he had been shot, another that he was tomahawked. In any case the marks of violence were plain to the men who discovered him.

The drovers fastened the body on a horse and carried it along with them to the first house to which they came. It chanced to be Farris's tavern, the very place where Langford was last seen alive as he departed toward the west with the Harpes.

Both John Farris and his daughter-in-law Jane Farris looked at the body and both identified it as that of their guest of two or three days before. Marks upon the clothing gave them his name: Stephen Langford.

He was buried not far from the tavern, and word of the murder quickly was carried to the nearest settlements. Although Farris did not know the names of the five who accompanied the victim when he left the tavern, he furnished a tolerable description of the two men and three women, and gave details as to how Langford joined their company—through his own kindheartedness.

The report of the murder "spread like wildfire," and the *Kentucky Gazette*, in its issue of January 2, 1799, had an article describing it, in all its macabre details. But already, before this newspaper was printed, the Harpes and their women had been captured and were being held in custody for trial.

4.

Logan's Station—so referred to both by the Harpes and the Marylanders—had lately changed its name to Stanford. In 1798 it had a
population of about two hundred, "including slaves," and a log courthouse and jail. It also had a leading citizen, Captain Joseph Ballenger,
a veteran Indian fighter, a merchant, and also a man of action.

Word reached Ballenger, December 19 or 20, that a murder had
occurred on the Wilderness Road, and that a party of vagrants, not
then known by name, was suspected of it. At once he called together
some men, on his own authority formed a band of "regulators"—that is,
an informal citizens' posse without legal authority or status—and set
out in pursuit of the vagrants who already had passed through Stanford.

As before, the Harpes made no effort to conceal their trail. Ballenger followed them across Brush Creek, a branch of the Green
River, then across the Rolling Fork of the Salt River, and finally, on
Christmas Day, December 25, 1798, he overtook the hunted party
somewhere in Hardin County.

The Harpes seemed to have relapsed into one of their periods of
brutish apathy. With their three women they were sitting in a row
on a log when the regulators rode up. As at Knoxville, although they
were armed, they offered no resistance but permitted their weapons
to be confiscated, themselves to be bound.

A search of their persons and their baggage revealed a pocket book
with the name of the dead man, Stephen Langford,[3] and various
other articles, some of which may have belonged to Peyton or the
two Marylanders, whose deaths had not as yet been discovered. But
the most damning piece of evidence to these frontiersmen was one
of the horses in the captured party, an animal which shortly was
proved to be the property of the murdered Langford.

All five prisoners were taken back to Stanford and lodged in the
two-room log jail, the men in one room, the women in the other.

Meantime, positive identification of Langford had been made by a
friend, David Irby, who hearing of the murder went to Farris's, and
with John Farris "raised the body." He thereafter swore positively it
was that of his friend, with whom he had come from Virginia and

[3] The name also is rendered as Lankford and Thomas Langford in various of the
old accounts.

from whom he had parted only a little while before the fatal meeting with the Harpes.

At Stanford the prisoners were objects of intense curiosity. When they were brought into the log courthouse for a hearing before three squires, the place was crammed with spectators. The squires, Hugh Logan, Nathan Huston, and William Montgomery, called upon the prisoners to plead guilty or not guilty to the charge.

All five denied their guilt, and gave their names as Micajah Roberts, Wiley Roberts, Susanna Roberts, Sally Roberts, and Elizabeth Walker. The name Roberts—adopted as an alias—was of course that of the two sisters. Oddly, one of the sisters, Elizabeth (or Betsey) who was legitimately entitled to the name, was the only one who did not use it, giving her name instead as Walker.

Proof against the defendants was overwhelming. Ballenger testified as to how he heard of the murder and captured them. Irby gave his previous acquaintance with and positive identification of Langford. Farris and his daughter-in-law also testified as to the identification, and stated under oath that the dead man was last seen with the defendants. Articles stolen from the victim, including the horse, were described and sworn to, as being in the possession of the prisoners when they were captured.

Through all this the Harpes, and their women as well, sat with faces "singularly set and lacking in all expression," as if they hardly understood that the proceedings affected them. At the end of the hearing the squires remanded the prisoners to jail "to be tried for the murder of the said Thomas [sic] Langford before the Judges of the District Court holden for the Danville District at the next April term."

In spite of their stupid, almost torpid behavior during the hearing, the two Harpes evidently were considered desperate men, for there is an item of expense listed by the sheriff: for the making of handcuffs for Wiley Roberts and Micajah Roberts, and putting them on and taking them off, a total of nineteen shillings (equivalent, roughly, to $4.50). There also was a bill submitted by the sheriff for the pay of eight men who took turns guarding the prisoners for fourteen days, at four shillings six pence ($1.12) per day for the services.

Before the district court began its sittings at Danville, Kentucky, the five prisoners were conveyed to that town, on January 5, 1799, and lodged there in another jail, the walls of which, according to the specifications given were "of hewed or sawed logs at least nine inches thick."

By this time the male prisoners seem to have recovered from their inertia, and were proving unruly, for on January 20 the jailer, John Biegler, bought "two horse blocks to chain the men's feet to the

ground," and also a new lock for the jail door and three pounds of
nails "for use of the jail." These precautions, unfortunately, were insufficient as events proved.

And now occurred an inevitability of nature, as shown by the jailer's itemized account of his expenses.

On February 8, tea and sugar were bought "for Betsey Walker, she
being brought to bed by a son the preceding night," also cash for a
midwife and other necessaries, the whole amounting to "1 pound,
8 shillings, 10 pence" (about $7.10).

March 8, a similar outlay of expenses was made "for the use of
Susanna Harpe brought to bed by a daughter the preceding night."
In this case the expenditure was "1 pound, 1 shilling, 4 pence" ($5.33).

Two babies had been born in the wretched little log jail, in cold
weather, by mothers charged with murder. And the poor women
probably could not even name the fathers of those babies with any
certainty, since either of the Harpes could have sired the children
to whom they gave birth.[4]

The two men, in the other jail cell, were by this time accustomed
to having people peer at them through the bars. One day to a crowd
of these morbidly curious persons Big Harpe "proposed to whip at
fisticuffs the two best fighters in Kentucky, provided he would be set
free if he succeeded in whipping the two men, and should he fail he
would abide by the decision of the court."

A wild, ranting boast; but the Harpes had their moments of calculated cunning, too.

Suddenly they were gone—broken out of jail, leaving their women
behind. The only hint of how they made their escape is a crestfallen
entry by the jailer, "to mending the wall in jail where the prisoners
escaped, 12 shillings."

This item was dated March 16. The day of their trial had been set
for April 15. But between the time of their escape and the trial date,
new, grim discoveries were made.

The decomposed bodies, partly devoured by wolves, of the two
Marylanders, Bates and Paca, were found in the woods somewhat off
from the Wilderness Road; and later that of Peyton. The Harpes were
at once suspected of these murders, but they were gone, no man
knew where, by the time the news arrived at Danville.

Meantime the third of the forlorn women appeared in the jailer's
account book with an entry of expenses for tea, sugar, and one quart
of whiskey "for the use of Sally Harp brought to bed the preceding

---

[4] It is to be noted that by this time Susan had accepted the name of Harpe,
although Betsey still called herself Walker. Why?

night by a daughter." In this case no midwife is mentioned. Presumably the girl, not yet twenty years old, was helped through her ordeal by the other two feminine prisoners; and the quart of whiskey (which cost one shilling six pence, or, say, thirty-seven cents) may have been as much for the refreshment of the Roberts sisters as for Sally, in this trying period.

Sally had by this time acknowledged the name of Harpe (or Harp) which indicates that the true name of the murderers was known. Yet when the three women were brought before the district court, presided over by Judges James D. Hunter and Samuel McDowell, April 15, 1799, they were entered as "Susanna Roberts, spinster, Elizabeth Walker, spinster, and Sally Roberts, spinster." Presumably they were thus classified as spinsters because of their own statement that they were not married, which indicates that they had no formal or legal matrimonial connections with the Harpes. It is probable that Susan's previous claim to be Big Harpe's wife was under the common law definition, and the same may have applied to Sally Rice's assertion that she was the wife of Little Harpe. Betsey Roberts, then and later, humbly accepted a role as a "supplementary wife" in the little harem.

Susan, the first to be tried for the murder of Stephen (or Thomas) Langford, was found guilty of complicity. But the other two were found innocent on the same charge, whereupon Susan, applying for a new trial, was set free. Evidently the murders of Bates, Paca, and Peyton, by this time disclosed, were not charged against the women, and it was not until later that Susan gave the details of the killing of the Marylanders.

Now public opinion came to the aid of the three miserable women. Abandoned by their men, each with a small child to care for, destitute and helpless, they were objects for pity. The women all said they were finished with the Harpes, were glad to be rid of them forever, and wished only to return to Knoxville, Tennessee, there to begin life anew.

When they were released from the jail, kindly citizens of Danville made up a collection of clothing and money, and provided an old mare for them. On April 20 the three forlorn creatures, carrying their babies and leading the old mare which bore their belongings, set out on foot on the trail toward Crab Orchard.[5]

But the protestations of the women that they were "through with

[5] The jail record showed that the two Harpes were confined for seventy-one days before they made their escape. Of the women, Sally and Betsey were imprisoned for one hundred and two days, and Susan one hundred and three days. Their infants were confined as follows: Betsey's sixty-nine days, Susan's forty-three days, and Sally's nine days.

the Harpes" proved insincere. One wonders what magnet continued
to draw them to the men who had subjected them to abuse and hardship, got them with child, and then abandoned them in jail to face
their fate alone. Surely the Harpes must have been the most depraved,
evil men they knew in all the world. They could expect nothing but
dreary wanderings, squalor and filth, submission to the lust of whichever man took a fancy to either of them whenever he desired, constant danger, exposure to the elements, hunger at times, rags for
clothing, and perhaps blows in the bargain when the Harpes were
raging. Yet like faithful dogs which lick the hand of the master even
when he kicks them, they returned to those wild men and that wild,
terrible life.

There must have been an agreement upon a meeting place before
the Harpes broke jail, for it was learned later that the three women,
as soon as they reached the Green River, traded their mare for a
canoe, loaded their babies and goods into it, and set off to paddle
down that river.

The Green empties into the Ohio River a little above the present
town of Henderson, Kentucky, then called Red Banks. Below Red
Banks, on the Ohio, were three points of sinister interest in the early
frontier days.

Just a few miles downstream was Diamond Island. A little farther,
in the wide Ohio, was Hurricane Island. And between the two, looking down from a cliff on the right bank of the river, was a strange
freak of nature called Cave-in-Rock. All three places were hangouts
of the dreaded river pirates, and it was in that area of cruelty and
wickedness that the women had agreed to meet their masters, the
Harpes.

5.

Long before their reunion, however, men had connected the murders of Bates, Paca, and Peyton with that of Langford. It became plain
now that the two men who escaped from the Danville jail were even
more dangerous than had been supposed.

All of Kentucky was aroused, angered, terrified. Householders
barred their doors and shuttered their windows at night. Lone women
lived in hourly dread.

All sheriffs, constables, and other officers of the law were notified
by the state to be on the constant lookout for the criminals and if possible to capture them. Governor James Garrard dispatched a special
commission to Captain Ballenger—who had once arrested the Harpes

and therefore knew them—authorizing him "to pursue them into the state of Tennessee and other states, and to apply to the executive authorities of such states to deliver them up."

Ballenger at once called together a posse, and led his party of armed horsemen toward the country where he found the Harpes before. Amazingly enough, he actually found them there, near the headwaters of the Rolling Fork, on April 10—ten days before the women in the Danville jail were released.

And there and then occurred a strange, almost ludicrous, incident.

To describe the peculiar horror and fear which the people felt for the two subhuman monsters ranging through their country is difficult. It is the unknown, the incomprehensible, that terrifies, and the actions of the Harpes were so weird, so shocking, as to place them outside the category of the behavior of normal men.

Strange stories and wild rumors circulated through the settlements: that the Harpes had revolting habits akin to cannibalism, if not cannibalism itself; that they possessed the evil eye which could cast deadly spells; that they were mad—and mad in the sense of rabid dogs, the bite of which was death.

The cruelty of the Harpes, their treachery, their pitiless killings, the very absence of motive at times, were acts of what we today would call compulsive murderers. But the frontier, lacking this and other catch-words of modern psychiatric jargon, considered them demented. And dealing with madmen, to the simple folk of the forest, was the next thing to dealing with the supernatural—perhaps these men were subjects of the foul fiend himself, living under his protection.

The result of this superstitious speculation now became apparent. When Ballenger and his posse found themselves suddenly and quite unexpectedly confronting the Harpes, face to face, they halted in their tracks. The two grim outlaws had their rifles ready—guns stolen after their escape from jail. But they had no need to use them.

Before the blood-chilling menace of the blank, wild stare in their eyes, the possemen were stricken with panic. Without firing a shot they fled from the awful presence of those madmen.

The Harpes at once plunged into a canebrake and disappeared.

It was no ordinary cowardice that gripped Ballenger's men. Theirs was simply a case of overwhelming awe and horror. A similar situation was to arise again, with a different group, and with the same result.

Just before they confronted the Harpes, a man from the immediate vicinity had joined Ballenger. He was Henry Scaggs, a leather-faced frontiersman, one of the "long hunters" who came to Kentucky as early as 1770—before either Boonesborough or Harrodsburg were founded—and fought Indians by the side of Boone himself. Scaggs, who had faced yelling painted warriors without flinching, fled from the presence of the Harpes as precipitately as the others.

As soon as the party recovered its breath after its flight, however, men began to look somewhat shamefacedly at each other, and Scaggs began to think. Presently he suggested that they go to his cabin, not far from where the Harpes were seen, and get some trail hounds he had there, to help the pursuit.

This was done. The dogs found the trail and followed it to the canebrake. But there Ballenger's men refused to go farther. To plunge into that thick and almost impenetrable tangle, where the insane killers might be waiting for them at any turn, was too much to face. Some of them at this point "resigned"—and went home.

With those he had left Ballenger continued the hunt, though he skirted the menacing canebrake. Scaggs, however, was sure the murderers were in that canebrake, and nowhere else. At whatever risk, it ought to be combed for them.

He bethought himself that within a few miles a "log rolling" was in process. It was a day when log cabins were commonly built by community effort. Families gathered from near and far. The men joined in rolling the logs to place, raising them on the walls, chinking them, fastening them with wedges, and roofing them with slabs, so that a cabin was easily completed in one day. The women prepared a feast of frontier delicacies, for the affair was always a social one. Among the workers the whiskey demijohn passed freely, there were boisterous jokes and laughter, and after the cabin was "raised" and the food eaten, the fiddles began to squeal and in the clearing dancing began, with a general jollification and "sparking" between youths and maidens.

Henry Scaggs rode for the clearing where he knew this process was going forward. When he arrived, most of the work was done and the festivities were about to begin.

A score or more of men were present, all no doubt with rifles handy, for men seldom ventured far without a weapon. To these Scaggs told of the Harpes in the vicinity, hiding in the canebrake, and asked them to help him flush the outlaws out.

But the log rollers were perhaps by this time a little tipsy, and just beginning to have a good time. They told him that they "had lost no Harpes"; and in any case the chances of finding them in that canebrake were too slim to be worth all that trouble; and besides there was a barrel of liquor to be drunk; and a bountiful supper to be eaten, and pretty girls to squeeze, and dancing to come; and in the end they invited him to sit down and have a pull at the demijohn and help them consume the feast. But they refused to go with him.

Discouraged, the old Indian fighter left them to their revelry.

6.

As it turned out, Henry Scaggs was mistaken about that canebrake.

The Harpes were in one of those periods of incredible activity that sometimes characterized them. They had emerged almost at once from the canebrake on the other side from where they entered it. And speedily the next tragedy took place.

Walking along an old buffalo trail not far from the canebrake, and probably whistling a cheerful tune as he went homeward, was a young lad with his little dog frisking about him. He was Johnny Trabue, thirteen years old, son of Colonel Daniel Trabue, a Revolutionary officer, who had a place about three miles west of the present Columbia, Kentucky. Johnny carried a sack on his shoulder and a bag in his hand. The sack contained a few pounds of stone-ground flour, which he had been sent to borrow, and the bag some seed beans—neither of them heavy enough to weary a boy of his age.

We can only imagine the scene: the whistling lad, not dreaming of any danger, coming along the trail with his dog; the two ferocious visages glaring at him from out of a thicket; the sudden spring, the terror, the sickening blows, the feeble twisting of the young legs in death. The little dog evidently tried to help his master and was struck brutally. As it ran limping and yelping away, the robbers leaned over their victim.

Scaggs, returning from the log rolling, had stopped at the Trabue place to talk with his friend the colonel about the menace lurking in the neighborhood. Trabue was willing to help, but he was then waiting for his son, who was overdue on his errand. As they talked, Johnny's little dog limped into the yard, evidently badly hurt.

Now the colonel was alarmed. He saddled a horse and with Scaggs rode to the neighbor's where the boy had gone. Yes, Johnny had been there; but he left some time before by the old buffalo trail. It was growing dark, but a search began which lasted throughout the night.

The Harpes! That was the thought in people's minds. Yet the father at first believed only that the Harpes had kidnaped his son. That they could be so fiendish as to kill a harmless lad who had nothing of value on him, he could not at first credit.

The search failed. Not for days was Johnny Trabue's fate known.

Then he was found—what was left of him. His body, disemboweled
and hacked to pieces as if in insensate rage, had been thrown into a
sinkhole. With it was the little bag of seed beans. The murderers took
only the small sack of flour. It was a slaughter for the sheer lust of
killing.[6]

From signs discovered fifteen miles southwest of the Trabue place
—where the Harpes had killed a calf, camped, had a meal of veal
and crude bread baked of Johnny's flour, and also made moccasins
of undressed calf's skin—it was believed they had gone up the Little
Barren River.

New excitement and fear swept over the state. At Frankfort, Governor Garrard issued a proclamation offering three hundred dollars'
reward each, for the capture of Micajah and Wiley Harpe. This
proclamation was signed April 22, twelve days after Johnny's murder,
and presumably after his remains were found. It gave the following
description of the two outlaws:

> MICAJAH HARP alias ROBERTS is about six feet high—of a robust
> make, and is about 30 or 32 years of age. He has an ill-looking, down-
> cast countenance, and his hair is black and short, but comes very much
> down his forehead. He is built very straight and is full fleshed in the
> face. When he went away [from the Danville jail] he had on a striped
> nankeen coat, dark blue woolen stockings, leggins of drab cloth, and
> trousers of the same as the coat.
> WILEY HARP alias ROBERTS is very meagre in his face, has short
> black hair but not quite so curly as his brother's; he lookes older,
> though really younger, and has likewise a downcast countenance. He
> had on a coat of the same stuff as his brother's, and had a drab surtout
> coat over the close-bodied one. His stockings were dark blue woolen
> ones, and his leggins of drab cloth.

The description was inaccurate in one respect: Wiley Harpe certainly had red hair. But it furnished an interesting additional point
regarding Big Harpe's appearance: "his hair . . . comes very much
down his forehead." He must have had an extremely low, almost
apelike, brow. The garments described were, without much question,
the clothes taken from the bodies of the Maryland men, Bates and
Paca, which the Harpes had been wearing since those murders, including their period in jail.

[6] Long years after, Colonel Trabue, in his autobiography, wrote: "It is a pity they
(the log rollers) did not continue the pursuit, for then John Trabue might not
have been killed." Probably he was wrong in this surmise, for the murder of
Johnny took place before the pursuit could have begun, and in a spot the pursuers
would not likely have thought to find the men they hunted.

7.

Before the governor's proclamation had 'a chance to circulate, the Harpes already had left a further trail of indiscriminate slaughters, to mark their insane progress.

The conjecture that they were heading up the Little Barren River proved shockingly true. Not far from present-day Edmonton, fifteen or twenty miles from the Trabue place, they killed a man named Dooley. Not much is known of this victim, except that he was a settler who had the grave misfortune to be in their path as they skulked through the country.

After the Dooley slaying they crossed over the height of land to the Big Barren River, and there, about eight miles below Bowling Green, Kentucky, they committed another murder, peculiarly heartless.[7]

This victim's name was Stump; a harmless, indolent shanty dweller, who owned a fiddle, usually went about in a shirt and linsey-woolsey pants without hat or shoes, and spent most of his time hunting or fishing.

Sitting on the bank of the river, with his cane pole and line, he had hooked several fish when he happened to notice smoke rising in the woods on the other side of the stream. Stump was a convivial soul. Thinking that the strangers might enjoy company, he stopped fishing, went to his cabin which he occupied alone, and taking his fiddle, a wild turkey he had shot recently, and the string of fish, he crossed the river in a skiff to say howdy, and make the newcomers welcome with a little music, some gossip, and a tasty fish and game supper.

Poor Stump had no way of knowing that it was the terrible Harpes upon whom he innocently intruded. When he was found later, he had been stabbed to death, and his body sunk in the river with the Harpe "invention." The corpse was washed up against a bar so that it was discovered. Some of Stump's neighbors at first were suspected of the killing, but proved their innocence. In any case, the ghoulish treatment of the body was enough to identify the Harpes as the guilty ones.

A great hue and cry arose. Lynching parties were organized, for matters had gone beyond the ordinary processes of law. But once more the Harpes disappeared.

[7] The details of this murder later were related by Big Harpe himself as he lay dying.

They were heading either for Diamond Island or Cave-in-Rock, where their women faithfully awaited them. But first they left one more mark of their murderous mania.

When they reached the Ohio River they must have stolen a boat to cross over to the Illinois side, since they probably knew their descriptions were so widely broadcast that they stood great risk of recognition if they used one of the regular ferries.

At any rate, their next act was a triple murder. The very names of these victims have been lost, but an account of the bloody affair was published in the *Illinois Gazette* some time after it occurred. The three men were camped near the mouth of the Saline River, on the land of Billy Potts.[8] Evidently the Harpes crept up on the camp, shot two of the men by the light of their own fire, and tomahawked the third.

By this time the Harpes, since fleeing from Knoxville, Tennessee, had murdered eleven persons *who had been accounted for*. How many others were their victims will never be known. The new country was thinly settled, and there were lone travelers whom nobody knew. Though in two cases bodies, sunk in rivers with stones crammed into the raw and bloody abdominal cavities came to light, it is highly improbable that all whom the Harpes so treated did so. There may have been half a dozen more murders never disclosed.

With the triple killing on the Saline, the bloody brothers entered the no-man's-land of outlaws on the lower Ohio.

[8] A place of sinister reputation because of the "murder tavern" Potts operated there later, in cooperation with the James Ford gang of highwaymen.

IV.   *Where Crime Was Spawned*

1.

Cave-in-Rock.

On the north bank of the Ohio River, in what is now Hardin County, Illinois, it still opens its huge arched maw, like the jaws of some gigantic man-devouring fish, in the face of a sheer one-hundred-foot rock cliff overlooking the stream.

What tales of blood spilled, of distress and suffering, of heartless cruelties, of treacheries and deceptions, of robberies and rapes and murders, that cave might reveal if it could speak, would curdle the blood if all were known. In its day it was the lair and stronghold of the worst cutthroats, freebooters, and gallows-birds this continent ever witnessed. First and last it exerted an influence of bale and woe for a full generation and more of time, saw innocent deaths beyond counting, and held all of interior America in a web of terror.

The cave is not enormous, as caves go; nothing, for example, like Mammoth Cave of Kentucky. It was its strategic location and the kind of men who seemed attracted to it that made it ill-omened beyond all other places in America.

Today, maintained as a state park by Illinois, its mouth is about fifty-five feet wide at its base, perhaps half that in height at the highest point in the arched opening, and it extends back into the solid rock for about one hundred and forty feet, with a small chamber branching off at the rear.

At one time the cave probably had a level floor and was much greater in interior length, for it was in remote ages the egress of an underground river. But its rearward portions have been filled by sand and silt and its floor now slants upward toward a small sinkhole which opens to the surface at the back, through which a man could climb up and out of the cave—a sort of escape hatch for lurking criminals in case the front was besieged by a force too strong to be resisted. At the mouth of the cave is a rocky shelf, relatively level, which falls off precipitately at its verge into the deep coursing river at its feet.

First at the cave may have been a certain John Duff. This Duff was a shadowy character, a wanderer beyond the rim of the settlements, perhaps wanted by the law. He was surprised on the lower Ohio and "brought in" by some of the scouts of General George Rogers Clark, when that bold adventurer and his little army floated down the Ohio in 1778, on the first leg of their famous expedition against Kaskaskia and Vincennes, during the American Revolution.

Duff may have been a spy for the British.[1] He in fact admitted under Clark's questioning that he had recently been in Kaskaskia, and had there been ordered by the commandant for the British, the Sieur de Rochblave, to "keep a close watch for rebels, and lose no time in bringing news of their approach." These instructions Clark's alert scouts set at naught; in fact the fierce-eyed Clark "induced" Duff to act as a guide—under the close watch of riflemen with itchy trigger fingers—on the march to Kaskaskia, which the little frontier army presently captured bloodlessly before going on to Vincennes.

Thereafter Duff dropped out of formal history. But the name recurs. Before 1790, a Duff, described as "a notorious counterfeiter" was at Cave-in-Rock. According to Rothert it is probable that this Duff and the John Duff of George Rogers Clark fame were one and the same.[2]

What makes the blending of identities more probable is that a Duff —one who knew the lower Ohio surpassingly well, as would John Duff of the shadowy frontier character—established near or in the Cave-in-

[1] Frederick Palmer, *Clark of the Ohio.*

[2] Otto A. Rothert, *The Outlaws of Cave-in-Rock.*

Rock a place known for a time as Duff's Fort, and later became a brother-in-law of Samuel Mason.

All of which brings us to as fascinatingly villainous a scoundrel as ever existed, Samuel Mason himself.

2.

Samuel Mason, in his prime, was a burly man, "weighing about two hundred pounds," but not fat, for he was active and muscular. His face was bland and smooth, except for "a tooth which projected forwards, and could only be covered with his lip by an effort." That protruding fang at times gave him a sinister wolfish look, but usually he was in good command of himself, and he succeeded at first in passing as an upright and even benevolent citizen.

Born in 1750, of a good Virginia family, he was wild and reckless in his youth. On one occasion he was wounded while trying to steal some horses belonging to a Colonel Hite of Frederick County, Virginia. Somehow he escaped any further penalty, and when the Revolution erupted in 1775, he found in the war an outlet for his turbulent spirits. He was then twenty-five, and he enlisted in the American army, serving with credit and rising to the rank of captain.

While stationed at Fort Henry (later Wheeling, West Virginia) he was twice mentioned in military correspondence for bravery in fighting the hostile Indians who were aiding the British. On one occasion he was wounded in a battle against overwhelming numbers of savages, in which twenty-three of the twenty-eight men of his unit were killed.

When George Rogers Clark set out against Vincennes, Captain Mason and two of his brothers were with him. Records show that Mason was at Fort Henry April 27, 1778, and returned in time to march with Colonel Daniel Brodhead's command against the Seneca Indians on August 11, 1779. Between those dates Mason was with Clark, in the campaign which began June 24, 1778 and ended with the final capture of Vincennes, February 24, 1779.

In one of his reports Clark stated that when he arrived at the falls of the Ohio (now Louisville, Kentucky) and began to enlist men in his army, he "scattered some of his men among the neighboring stations (probably on recruiting missions) . . . Of this party were . . . Thomas and Joseph Mason, brothers of Captain Samuel Mason." This going out of his way to mention Captain Mason indicates that the latter was held in some respect by George Rogers Clark.

During the Kaskaskia-Vincennes foray, Mason certainly became ac-

quainted with John Duff, the somewhat suspected guide; and since
Clark landed at the old French fort called Massac, which was only a
few miles downriver from Cave-in-Rock, he very likely at that time
became acquainted with the cave, too.

An ex-horse thief, turned patriot, his craving for excitement when
the war ended caused Mason's restless nature to turn to outlawry. And
with his inclination toward robbery he discovered a new ability to
present a face of innocence to accusers.

For a time he operated a tavern near Wheeling, thus learning a
business which he was able to utilize to advantage, as will be seen, in
his later criminal years. But horses were being stolen in the vicinity,
and whispers kept connecting Mason with some of these thefts. At
last his reputation became so unfragrant that he left the country, and
after various misadventures appeared on the lower Ohio—drawn as if
by a magnet toward Cave-in-Rock.

At first, however, he lived in Red Banks, a little wilderness community at that time. His pompous and impressive manner caused men
to accept him as a citizen of importance and worth. He even assisted
in organizing a new county government, and was appointed justice
of the peace—a "squire" in the language of the time. He possessed a
house and a family—his wife, four sons and an unmarried daughter.
And he also had a group of hangers-on of a strangely disreputable
character. One of these was Duff, who married Mason's sister perhaps
at this time, and who had learned in some manner to be a "coiner"—
the phrase then used for a maker of counterfeit money. Another was a
tavern keeper, Nicholas Welsh, of dubious methods. A third was
Henry Havard, a young Tennesseean with murderous instincts. There
were at least two others, equally unsavory, named Barrett and Hewitt.

Such a jackdaw company was sure to collide sooner or later with
the law. Captain John Dunn, the Red Banks constable, smelled out a
relationship between the supposedly respectable Mason and some of
the sneak thievery and property depredations occurring in the
countryside. The stouthearted old captain publicly called Mason "a
rascal," and refused to sign some legal papers for him. A few days
later some of Mason's men set on him and beat him into insensibility.

Hardly had Dunn recovered from his beating enough to be about,
than the Mason gang similarly assaulted Hugh Knox, a young lawyer,
who later became a judge at Henderson. It was being made clear to
all and sundry that there was danger in incurring the ill-will of Samuel
Mason.

From beatings it was only a step to murder. On July 9, 1794—the
year the Harpes committed their first murder, that of Moses Doss in

southern Tennessee—a young man named Benjamin Van Cleve stopped overnight at Red Banks. Van Cleve kept a diary and in it he recorded his impression of the hamlet:

> This place is a refuge, not for the oppressed, but for all the horse thieves, rogues, and outlaws that have been able to effect their escape from justice in the neighboring states. Neither law nor gospel has been able to reach here as yet . . . I inquired how they managed to marry, and was told that the parties agreed to take each other for husband and wife before their friends. I was shown two cabins, with about the width of a street between them, where two men a short time ago had exchanged wives. An infair was given today by Mason to a fellow named Kuykendall who had run away from Carolina on account of his crimes, and had run off with Mason's daughter to Diamond Island station, a few weeks ago. The father had forbid him the house and had threatened to take his life, but had become reconciled and sent for them to come home. The parents and friends were highly diverted at the recital of the young couple's ingenuity in courtship, and laughed heartily when the woman told it. She said she had come downstairs after all the family had retired, having her petticoat around her shoulders, and returned with him through her parents' room, with the petticoat around both; and in the morning she brought him down in the same manner before daylight.

The company may have been "highly diverted," and Mason himself may have "laughed heartily" when his daughter told how she made a fool of him by smuggling her lover up to her bed under his very nose. But secretly he was far from amused. He was in fact raging inwardly at being thus made a laughing stock, for he had all of a pompous man's vanity.

Yet he masked his feelings, for Kuykendall was a dangerous man. Wrote Van Cleve in his diary:

> This Kuykendall, I was told, always carried in his waistcoat pocket "devil's claws"—instruments, or rather weapons, that he could slip his fingers in, and with which he could take off the whole side of a man's face at one blow.

Kuykendall also was a daring robber, who used Diamond Island, between Red Banks and the Cave, as an operating point. Obviously Mason, who had a fair share of consideration for the safety of his own precious skin, did not care to risk an open quarrel with such a man.

Besides, he had a better way of dealing with him. During the all-night celebration he played the role of smooth host, smilingly urging the guests at the celebration of his daughter's "marriage"—which was without benefit of license or clergy—to make free with the dippers at the open barrel of whiskey, to help themselves to more of the roast venison and wild turkey on the side table, to disport themselves more merrily in the dance numbers while the fiddles squealed and whimpered.

Before dawn Kuykendall said farewell to his "father-in-law" and the assemblage, and with his "bride" started the fifteen-mile ride which would take them to the boat in which they would cross to Diamond Island. He never reached there.

Somewhere along the way rifle flashes lanced the darkness out of an ambush and Kuykendall, "devil's claws" and all, pitched to the ground, dead. Who killed him? The actual murderers are not known; but the instigator certainly was Mason, and the men whose lead slugs cut down Kuykendall either were his two elder sons, or some of his gang of followers.

It did not pay to cross Samuel Mason. And especially it did not pay to bring laughter upon him and wound his vanity.

Just what happened to the daughter we do not know. Perhaps she returned to her father's roof, frightened and chastened, for she had nowhere else to go. We do know that a few years later Mason was to mention a daughter married to "a respectable man" named Thompson, then living at Cape Girardeau, Missouri, a short distance above the confluence of the Ohio and Mississippi Rivers and therefore not far from Red Banks and Cave-in-Rock. This daughter may have been the relict of the slain Kuykendall.

3.

One murder had been committed on Mason's orders. Others soon followed.

Lawyer Knox, already the recipient of a beating from Mason's gang, discovered that a Negro woman and her two children, his slaves, had been stolen. He informed Captain Dunn, who assembled a posse and with Knox rode straight to the Mason place. The three slaves were recovered, and Mason's rancor against Dunn festered and grew.

By now it was apparent to the outlaw boss that Red Banks was growing too hot for him. Late in 1796 or early in 1797, he and his entire ill-favored entourage of family and followers abruptly left the settlement and went downriver to Diamond Island, probably taking up residence in the very quarters once occupied by Kuykendall. They were not, however, through with Red Banks.

One day the following fall of 1797, Thomas Mason, eldest son of Samuel Mason, appeared in Red Banks. He was drunk, carrying his rifle, and making loud threats against John Dunn's life. Thomas Durbin, a cousin of the constable, and a newcomer to the village, tried to reason with the man and induce him to depart. Young Mason replied by shooting him down, then rode away. Murder number two had been committed.

The third slaying soon followed. Late in December Captain Dunn with a friend named Thomas Smith, riding on business, began to cross a creek south of the town. As their horses forded the stream Dunn casually remarked that "in former years he dreaded the crossing of that creek on account of the Masons, since it was so well fitted to waylay the unwary."

Hardly were the words out of his mouth when the whiplash crack of a rifle was heard and Dunn, mortally wounded, plunged from his saddle into the creek. He managed to say that his murderer was "that bad young man" before he died. It was taken that he meant Henry Havard, one of Mason's more reckless followers.

Havard knew he was suspected, and fled from the country to his father's home on the Red River in Tennessee just south of the Kentucky border. But to the grim posse which rode hard on his trail, state lines meant nothing.

The fierce horsemen surprised him at his father's cabin. Havard, who had expected no such quick pursuit, tried to hide between the feather mattresses of a bed as the posse galloped up. The pursuers simply blasted a volley of bullets through the feather bed. Then "they made the old man pull out the body of his son and when they found his brains oozing out they knew he was quite dead." Captain Dunn, respected and well liked, was avenged, frontier style.

Shortly afterward Hewitt, one of the Mason gang, was captured opposite Diamond Island on the Kentucky side of the Ohio River. The regulators were strongly inclined to lynch him, but having no direct proof of his participation in the Dunn assassination, smashed his gun and told him to "make tracks" out of the country, which he did. Nicholas Welsh, the shady tavern keeper who served drinks to Mason's gang, and probably acted as a fence and a spy, also "disappeared immediately after Captain John Dunn was shot and was never again heard of."

But Samuel Mason himself still was very much to be heard from. As to the three murders it is to be noted that he was not present at any of them. A very crafty man, he much preferred having others do his dirty work. He was in fact to say long after, in his own extenuation, that he "had never killed a man . . . except when it was necessary to defend his own life."

4.

Diamond Island was not headquarters for the Masons very long. The Cave down the river was far better adapted to their purposes. They did, however, keep the island as an upstream outpost for robbery and at times used it for a curious form of allurement by homespun sirens.

For a long time Samuel Mason had looked greedily upon the flatboats loaded with goods that floated down the river. Now he proposed to rob those boats and hit upon a scheme which would bring them easily into his power.

He knew the river men, and he knew that the long, tedious float down the Ohio could build up thirsts and appetites of various kinds. So he drew upon his previous experience as a tavern owner, put a stock of liquors into the Cave, and erected a sign advertising them.

But his true name was too well and unfavorably known upriver, so for the purposes of the sign he assumed an alias. The sign was planted on the water's edge before the Cave and read in bold letters:

WILSON'S LIQUOR VAULT AND HOUSE FOR ENTERTAINMENT.

The last three words, "House for Entertainment," had a clear and unmistakable meaning in that day: that there were women there whose smiles could be bought. By this time Mason had gathered quite an assemblage of "choice" underworld characters of both sexes. Not improbably his own daughter, who already had shown that she regarded sexual morals but lightly, was among those who sold their favors. Both of Mason's elder sons were married, and their women lived in the Cave aggregation. One of them may have participated in these revels, for it was later indicated at one of his trials that she had inclinations along this line. There were others of the sex, including some Negro slave women, and the three members of the Harpe harem who arrived in 1799,[3] as well as doxies from upriver of various ages and proclivities. Some of these may not have been exactly beautiful; but canal boatmen, after weeks without the sight of a woman, were not too exacting in the matter of feminine pulchritude.

"Thieves and gamblers [also] stopped off here and in a few months the place became infamous for its licentiousness and blasphemy."

One thief who joined Mason's crowd in this period was named May

[3] It is doubtful that the Harpe women did any actual prostitution. The deadly jealousy of their men was too well known. And Samuel Mason's own wife seems to have been "virtuous" in this regard at least. She obeyed him but she disapproved of his new kind of life as she later demonstrated.

—James May. It is a name to remember for this man played a grim
role in Mason's final fate.

When May first arrived at Red Banks, he was accompanied by a
woman. He said she was his sister, but there were those who appear
to have doubted it, "for it occasioned some remarks." More likely she
was his mistress. The two finally stole some horses, and the woman
disappeared with the animals. May, however, was captured and returned to Red Banks. Before he could be tried and given the whole-
some thirty-nine lashes, he escaped "by making an extraordinary leap,"
and sought safety with the outlaws at the Cave. Thereafter he was
more or less constantly with Mason.

It was during this era that the cavern gained its distinctive name,
Cave-in-Rock. First it was known as Wilson's Tavern, then as Cave
Inn, or Rock Cave Inn, and presently as Cave Inn Rock, from which
emerged its final title Cave-in-Rock.

5.

After a time the sign disappeared, either removed or destroyed by
storm or flood. But Mason no longer needed it.

His plans had become more ambitious than the mere defrauding of
river men in the bar, gambling room, or brothel. He was greedy to
make bigger and better gains, and the strategic position of Cave-in-
Rock was exactly suited to his evil purposes.

The Cave is situated at a point where the Ohio becomes narrow and
swift, making navigation difficult. Above it lies Diamond Island, below
it is Hurricane Island, and there were at that time many snags, hidden
rocks, and reefs in the river bed, some of them since cleared away.

Even before the arrival of Mason, small gangs of river pirates made
a practice of lying in wait for any cargo boat which by misfortune
wrecked itself on one of these obstructions. In such case a boatload
of thugs would descend upon it, kill or capture the crew, and thoroughly loot it.

To Mason, however, this method was too slow, and too dependent
on chance. He was a man with ideas: the first criminal on the frontier
in fact with really grandiose plans which conceived of robbery as a
wholesale operation.

Of some education, he may have read the fable of the Lorelei who
lured boatmen to their destruction on the ancient Rhine. In any case
he knew the susceptibility of woman-hungry men. Out of this he
evolved a cunning scheme.

Upstream, at the head of Diamond Island, he was wont to post one of the more attractive women of his band. When a flatboat came drifting down the stream, she would wave and call out to it, making signals of distress. Almost invariably such a boat would come to the shore of the island near her. She would then tell of being stranded and beg to be taken to her friends down the river a few miles—at the Cave.

Cave-in-Rock had not yet become notorious. Its existence in fact was hardly known at the time. Quite willingly the flatboatmen would take the "stranded" woman aboard, and steer on downstream. A landing would be made at the shelf before the cave, to set her ashore.

Then would come the fearful closing of the trap. Out of the cave would pour a gang of murderous river pirates armed with guns and tomahawks. The crew would be butchered on the boat. The goods would be appropriated.

Occasionally a rogue who was hardy enough, was allowed to join the pirates; and the fate of any women captured can be imagined. Some, perhaps, agreed to become part of the Cave's reservoir of sex. For the others, rape and death were the alternatives.

Not all boats of course fell victims to this treachery. Sometimes as he watched one of them passing the cave without stopping, Mason would smile grimly, the wolf fang showing, and say "These people are taking my produce to market for me."

He had cause for that saying. Below Cave-in-Rock was Hurricane Island, where lay in wait another crew of Mason's robbers. And below Hurricane Island, not far from the juncture of the Ohio and Mississippi was Wolf Island, where still another gang lurked. Wolf Island has since disappeared, being submerged or cut away by floods of the Mississippi, but in its day John James Audubon, the famous naturalist, recorded in his journal that "to pass Wolf Island was not less to be feared than to anchor under the walls of Algiers." Lucky were the boats that managed to safely run the gantlet of these several stations.

When the crew of a flatboat was massacred a new crew—of Mason's men—frequently took the boat on down to Natchez, where the horses, Negroes, and other cargo it carried were sold. With the money the rogues were expected to return to their headquarters and divide their profits with the others of the gang.

How many persons of both sexes were murdered at Cave-in-Rock can never be known. One writer states that in later years sixty human skeletons were found buried in the rear of the cavern. From this he deduces "at least sixty boatmen had fallen victims to the outlaws of the lower Ohio."[4]

[4] Thomas D. Clark, *The Rampaging Frontier*.

He may be referring, however, to burials discovered just back of the cave, where five grave sites, "each containing five to ten human skeletons," placed in stone-walled sepulchers, were exhumed. These have since been identified as Indian burials, placed there long before Mason's day.

Certainly the usual method of disposal of bodies of victims at the Cave was easier than grave digging. It was the method the Harpes invented, and the Harpes themselves may have demonstrated their singularly gruesome technique in person to Mason. For by this time the two Harpes had become members of the Cave-in-Rock gang, though for a brief time only.

6.

In their bloody raid through the Green River country of Kentucky, previously narrated, the Harpes without question were heading for an agreed rendezvous with their women.

Those women, with their babies, paddled all the way down the Green, stopped briefly near Red Banks, and then went on down the Ohio to Cave-in-Rock. Their men had not yet arrived there, and shortly after they arrived at the Cave, two of them were taken upriver, to Diamond Island, to act the siren role already described.

The two, it is probable, were the younger and comelier members of the trio, Sally Rice and Betsey Roberts. Susan Roberts, elder of the two sisters, was described as "rather tall, rawboned, dark hair and eyes, rather ugly," scarcely the type to lure men to their downfall. On the other hand Betsey, "blonde, blue-eyed, a perfect contrast to her sister," and Sally with "frail blonde beauty,"[5] were well cast for the roles.

They performed the duties expected of them until the Harpes, after the three murders they committed at the mouth of the Saline, reached Cave-in-Rock.

Neither they nor any of the other criminal denizens could remain longer on Diamond Island, for the trail of murders left by the Harpes had thrown Kentucky into a frenzy. Captain Ballenger, after a furious pursuit, was thrown off the chase; but it was taken up by Captain Young of Mercer County, who with a company of regulators swept across the northern part of the state, hung a reported fifteen men for

[5] These descriptions, furnished by Sheriff William Stewart who had the women in custody for a time, evidently are based on their appearance after they were thoroughly scrubbed and cleaned up. Even then his words may have been tinged a little by frontier gallantry.

major crimes, administered some deserved floggings here and there, and drove the outlaws before them.

They cleared out Henderson County, including that hotbed of lawlessness, Red Banks. Then they crossed over to Diamond Island, considered a part of Kentucky, where their appearance caused every criminal to depart in haste for "across the river," which of course meant Cave-in-Rock on the Illinois side.

There the outlaws were safe from Captain Young and his Kentucky regulators who did not feel that they could invade a neighboring territory without more authority than they possessed.

The Harpes, Micajah and Wiley, and their three women, Susan, Betsey and Sally, with the three infants, thus found themselves inhabiting the Cave with other outlaws, male and female, who filled it to the point of overcrowding.

This situation did not long exist. Even the depraved scoundrels of the Cave found the Harpes too macabre to be tolerated.

About the end of May, 1799, not more than a week or two after the unholy Harpe tribe was reunited, a flatboat carrying two families was captured by the river pirates. How many souls were on the unfortunate craft we are not told, but "two or three passengers who were not killed in the battle preceding the robbery were brought ashore." One of these was a man. The others may have been women, for the outlaws had their uses for pretty feminine prisoners.

The Harpes cared nothing about the loot, or the women. But they claimed the man as their particular prey.

While the bandits celebrated around a huge fire on the shelf before the cave, the skulking brothers disappeared with their unhappy captive. It was night. The leaping flames of the fire lit up the face of the cliff and the hard visages of the criminals around it. All at once yells, followed by a scream of mortal terror, were heard from above.

Even the hardened outlaws were transfixed by the chilling sight they saw when they glanced upward. A horse, blindfolded and driven to a frenzy of fear by shouts and proddings from behind, was seen to leap suddenly outward from the top of the cliff, into the gulf below. On its back sat the prisoner from the flatboat, stark naked now, lashed to the animal's back, with an expression of utmost horror on his face.

For a moment the blinded horse and helpless rider seemed to hang in the air. Another instant and they crashed to the rocks below, both killed by the terrible fall.

Now, from above, came peals of maniacal laughter and presently the Harpes came down from the cliff by a side slope, still holding their sides in their dreadful mirth. It was a capital joke, they believed, which they had played not only upon their victim, but on their fellow outlaws, who got such a start out of the episode.

But though Mason and his men dealt in murder, this "prank" was too much even for them. It revealed a wild and insane cruelty that chilled their blood.

The Harpes and their women and children were ordered to leave Cave-in-Rock forthwith. And there must have been fierce menace in the faces of the men with the guns who so bade them, for they made all haste to obey.

V.   *Werewolves in the Wilds*

1.

Exactly what route the Harpe tribe followed after it was ejected from Cave-in-Rock is not known. But it is probable that they took a boat of some kind, floated down the Ohio, and then for a distance down the Mississippi, because next they were heard from in Tennessee—and in *eastern* Tennessee.

Since this required a land journey of considerable distance from the Mississippi, there is also the possibility that they went downriver only as far as the mouth of the Tennessee, then paddled up that stream to perhaps where Duck River flows into it. In high water time—and this was late May or early June—they might then continue by boat a considerable distance east in the direction of Columbia, Tennessee.

The defect in this course, from the viewpoint of the Harpes, was that they were very much wanted in Kentucky, with everybody on the lookout for them; and it would seem wise to shun that state, for they were heading for Knoxville, Tennessee, the scene of their earlier adventures.

However they went, the two savage men, their three women, and the three children passed through the country like a shadow. Nobody saw them.

Then, about the middle of July, the dead body of a farmer named Bradbury was found some fifty miles west of Knoxville in Roane County, right beside a country road where it ran over a rise of ground which since that day has been known as Bradbury's Ridge.

There were no witnesses of the murder, or the murderers. As for the Harpes, Tennessee had been comfortably lulled into the belief that it was rid of them for good. Nobody dreamed they were in the country. A few days later, however, the mystery of this slaying was solved.

A young boy, the son of Chesley Coffey, was intercepted while he was riding along the road near Black Oak, about eight miles northwest of Knoxville on an errand to borrow a fiddle for his father. "Those terrible men (the Harpes) smeared a tree with his brains, making out that his horse had run against the tree." The body was left beneath the tree, but the murderers took the gun the boy carried and the shoes he wore—the latter probably for one of the women since the men could hardly have worn the footgear of a mere lad.

Two days later, almost in the environs of Knoxville, a man named William Ballard was killed. This time the mark of the fiends was too clear for any mistake. Ballard's body had been cut open, filled with stones, and sunk in a stream—possibly the Holston River—but not deeply enough, for it was soon discovered.[1]

That disemboweled body and the stones! It was enough to alarm everyone in the country around. But in their strange, unpredictable way, the Harpes were gone—on their own back track. Somewhere, in a hidden and unfrequented part of the wild country, they made a camp, left the women and children, and went "hunting"—literally—in Morgan County.

The word "hunting" is horribly appropriate. Like werewolves the two blood-mad murderers had begun to kill for the sheer lust of killing. Robbery? A few worthless articles were taken here and there, but money was no consideration. A weapon now and then, chance items of apparel, or a horse—necessities, no more—these they took carelessly when the mood suited them. But the cunning they displayed, the pa-

[1] This was the third body the murderers thus sank which came to light—Johnson's and Stump's, and now Ballard's. It is not probable that this sort of "bad luck" attended all of their disposals in this manner. Unnamed victims, to a number which is anybody's guess, must never have been discovered, swelling the fearsome list of Harpe killings.

tience and endurance, and the rage of desire, all were for the terrible pleasure of slaughtering human beings.

Wrote Judge James Hall, in his *Story of the Harpes,* published in April, 1824, when the events were still vivid in his memory:

> Neither avarice nor want nor any of the usual inducements to the commission of crime, seemed to govern their conduct. A savage thirst for blood—a deep-rooted enmity against human nature, could alone be discovered in their actions . . . Plunder was not their object; they took only what would have been freely given them, and they destroyed without having suffered injury, and without the prospect of benefit . . . They plunged into the forest, eluded pursuit by frequently changing their course, and appeared unexpectedly to perpetrate new horrors, at points distant from where they were supposed to lurk.

2.

In Morgan County, at a place since called Brassel's Knob, the murderers overtook, July 29, two brothers named James and Robert Brassel. The first was afoot, carrying a gun. The other was mounted but unarmed.

Here the Harpes displayed one of their eerie streaks of cunning. They were riding two good horses—stolen, of course—and they drew up beside the brothers with a salutation, usual at that time, of "What's the news?"

The Brassels were full of news. They told of the murders of the Coffey boy and Ballard, which were topics of the day. With glittering interest the Harpes listened to this tale of their own crimes. Meantime they observed that only the young man on foot was armed.

"We're after the men who did those murders," one of them said, and added that others, "helping in the pursuit," were just behind, suggesting that the Brassels wait for them.

The brothers agreed. But suddenly Big Harpe glared at them. "I believe you're the Harpes yourselves!" he exclaimed.

With that, before the Brassels could recover from their astonishment, he and Little Harpe leaped from their horses, wrested James Brassel's gun away from him, and began tying the young man's hands and feet.

Now, with sudden freezing horror, Robert Brassel realized the truth: *these were the fearful Harpes themselves!*

He might easily have whipped his horse and escaped, but instead he tried to help his brother. Jumping down from his saddle, he snatched at the gun which the outlaws had thrown to the ground as they tied James Brassel. But Little Harpe was too quick for him, and seized it instead.

Life or death now! There was no mercy in those terrible countenances. Robert Brassel fled in terror for the nearest cover. Behind him he heard the pounding feet of Little Harpe pursuing him; at every instant he expected to feel a bullet in his back.

Presently the gun's report did sound; but the bullet missed. Gasping and leaping forward at his utmost speed he managed to outrun Wiley Harpe and plunged into the woods.

At that his pursuer ceased the chase and went back to where Big Harpe stood over the bound and helpless James Brassel. The brief flash of forethought and cunning had passed. It did not seem to occur to either of the Harpes that Robert Brassel, escaping, would arouse the country against them.

Instead of trying to find where he might be hiding, they turned to what was more congenial—slaughter.

It was ten miles before Robert Brassel, continuing his flight, met anyone. Then he encountered a party containing a man named Dale, his wife, and three other men, all traveling toward Knoxville.

At his story, gasped out, the men agreed to go with him and see if they could rescue his brother. Strangely, in this frontier land, they had only one gun in the party. Nevertheless, after putting Mrs. Dale in a place of safety, perhaps in a cabin of some roadside family, they followed Robert Brassel to the scene of his encounter with the Harpes.

The murderers were gone, but James Brassel was there—dead and hardly recognizable, his head beaten in and his throat cut. His gun, the only thing of any value he carried, had been smashed, evidently used as a club to batter him as he lay bound and helpless. It was on the ground beside him, useless now.

The sight was horrifying to the beholders, but rather haphazardly they started out to see which way the Harpes had gone. A trail of horses' hoof marks, plain enough, led toward Knoxville.

Now suddenly came a hair-raising occurrence. Riding back on their own trail appeared the Harpes, and confronted the little party of pursuers. Though they were alone when they killed Brassel, they now were followed by their three women, mounted like themselves on good horses and carrying their young children. There also were a couple of pack animals, loaded with clothing and provisions, "apparently for a long journey and for battle and siege."

To an abrupt halt came the pursuers. Once before a posse had been overawed by these terrible men, and this party had only one gun. One of the men near Dale whispered, "If they don't show signs of fight, let's leave them be." With heartfelt unanimity the suggestion was adopted.

On came the Harpes. They "looked very awful at them" (the pursuing party), then rode by followed by their little cavalcade, and on into the forest beyond.

So dire was the impression made on them that Dale and his men continued on their way—opposite to that taken by the Harpes. They were careful to ride in silence "lest any words they should utter might be overheard and mistaken by the Harpes as a threat." Only young Brassel was vocal, crying out at the cowardice of his companions. But he had no weapon and could not carry on the pursuit by himself.

Later James Brassel's body was properly buried. But by then the Harpes once more had disappeared. With their women and children, their stolen horses and other plunder, the savage werewolves of the wilds were heading north, "with ever-increasing desire to shed blood."

3.

It is presumed that they crossed into Kentucky through what is now Pickett County, Tennessee. Somewhere near the interstate line they found their next victim, a settler named John Tully.

There is mystery about this Tully. According to the memoirs of Colonel Daniel Trabue—whose young son was murdered the year before—Tully not only knew the Harpes, but once carried messages to them from the Harpe women, when the outlaws were heading for Cave-in-Rock. If he had thus rendered the Harpes a service it did not help him when they found him alone. Without pity they slew him, and dumped his body behind or under a log, as they previously had done with Langford.

Meanwhile Robert Brassel had rallied "William Wood and others" and was trailing his brother's murderers north through Tennessee. The party arrived at the state line soon after the Harpes had gone on. They found Nathaniel Stockton and other neighbors searching for a missing man, and made the melancholy discovery of Tully's dead body, hidden behind the log where it had been thrown.[2]

After Tully was buried, most of the Tennesseeans turned back into Tennessee. We lose track of Robert Brassel at this point, perhaps because he was one of those who returned to their homes. But William

[2] If Tully did indeed befriend the Harpes, the State of Kentucky was not made aware of it. On December 18, 1800, the legislature passed a bill for the relief of "his wife, Christiana Tully, a desolate widow with eight small children," which aided her in maintaining her home.

Wood took council with Nathaniel Stockton, Tully's neighbor, and they decided somebody should warn Colonel Trabue, who had been active in spurring the hunt for the Harpes after his son was murdered, and who might be the next object of their malice.

Cutting across country where horses could not travel, in order to arrive in time, Wood and Stockton made the journey of forty miles on foot to Trabue's place, where they found the colonel and his family unharmed.

The colonel, who also was a justice of the peace, acted promptly and with sense. First he prepared a statement, to which the two men swore, reciting the four murders thus far discovered since the Harpes reappeared (although he got the name Hardin, instead of Ballard). With copies of this he sent out two mounted messengers in different directions.

One man rode hard for Frankfort to see the governor and secure publication of the notice in the newspapers. The second galloped toward Red Banks, with a warning message to General Samuel Hopkins, the most prominent citizen of the place, a known foe of the Harpes and Masons, suggesting that the murderers might head back that way.

The Harpes did go toward Red Banks, eventually, but at this time they were in the very country through which John Ellis, the messenger to the governor, must ride. As he rode, Ellis spread the news to people he met: "The Harpes are back! The Harpes are back!"

It was ninety miles to Frankfort and the Harpes themselves learned of Ellis' errand. Somewhere along the road the messenger looked back and saw two savage-looking men spurring their horses after him at the dead run. The dread Harpes were pursuing him!

He put spurs to his own horse, and later was devoutly thankful that he was mounted on a superior animal. The Harpes had good horses too, and they rode like wild Indians to overtake him. But Ellis was a rider also. Leaning forward over his horse's neck, and watching the rough trail ahead to avoid holes or barriers over which his animal might stumble and bring about his ruin, he kept ahead of his pursuers for miles. At length his horse drew farther ahead, and the Harpes, furiously shaking their rifles at him, turned aside and once more disappeared into the forest. Ellis reached Frankfort in safety.

News that the murderers were on the prowl in western Kentucky traveled with speed inspired by an electric shock of fear. All Kentucky and even persons in other states were aware of the deadly menace in the country, and newspapers published the story, adding to the general alarm and disturbance. Where were the Harpes? This was the subject of universal fearful speculation.

The grisly trail of the man-killers soon made itself evident. About twenty-five miles from Trabue's place, on Marrowbone Creek, they came upon a cabin so isolated that news of their depredations had not yet reached it. In the cabin lived a man named John Graves and his thirteen-year-old son. They were putting a crop in a new "patch" and expected the rest of their family to join them before long.

After dark the Harpes approached this place and asked permission to camp beside it for the night. Permission was granted; probably, in the hospitable manner of the frontier, food also was given to the little group of strangers.

But gratitude was utterly foreign to the Harpes. In spite of the kindness of the cabin man and his son, they crept into the cabin early next morning, while John Graves and his boy still slept, and with Graves's own axe, "split the heads of both open and threw the bodies of both into the brush fence that surrounded the house."

Days later a suspicious gathering of buzzards, soaring and swooping and settling in the trees near the Graves cabin, led to an investigation. The bodies were found, decomposing and much torn by the devouring vultures, yet with the marks of violence clearly evident. These murders occurred some time in the week before August 22.

Throughout the country, parties of armed men were searching for the Harpes and there was no question that lynching would be their fate if they were captured. But capturing the murderers was a necessary prelude to a successful lynching, and in the tangle of wooded west Kentucky that was a dangerous and difficult task.

From the Graves cabin the Harpes headed north for some twenty miles into Russell County, where lived "Old Man" Roberts—that is all of his name we know—the supposed father of the two Roberts girls, and therefore the "father-in-law," without legality, of Micajah Harpe. The women had stopped there once before, for a brief period, in their flight from Danville, when they took their long canoe trip down the Green River into the Ohio, and thence to Cave-in-Rock. Perhaps it was Old Man Roberts who furnished the canoe and took their mare in payment.

On this occasion he gave them shelter once more, though it was for a short time only. The Harpe men were uneasy, and wanted to be on the road. Hardly giving their wretched women time to rest, they headed off again, this time westward toward Logan County. Evidently they still hankered for the outlaw range of the lower Ohio.[3]

For some time now the Harpes had not killed anybody and their

[3] Perhaps on this journey they spent a little time in Mammoth Cave. One of the women later said they sojourned either in Mammoth Cave, "or some other large cavern."

thirst to inflict bloodshed and misery was preying on them. Under such circumstances they were not selective.

Their first victim was a little Negro boy. He was riding on an old horse with a bag of grain intended for a mill when they halted him. In sheer deviltry "they dashed the boy's brains out against a tree, but left the horse and bag of grain untouched."

The murder of the Negro boy was senseless. He not only was harmless, but he was a slave—property, like the horse. They might have taken him along with them and sold him to someone for a good sum. But money was not what they were after. It was blood and death that counted.

Next came another child. We do not even know her name. All we know is that she was "a little girl found at some distance from her home, whose tender age and helplessness should have been protection against any but incarnate fiends."[4]

4.

Up to this time the Harpes had committed their murders singly, or by twos, in one instance three men at a time. But now came a wholesale murder the details of which are described by T. Marshall Smith; who frequently depends on tradition, but which are accepted by Otto A. Rothert, a serious and accurate historian, indicating there is basis of fact in the incident.

They had crossed Big Whippoorwill Creek, about eight miles west of Russellville, in Logan County, and were camping in a cave, when at about sundown they saw a caravan which consisted of two brothers named Trisword, their wives, "several children, and a few black servants." The exact number in the party is not stated in the account,[5] but it must have been at least a dozen strong.

When the Triswords made camp, "at what was for many years called the point of Clay Lick woods," the temptation offered by so many unsuspecting and virtually helpless human beings became overpowering to the blood-crazed creatures who watched them.[6]

[4] Lewis Collins, *Historical Sketches of Kentucky*.

[5] T. Marshall Smith. His chronology is badly mixed. I have followed that of Otto A. Rothert, a careful student of the period.

[6] One account, T. Marshall Smith's, says that at this point the Harpes were joined by "two Cherokees"—companions of their early outlawry. But this is unlikely, since there is no mention of the Indians in the events preceding or immediately succeeding this episode.

At daybreak the assassins crept up on the sleeping camp. As soon as it was light enough to see the sights of their rifles, the Harpes fired at the recumbent figures. Two persons were killed instantly—one of the Trisword brothers and one of the wives. A child was mortally wounded.

Now, with wild yells, the Harpes bounded forward to finish their slaughter. The unhurt Trisword brother, supposing they were attacked by Indians, managed to get to a buffalo trace, and "quite in his undress," raced eight miles to Drumgool's Station, today's Adair, Kentucky, to give the alarm.

A hastily assembled party of nine armed men accompanied Trisword back to the camp site to meet the "hostile Indians," and if possible to rescue the survivors. They were too late. At the place of the massacre they found "the ground covered for a space with the bodies of men, women, and children, white and black. Some of them dreadfully mangled; and some stripped to the skin."

The only survivor of the party was the man who fled.

The dead were gathered and buried in a common grave near the scene of the slaughter.

The following day Colonel William Stewart, sheriff of Logan County, organized a posse of a dozen men and set out to hunt the murderers, and "if Indians, destroy them, or if white, to bring them back to Russellville for punishment."

The track was easily found—as so often before the Harpes, who were at times cunning woodsmen, lapsed into that strange carelessness of theirs. It led north and east to Mud River, which runs northward from Russellville.

Later it was learned that on the first night after the Trisword massacre the Harpes camped at the grounds where a big revival camp meeting had been held only a few weeks before. The brutal outlaws were "edgy." Perhaps the wholesale nature of their last slaughter made them apprehensive.

And here we have a sudden flash of insight into the abysmal nature of these beasts.

That night the children were fretful and wailing. Often the Harpes had snarled at the women about the whimpering infants. Big Harpe once had said that the babies might bring the attention of pursuers to them, and threatened to kill them. Sometimes when the two Harpes were in a drunk and surly mood, the women would steal away with their little ones, far enough into the woods so that their unnatural fathers could not hear them.

But on this occasion, at the camp meeting grounds, the bigger outlaw's patience snapped.

"The infant of Susan . . . about nine months old, being very sick and crying all morning, so that nothing could quiet it, Big Harpe snatched it from its mother's arms, slung it by the heels against a large tree by the path-side, and literally bursting its head into a dozen pieces—threw it from him as far as his great strength enabled him, into the woods."[7]

In this connection there is an error in identification. The children of both Susan Roberts, a girl whom she called Lovey, and Betsey Roberts, a boy whom she named Joe, survived. It was the child of Sally Rice, a little daughter, who was so brutally killed.

Was it Big Harpe's own child? Before his death, he said it was, although Sally was "married" to Little Harpe. But then he probably did not know, could not possibly know, because of the promiscuity in which he and the other indulged with the three women.

Thus the "swinging by the legs against a tree" reached its most revolting and dreadful culmination. Writing in 1923, Otto A. Rothert, a very careful historian, said, "A large maple tree still marks the spot where this deed was enacted."

Yet the mother, probably weeping, still followed the man who slew her child. Why did the women do so? Why did any of them remain with the Harpes after the sickening deeds they had witnessed?

Were they afraid to leave their masters? Once before, when they had every opportunity to be rid of the brutes for good, they made a long and dangerous journey to rejoin them. Perhaps it was sheer animal magnetism by which the Harpes held them. Perhaps the women even obtained a crazy vicarious thrill out of the life they led, the things in which they took part.

The fact that they did remain, did continue to follow and obey and participate in the deeds of blood, if only as onlookers, measurably waters down any sympathy one might be inclined to feel for them.

[7] T. Marshall Smith, *Legends of the War of Independence.*

VI.   *A Bloody Head on a Stake*

1.

He did not know it when he killed Sally Rice's baby girl, but time was beginning to run short for Micajah Harpe.

True, Sheriff Stewart's posse was given the slip. It went off toward the south, following a report that the outlaws were heading back toward Tennessee. But the respite was only temporary, although more lives would be snuffed out before he paid with his own in a singularly horrible way.

Most people did not believe that the Harpes would be so foolish as to return to Henderson County, where not many months before Captain Young and his regulators had so wholesomely decimated the outlaws of the area, and driven others out of the country. But in their crazy way, the Harpes seemed to realize that the unexpected was their safest course.

At a place known as Knob Lick, not far from present-day Sebree, Kentucky, in northern Webster County (then a part of Henderson County), two families of supposed settlers appeared and quietly took up residence on Canoe Creek. At first nobody paid any attention to them, but this did not last for long.

One day John Slover, an old hunter and Indian fighter, who had killed a bear in the area, was riding along a path through the woods toward his cabin, with some of the meat and the skin, when he heard the unmistakable sound of the click made by a rifle hammer when it falls and misses fire.

Instantly glancing around, he saw two men glaring at him through the bushes. Slover sank his spurs into his horse and the animal bounded forward. In a few moments he was far enough along the twisting trail to be out of sight of the strange and now suddenly menacing pair.

That one of those men had tried to shoot him he was sure. Why, when the first failed, the second did not fire, he could only explain to himself by the conclusion that the second—fortunately for him—was not at the time carrying a gun.

When Slover recounted the incident to some of his friends, they agreed that an attempt had been made to assassinate him, but they refused to believe the Harpes were in the country, so sure was everyone that from very fear the outlaws would give the area a wide berth.

Nor, apparently, did anyone suspect the "two harmless families" so newly arrived in the neighborhood. At this time in fact the Harpes were in another of their periods of cunning and caution. In their adventurous journeyings, they had managed to clothe themselves in sober dark garments taken from the bodies of some of their victims, so that they appeared fairly clean and well spoken. They lived in a manner so secluded that not even the presence of a third woman with them, which might have created speculation, was noted. They seemed to be quiet, peaceful settlers, far different from what the terrible Harpes must be like.

But a day or two after Slover's adventure, a man of the neighborhood named Trowbridge disappeared. He had "made salt" at Robertson's Lick, at the headwaters of Highland Creek, and when last seen was setting out to convey the salt to his farm, which was near the mouth of the creek where it emptied into the Ohio River.

A search was made for him, but not for months was his fate known. Then one of the Harpe women, after her arrest, revealed that although Trowbridge's route took him eight or ten miles west of Canoe Creek where the Harpes were camping, the two outlaws crossed the height of land, waylaid him, murdered him, and disposed of his body in their favorite ghoulish fashion.

Up at Red Banks, General Hopkins, a Revolutionary officer, land company representative, a squire, and later a Congressman, was a personage of unusual force and brains. He had been alerted by the message from Colonel Trabue, and when he heard the report of Slover's singular adventure, and soon after, of the mysterious disappearance of

Trowbridge, he began to have a strong suspicion that those supposedly peaceful settlers on Canoe Creek were in fact the Harpes.

Accordingly he sent scouts up the stream to check on the suspected people. But the scouts, watching the place, saw only two men, dressed rather better than average frontiersmen, and no sign of women or children. What they did not know was that the Harpes had grown apprehensive and had sent the women and children away shortly before, to a rendezvous previously decided upon. This was a cave, on or near Pond River, an affluent of the Green, some thirty or forty miles from the Canoe Creek camp.

There was something else the scouts did not know: the Harpes were aware all the time that they were being watched, and took good care to behave in such a manner as to excite no suspicion.

Hopkins' men even brought John Slover to a place from which he could observe the two suspects, unseen. But the Harpes were wearing different, more respectable clothing than they wore in that one brief glimpse he had of them, and he at last decided that they were not the ones who attempted his life. After a time the scouts returned to Red Banks, to report that there must be some mistake in thinking the men they had watched were the outlaws.

The very next day the Harpes left the cabin to join their women.

But first they had some business to attend to. On Deer Creek, south of Canoe Creek, in what is now Webster Country, lived Squire Silas McBee, a justice of the peace who had been fearless in leading the fight against the outlaws of the lower Ohio. To kill this man was the Harpes' first objective.

The afternoon of the day they left Canoe Creek, August 21, 1799, they arrived at the cabin of James Tompkins on Deer Creek. Here once more they displayed the unusual gift for dissembling which sporadically revealed itself in their actions.

Tompkins lived alone, and they could easily have killed him; but his house was only half a mile from McBee's place, and butchering this man might alarm the more desired quarry. Assuming, therefore, unctuous manners very strange for them, the Harpes introduced themselves as itinerant Methodist preachers. Their garments were sober, and the fact that they were armed occasioned no surprise since everyone, ministers included, carried weapons in that wild country at the time.

Tompkins gladly welcomed the "reverends," and invited them to supper. When they seated themselves at the table Big Harpe, as a capsheaf to all this play-acting, bowed his head and said a long prayer, to which Little Harpe and Tompkins, in the manner of that era, uttered hearty "Amens."

The supper was poor, lacking meat, and Tompkins apologized, saying he had none.

"What about deer? Plenty of them around here," said one of the Harpes.

"I've run out of powder," confessed the shamefaced Tompkins.

Now occurred the most surprising act in this sequence.

"We can't let a man go without powder," said Big Harpe. And from his own powder horn he poured out a cupful of powder for his host.

That cupful of powder—the only gift, so far as is known, that Micajah Harpe ever made to anyone—was later to play a strangely fateful role in his career.

Darkness was descending, and though Tompkins urged his "ministerial" friends to remain for the night, they told him they still had ten miles to travel, and after bidding him a farewell, complete with pious pulpit phrases, set off toward the south.

As soon as they were out of sight of his house, however, they made a quick swing toward the northwest in the direction of Squire McBee's residence. Night had fallen, the moon was shining brightly, and it is probable that they planned to shoot him through a window.

McBee, however, kept a pack of savage bear dogs. All at once he heard them break into fierce barkings and snarlings, and going to the door saw the pack attacking two men in the moonlight. The squire was canny. He was expecting no visitors and these appeared to be on some errand unexplained and strange. What was more odd, the men made no shout to the house for help. The squire did not, therefore, call off his dogs.

Presently, after fighting off the pack, the Harpes departed. It may be wondered why they did not use their guns on the dogs. The explanation is that such an act would certainly reveal them as enemies, since no man, in that day, shot another man's dog, unless he expected to defend himself from sudden retribution. The Harpes preferred not to reveal their true identities or their schemes just at that time.

2.

About four miles northwest of Squire McBee's place, not far east of the present town of Dixon, lived Moses Stegall,[1] with his wife and their four-months-old baby son. This family, it later developed, was decidedly curious in its dealings. Both Stegall and his wife knew the

[1] Sometimes spelled Steigal.

Harpes, and Mrs. Stegall had been told by them never to address them by their real names in the presence of a stranger.

To show the connection still further, just a day or two before the three Harpe women and the two children had stopped at the Stegall place, for a meal or for a night's shelter. At that time Susan was paid one dollar on an order given her by John Leiper, also of this neighborhood, for "services unspecified."

Adding to the general mystery of the succeeding events is the fact that Leiper, who played an important part in them, also knew the Harpes, having at one time lived near Colonel Trabue in Adair County. There is reason to believe that Leiper had in some manner incurred the enmity of the Harpes and feared they would kill him, which would explain the zeal of his later pursuit of them.[2]

The women and children had gone on, to the secret rendezvous, but on the night of August 22, after they had been repelled from McBee's place by the bear dogs, Micajah and Wiley Harpe appeared at the Stegall cabin and knocked on the door.

Mrs. Stegall opened the door and readily admitted the two night callers. There was some conversation. She told them that her husband was away but would return before long. Meantime she already had another gentleman guest.

This was a Major William Love, a surveyor who lived in southeast Kentucky and had business to discuss with Stegall. Major Love already had retired in the loft above, but he now descended and was introduced by Mrs. Stegall to the newcomers under fictitious names. Then, since she had no other sleeping room, she invited all three male visitors to share the loft together.

They climbed above, and made ready to sleep. The major, indeed, was soon slumbering. But he had an unfortunate habit—he snored. The Harpes were enraged by this. Presently one of them tomahawked him as he lay.

Now the two descended the ladder to the main floor. Mrs. Stegall rose from her bed with some surprised inquiry. Their madness had returned upon them.

"What do you mean putting us in the same bed with a man who snores?" one of them growled.

---

[2] Could the "services unspecified" for which Leiper gave Susan the order for one dollar have been of such nature as to arouse the jealousy of the Harpes, as their jealousy was aroused against Moses Doss? Leiper was a known skirt chaser. He had been indicted the previous July for "living in adultery with Ann L. Allen, from the 20th of last May." This case probably still was pending at the time of the hunt for the Harpes which took place in the latter part of August.

This woman was a friend, who it turned out had befriended their own women and children, and was now befriending them. But they murdered her and the baby then and there.[3]

The Harpes next gathered up a few articles of clothing to carry away, and set the cabin on fire with the murdered man, woman, and child inside it. The baby's death may have been quick when its throat was slashed, but Mrs. Stegall seems to have died hard. When later on her charred body was examined, three case knives were found stuck into it, one buried so deeply that the fire which consumed the house did not burn the handle.

Something more than mere mad desire for destruction prompted this arson after the murders. The Harpes knew the responsible and generous nature of their enemy, Squire McBee. He was at this time a mature man, and very corpulent. One account says "he rode heavy in his saddle." But he was fearless, had fought at King's Mountain and other Revolutionary battles, as well as against the Indians, and his public spirit and character made him a natural leader.

Since it was still night when the cabin was set on fire, the Harpes believed he would see the flame-lit skies as the structure burned, and would at once ride to the place to see if he could be of any assistance to the family, whereupon they would ambush him.

From the barn they took a gelding belonging to Stegall and a fine mare belonging to Major Love, and hid them in the woods. They then concealed themselves in the bushes along the road by which they supposed Squire McBee would come.

[3] One version of this killing, given by J. W. M. Brazeale, in his *Life as It Is*, is as follows: After the Harpes killed Love, they peacefully slept the rest of the night beside the dead man in the loft. In the morning they went below, and asked Mrs. Stegall to get some breakfast for them. She supposed that Major Love was still sleeping, and said she would do as they asked, but her child was ill, and needed attention, and it would therefore take her some time to cook the meal. At this the Harpes suggested that she put the baby in the cradle and let them rock it. She did so. "After Mrs. Stegall had prepared their breakfast and the ruthless and savage murderers had partaken of her hospitality, she went to the cradle to see if the child was asleep, expressing some astonishment (as Micajah Harpe acknowledged when he was afterward taken) that her child should remain quiet for so great a length of time . . . She beheld her tender, harmless, and helpless infant lying breathless, with its throat cut from ear to ear . . . But the relentless monsters stayed not their bloody hands for the tears and heartbroken wailings of a bereaved mother. They instantly dispatched her, with the same instrument (a butcher knife) with which they had cut the throat of the child." This story, which is ascribed to Big Harpe himself when he lay dying, when he made several disclosures of his past, gruesome as it is, may well be the true account.

3.

It so happened, however, that McBee did not see the distant fire that night; he did not, indeed, know anything about it until the following day.

Meantime the Harpes did not remain idle. At early daylight next morning, two men, named Hudgens and Gilmore, coming from Robertson's Lick with packs of salt, were suddenly halted when the two outlaws stepped into the path with rifles ready to fire.

"We're looking for the men who murdered the Stegall family and burned their house," said one of the Harpes.

The two men, with astonishment, denied any knowledge of it.

"Well," said the Harpes, "you'll have to go before Squire McBee and prove you're innocent."

To this Hudgens and Gilmore agreed. They surrendered their guns and obediently marched along the trail toward the squire's house.

Suddenly Big Harpe dropped a few steps behind the prisoners, raised his rifle and shot Gilmore through the head. The man pitched forward on the ground, dead in an instant.

Now Hudgens, with one startled glance around, realized for the first time who his captors were. He tried to run for it, but Little Harpe was faster than he. In a few yards he overtook him and beat out his brains with his own gun.

The diabolic violence of these two added murders seemed for the moment to assuage the blood lust of the killers. After concealing the bodies so that persons passing on the trail would not see them, they again took up their hiding place.

Within a short time a party of five men, headed by John Pyles, also returning from Robertson's Lick, passed down the trace. These men had seen the smoldering ruins of the Stegall cabin and were hurrying to report the matter to Squire McBee.

The Harpes, lying motionless in ambush, let them pass. Perhaps five men were too many for them to molest. More likely, however, the outlaws thought that Squire McBee, when informed of the fire, would come riding and they would gain their end of assassinating him.

But a special guardian angel seemed to watch over the squire. Instead of taking the direct trail to the Stegall place, he rode by a short cut to another neighbor's, William Grissom, to get help. Thus, without knowing it, he escaped death at the Harpe ambush on the main trail. He and Grissom, with other members of the Grissom family, then rode by a different route to the Stegall cabin.

The squire was a thorough man. He investigated the ruins, and to his horror found the half-consumed bodies of Mrs. Stegall and Major Love. No mention was made at the time of the baby. Perhaps its small form was entirely reduced to ashes.

Examination of the bodies revealed the three knives buried in the woman's corpse, and also that the man's head had been split by a hatchet blow. This was so clearly the work of inhuman killers that everyone present reached the dread conclusion that the Harpes were on the loose again—and in this very neighborhood.

Squire McBee and the Grissoms buried the bodies, then rode back to the Grissom place. From there, accompanied by William Grissom, the squire returned to his own home, taking once more the short cut and thus disappointing the Harpes.

Barely had they dismounted at McBee's when Moses Stegall himself rode up. For the first time he now learned the fate of his family. Understandably, he was furious. It had to be the Harpes, he fiercely said. And he volunteered to go and find a posse of men to hunt them down, proposing to ride to Robertson's Lick[4] where several men were at that time working. This was agreed and he rode away.

Some time that afternoon the Harpes, who by now must have known that their presence in the area was suspected, slipped away and were gone. Not long afterward the bodies of Hudgens and Gilmore were found and buried, increasing the extent of the horror which had taken five lives within a few hours in the small neighborhood.

By next morning Stegall was back from Robertson's Lick. He brought with him three men, John Leiper, Matthew Christian, and Neville Lindsey. At Squire McBee's were waiting the squire himself and William Grissom. Also James Tompkins, he who had given hospitality to the supposed "Methodist preachers," and who now for the first time was aware of the true identity of his dreadful visitors.

4.

Seven strong, the posse set out on a search so fierce and remorseless that it is even yet a legend of the country.

They were all veteran woodsmen, and all well mounted and armed, but they differed markedly in character. McBee was the leader. An

[4] A "lick" in the language of the frontier was a place where salt was found in deposit on the surface of the earth, or in a saline spring, so that animals came to lick the ground for the mineral. Such places were well known as hunting grounds, and at such places the frontiersmen by primitive methods of evaporation "made salt," a necessity for their homes. Robertson's Lick was within a few miles of Squire McBee's home.

alert, responsible man, before he left his house he gathered in it the members of his own and Grissom's families, saw that the windows were shuttered and doors barred, armed the women and youngsters with a few old guns, and told them not to leave it until he returned and to defend the temporary little fort if it was attacked.

William Grissom also was a substantial man, brave and ready. Matthew Christian belonged to a good family, and went to some trouble to reach the rallying place at McBee's, having first gone to Grissom's to offer his services, where he found the place deserted. Neville Lindsey was intelligent and alert, so much so that later he became a successful land developer.

After these, the quality deteriorated. James Tompkins appears to have been mentally slow, a man who allowed others to lead, and acceded too readily to suggestions, though honest enough.

But what about Moses Stegall and John Leiper? Both of them had the guilty knowledge that they were acquainted with the Harpes and had hitherto done nothing to bring them to justice, indeed had assisted them. Now they were eager enough to kill the outlaws, but this was perhaps as much for fear they might themselves be exposed as from desire to bring the Harpes to justice. Stegall, to be sure, had a grievance—his wife and child had been murdered. But this, as later events proved, did not seem to prey too heavily upon him. Stegall and Leiper, it must be concluded, were treacherous and untrustworthy, yet they played a major part in what followed.

The trail of the Harpes' horses was found and followed. At one place it was obliterated by the hoof marks of a herd of buffalos—which at that date still roamed in Kentucky. But the party divided and circled until the track again was found beyond this interruption.

Somewhat farther on the trail forked. Here the pursuers had to divide, part following each fork. After a time the forks rejoined, and from then on the main track made by horses' hoofs was clear. This appears to be the only time when the Harpes made any real attempt to confuse potential pursuers. And even this effort was childishly ineffective.

That night Squire McBee and his men camped beside Pond River, on the west bank. They had, of course, no tent or even coverings except for saddle blankets. During the night a heavy rain came up and all were drenched. This was not in itself a matter of moment: all the men were accustomed to outdoor inconveniences. But it had one interesting effect. The soaking so swelled the wooden ramrod of John Leiper's rifle that later, at a critical moment, he was not able to draw it out to reload his weapon.

Next morning the party forded the river into what is now Muhlenberg County. Very shortly, "about an hour after sunup," they found two dogs both dead. The animals were recognized as having belonged to Hudgens and Gilmore, the men murdered by the Harpes in the McBee neighborhood. Either they had followed the outlaws or been taken along on leash. Evidently they had been killed for fear they might attract attention by barking. So recently had they been killed that the carcasses were still warm.

This circumstance caused the possemen to believe they were now close to their quarry. Four of the party, Leiper, Stegall, Christian, and Lindsey, dismounted and went ahead on foot, Indian style, to scout with as little noise as possible, while McBee, Grissom and Tompkins followed, bringing along the horses. After a mile or so the men on foot mounted again and they rode on as before, the squire in the lead.

All at once McBee gave a cry: "There they are!"

On a hillside ahead he saw three men, and even at the distance he recognized two of them as the Harpes. The outlaws were standing on the ground, though one of them held a horse by its bridle, talking to a third man whom the squire did not recognize, also on foot.

Instantly McBee spurred his horse forward and the whole posse rode at a full gallop for the place where he had spied the outlaws.

In the next few minutes things happened very rapidly. Big Harpe was seen hastily to mount his horse and ride off at top speed, while Little Harpe, on foot, dashed in a different direction.

The man they had been talking to ran toward the posse itself. As he neared, to a distance of about sixty or seventy yards, he suddenly leaped behind a tree.

So suspiciously hostile seemed the action that McBee, taking no chances, raised his gun, which was loaded with buckshot, and fired at part of the man's body which was exposed to view behind the tree trunk. It was an expert shot. Two of the shot took effect, one hitting the man in the right leg, and the other in the right arm.

He fell to the ground. At the same moment, Stegall exclaimed, "Don't shoot! It's George Smith!"

Smith was an honest settler who lived two or three miles up the Pond River from where they were at the moment. Stegall's shout saved his life, for others of the party had leveled their guns.

"Squire McBee!" cried out the wounded man, who recognized the leader of the party.

As McBee rode up with his men, Smith blamed himself for the mishap, was even apologetic about it.

"I was nearly bereft of my senses," he said. "I expected every minute that the Harpes would kill me, and when I *treed* [tried to hide himself] I was still so scared that I didn't realize what a fool act it was."

He was not seriously hurt. Later, after his wounds were bandaged, he was able to hobble home without assistance.

To McBee he said that he had been looking for strayed horses when he met Little Harpe "with his gun in one hand, and a kettle in the other, going for water"—down to the river a short distance away. Little Harpe stopped him and began to question him so loudly that Big Harpe heard him from where they were camped "not more than eighty rods distant," and came riding to join in the inquisition, on the fine gray mare which, the posse knew, had belonged to Major Love. Just as the second outlaw dismounted and Smith was mentally counting the minutes until his end, McBee's posse was seen riding toward them and the killers fled.

By the time Smith finished his story and had his wounds dressed, the Harpes had disappeared. But acting on his description that the outlaw camp was "not more than eighty rods distant" from where he had been talking with them, McBee's men began a search of the area. Very soon they discovered the hiding place. It was described as "a natural room, perhaps fifteen feet square, under a shelving rock projecting from the cliff of a ridge facing south, with a large rock in front, leaving but a narrow entrance—affording altogether a very secluded and safe retreat, susceptible of easy defence."

When the posse advanced "rather cautiously" upon this place they found in it only one person, Sally Rice, the "wife" of Little Harpe whose child Big Harpe murdered at the camp meeting grounds.

In spite of all her terrible experiences, Sally was still no more than a girl. She was terrified and ready to talk. After the outlaws first saw the posse, she said, Wiley Harpe disappeared and she had not since seen him. But a few minutes before McBee's men discovered the outlaw retreat—perhaps while they were still talking to the wounded Smith—Micajah Harpe rode up to the cave leading two horses, evidently by such a route that the men down in the valley did not see him. On the led horses he mounted his own two "wives," Susan and Betsey Roberts, and their two children, and all rode away in the same direction from which he had come. There was no horse for Sally, so she was left behind.

She pointed out the direction in which Big Harpe had gone, and stuck to her story even when McBee threatened to shoot her dead unless she told the truth.

Most of the posse set off in pursuit. Squire McBee, because his great weight in the saddle precluded a long ride at a fast pace, remained behind to take charge of the prisoner. He placed Sally on a spare horse, perhaps a pack animal of the posse, and with her followed his men, who by this time were far ahead on Big Harpe's trail. The whereabouts of Little Harpe of course could not be determined.

5.

Big Harpe's effort to carry off his women was a fatal mistake. They so slowed him down that within two miles the posse sighted him ahead on a small ridge.

"Stop, or we'll fire!" one of them yelled.

At that Micajah Harpe abandoned the women and dashed away at the full speed of his mare. The women halted, trembling, and quickly surrendered.

Meantime Leiper, riding at the head of the posse, took a shot at Big Harpe, but missed. He was a good marksman, and rode a fine horse, and he was determined, for his own reasons, to get the murderer. But when he tried to reload his rifle he found the ramrod stuck, due to its swelling caused by the soaking rain of the night before. With a curse he called on Tompkins to lend him his gun. Tompkins, in his slow-witted and obedient way, complied.

Tompkins and Lindsey were detailed to guard the two women and their babies, and were presently joined by McBee, bringing Sally. The remaining four, Leiper, Stegall, Grissom and Christian, spurred hard after the big outlaw.

At first it was a headlong race, but the excellent mare Big Harpe was riding evidently had been ridden until her strength was about gone. After a time she began to fail and the pursuers drew up on him.

As they came within range, three of them—Stegall, Grissom, and Christian—halted their horses to fire at him. Christian's bullet wounded him slightly in the left leg but did not halt him.

Leiper, however, did not slow his mount or fire his rifle. As he drew ahead of the others and gained on Harpe, the outlaw, who seemed to think that all his pursuers had emptied their guns, brought his mare to a plunging halt, and turned fiercely in the saddle to shoot down his nearest enemy.

But first he spent a moment looking to his priming. That delay was fatal. Leiper took aim and fired.

The leaden ball, from the gun borrowed from Tompkins, struck Harpe in the body, shattering his spine.

The wound was mortal, and here is a singular thing: the bullet that caused it *was sped by his own powder.* It was fired from Tompkins' gun which Leiper had borrowed, and was loaded with the very powder Big Harpe had poured out into a cup a few nights before at Tompkins's house.

In spite of his paralyzing wound, the enormous vitality of the outlaw kept him in his saddle where most men would have fallen to the ground.

By no means was he finished. Levelling his gun at Leiper, he pulled the trigger. But he had not been able to prime the weapon carefully, and it snapped without firing. In bitter disgust he hurled it away from him.

Micajah Harpe, his backbone and spine smashed above the hips, was now paralyzed from the waist down. Yet by sheer balance he still managed to keep his saddle, and brandishing a tomahawk, urged his jaded mare forward.

His pursuers called on him to halt. He shook his tomahawk at them.

"Stop your horses and I will," he yelled back. They noticed that his voice shook as he said it.

They pulled up their mounts, and Leiper and Stegall, who wished to be most certain of the outlaw's death, dismounted to reload.

But Big Harpe was a trickster to the last. Suddenly swinging the mare into a small canebrake, he rode into it and was lost to sight.

Meantime Leiper's horse, frightened by the shooting and shouting, broke away and ran. Some time was required before Christian, who remained mounted, rounded up the animal and brought it back.

All had reloaded their guns now, and they followed the outlaw into the canebrake. It was easy to trace the mare's course, where she bent the cane as she plunged forward. But she was almost finished, and just as she and her rider emerged on the other side, not half a mile from where they entered the canebrake, they were overtaken.

The mare, head down, was walking slowly. Slumped on her back, the man was almost unconscious. The tomahawk had fallen from his nerveless fingers, and his mouth was drawn and black.

They hauled him easily from the saddle, and he fell thumping to the ground.

There he lay while the entire posse, including Squire McBee, gathered round him.

"Water!" he gasped. And Leiper, the man who brought him low, for lack of any other container took off one of the outlaw's shoes and in it brought water from a muddy pool in the marshy canebrake.

"Have you any money hidden?" Squire McBee asked.

Feebly Big Harpe replied that he had secreted a pair of saddlebags with money near the head of Pond River, some twenty miles from where he then lay.[5]

[5] Though the posse paid little attention to this since his description of the exact locality was vague, it was later reported that a considerable amount of specie was found by accident near the headwaters of Pond River. This may have been Harpe's treasure, the amount of which was never disclosed.

"You're already dying," said McBee, "but we can't wait all day for you to do it. So if you want to say a prayer before you go to the next world, we'll give you time for it."

To this the outlaw made no reply, "appearing quite unconcerned."

Now Stegall came and stood over the prostrate man. He and Leiper both very likely were fearful of some disclosure Harpe might make.

"You killed my wife and baby!" Stegall growled, and drew a great knife from his belt. "See this knife? I'm going to cut your head off with *this!*"

"I'm a young man," said the dying outlaw faintly, "but I feel the death-damp already. Before I die I wish you'd bring old Baldwin here, because he got me to commit all my crimes."[6]

Either then or just prior to Stegall's threat, Harpe made several confessions. To quote a news item from the *Carolina Gazette,* under a date of September 10, 1799:

> He (Micajah Harpe) confessed the killing of Mr. Stump on Big Barren; he also confessed of their killing 17 or 18 besides.

Another source, Colonel G. W. Sevier, later stated the number was thirty-one. Otto A. Rothert lists the total, up to Big Harpe's death, at "twenty-eight, exclusive of the Triswords, of whom there were probably about ten"—say, thirty-eight.[7]

---

[6] At this date Micajah Harpe was thirty-one years old. The Baldwin of whom he spoke was a "suspicious character" who lived in Livingston County, not far from Cave-in-Rock. He was later arrested and tried as an accomplice of the outlaws but for lack of sufficient evidence was acquitted.

[7] The exact number killed in the Trisword massacre is not known. The party was described as being comprised of "two Trisword brothers, with their wives, several children, and a few black servants." None of these survived except the one Trisword brother who escaped. "Several" children could mean anything from three to half a dozen or more. "A few" black servants could indicate the same vague numbers. But counting only absolute minimums, I believe that Rothert's figure, if anything, is too conservative.

Assuming ten were slaughtered in the Trisword massacre, I made the total figure of murders thirty-nine, as follows:

Moses Doss, Johnson, Peyton, Stephen Langford, Bates and Paca—six murders before the Harpes were arrested in Hardin County, Kentucky.

Johnny Trabue, Dooley, Stump, and three unnamed men at the mouth of the Saline River in Illinois—six more, or a total of twelve—after the Harpes escaped from the Danville jail and before they reached Cave-in-Rock.

The man they drove on the blinded horse over the cliff at Cave-in-Rock, raising their score to thirteen.

Bradbury, the Coffey boy, William Ballard, James Brassel, John Tully, John Graves and his son, an unnamed Negro boy, a little girl also unnamed, ten in the Trisword slaughter, Big Harpe's own child by Sally Rice, Trowbridge, Major Wil-

It must have been in the course of these confessions that the details of the murders at the Stegall house, and the killing of harmless old Stump, with his kindly offer of a turkey, fish, and fiddle music came out.

During this account, also, Harpe said that he "regretted none of the murders he had committed except the killing of his own child."

That could only be Sally Rice's daughter, brained against a tree at the Mud River revival grounds. It vividly illustrates how the three women were held in common by the outlaw brothers, for though Sally was ostensibly Little Harpe's wife, Big Harpe, dying, felt very sure that he had sired her infant.

By this time the outlaw had grown so weak that he could no longer raise himself on his elbow, but he was dying too slowly to suit Stegall, who probably feared that at any moment something might be said that would involve himself. There is no record that Harpe made any accusations. Perhaps he felt that since he had murdered Stegall's wife and child anything he said would be put down as falsehoods by these men. At last, however, Stegall grew impatient, cocked his rifle and aimed it at the head of the expiring murderer.

Harpe, seeing the gun pointed at him, summoned enough strength to twist his head this way and that, seeking hopelessly to avert the bullet and prolong his miserable life a few more minutes. What ensued is related in several ways.

According to one version, by J. W. M. Brazeale, Stegall said after a few moments of this, "Well, I won't shoot him in the head for I want *that* as a trophy." He thereupon shot him in the body, and the outlaw died from the bullet, after which Stegall cut off his head.

Another version, cited by Robert M. Coates, which sounds terribly realistic, goes as follows: Stegall did not shoot the outlaw. Instead he "took Harpe's own butcher knife, which Leiper had compelled him to deliver up, and taking Harpe by the hair of the head, drew the knife slowly across the back of his neck, cutting to the bone; Harpe staring him full in the face, with a grim and fiendish countenance, and exclaiming, 'You are a God damned rough butcher, but cut on and be damned!' Stegall then passed the knife around his neck cutting to the

---

liam Love, Mrs. Mary Stegall and her baby son, Hudgens and Gilmore, before Big Harpe's death—making twenty-six after they left Cave-in-Rock, or a grand total of thirty-nine, *of whom there is some record.*

But nobody knows if even these were all. There probably were more, for the Harpes must have participated in murders while waylaying flatboats with the outlaws at Cave-in-Rock, and there almost certainly were others, slain in their various "raids," whose bodies were never found in that primitive country.

bone; and then wrung off his head, in the same manner a butcher would of a hog."

It somehow sounds gruesomely circumstantial, and fits the time and place and also Stegall's bitter hatred and perhaps anxiety to silence the dying man.

6.

There are other details, some of them horrific.

When they started back, they made hatchet-faced Susan Roberts, who claimed to be Big Harpe's wife, carry the bloody head by the hair for some distance. "While slinging it along she kept muttering, 'Damn the head!'"

Later the head was put into a bag or wallet, slung at Squire McBee's saddle bow. That day, heading back and knowing they must camp with the three women and two children as prisoners to be fed, they found themselves short of food. They therefore stopped at a neighboring corn field and helped themselves to some roasting ears. Having nowhere else to carry the corn, they dumped it unhusked in the sack which already contained the bloody head.

That night the corn was taken out of the sack to be husked and cooked for supper. One member of the posse refused to eat any of it "because it had been put into the bag with Harpe's head." His companions considered him finicky. After all, the corn still was in the husks, wasn't it? They ate with gusto.

Whether any of the women or children partook of it is not of record.

Returning to their own neighborhood, the men took Harpe's head near to where he committed his last crimes: the murders of Mrs. Stegall, her infant, Major Love, Gilmore and Hudgens.

At the side of the road about three miles north of what later became the town of Dixon was a large oak tree. Some of the men sharpened the end of a projecting limb on this tree into a sort of a stake, and stuck the ghastly trophy on it "as a warning to other outlaws." Upon the trunk of the tree they carved the letters H.H. for "Harpe's Head." For many years, and perhaps still today, the place was known as Harpe's Head, and the road that passed it was called the Harpe's Head Road.

Time passed and the horrid object remained, the skull and jawbones still grinning at the passer after all the flesh had decomposed or been carried away by birds of carrion tastes.

Then came a last touch of the macabre. Years later an old woman of the district, a sort of backwoods witch, had a nephew who was sub-

ject to fits. She was told by a "conjuring doctor" that the "bone of the
human skull, pulverized and properly concocted," would cure the
malady. One dark night the old woman stole out to the Harpe tree,
took down from it the bleached skull, and powdered it for this purpose. There is no record as to the success or failure of this "cure" in the
case of the nephew with fits.

As to other major actors in the last days of Micajah Harpe:

The seven men of the posse received the reward of three hundred
dollars offered by Governor Garrard. Leiper, because he actually felled
the outlaw, received the larger share—one hundred dollars—the re-
mainder being divided among the other six.

Five of the pursuers of Harpe lived out lives well respected. But
against two of them, Leiper and Stegall, public suspicion turned. It
was whispered, probably with truth, that they joined the chase to kill
the Harpes in order to silence them about crimes in which they themselves had participated.

Leiper was at first something of a hero, but the public soon began
to shun him. He "died suddenly of winter fever (pneumonia) some
time during the winter of the cold Friday." The "cold Friday" in old
chronicles was February 6, 1807.

Stegall, at first sympathized with for his loss and praised for the
actual finishing off of Harpe, fell under the same suspicion. He met his
fate even earlier than Leiper. In 1806 he induced a girl living with her
family, Maddox by name, on or near the Tradewater River, to run
away with him. They made their elopement successfully, fled north
and crossed the Ohio River into Illinois. There, apparently feeling they
were safe from pursuit, they stopped with some "highly questionable"
acquaintances near Ford's Ferry, about two and a half miles upstream
from Cave-in-Rock itself. These acquaintances undoubtedly were some
of the Ford's Ferry bandits, of whom we will hear more later.

But the pursuit did not halt at the river as Stegall and his new mistress expected. The girl's brother and a friend named Peak Fletcher—
who was one of her admirers before she ran off with Stegall—traced
them to their new abode, a log cabin.

Looking through the chinks of the cabin they saw by the light of a
single candle in the room, the amorous Stegall with the errant damsel
sitting on his lap in close embrace. The two young men did not hesitate
because of this proximity. Aiming through the chinks they both fired,
killing Stegall. Miss Maddox was not injured by the shots, though
she was frightened nearly to death. Her brother took her back home.

The three women of the Harpes were given a preliminary hearing at
Henderson (Red Banks), General Hopkins presiding, and held for trial
at the district court in Russellville as parties to the Stegall murders.

Sheriff Stewart who once had vainly hunted the Harpes, had the women in his custody and showed kindness toward them. Finding that since they were "lodged in the old log jail, they were becoming dirty and lousy," he gave them liberty in the town under close watch, collected some necessary clothing for them, had them and the children cleaned up, and put the women to spinning on a couple of spinning wheels in the courthouse. This gave the sad creatures some occupation to relieve their monotony.

Later, when Stewart learned that Moses Stegall had arrived in the town, intending to kill the three women if they were acquitted, he hid them for a time in a cave five miles outside of town, until Stegall departed—to his eventual death.

They were tried under the names of Susanna Harpe, spinster, Betsey Roberts, spinster, and Sally Harpe, spinster. Sally, in her testimony, related that on the day he was killed Big Harpe wanted to murder the two remaining children to facilitate his own escape. She protected them by placing them in a niche in the rocky cave which was their retreat, and lay with her own body between them and the blood-mad outlaw until his crazy fury abated. Later on he took the children and the other two women with him on his last flight.

All three women were acquitted, since it was clearly shown that they were nowhere near the scene when the Stegall murders occurred. All were released, and all lived for years after their trials.

Susan Roberts, the eldest, lived on a plantation owned by Colonel Anthony Butler, earning her way by spinning and weaving. No man seemed to desire her in marriage. Her daughter, whom she called Lovey, grew up to be "very pretty, common size, round features, handsome form, black hair, rather dark skin and had a dark and sometimes bad, devilish eye." She was a true daughter of her father—whichever of the Harpes he was—in that she lacked any kind of morals. So promiscuous did she become with men that at last she and her mother were driven out of the country. Susan died and Lovey drifted to Pearl, Mississippi, and from there no man knows where, but it may easily be surmised that she ended in one of the Natchez or New Orleans bawdy houses.

Betsey Roberts, who was prettier than Susan, married a man named John—or Sol—Hufstetter. She apparently lived conventionally and industriously the rest of her life. Her son—by one or the other of the Harpes—was known as Joe Roberts. He grew up, enlisted in the army, and after that his fate is unknown.

Sally Rice, in some respects the most pathetic of the feminine trio, was rescued by her father, the Reverend John Rice, described as "of irreproachable character." He took her home to his farm near Knoxville, Tennessee, where Wiley Harpe first saw her and wooed her. Sally must have regarded her "marriage" to Little Harpe as extra-legal, for though he was still living she took another husband and with him moved to Illinois. By this new spouse she had a second daughter. This girl was described in 1820 by William Stewart, the former sheriff—without, however, giving her first name—as "a fine looking young lady." Other children followed the daughter.

But what became of Wiley Harpe?

At the death of his brother Micajah he was nowhere in evidence. None of the women could give a clue as to his whereabouts. Like a coward and a cur he slipped away, leaving the others to their fate. For a time all track of him was lost.

But he was to reappear, continue his criminal career, gain new notoriety, and at last meet a fate as grim as that of Big Harpe himself.

VII.   *Genius in Treachery*

1.

The Harpes left an unprecedented record of murders. Yet dreadful as it was, one even more terrible was being compiled by a smooth, seemingly genial man on the Ohio River at Cave-in-Rock.

Samuel Mason was the first real genius of outlawry on the frontier. And he was even more terrible than the Harpes in this respect: where they slaughtered out of blood-lust, he coldly murdered for money and loot, cunningly concealed the dead, and organized a band of criminals, the spawn of evil that cursed the Mississippi Valley for more than forty years.

This man, smiling with his wolf fang, eyes hooded to hide the glitter of greed and death in them, was the very archetype of the pious hypocrite, so that one can hardly endure reading about him and assessing his evil deeds.

How many perished at the hands of his gang of outlaws? It can never be determined. The deep swirling Ohio River swallowed them—and Mason was more careful than the Harpes in his disposal of the corpses.

The disappearance of people, even whole boat-loads of them, including women and children, was at first hardly realized either upstream or downriver. Families departed on their flatboats and their acquaintances lost all track of them, even when they were fortunate enough to run the outlaw gantlet in safety and reach their destinations. They settled, perhaps, or went to other parts of the South, or were lost in one way or another, and since few could read or write, correspondence was almost entirely absent.

In time, however, the frequent non-return of boatmen and especially the loss of valuable cargoes, caused inquiry to be made. This eventually led to armed action against Cave-in-Rock. But by then Mason already had transferred his activities elsewhere.

His usual method of handling captured cargoes, as has been seen, was to replace the murdered crews of the boats with his own men, who then took the craft on down to Natchez or New Orleans, sold the cargoes, and with the money returned—presumably—to Cave-in-Rock for a division of the spoils.

This plan, however, had the defect of placing a considerable strain on the "honesty" of fellows who were fundamentally dishonest. Too often they spent the money they received for the stolen cargoes in various riotous ways, or simply decamped with it.

Spending your money in New Orleans or Natchez was easy—if you had a chance to spend it. The money might just as easily be taken away from you by any of various smooth or violent rogues who infested those places.

Both cities had notable underworlds where the gambler, the prostitute, the confidence man, the pickpocket, the thug, and the highwayman all flourished almost without restriction. In New Orleans the chief red light district was known as the Swamp. In Natchez it was called Natchez Under the Hill to distinguish it from Natchez on the Bluff, where the respectable part of the population dwelt. Of the two the Swamp was rather the larger, but man-for-man—and woman-for-woman—they were at least equal in general iniquity.

The "capitals" of these districts of vice were the biggest and plushiest brothels they contained. In their heyday these palaces of sin were gaudy enough, with velvet curtains, luxurious furniture, pier glass mirrors behind the bars, crystal chandeliers, and paintings of sinuous nudes adorning the walls, so that the greenhorn river boatmen, who never before had seen such sybaritic surroundings, were fairly dazzled. Such bagnios were the meeting places of the underworld, where the combinations of liquor, gambling and sex furnished the allurements, and where most of the deviltry was hatched.

In Natchez, for a time, the leading "madame" was Marie Dufour. She had a lover named Jim Girty, brother of the infamous Simon Girty, and a terrible fighter who was said to be armored by nature so that he could not be killed with a knife, "because his ribs grew together making a bone sheath for his body." This report was proved fallacious one day when someone from upriver, who had not heard the fearsome tale of Girty's invulnerability, during a fight tried a knife on him, and found that the blade slid between his ribs as easily as it would on anyone else. Marie committed suicide over her lover's dead body by shooting herself in the mouth with a pistol.

After that other harlots and operators of pleasure houses at Natchez, were rivals for pre-eminence, including such feminine personages as red-haired, green-eyed Madame Aivoges, and a six-foot Amazon named Annie Christmas. One and all they succeeded passing well in attracting the gullible and lustful young men from upriver to their gilded joy palaces.

In the Swamp at New Orleans, for several years, a madame called Mother Surgick took precedence over all others. And such precedence meant something really dazzling in tinsel glory. Mother Surgick's girls attracted the most select of the underworld notables, including the terrible John A. Murrell[1] himself, as well as a constant stream of the raw and eager river men who formed the basic crop for such places.

The Swamp, of course, had many other bawdy houses in addition to Mother Surgick's house of luxury, some of them closely rivaling her establishment in decor and damsels. In such "houses" everything went. There were the girls, half nude and smiling an invitation to every male guest; peep shows, too, for those who liked that form of entertainment; sleek gentlemen with nimble fingers operating cards or dice; long mahogany bars dispensing drinks, sometimes exotic, and too often containing what later was called a "mickey finn" to prostrate the drinker and make him easy prey for deft-fingered thieves; and music, continual music, usually rendered by Negro musicians.

In addition to the top-flight "parlor houses" in New Orleans and Natchez Under the Hill, there were many rowdier and seedier places, running the gamut all the way down to Negro "cribs," where the favors of dark bawds could be purchased for as little as ten cents.

Crime flourished, and merely to enter the Swamp or Natchez Under the Hill could be dangerous. Sometimes in the dark alleys knives flashed, bodies fell to the ground, and shadowy figures crouched over them momentarily to rifle the pockets.

There were frequent fights in the streets of the Swamp, and on the

---

[1] See later for an account of Murrell and his activities.

muddy shelf of Natchez Under the Hill. Once, in New Orleans, two men shot it out in a duel over the favors of a particular courtesan, who with her girls watched from a window above, while in the rear of the establishment her cooks prepared a dinner in honor of the one of her bellicose lovers who emerged victor. One man was killed; the other sat down to wine and viands with his light of love.

On another occasion a river man named Bill Sedley, in a gambling house owned by the Contreras brothers, accused Rafael Contreras, during a faro game, of hiding a card up his sleeve. Contreras and his brother Juan thereupon closed and locked the door of the room, shutting Sedley in with the two of them. Those outside heard the sound of blows, yells, and shots. Then the door opened and Sedley emerged. One arm was broken by a pistol ball, and he was bleeding from several cuts. But he gestured toward the bar.

"Help yourselves, gentlemen," he said, "and drink hearty. The proprietors of this here place have gone on a journey and left me in charge."

Both Contreras brothers were found dead in the room, killed by Sedley in what must have been a furious battle of one against two.[2]

Most frequently, however, the fights were hand-to-hand battles between those notable brawlers, the "bullies" of this or that flatboat. Then eyes were gouged out, noses bitten off, skulls fractured, or necks broken. By morning the districts often had their quota of dead. But of these deaths the police were not informed. The underworld took care of its own casualties, and the lordly Mississippi was always there, rolling by, to bear corpses downstream and out of mind.

2.

Even if a man succeeded in evading the perils of the Swamp or Natchez Under the Hill, danger always awaited him on the road home. Return travel from southern markets was usually overland, since rowing or poling a boat up the turbulent Mississippi was toil both backbreaking and lengthy.

In riding or walking back to Kentucky, Tennessee or the Ohio country, travelers generally used the celebrated Natchez Trace, most famous of the frontier trails. That path was known in early days, according to one historian, as "The Devil's Backbone,"[3] and right well did it deserve such a title.

[2] Herbert Asbury, *The French Quarter*.

[3] Jonathan Daniels, *The Devil's Backbone, the Story of the Natchez Trace*.

Running for some five hundred miles northeast from Natchez, Mississippi, to Nashville, Tennessee, it was wild and perilous almost every foot of its way. For most of its length it followed an old Indian path known as the Chickasaw Trail, through the country of the Chickasaw and Choctaw Indians who were none too friendly toward white travelers in the earliest years.

The trail passed through woods "thick laced with wild grape vines and hanging with Spanish moss," or penetrated canebrakes where the cane stood ten to twelve feet high and so thick that the only vision was along the narrow path ahead—perfect ambush by lurking foes. Here and there were caves and depressions; one known as the Devil's Punchbowl, which was to have an alarming significance over the years. It is described by Harnett Kane, in one of his delightful books on the South:

> Along this river just outside Natchez . . . (is) a peculiar, to some awesome, phenomenon called "The Devil's Punchbowl" . . . About five hundred feet wide . . . thickly grown, it provided a dim, almost impenetrable place of concealment. Natives thought a heavy meteor might have once plumeted there . . . Steamboatmen claimed that their compasses behaved crazily when they passed.[4]

On such a path, beset by countless natural ambuscades, a man set out at his own risk. Though the Indians at first caused some trouble, white outlaws became a more serious peril later.

First of the robbers to make extensive practice on the Natchez Trace was Samuel Mason. His discovery that some of the outlaws he had "trusted" did not return with the money when they sold stolen cargoes with which he sent them to the markets, probably had much to do with his decision to leave Cave-in-Rock. But Mason also had a remarkably sensitive feeling for saving his own precious skin. He had left Red Banks just ahead of punitive justice. He deserted Diamond Island just before Captain Young's regulators swept it like a storm. Now he was the first to anticipate that before long Cave-in-Rock might become an unhealthy abiding place for such as he.

The hue and cry over the Harpes in the latter part of 1799 must have alarmed him, for either in that year or early in the next, he departed from Cave-in-Rock forever. From then on he became a scourge both on the Mississippi River and along the Natchez Trace.

John James Audubon, the naturalist, writing in 1815 when recollections of Mason were very fresh and information as authentic as recent occurrence could make it, said:

[4] Harnett Kane, *Natchez on the Mississippi.*

The name of Mason is still familiar to many of the navigators on the lower Ohio and Mississippi. By dint of industry in bad deeds, he became a notorious horse stealer, forming a line of worthless associates from the eastern part of Virginia (a state greatly celebrated for its fine breed of horses) to New Orleans, and had a settlement on Wolf Island, not far from the confluence of the Ohio and Mississippi, from which he issued to stop flatboats and rifle them . . . His depredations became the talk of the whole western country.[5]

This was written twelve years after Mason's death, when the true extent of his operations was just being realized. The network reaching from "the eastern part of Virginia . . . to New Orleans" is no exaggeration. Whatever his other failings, Mason was able to persuade men to his way of thinking and doing, and there is good reason to surmise that both Sile Doty's great horse stealing ring which flourished from 1818 to the Mexican War, and the far more sinister Mystic Clan of John A. Murrell may have used this earlier organization of Mason's for a foundation on which to rise and expand.

The first official record concerning him, after he left Cave-in-Rock, is contained in a report of the Spanish administrator at New Madrid—now Missouri, but then Spanish territory, as was all the country west of the Mississippi prior to the Louisiana Purchase, in 1803. Mason, plausible, smooth, apparently sober and respectable, appeared at New Madrid in March, 1800, and applied for a passport to permit him to settle in Spanish territory.

The passport was granted. It was the first step in Mason's new policy. By living in Spanish territory and taking refuge in his new home after each depredation, and by robbing only American citizens, in American territory, or on the river, he believed he would be safe from warrants, and particularly from those unpleasantly determined gentlemen with ropes in their hands, the regulators. For his new outlaw headquarters he chose a small settlement called Little Prairie (now Carruthersville, Missouri) some thirty miles downriver from the administrative headquarters at New Madrid.

Even before this, Mason probably was active along the Natchez Trace. Nobody really knows, for robbery in the wilderness was almost always accompanied by murder. "Dead men tell no tales," and the disappearance of travelers occasioned little comment beyond idle wonder as to what direction they may have gone.

In July, 1800, four months after Mason received his Spanish passport, John Swaney witnessed a murder and robbery which he declared was the work of the Mason gang.

[5] John James Audubon, *Delineation of American Scenery and Character.*

Swaney was the official mail carrier between Natchez and Nashville. A wonderful rider and woodsman, he enjoyed a curious immunity from molestation either by renegade Indians or white outlaws, so that other travelers sometimes sought his company for safety.

On this occasion he was alone and slept in the woods. At dawn, as he resumed his journey, he suddenly heard men's voices. Thinking it might be a group of travelers, he blew his horn—the signal that told denizens of the wilderness who he was and what was his errand—and galloped his horse toward the sound.

Before he came in view he heard a shout: "Surrender!"

It was followed by a shot, then another.

As he burst into view, he saw a tableau that lived with him all his days. A gentleman, pale and "cursing helplessly," sat on a shying, side-stepping horse, with two pistols in his hands, still smoking. He had missed both shots.

Before him stood a bandit, stripped to the waist, his face covered with war paint like an Indian's, so that he could not be recognized. Deliberately the bandit raised his rifle and shot the horseman through. Down from the saddle pitched the victim, dead.

But Swaney's appearance changed the situation. The murderer's gun was empty. He dived into the forest and disappeared.

Swaney's horse was plunging, startled by the shot. This was no place to linger. Somewhere in that tangle of trees and vines beside the trail lurked a man who would assuredly reload and who already had proved that he was a killer.

Without dismounting Swaney galloped on down the trail to get help. Soon he overtook the companions of the dead man, who had ridden on ahead of him. One he knew, a Major Ellis. The other proved to be the murdered man's son.

They heard his startling story. The man who had been killed, it developed, was Robert McAlpin, a Carolinian, who was on his way with them to purchase land in the Mississippi territory.

The son wanted to return at once, but Swaney persuaded the two that they should get help. Not far away was an Indian village called Pigeon Roost, because of the great flocks of passenger pigeons which came there periodically to feed and nest. Thither Swaney led Major Ellis and young McAlpin.

With some of the Indians they returned to the scene of the murder. The robber, or robbers, had been there before them. The dead man lay, stripped to his underwear. All his money and valuables that were visible were taken. But the outlaws had overlooked a money belt, containing most of his cash, which he wore next to his skin.

The victim was buried at that place, and his young son, white-faced and bitter, cut the bark from a tree to make a smooth place, and on it carved this inscription:

ROBERT MCALPIN

MURDERED & KILLED

HERE JULY 31

Swaney could not name the specific individual who shot McAlpin, but he knew some of the Mason gang and their work, and he swore the deed was done by those bloody freebooters.

3.

Having now a retreat which he believed was safe on the Spanish side of the river, Mason decided to establish a couple of advanced posts closer to operations, for the Natchez Trace was a long hard journey from Little Prairie and New Madrid. One of these was a camp on Stack Island, also called Crow's Nest, about fifty miles above Walnut Hills (today's Vicksburg, Mississippi). A second camp, but for emergency use only, was near Rocky Springs on the Natchez Trace itself, in what is now Claiborne County, Mississippi.

He had a gang of desperate scoundrels about him, including his sons. Two of these merit especial attention. One was James May, who joined Mason at Cave-in-Rock and followed him when he went south to prey on the Mississippi River traffic and the Natchez Trace. The other was a smallish man with fox-red hair, a countenance "meagre and downcast," shifty eyes and a peculiarly furtive manner, who went by the name of John Setton. His real name was Wiley Harpe.

That Big Harpe dominated the dual team of killers in their bloody raiding before his death now became apparent. Micajah had never gone in for robbery for its own sake. He took money, more often odd articles of clothing, weapons, sometimes horses, once something as insignificant as a small sack of flour. Killing—the infliction of death—was the impelling motive in his crazed, inhuman mind.

During all their years together Wiley, the younger and smaller member of the eerie pair, followed, obeyed, and seconded his brother in his deeds, evidently very much the subordinate. From the time of Micajah's death, however, Wiley Harpe's interests took a different turn. He still killed, but greed dominated him. Micajah Harpe murdered for murder's sake; Wiley Harpe murdered for avarice.

There was another factor, a conclusion drawn from the later evidence: while Wiley Harpe took a back seat, so to speak, when Micajah was alive, it must have been Wiley who was the cunning one, the "brains" of the pair. He probably was chiefly responsible for the flashes of dissembling, of malign treachery, of escapes and surprises and strategems. This shifty trait extended to his act of simply fading from view when retribution was closing on his brother. Thus he escaped from Squire McBee's posse, and lived to win additional evil infamy for himself and the Harpe name.

Where had he been since his brother was killed? He skulked in hiding for a while, then appeared furtively in Tennessee under the name of Setton. According to Lyman C. Draper,[6] he made friends with a young man named Bass living in Williamson County, Tennessee, and courted then married Bass's sister—although his "wife," Sally Rice, was still very much alive. The couple departed, ostensibly on a honeymoon journey to North Carolina, but the bride never arrived there. At the Holston River, in extreme northeast Tennessee, Setton brought her dead body to a house. The white residents were absent, but he told the Negroes there that his wife had fallen from her horse, been dragged by a stirrup, and so killed.

The Negroes helped him bury her, after which he sold her clothing and saddle, and left hurriedly with her horse as well as his own. When the white family returned and heard the story from their servants, they exhumed the body and discovered that the girl actually had been killed by heavy blows on the head. A pursuit was organized but Setton was gone and no trace of him could be found.

Presently he appeared at Fort Pickering, on the present site of Memphis, Tennessee, where he enlisted in the army, remained for a brief period, and one day "borrowed" the fine rifle of the captain, Richard Sparks, and disappeared. Somewhere he met James May once more, and each finding the other's brand of criminality congenial, they became associates and allies.

Samuel Mason, at that time, was somewhere in Arkansas, for it was "up the Arkansas River" that Harpe, alias Setton, paddled to join him. Wiley Harpe and his brother had once been ejected from Cave-in-Rock for their shocking cruelty; but Mason now may have been glad to gain a follower of such hardihood and lack of scruples. The bandit chief might even have considered it an advantage to be able to strike terror in frontier hearts by allowing the report to go abroad that one of the terrible Harpes was now among his henchmen.

He could not have foreseen the bloodcurdling denouement in his career and their own that Wiley Harpe (John Setton) and James May would play before their association came to an end.

[6] Mss. now in the collections of the Wisconsin Historical Society.

4.

Along the Natchez Trace, Mason's gang became the darkest of
threats. More than once the boss outlaw stopped John Swaney on his
mail-carrying rides, but never once did he harm him. On the contrary
he assured Swaney that "no mail carrier need fear being molested by
him and his men," and that he "did not desire to kill any man, for
money was all he was after and if he could get it without taking life,
he certainly would not shed blood."[7]

Still the pious hypocrite, the man who had on his conscience an uncounted number of murders mouthed a technical morality. He had
not at this time—by his own statement—ever shed blood with his
own hands; but this was because he was careful to leave the actual
killings to his agents and followers.

It was through these stoppages that Swaney came to recognize
members of the gang, who hung sullenly about while their leader
questioned him. At a guess, the man whom he saw murder McAlpin
was Wiley Harpe; and he did not identify him because that may have
been part of his passport agreement—that he would mention no names
so long as they let him pass unmolested in his errands for the mail
service.

Not long after the McAlpin murder Swaney saw another of Mason's
robberies—with a whimsical turn to it this time.

A crew of flatboat men from Kentucky, having disposed of their
produce at Natchez, were making the usual overland return by the
Trace. They camped for a night at Gum Springs, in the Choctaw
country, and after eating supper decided to put out pickets for the
night to guard the camp while it slept.

One of the pickets, going to his post, trod—to his enormous consternation—on a human body, hidden in the grass. The body was
alive, it gave a yell, and fired off a gun, shouting "Shoot and kill every
man here!"

The trodden person was, of course, a member of Mason's gang
which at that moment was creeping up on the camp; and the gunshot
and yell were too much for the composure of the Kentuckians. In
complete and unanimous panic they galloped off into the forest, leav-

[7] Robbing the mails was a federal offense, punishable by death. Mason probably
had no desire to have the government interest itself in his case. He preferred dealing with state or territorial officers, who were few and at times might be bought
off.

ing behind everything—money, guns, knives, even much of their clothing. Mason's men appropriated this property and disappeared in the
opposite direction.

Next morning, when Swaney arrived at the place, the Kentuckians
were still hiding in fear; but seeing their campfire he blew a blast on
his horn. At the sound the disconsolate crew appeared, one or two at
a time. He afterward described them as "the worst scared, worst looking set of men he ever saw." Some were only half-dressed. One tall
fellow wore only a shirt.

They discovered at once that their camp had been looted, and the
discovery appeared to give them a little courage, especially the big
Kentuckian who had lost his breeches. Having no other arms, they
cut some stout cudgels, and with the trouserless Kentuckian in the
lead set out to pursue the robbers, hoping to catch them off guard
and attack them with these primitive weapons.

But on the way the tall Kentuckian stumbled across his lost pants,
which the outlaws somehow dropped in their retreat; and to his great
joy his money was still there—sewed in the waistband. Now his zest
for the pursuit showed a considerable decline, and having donned his
nether garments he became the tail, instead of the head, of the club-
wielding contingent.

Suddenly a harsh voice challenged them from a thicket ahead.

"We've got our guns on you! If you come a step farther, we'll kill
every last one of you!"

Courage melted. The boatmen stampeded wildly away—and the
big Kentuckian "out distanced the whole party in the race to the
camp."

But to his credit, Swaney later recorded, the big Kentuckian spent
all the money he had recovered, buying supplies for his friends.

This was only one of many such forays by Mason along the Trace.
The ones that gained the greatest publicity, however, were two robberies of the same man—Colonel Joshua Baker, of Kentucky.

First of these occurred on the Natchez Trace, August 14, 1801. It
was a routine coup for Mason's men. Colonel Baker, with William
Baker, perhaps a relative, and a man named Rogers, having sold a
valuable cargo of horses and mules downriver, were returning to Kentucky when they came to a creek with very steep banks down which a
deep-cut bridle path led to a ford.[8] Stopping at the bottom of this

[8] Then called Twelve Mile Creek, but since that day known as Baker's Creek, in
Hinds County, Mississippi, the scene, incidentally, of a battle during the Civil
War.

ravine to water their horses, the three men heard a command from
above to surrender. Four men "blacked"—that is, their faces smeared
with charcoal to make identification difficult—were aiming their guns
at them.

At the mercy of their assailants, the three men gave up their arms
and saw the robbers, of whom Samuel Mason was certainly the leader,
make off with their horses, pack mules, and valuables.

One of the pack mules, however, became frightened and broke
away. After the robbers were gone William Baker caught the animal,
which carried some of his property, including, according to an account in the *Kentucky Gazette* of September 14, 1801, "a considerable
sum of money."[9]

Colonel Baker was no ordinary meek victim of the bandits. He made
his way to the nearest settlement, got help, and pursued the robbers,
following their trail to Pearl River, not far from today's Jackson, Mississippi.

They halted, on the banks of the stream, for a noonday rest, and
there they had a taste of Mason's ingenuity. The day was quite warm
and two members of the posse decided to take a swim. All was quiet
and they did not dream an enemy was near. As they splashed and
laughed in the water, they neared the other bank.

Suddenly their laughter ceased. They found themselves looking into
the muzzles of guns, aimed at them through bushes on the shore.

"Come out!" was the order.

They obeyed, climbing up on the bank, naked and dripping. When
they were led a little way into the woods out of sight of their friends,
Mason himself appeared, "a hale, athletic figure clad in leather shirt
and leggins, common to the Indians and hunters of the frontier."

He gave them a sarcastic grin, the wolf fang showing, and said with
mock politeness, "I'm glad to see you, gentlemen, and though our
meeting did not promise to be quite so friendly, I am just as well satisfied; my arms and ammunition will not cost as much as I expected."

Thereupon he shouted across the river to the rest of Baker's party,
"If you approach one step or raise a rifle, you may bid your friends
farewell. There's no hope for them but in your obedience. I want
nothing but security against danger for myself and party and this I
mean to have. Stack your arms and deposit your ammunition on the

[9] It may be difficult to understand why money should be entrusted to a pack mule
to carry. But it should be remembered that most of the transactions of the time
were carried on in specie, and coin in the sum of several hundred dollars, especially if it be silver, the common coinage of the period, makes a very heavy
weight.

beach near the water. I'll send for them. Any violence to my messenger, or the least hesitation to perform my orders, will prove certain and sudden death to your companions. Do what I say and I'll let them go."[10]

To save the lives of the two prisoners there was nothing for Colonel Baker to do but obey. His men placed their arms and ammunition as ordered. Two of the robbers crossed over and took possession of the guns and powder and ball, while a rifle was held at the head of each of the prisoners, now placed in full view. When all this was accomplished, "the prisoners were dismissed with a good humored farewell; and the dreaded Mason, true to his word, was soon lost in the depths of the wilderness."

Crestfallen, Colonel Baker and his men, weaponless, could only return to the settlement whence they came. It was Baker's first experience with Mason, but he was to have a second adventure, and Mason would in the end find him a vengeful enemy who had much to do with his final downfall.

These two episodes—the trouserless Kentuckian, and Colonel Baker's encounters with the bandits—were bloodless, and indeed revealed a kind of grim humor in Mason. But they were not typical of all his operations. Travelers were murdered on the Trace, and flatboat crews on the Mississippi were massacred in the operations of the gang in the next months.

5.

Always the business man, Samuel Mason knew he had to have some means of disposing the valuables and other loot he gained from his victims, aside from the cash itself.

One of his contacts was with a certain Anthony Glass, an ostensibly respectable merchant, who operated a general store in Natchez. Glass had helped in laying out the Natchez Trace and was received in the best society; but secretly he was a "fence" and also an informer for Mason and other robbers.

At times it was necessary to visit this man, to receive from him money for stolen goods delivered, and probably for this reason Mason

---

[10] This speech sounds somewhat stilted for a robber in the wilderness, even an orotund robber like Mason. It was thus recorded in the *Natchez Galaxy*, by a contributor who wrote of the robbery twenty-eight years later, in 1829. Very likely the bandit talked more crisply and colloquially. But however he said it, he made his point crystal clear.

and his son John[11] entered Natchez one day, not long after the Baker robbery. Someone, very likely a member of the posse that pursued them to Pearl River, spotted them and denounced them as robbers.

They were arrested, and in spite of the eloquence of their lawyer, a man named Wallace, were sentenced to receive thirty-nine lashes and be exposed on the pillory.

To the end they persisted in their denials of guilt, and George Wiley, who was present at their punishment, later wrote, "I . . . shall never forget their cries of 'Innocent!' at every blow of the cowhide which tore the flesh from their quivering limbs, and until the last lash was given they shrieked the same despairing cry of 'Innocent! Innocent!'"

After they were punished Mason turned to the crowd and said, "You have witnessed our punishment for a crime we never committed; some of you may see me punished again but it will be for something worthy of punishment!"

With that threat, they were locked in jail, but shortly after, through the help of some of Mason's confederates, they escaped and fled into the wilderness.

Another instance of Mason's bitter humor occurred shortly. During his trial one of the jurors (name not given) was outspoken in his condemnation. A few weeks later this man, returning from an errand and on his way to Natchez, was riding down a bridle path through a canebrake when Samuel Mason himself stepped out of the cane and aimed his rifle at the juror's head.

"I've waited two days here to blow your brains out," he said coldly.

Terrified, the juror begged to be spared for the sake of his wife and children.

"Did John Mason ever do you any harm?" asked Mason. "Did I myself ever do you any injury? Did you ever hear of me committing murder, or suffering murder to be committed?"

"Never in my life," whimpered the craven juror.

"Thank God, I have never shed blood," said Mason piously, and with complete mendacity. "But now, come down off your horse, sir. If you have anything to say to your Maker, I'll give you five minutes to say it."

The poor man got off his horse, went down on his knees, and began a tearful prayer, "addressed rather to the man who stood beside him with his gun cocked." The exhibition seemed to disgust Mason.

[11] Rothert denies that Samuel Mason himself was present on this occasion, but two other accounts, by George Wiley and William Darby, both of whom were actual witnesses of the events, state flatly that he was.

"With a bitter smile, he swore his (the juror's) life was not worth taking, wheeled around and in an instant disappeared amongst the cane."

From the time of the whipping in Natchez, onward, the robberies of the Mason gang increased in boldness, and also in bloodshed. How much money they got is only to be guessed. At the Baker robbery they got twenty-five hundred piasters, according to later testimony.

A young man "with six hundred dollars quilted into his coat," disappeared on the Trace and was never seen again—without question a victim of Mason's men.

Another, later, robber, Joseph Thompson Hare, who ended his career on the Trace about 1813, left a somewhat more specific record on this point. In one robbery he took "300 doubloons, 74 pieces of different sizes, and a large quantity of gold in bars—thirty-weight of it." In another he got "700 doubloons and five silver dollars and 400 French guineas, and 67 pieces of value." In a third he netted "twelve or thirteen thousand dollars . . . all in gold." In still a fourth, "seven thousand dollars was a total of the haul."[12]

The Mason robberies may well have reached such proportions at times, and there also were the goods and livestock they took in their piracies on river boats, which they converted into cash through the sleek Mr. Glass and others.

What did they do with these profits? In the first place there were many of them to divide among, and the girls and gambling halls in the New Orleans Swamp district and Natchez Under the Hill caused money to disappear rapidly. Some of it, according to long-time tradition, was hidden across the river from the present Vicksburg, Mississippi, in the highlands called the Mason Hills of Louisiana. Many searches have been made for this booty, but if any of it ever was found the discoverers revealed their luck to nobody.

6.

Ever bolder grew the Mason gang. Once Anthony Glass, the Natchez "fence," reported that he was held up as he rode with a Kentuckian named Campbell, driving a herd of horses. Glass was spared

[12] A piaster was a Spanish silver coin, roughly equivalent, at the time, to the American dollar. A doubloon, Spanish and gold, was sixteen piasters—or dollars. A guinea, British, was worth 21 shillings or five dollars and a quarter, although what a "French" guinea was is obscure.

and allowed to go on, but Campbell was murdered and robbed, and the horses were taken.

Later, on a tree beside the corpse, was found a sign reading:

DONE BY MASON OF THE WOODS.

John Setton (Wiley Harpe) at a subsequent date asserted that Mason did indeed commit this crime. But the story sounds fishy. Knowing Mason's cunning it seems improbable that he would put up such a sign accusing himself, for he made a great point of trying to impress people with the assertion that he was "not a man of blood." It seems more likely that Glass led his companion into an ambush, and that Wiley Harpe himself committed the murder and put up the sign.

Early in 1802 Mason had the misfortune—for him—to again encounter Colonel Joshua Baker, of Kentucky. This time it was on the river, for Mason made a regular practice of looting boat traffic on the Mississippi as he had done since the Cave-in-Rock days, his headquarters for such forays being Stack Island.

Colonel Baker, floating downstream in a flatboat loaded with merchandise, had learned much from his previous experience with the robbers. This time he armed his crew with guns, and grimly kept watch for pirates.

It was some time in April when the expected happened. Somewhere near Stack Island the outlandish river pirates started out toward the flatboat in their pirogues. But they had not counted on armed resistance. At the sight of the guns on the flatboat they sheered away and Baker's men continued safely on to Natchez, where the colonel made a written report of the attempt. Apparently he knew that Mason and even Wiley Harpe were among his assailants, as is shown by a letter written by Governor William C. C. Claiborne, a man of force and ability, who very recently—late in 1801—had become governor of the Mississippi Territory.

As soon as he received Baker's report, the governor wrote to commanders of militia and regular troops stationed in the territory letters similar in context. One of these, to Colonel Daniel Burnett, at Port Gibson, Mississippi, shows the tenor of all:

Sir,—I have received information that a set of pirates and robbers who alternately infest the Missisippi River and the road leading from this district to Tennessee [the Natchez Trace], rendezvous at or near the Walnut Hills [later Vicksburg] . . . a certain Samuel Mason and a man by the name of Harp [sic], are said to be leaders of this banditti: —they lately attempted in a hostile manner to board the boat of Colo [nel] Joshua Baker, between the mouth of the Yazou [Yazoo] River, and the Walnut Hills, but were prevented by Colo[nel] Baker's making a shew of arms, and manifesting a great share of firmness. These men must be arrested; the honor of our country, the interest of society, and the feelings of humanity, proclaim it is time to stop their career; the crimes of Harp, are many and great, and in point of baseness, Mason is nearly as celebrated:—While these sons of rapine and murder are permitted to rove at large, we may expect daily to hear of *outrages* upon the lives and properties of our fellow citizens.

At this time rewards were offered for the apprehension of the criminals: four hundred dollars by the Secretary of War, and five hundred by Claiborne as governor of the territory. A wide hunt immediately began, soldiers, posses of civilians, and friendly Indians, all joining in the search.

Unfortunately Mason, hiding at that time on Stack Island, intercepted a traveler, robbed him, and found in his possession a copy of Claiborne's proclamation of reward. He read it aloud to his followers, with a chortle. How could American authorities catch him, when all he had to do was slip across to the Spanish side of the river, which was his right under his passport?

Nevertheless, that reward was his death warrant; as other rewards proved to be the death warrants of other outlaws in history, including, later on, Jesse James.

And here we come upon an interesting and important note. Sometimes the Mason band used other than violent means to rob travelers. Zadock Cramer, whose book *The Ohio and Mississippi Navigator* was a bible to all who risked the dangerous channels of those rivers, had this comment in the 1818 edition of his work, the first edition of which was printed in 1803:

> Stack or Crow's Nest Island has been sunk by the earthquake [of 1811] or swept by floods . . . Stack not long since was famed for a band of counterfeiters, horse thieves, robbers, murderers, etc., who made this part of the Mississippi a place of manufacture and deposit. From hence they would sally forth, stop boats, buy horses, flour, whiskey, etc., and pay for all in fine, new notes of the *"first water."*[13]

In other words, counterfeit money. That money, or at least a great share of it, came from Cave-in-Rock, which was now inhabited by a different order of law-breakers, concerning whom we shall presently learn more.

[13] But Stack Island must have re-emerged later. Mark Twain in his *Life on the Mississippi*, speaks of it as a well-remembered navigation point during his days as a steamboat pilot.

VIII.   *Three More Heads Roll*

1.

Although he laughed at the notice that a reward was posted for his capture, Mason must have realized that the chase would now grow hotter. So early in January, 1803, he moved with his family and part of his followers across the Mississippi to the Little Prairie rendezvous.

In this move, however, he made one serious oversight. Since he obtained his passport from the Spanish authorities, the Louisiana province had changed hands. It now belonged to France, through the secret treaty of San Ildefonso, signed October 15, 1802. A still more drastic change in status of the province would occur soon when it became United States territory through the Louisiana Purchase, ratified October 21, 1803.

Mason, of course, had no way of foreseeing the latter contingency, and the troubles he now encountered were enough to keep his mind occupied with present worries. He had counted on the fact that Spanish officials, while willing to arrest persons who committed crimes on their side of the river, took small interest in apprehending persons charged with felonies on the American side. The French administration, however, had a different policy.

The commandant at New Madrid was Captain Henri Peyroux de la Coudrenière. When George Ruddell, a citizen of Little Prairie, appeared before him and told of a mysterious party of "eight men and one woman," all mounted and armed, which had ridden into his town and taken up residence in an empty house, the commandant took immediate interest—especially when Ruddell, who had seen Samuel Mason before, expressed the belief that if this was "not all the Mason band, it was probably a part."

Peyroux at once ordered a detachment of militia, accompanied by Ruddell, Joseph Charpentier, an interpreter, and two other citizens, to Little Prairie. They arrived just in time. The Masons were still there, but their horses were saddled and their pack animals loaded as if for immediate flight.

Probably they had been warned of the move against them. At the appearance of the militia, Mason assumed his most pious and injured air, and asked what "unjust imputations" had been made against him. For answer, Captain Robert McCoy, in command of the militia, ordered the whole party put "in handcuffs and chains."

Once secured, they were asked their names. Mason gave his readily, as did Thomas and John, his older sons, Samuel, Jr. (then aged eighteen), and Magnus (sixteen years old). The woman had three children with her. She said she was John Mason's wife, her former name being Marguerite Douglas.[1] There was one other man in the party. He said his name was John Taylor. Later, during the trial, he admitted to being John Setton. In reality he was Wiley Harpe.

Self-righteously, Mason produced the passport of March, 1800, to prove the legality of his entry into the territory. Of this Captain McCoy took charge, and ordered an inventory made of the group's possessions, to prevent any from being illegally taken.

These possessions included "eight horses, new and old clothes, many yards of silk, muslin, and cotton, old and new pistols and guns, a field stove, a box of salt, three horns of powder, six barrels of flour, English cutlery, various other imported goods totalling more than a hundred items, and more than seven thousand dollars in United States money (bills), of which the serial numbers and amounts of each were taken." There also were found "*some twenty twists of human*

[1] Samuel Mason's wife, by this time, had left him, and was living near Bayou Pierre, not far from Point Gibson, in Mississippi, where "she was generally respected as an honest and virtuous woman, by all her neighbors."

hair of different shades which do not seem to have been cut off voluntarily by those to whom the hair belonged."[2]

Trophies, these last? Perhaps of victims along the Trace or on the river?

Later it was determined that much of the money "appears to be counterfeit."

At New Madrid, when the prisoners were questioned by Peyroux, an astounding series of charges and countercharges, perjuries and fabrications, ensued. Specifically they were asked about the two robberies of Colonel Baker, the murder-robbery of Campbell, and the robbery of a boat belonging to a certain Owsley.

Mason said the man called "John Taylor, alias John Setton . . . and sometimes going by other names he, Mason, could not recall" committed the robberies. Asked if the money in his possession was counterfeit, he did not deny it, but asserted that since he had made no attempt to pass any of the bills he could not be punished for carrying them—an error, for under the law any persons having possession of counterfeit money, knowing it is counterfeit, are guilty of felony.

Setton, brought before the commandant, just as freely charged the Masons with the crimes, and told a fantastic story that "the banknotes were found in a bag hanging in a bush, near the road where we happened to be camping." He gave an untruthful account of his previous life, and then told a tearful tale of abuse: how the Masons on one occasion gagged him, bound his hands and feet, and held him down on the floor of a house for about three hours to prevent his warning a prospective robbery victim. The person they intended to rob was a man named Koiret, and he escaped.[3]

On one detail of this episode, the Masons and Setton astonishingly agreed: They marched him at a pistol's point to the house of "William Downs, a magistrate," about twelve miles below Nogales (another name for present-day Vicksburg) and there caused him to sign a confession that he was guilty of three crimes, keeping the confession as a means of holding Setton under control.

Of Marguerite, John Mason's wife, Setton indicated that she was of "a sportive nature," and made excuses to be "left alone in the house with a Dr. Wales for whom she seemed to have a fondness." Once, he said, when a man named Barrett, a member of the gang, threatened to denounce the family, Marguerite seized a long knife and

[2] McCoy's official report.

[3] Later it developed that Koiret was a secret service spy for the government, gathering evidence against the gang.

would have killed him had not Thomas Mason interfered and prevented her.

In addition to Barrett, Setton named as other members of the gang Wiguens (an army deserter), Bassett (not to be confused with Barrett), Gibson, Fulsom, Philips, and others. Interestingly, he did not name May, though May certainly was with the Masons. Perhaps he went under one of the names already cited. Both Samuel Mason's and Thomas Mason's wives had refused to follow their husbands in their careers of crime, he said, and were living "across the river."

Now came a sudden, shocking question.

"Are you acquainted with the man, Harpe?" asked the commandant.

Setton hesitated. Then he replied that "he had met a man by that name in Cumberland who had since been killed, but had left a brother, whose whereabouts were unknown to him . . . He did not know whether Harpe and any of the Masons ever had any dealings together or had ever met, but he felt confident that Harpe had not been around since he had the misfortune to fall into Mason's hands."

The name of Anthony Glass was brought into the testimony by Setton, who named him directly as the fence to whom Mason sold goods, being paid "cash for half its actual value." Glass, according to Setton, "had been a poor man . . . until he came into contact with the Masons."

There was other testimony by other witnesses, including one interesting echo of the Cave-in-Rock killings related by a man named Pierre Billeth. He said that in August, 1798, near the mouth of the Cumberland River, he heard a Negro woman tell how her then master, Samuel Mason, "after stabbing and robbing a man, commanded her to help tie a rope around his neck and drag the body to the Ohio, where they threw it in the water." This woman, said Billeth, had been stolen by Mason and later sold to Father Manuel, a Catholic priest, who presumably was her owner when she related this story.

The court, however, could not admit this testimony, since it not only was hearsay, but told by a slave.

Summing up all these conflicting stories, Peyroux decided (a) there was no proof that the prisoners had committed any crime on the French side of the river; (b) on the other hand it was apparent that they were guilty of crimes on the American side.

He had no power to punish them for violations of law in the United States. But the Intendant, at New Orleans, Manuel de Salcedo, did have the power to deliver them over to American officials for trial. Peyroux therefore ordered the whole group to be conveyed down the Mississippi to New Orleans.

Since it was about nine hundred miles from New Madrid to New

Orleans, a flatboat was provided for the journey. On this went the ten persons of the Mason party—including Setton—Captain McCoy and five soldiers, the interpreter, and a crew to navigate the craft, which quite overcrowded it.

There is a version that on the voyage Setton was chained "in the most conspicuous place," on the deck. McCoy did not want to lose him—he might turn state's evidence.

Setton (Wiley Harpe) knew that his enemies were two-fold. On the one hand, Mason and his sons were ready to slit his throat. On the other hand Captain McCoy and the guards were "frowning on him as they would at a chained, sheep-killing dog." His appearance at this time was described as repellent, his countenance "always downcast and fierce," his hair red, his face "meager," his figure "below that of the average man," but well-knit and cable of strenuous action. His age then was about thirty years.

The journey downriver to New Orleans was made safely, and the prisoners in due time were handed over to American authorities. In March, 1803, they were sent, this time on a sailing craft, upstream to Natchez for final trial.

So far everything had gone smoothly. The prisoners seemed reconciled to their fate, sitting in a sort of apathy, no words passing between Setton and the others.

But March 24 the boat's mast broke and a halt was made at Pointe Coupee, above Baton Rouge but below Natchez, for repairs. Some of the soldiers and crew were sent ashore to cut a tree for the mast.

This was the chance for which Mason and Setton were watching. If the guards believed the two were not in communication, they were vastly mistaken, for they acted with instant unanimity which indicated careful planning for just such an event. How they managed to free themselves from their irons is a mystery, but there must have been bribery or treachery somewhere.

McCoy was in his cabin when the Masons and Setton, rising unexpectedly, seized the gun of what apparently was the single guard set over them. A shot was heard, and McCoy came leaping on deck.

As he did so, Mason, at point-blank range, shot him "through the breast and shoulder"—perhaps a single bullet making the wound. Back staggered McCoy, mortally hurt. But though he was hardly able to stand, he fired his pistol, hitting Mason in the head.

Mason fell, rose, fell, and rose again. But McCoy was sinking down, dying.

Covered with blood, Mason led his party in driving all others off the boat. One of them, the guard who was disarmed and then fired upon with his own gun, had an "arm shot to pieces."

Quickly the outlaws put off from shore, and worked the captured boat along the river until sunset of that day, March 26, 1803.

Before dark Mason and Setton could see boats pursuing them, an overwhelming number of armed men in them. They put in to shore, and the entire party plunged into the woods.

The pursuers found nobody on the boat, except perhaps the body of McCoy. There could be no chance of overtaking such expert woods-men as the fugitives, even with the woman and the children. And if they did happen to overtake Mason's gang it would be death for some of the pursuers in the darkness. Baffled and furious, the possemen re-turned to their homes.

Once more, and after one of the most daring exploits of his career, Samuel Mason was on the loose with his murderous gang.

2.

James May was not with Mason at the time of his arrest at Little Prairie. But he rejoined the boss bandit shortly after the escape at Pointe Coupee.

The outlaws had landed on the American side of the river, and from Pointe Coupee they made their grim and furtive way north through Mississippi. In spite of their secrecy, however, they were seen and reported about June 6, on Cole's Creek, near the Natchez Trace, a few miles north of Natchez itself. Militia immediately were sent in pursuit, but lost track of them.

Now the chase was spurred by an increased reward, on new terms: an offer of one thousand dollars for "taking old Mason dead or alive."

Dead or alive! That one phrase added the needed incentive. Fetch-ing a desperate man in dead was much easier than bringing him in alive, and allowed considerable leeway in the manner of taking him, especially to the unscrupulous and bloody-minded.

Within a little more than a month James May appeared at Green-ville, Mississippi,[4] with some articles of property and money, and there swore before a magistrate that he had taken from Samuel Mason "after shooting him in the head just above the eye."

He thereupon recounted a tale as wild as Wiley Harpe's, about being robbed, kidnaped, and "forced" to join the gang and participate in its crimes. Finally, when he heard shooting on the river—one of Mason's piratical attacks on a flatboat—he concealed himself in a skiff with his gun. After the alarm passed, "whilst Mason was counting his

4 This was old Greenville, later called Hunston, not the present Greenville, of Washington County.

money and property to divide with the party, he (May) shot him, put
the money and property on board the skiff" and fled to Greenville.

A highly unlikely story; but the fact that he turned over actual
money—how much is not stated—lent an air of credibility to it. The
wound described by May on Mason's head was authentic enough, but
May did not inflict it. It was caused by Captain McCoy's dying shot
when Mason and the others escaped at Pointe Coupee. Evidently it
was a flesh wound only, visible but not too serious, because the outlaw
was very active thereafter.

May hoped to collect the reward, but since he had no proof that
Mason was dead, it was not paid to him and he soon left Greenville.
Next time he would make more sure before calling for that reward.

Some time after the escape from McCoy's boat, Wiley Harpe and
Mason separated. It was with May that Harpe now joined. How they
found each other in that wilderness we do not know, but from this
time forth they were in constant company, and it is very clear that
they were kindred spirits. May, frustrated in his effort to collect the
reward for Mason, perhaps infected his associate with a desire to get
that money—or perhaps it was the other way around, because it is quite
well established that the two were in partnership before May's visit to
Greenville.

They might have done well enough as bandits on the Trace, had not
the allurements of Natchez Under the Hill proved irresistible to them.
One of their robberies was of a man named Elisha Winters, whom
they waylaid below Natchez, on his way north from New Orleans.
They took his money and other valuables, but for some reason spared
his life, a circumstance most unusual for them.

It was an unfortunate circumstance, too, for Winters proceeded to
Natchez, when they expected him to return to New Orleans. He was
still there when May and Harpe appeared in the town, to have a fling
with the girls and the dice, on the muddy strip below the respectable
part of the city. A newspaper article in the *Kentucky Gazette* gave a
meager account of what thereupon took place:

> A letter from a gentleman at Natchez, to his correspondent in this
> town [Lexington], dated 20th October, contains information that the
> men who robbed Mr. Elisha Winters, on his way from New Orleans,
> have been taken and committed to jail; so that there is a probability of
> his getting his money. They had in their possession sundry articles taken
> from the party who were robbed at Bayou Pierre.[5] One of the robbers

[5] Bayou Pierre was a favorite hunting ground of Mason. There his wife lived, and
also one of his daughters-in-law, Thomas's wife. Not far from Bayou Pierre he had
robbed Colonel Baker's party, but this robbery reported was a later depredation of
the gang.

has turned state's evidence against the rest; and says that if he can be suffered to go out with a guard, he will take them where all the papers were hid and a number of other things with some money. The place is not more than a two days' ride, and application has been made to the governor for the above purpose, which will doubtless be granted.

The "men who robbed Mr. Elisha Winters," were May and Harpe, and Winters himself must have seen and identified them, after which they were arrested. Indeed, May and Harpe may have been in Natchez partly for the purpose of disposing of some of the "sundry articles" to the smooth Mr. Glass, who would take them for "half their value."

The man who "has turned state's evidence against the rest," was Wiley Harpe. He claimed, as soon as he was arrested, that he had come to Natchez for that very purpose—a most improbable story.

But both prisoners were plausible, and seemed in earnest. They said that they alone knew where to find Mason; and if they were released they would get him and bring indubitable proof they had done so.

They sounded convincing and since numerous parties had scouted for the boss bandit without finding a trace of him, the authorities at length decided to release the two unfragrant characters, on the gamble that they might succeed where others had failed.

May and Harpe set forth, presumably early in November.

3.

Evil though he was, one can almost feel a slight stir of sympathy for Samuel Mason with those two skulking scoundrels descending upon him. They knew no loyalty, no pity, no honor—not even the type of honor that is supposed to exist among thieves.

What transpired has been the theme of several versions. The most probable of these is that Harpe and May found Mason in one of his hideouts—a place which both of them knew. Perhaps it was the one just south of Bayou Pierre in Jefferson County, Mississippi; or the one in Mason's Hills across from Vicksburg in Louisiana; or at Lake Concordia, over the river from Natchez. All of these places have been mentioned, but there is no way of being sure.

In any event, and wherever they found him, Mason evidently was alone and desperate. The chase for him had been thickening, his band had scattered, and he probably was glad to see Harpe and May. It was easy for them to convince him that they were fugitives who had escaped from prison and wished to join him again as followers.

Under ordinary circumstances, Samuel Mason was a suspicious man, quick to see a flaw in the story or acts of another; but these two

had been with him for years, they had participated with him in countless crimes, and they were too deeply involved to turn against him—or
so he thought. He had that confession of Wiley Harpe's, which he
could produce if he needed it; and perhaps something of a similar
nature concerning James May, to hold over his head and compel
obedience. Mason needed men; any kind of men, and he accepted
them. It was the greatest and last mistake of his life.

We can almost see them, smiling, fawning on him, pledging their
friendship and loyalty—awaiting their chance. The chance finally came,
and late in November or early in the following month, the conscienceless scoundrels returned to Natchez by canoe. In the bow of their craft
was a hideous trophy. "Rolled up in blue clay to prevent putrefaction"
was the grim and ghastly head of Samuel Mason.

The man who had dealt in treachery all his life at last had fallen
victim to a treachery worse than any of his own.

According to one account, "While Mason, in company with the two
conspirators (Harpe and May), was counting out some ill-gotten
plunder, a tomahawk was buried in his brain. His head was severed
from his body and borne in triumph to Washington (near Natchez) the
seat of the territorial government."[6]

Enormous public excitement was created when Harpe and May
brought the head to Natchez. At once a large crowd gathered to see
the horrid trophy. It was identified by numerous persons "by certain
scars and peculiar marks." One of the scars must have been that caused
by Captain McCoy's pistol ball, and at least one of the "peculiar marks"
would be the telltale projecting tooth. May and the supposed "Setton"
were for the moment public heroes, "whose prowess had delivered the
country of so great a scourge."

One important witness, however, denied the identity of the trophy.
Mason's own wife, living then on Bayou Pierre, was brought to
Natchez, Governor Claiborne sending his own carriage for her. She
gazed at the rotting head without a single change of expression, then
turned away.

"That's not Samuel Mason," she said.

The reputation she had succeeded in building for herself since she
left her husband was so good that her denial caused doubts to be
raised. Later on some theorized that "one of Mason's gang killed an
innocent man, cut off his head, carried it to the Governor of Mississippi
and claimed the reward.[7]

[6] John W. Monette, *History of the Discovery and Settlement of the Valley of the
Mississippi*.

[7] Robert Lowry, *History of Mississippi*.

It should be pointed out that such denials as that of Mrs. Mason are not uncommon in the history of crime. Years later, Belle Starr, the Oklahoma woman outlaw, looking at the body of her dead lover, Jim Reed, refused to identify him "because she wouldn't have his killer get the reward."

In this instance, however, the evidence was too overwhelming. It was Samuel Mason's head without question. May and Setton now demanded the one thousand dollar reward offered for the outlaw "dead or alive," and went before a magistrate to swear to an affidavit with which to collect the money.

It looked as if all was smooth sailing for the scoundrelly pair. They would receive the money—equivalent in value to perhaps ten thousand dollars in today's terms—would be praised and admired, would be able to swagger about the streets of Natchez and disport themselves in the district down under the hill, without anyone to interfere with their pleasures.

But just here a strange quirk of fate intervened.

4.

It must have been at about the same time they robbed Elisha Winters—for which they were arrested—and before they began their hunt for Samuel Mason, that May and Harpe had committed another robbery—and a murder.

There were two men this time. Their names are not of record, but one of them was killed. The other was lucky enough to escape with his life. Harpe and May took the valuables of the murdered man.

Now, at the very time the two were signing the affidavit before a judge at the courthouse, the survivor of their banditry registered at a tavern in Natchez, and took his horse to the stable. There he saw, in their stalls, two horses which he recognized "by peculiar blazes on their faces," as the animals ridden by the outlaws who robbed him two months before and murdered his companion.

At once he asked who owned those horses. When he learned who the men were, and that they were at that time in the courthouse to collect the reward for a deed which was ringing through the whole country, he went to the courthouse himself. There they were—the very bandits who murdered his friend.

He denounced them, but he had no proof to back his accusation. Harpe as "Setton," and May, were at the moment public heroes. No arrest was made, though suspicion was aroused.

At this point a hitch occurred—a serious one from the standpoint of

May and "Setton." Governor Claiborne, acknowledging the debt for the reward, found that the territorial treasury was too low to pay it at once, and told the men they would have to wait a few days until more funds arrived. They had to abide this delay, but they were uneasy and with good reason.

At this very period, due to Jefferson's purchase of the Louisiana Territory, the government was in the act of taking over the former Spanish-French province. Soldiers were being sent for garrison duty, and a company of these, stationed at Natchez, was commanded by Captain Frederick Stump, a Tennessean and a friend of Governor Claiborne.

During the excitement over bringing in Mason's head, Captain Stump had a good look at the "heroes." He was in fact present with Claiborne when May and "Setton" presented their affidavit and claimed the reward. In particular his attention was riveted by the appearance of "Setton."

As he sat, watching the men talk with the governor, a trend of thought started. That red hair—the "downcast countenance"—the ferret-like look of cunning—other details which fell into place—all corresponded with the descriptions of a very much wanted outlaw.

When the two departed after being told they would have to wait for their money, Captain Stump turned to the governor and said, "Sir, I believe that man Setton is really Little Harpe!"

Claiborne was startled. But he was a man of quick and decisive action. He ordered the immediate arrest of the pair.

Setton, surprised at the accusation when he was taken into custody, denied he was Wiley Harpe, as he had done previously at New Madrid. May was silent.

Just at this time a flatboat from Kentucky was landing its cargo at the Natchez docks. When a public announcement was made that it was "believed that Wiley Harpe was taken, and if any Kentucky boatmen had any personal knowledge of him, they were desired to examine the prisoner," five Kentuckians responded.

These men had all seen the Harpes and part of them had been witnesses when the brothers were tried for murder and broke out of jail at Danville, Kentucky. They agreed that the prisoner looked like Little Harpe, and one mentioned a mole and two toes grown together on one foot as identifying marks, which the prisoner was found to have.

Even more direct was the identification of an older acquaintance of Wiley Harpe. Back in the Knoxville days, when the brothers were racing horses and gambling, before they really launched on their career of murders, Little Harpe had a knife fight with a man named John

Bowman,[8] and got the worst of it. He came out of the encounter with an ugly wound on his chest.

Bowman happened to be in Natchez, and he came forward to look at the prisoner. After studying him for a few moments, he said very positively, "You're Little Harpe."

The other denied the name.

But Bowman was certain. "If you're Harpe," he said, "you have a scar under your left nipple where I cut you in a difficulty we had at Knoxville."

With the words he tore open the accused man's shirt—and there was the telltale scar, exactly as he had stated.

5.

Wiley Harpe! The dreadful record of the murder trail in Tennessee, Kentucky, and Illinois, was part of the intimate knowledge of the whole frontier. The prisoner cowered and persisted in denying his identity. But now it was proved beyond any doubt.

And his companion? Not much was known about May, except that he had helped rob the men who identified him. His mere association, however, with a ghoul like Wiley Harpe, was enough to condemn him, and it would be only a question of time before the full story of his criminal activities at Red Banks, Cave-in-Rock, and up and down the Mississippi and the Natchez Trace would be known.

The two culprits were lodged in the Natchez jail. With consciousness of doom upon them, they were desperate. One night they managed—how, the record does not state—to break out and escape.

Immediately the country was wildly aroused. Wiley Harpe at large again! From very terror, he must be found and finished!

In every direction posses rode, up and down the Trace. Inquiries were made wherever the fugitives might have been seen.

The chase was unrelenting. Apparently the fugitives had been unable to provide themselves with horses. Northward went the hunt, led by reports of suspicious-looking persons seen in that direction. It ended suddenly. Near Greenville, only about twenty miles northeast of Natchez, the escaped prisoners were recaptured. They were unarmed, and had been able to make little distance from the city where they broke jail, because of the necessity of keeping concealed much of the time.

Greenville has long ago disappeared, but it was at that time an im-

[8] See Chapter II.

portant town on the Trace,[9] with fine homes and a courthouse. The
two prisoners were locked in the Greenville jail—presumably in irons
to prevent a new escape. Justice moved against them swiftly.

William Downs—that same Squire Downs who once had taken
Wiley Harpe's confession under the name of Setton, when the outlaw
stood with Mason's pistol at his back—was foreman of the grand jury
that considered their cases, January 13, 1804. An indictment of armed
robbery, *not* murder, was quickly brought against both prisoners. But
it amounted to the same thing in the end. The penalty was death on
either charge if conviction was obtained.

Soon after the indictments were rendered the actual trials began,
Harpe and May being tried separately, before different juries. The
presiding judges were men of the highest standing, Peter B. Bruin,
David Ker, and Thomas Rodney.[10]

The defendants secured the services of two well-known lawyers,
Breazeale and Parrott, who used every legal tactic to save them. They
attempted to quash the indictment; they denied that the court had
jurisdiction; they finally asked for a writ of *habeas corpus*. In each motion they were overruled.

May, the first to come to trial, was found guilty. Soon afterwards
Harpe heard the same verdict from his own jury. Now the lawyers
came forward with a "plea of former acquittal"—although where such
an acquittal was obtained, if ever, cannot be discovered. In any case,
the court once more overruled them.

On February 4, 1804, the two prisoners were brought before the
court, and heard their sentences pronounced in identical words, "that
on Wednesday the eighth day of the present month he be taken to the
place of execution and there hung up by the neck, between the hours
of ten o'clock in the forenoon and four in the afternoon, until he is
dead, dead, dead."

Today they still point out the "Gallows Field." It is a flat and bare

[9] The present Greenville, in Washington County, Mississippi, is not to be confused with this earlier Greenville, which was in Jefferson County, about twenty
miles northeast of Natchez.

[10] Their respected position in Mississippi is demonstrated by the fact that later two
of these same judges, Bruin and Rodney, sat on the case when Aaron Burr was
tried in Washington, Mississippi, on an indictment for treason. Ker, however, did
not sit in that trial. He caught pneumonia in the drafty courtroom during the
May-Harpe trials and died. The Burr case was transferred to the East, and conducted in Richmond, Virginia, with Chief Justice John Marshall sitting as federal
court judge. In this case Marshall's strict interpretation of "overt act" resulted in
acquittal.

area, with trees looming dark about it. In that day it was near the Natchez Trace.

The gallows for Harpe and May consisted simply of a timber or heavy pole, extending from the fork of one tree to a similar fork in another, thus thriftily eliminating the expense of a carpenter and materials for a more conventional gibbet, while achieving equally satisfactory results. From the crossbar two ropes with nooses dangled.

On the day of the execution everyone in Greenville and for long distances around gathered to see the double hanging. Hundreds of spectators, all agog, watched the condemned men, under heavy guard, marched on foot, their hands tied behind them, to the place where they were to die.

Ladders were placed, one at each tree, and the prisoners ordered to climb them, which they did. The nooses were adjusted about their necks.

As was customary, each was permitted to make a statement. May tearfully "complained of the hardship of his fate; said he had not been guilty of crimes deserving death and spoke of the benefit he had rendered society by destroying old Mason."

Harpe made some sort of a confession, "which had a tendency to implicate several persons not heretofore suspected as parties concerned with the Masons in their depredations." Perhaps he named, stumblingly from memory, some of Mason's far-flung accomplices. More of this sort of thing would later come out in the final statement of Henry C. Shouse; and its greatest exemplification would be brought about in the affairs of John Murrell years later.

Nobody took down the statements of Harpe and May verbatim, and they were not given much time for final words. Their arms and legs were bound, the ladders were kicked away, and they hung until, as prescribed in their sentences, they were "dead, dead, dead."

Until now everything had been according to legal process. But with the outlaws dead, the genuine hatred of the people manifested itself.

The bodies were taken down, the heads hacked from the trunks, and stuck on poles, which were placed beside the Trace, one at a short distance south of Greenville, the other a short way north of the same town, as "gruesome warnings to highwaymen."

Over the protests of persons who had relatives buried there, the headless bodies were placed in the same grave in a small cemetery beside the Natchez Trace. When the officers of the law insisted on using the place for the interment of the outlaws, those who had kin there—only about half a dozen graves existed—exhumed the bodies of their dead and moved them to a new burying ground half a mile south of Greenville, which is today known as the Bellegrove Church Yard.

Four decapitated outlaws. Four ghastly heads for exhibition to the morbidly curious.[11] We have seen what became of Micajah Harpe's head in Kentucky. Mason's head, after it served its turn as an object of curiosity, probably was buried somewhere near Natchez.

Nor is there any record of the eventual fate of Wiley Harpe's and James May's heads. Perhaps when the elements had bleached the skulls they were appropriated by morbid souvenir hunters.

Not even the bodies of Wiley Harpe and James May lay in peace. The two corpses were nailed up in a plank box together before being buried. Close to the graveyard ran the Natchez Trace. In later years the trail was improved into a wagon road. As it gradually widened and was deepened by traffic and erosion, at last the wheels which rumbled by cut into the shallow grave itself. Bones of the outlaws appeared now and then, protruding out of the bank beside the road and were dragged forth to be gnawed by dogs or wolves. Eventually even these last traces of the two criminals disappeared.

Mason's band was scattered, some of its members continuing, however, as parts of future gangs; for the lust for crime is not easily eradicated. But though Mason and the Harpes were gone, something more lasting than human lives continued to exert a maleficent influence for years to come. It was Cave-in-Rock itself.

[11] Audubon, in one of his journals, has an account of a Mason who was overtaken by a body of regulators, who killed him, cut off his head, and stuck it on "the end of a broken branch of a tree, by the nearest road to the place where the affray happened." This may be a garbled account either of Samuel Mason's death or that of Big Harpe, since no regulators had anything to do with killing the former. Rothert surmises it may have been the end of one of Mason's sons. If so, this would raise the total of decapitated outlaws to five.

IX.   *Counterfeiters in the Cave*

1.

The counterfeiting of lawful money was little known in the American colonies before the Revolution. "In the colonies," according to Frederick A. Bradford,[1] "what coin was in use was almost entirely of foreign extraction, while the bills of credit issued by the various colonies . . . were frequently so depreciated as to make counterfeiting impossible."

It was a war measure, introduced by the British general, Sir Henry Clinton, the object of which was to wreck the already shaky financial condition of the continental currency, that gave the first great impetus to counterfeiting in America. Congress, in 1776, authorized the printing and circulation of paper money, and one Smithers, an Englishman living in Philadelphia, was hired to engrave these bills of exchange.

[1] *Dictionary of American History.*

His effort produced currency, the units of which were guaranteed in terms of "Spanish milled dollars."[2]

Soon after Smithers began making continental currency he was suspected of treason, and fled from Philadelphia to New York, which was then in the hands of the British. He was gladly received by Clinton, who promptly put him to work making counterfeit money with which to flood the rebellious colonies. Smithers was able to produce "bogus" so close to the genuine that it was hard for an expert to detect it; while the ingenuous common citizen accepted it without question.

So openly and with such zeal did Clinton's counterfeiters work that tens of thousands of dollars of worthless paper was soon in circulation. Indeed, there were newspaper advertisements, soliciting agents to spread this bogus money. One, appearing in the New York *Mercury* and presumably paid for by the British, read as follows:

> Persons going into other colonies may be supplied with any number of counterfeit Congress notes for the price of the paper per ream. They are so neatly and exactly executed that there is no risk in getting them off, it being almost impossible to discover that they are not genuine. This has been proved by bills to a very large amount which have already been successfully circulated. Inquire of Q.E.D. at the Coffee House, from 11 A.M. to 4 P.M., during the present month.

This spurious flood so brazenly continued had much to do with the depreciation of continental currency which by 1781, before the end of the Revolution, had practically lost all value, giving rise to the phrase, still in use, "not worth a continental."

With the end of the war, the British supply of counterfeit money of course ceased. But by then the idea of thus making easy profits had been absorbed by numerous shady gentry, and in spite of the government's stern efforts to suppress it, counterfeiting continued.

A frequent and favorite location for a "coiner," as counterfeiters were often called, was in some remote cave. Sile Doty, a notorious and clever eastern outlaw, in his story of his own life,[3] described the hid-

---

[2] The Spanish dollar, sometimes called a "piece of eight," because it was valued at eight reals, was the usual standard coin before the government set up its own mint in 1793. It was a common practice to cut this coin with a chisel into eight pieces for smaller change. These pieces were called "bits," and the modern slang of "two bits" for a quarter of a dollar, "four bits" for a half, and "six bits" for seventy-five cents, is a relic of this practice. In earlier nomenclature there was a differentiation between "short bits," amounting roughly to a modern dime, and "long bits," or fifteen cents, which combined into "two bits." This usage obtained as late as Mark Twain's early years in the West, and reference to "short bits" and "long bits" was made by him in his journal of crossing the Isthmus of Panama.

[3] *The Life of Sile Doty, the Most Noted Thief and Burglar of His Time.*

den cave of a coiner named Lyman Parks in a cliff overlooking the Connecticut River, where he kept four men employed who "could imitate the coin of the United States so perfectly that it was a hard matter to detect it." This was in 1820, and Parks at that time gave Doty a list of "parties engaged in this rascally business" which included "residents of New York, Albany, Buffalo, Baltimore, New Orleans, and many other places."

During the Revolution one or more caves in Bucks County, Pennsylvania, were used by the Doane family of Tory outlaws for the storage and circulation of Clinton's bogus money, if not for its actual manufacture.[4]

Most famous of the counterfeiting caves, however, was our old friend, Cave-in-Rock. And the first of the "coiners," John Duff—the probable brother-in-law of Samuel Mason—seems to have operated in the Cave while Mason and his robbers were still there, and began those operations even before Mason moved in.

If he was the same Duff mentioned by George Rogers Clark, he was at first a hunter and fur trader. About 1790, while he was living in the Cave, a very sleek young gentleman named Philip Alston joined him there. Alston was a South Carolinian of polished manners and good education, perhaps a member of a Tory family, who early in his life learned the art of counterfeiting. His specialty was not bogus notes so much as bogus coins. Some years ago a coining die, for the making of counterfeit half dollars was found in the Cave, which may have belonged to Alston and later to Duff.

Alston's first misadventure of record was in Natchez. In the Catholic church there he saw a golden image of Christ. One day the image disappeared. Alston had stolen it. He might have melted down the gold and sold it in that form, but he knew a better way. By using alloys and making counterfeit coins he could make the metal go much further and be of greater value to him.

He was, however, suspected. Hastily fleeing from Natchez to escape the law, he settled near Russellville, Kentucky, where he "established a salt works and store . . . managed the Cedar House, a tavern . . . also farmed, preached, and taught school."[5]

Evidently he was a man of parts, who could turn his hand to many trades. He was well respected in the community—which later came to know the Harpes so fearfully well—until the country was flooded with spurious money, made by Alston. He thus became, according to Alexander C. Finley, "not only the first farmer, manufacturer, and

[4] *The New Doane Book.*

[5] Alexander C. Finley, *History of Russellville and Logan County.*

merchant, but he established the first depot of exchange and the first
bank, and also the first mint in western Kentucky."

A glittering record, surely. But the frontiersmen took a less than
kindly view of it. Again Alston was forced to flee—just ahead of some
indignant citizens. He appeared at Red Banks—later a hangout of
Mason—about 1788. Shortly after, about 1790, he was over the river
with Duff at Cave-in-Rock.

It must have been from Alston that Duff learned "coining"; and
Alston probably furnished the tools and dies for this manufacture,
since Duff would hardly have the skill. Duff was spurred to this new
activity by his discovery of a mine containing lead with a certain
amount of silver in it, on the banks of the Saline River, in Illinois,
which flows into the Ohio not far above the Cave.

Just what proportions of lead to silver Duff used in his coins is not of
record, but perhaps they were like those of the fabled butcher who
sold rabbit sausages, and was arrested for mixing horse meat with the
rabbit meat. When the judge asked him how much horse meat he used,
the butcher said, "Oh, about half and half."

"You mean," said the judge, "that you use one pound of horse meat
to one pound of rabbit meat?"

"Oh, no, your honor," said the prisoner at the bar, "one horse to one
rabbit."

Alston left the Cave for surroundings less primitive and more to his
taste, and died, according to the only available account, somewhere in
Spanish territory, where he had become quite prosperous.[6]

Left to himself Duff plied his trade as "coiner" with such zeal that
he frequently had to change his base of operations. For a time, after
Mason departed from Cave-in-Rock, he had a den near Caseyville,
Kentucky, just below the mouth of the Saline River; and at another
time he pursued his trade thirteen miles up the Saline River itself, to
be near his source of lead and silver ore. There, on one occasion, he
showed a woman named Mrs. Hammack—having first blindfolded her
so that she would not know how to find it again—the interior of a cave
containing boxes of "counterfeit silver and gold coins in boxes and
chests.[7]

[6] Finley says that "Peter Alston, Philip Alston's youngest son, became an outlaw
and robber, and joined Mason's band at Cave-in-Rock, and was allied with the
Harpes, and with one of the Harpes was executed at Washington, Mississippi, . . .
for the killing of his chief, Mason, for the reward." It is possible that James May
was an alias for Peter Alston, or vice versa. But the execution referred to took
place at old Greenville, not Washington.

[7] This story was related by Mrs. Hammack years later. Her memory may have
played her false in one particular. It is unlikely that Duff had any "gold" coins of
his own making. His manufacture was "silver."

At times Duff had to do some agile dodging to escape the authorities. Once he saved his life by a quick and unusual expedient. A posse cornered him at his house near Caseyville while his wife was down at the river doing the family washing. Duff ran down to where she was boiling clothes in a large iron kettle. Quickly dumping the washing out on the ground, he dipped the kettle in the river to cool it, then, holding it over his head, began to swim across the Ohio to the Illinois side.

The posse which had pursued him down to the bank began to fire at him as he swam; but though several bullets hit the kettle, none penetrated it. When he reached the opposite shore, he held the kettle at his back for protection, fled into the woods and was lost to view.

He met his death after his final move, which was to a place known as Island Ripple on the Saline River. Once he escaped from soldiers there, but at last a "Canadian" (French *courier de bois*) and three Shawnee Indians, hired by the commandant of a fort on the Illinois side of the river, shot and killed Duff while he was drunk.

In the years since there have been many searches for "Duff's treasure" in caves and other places along the Saline, but all have been fruitless, at least as far as any records show.

2.

Other counterfeiters followed Duff. Most notable of these was a man known as "Bloody Jack" Sturdevant, a gambler and gangster, who plied his illegal trade at Cave-in-Rock and its vicinity for years until put out of commission by one of the heroes of the frontier—James Bowie.

Sturdevant was described by Judge James Hall as follows:

> He was a man of talent and address. He was possessed of much mechanical genius, was an expert artist and was skilled in some of the sciences. As an engraver he was said to have few superiors; and he excelled in some other branches of art . . . He could, at any time, by the blowing of a horn, summon some fifty to a hundred armed men to his defense . . . He was a grave, quiet, inoffensive man in his manners . . . yet this man was the most notorious counterfeiter that ever infested our country. His confederates were scattered over the whole western country, receiving through regular channels of intercourse their supplies of counterfeit bank notes, for which they paid a stipulated price—sixteen dollars in cash for a hundred dollars in counterfeit bills.[8]

[8] Judge James Hall, *Sketches of History, Life and Manners in the West.*

One of Sturdevant's "confederates"—circulators of his bogus money—
was a young man with a satanic genius for crime which would one
day make his name dreaded throughout the country. He was John A.
Murrell, and though his connection was more or less indirect, Murrell's career, like so many others, could trace its start to sinister Cave-
in-Rock.

Sturdevant had a talent not mentioned in Judge Hall's summary,
but easily understood in a man of his dexterity and lack of honesty:
he was a card sharp.

He owned in fact a gambling place on the strip at Natchez Under
the Hill, where he went at times to fleece the unwary in crooked card
games. Perhaps he was considering retirement from the increasingly
dangerous trade of counterfeiting and to follow the safer pursuit of
gambling.

Some time during the year 1829 Sturdevant lured a young man
named John Lattimore into his establishment. The youth was a son of
Dr. William Lattimore, a highly respected planter and former territorial representative in the United States Congress. Because he was
busy with other affairs, Dr. Lattimore entrusted that year's cotton crop
to his son, to sell on the Natchez wharf. Young Lattimore did so and
received payment in cash.

Soon after this transaction was completed a plausible stranger—a
"runner" for Sturdevant—suggested a little amusement for the evening.
There were rounds of drinks in various places, which led at last to the
gambling room of Sturdevant himself. A turn at the cards was suggested, and the youth, with the confidence of the liquor in him and a
full wallet (of his father's money) agreed. Sturdevant rapidly fleeced
him.

Thereafter, according to the best-accepted account[9] the following
sequence of events took place:

As young Lattimore stumbled back up the hill to the respectable
part of the town, dejected, ashamed, and alone, he met, of all people,
Jim Bowie, who was a friend of his father's.

Bowie questioned young Lattimore, found what had happened,
and taking the youth with him went direct to Sturdevant's, sat in the
game, and quickly detected the cheat.

At once he rose, gathered all the money on the table, and put it in
his pocket.

"Are you drunk?" cried Sturdevant. "Put that money back on the
table!"

Bowie looked him in the eye, accused him of robbing the young

9 Raymond W. Thorp, *Bowie Knife*.

man, and said he had taken from the table enough money to repay Lattimore.

Sturdevant may have had a "grave, quiet, inoffensive" manner, but he was a very dangerous man. "He had twice killed with the pistol, and once with the dagger, [and] burned four houses of political enemies to the ground."

When the word "cheat" was flung in his teeth, Sturdevant wrathfully said he would fight. Bowie agreed and named his terms: Knives, left wrists tied together, antagonists in a ten-foot circle chalked on the floor, to begin stabbing at each other at a signal.

The fight hardly lasted five seconds. At the signal Sturdevant made a great slash with his knife. Bowie avoided the blow, and with a savage sweep of his own blade, cut his adversary's knife arm to the bone so that he dropped his weapon.

Sturdevant expected immediate death. But Bowie slashed the bindings on their left wrists, saying, "I won't kill a helpless man," and left the place with young Lattimore.

The outlaw chief was raging. Shortly after, when Bowie started on a journey that eventually would take him to Texas—and his final heroic death at the Alamo—three of Sturdevant's men ambushed him in a canebrake. Single-handed, in a furious battle in the dark, Bowie killed all three, although he himself was wounded in one leg.

Sturdevant left Natchez never to return. At Cave-in-Rock he nursed his wound. How long it incapacitated him is a matter for conjecture; but it probably handicapped him both as an engraver of counterfeit bills, and as a manipulator of cards, if the tendons of that arm, the right, were severed.

Soon afterwards he moved from the Cave, which was damp with dripping walls in wet weather, to a log house, a story and a half high on a bluff above the present town of Rosiclare, Illinois, near the foot of Hurricane Island.

There, in 1831, a party of Illinois regulators attacked him. Sturdevant and his men fought back. In the battle that followed one regulator was killed, and it was claimed that three counterfeiters also paid with their lives. But when the regulators made ready for a rush, they found a small howitzer trained down the stairway, and halted to wait for reinforcements.

During the night Sturdevant and his gang escaped. According to Rothert, "Sturdevant was never again heard of in that or any other locality. What became of him is not known. This attack on his headquarters ended forever counterfeiting in the Cave-in-Rock country."[10]

[10] Otto A. Rothert, *The Outlaws of Cave-in-Rock.*

Years later the bullet holes of this battle still could be seen in the logs of the building, which stood deserted and gradually fell to pieces. In 1876 some quarrymen, working in a quarry adjacent to the place, set off a blast which opened a hidden hollow in the stone. Within this hollow was found "a set of dies for making counterfeit half dollars"— the half dollar was a favorite piece for "coiners," because it passed more easily than the dollar.

X. *Ferryman of Death*

1.

While counterfeiters still operated at Cave-in-Rock, a figure almost as sinister as Samuel Mason himself made his appearance in western Kentucky, made contact with the "coiners," and cooperated with them.

His name was James Ford, and he took up residence near Tolu, a river town opposite the very head of notorious Hurricane Island and only five miles below Cave-in-Rock, about 1803. Such was his demeanor that it was not for several years that his criminal activities were suspected. An eyewitness described him as he looked in 1822:

"He was about six feet in height, and of powerful build, a perfect Hercules in point of strength; but he has now grown too corpulent to undergo much fatigue. His head is large and well-shaped; his sandy brown hair, now thin, is turning gray, for he must be fully fifty years old; his eyes, of a steel-gray color, are brilliant and his glance quick and penetrating; his nose rather short and thick; his upper lip remarkably long, his mouth large, and his lips full and sensuous. He has a broad, firm, double chin, and his voice is deep and sonorous. His complexion is very florid, and he converses fluently. On the whole, when in repose, he gives one the idea of a good natured, rather than a surly, bulldog; but, if aroused, I should say he would be a lion tamer."

That description was given by Dr. Charles Webb, a highly respected physician and citizen, who through a strange series of accidents married Ford's daughter.

For years before 1822—when Dr. Webb first saw him—the portly, impressive figure of Ford had been a familiar sight in the Cave-in-Rock country. Its possessor was considered a substantial man, a man of enterprise, an upholder of the law—for he was a squire, and had been so since 1815.

Several fine farms belonged to him and his holdings continued to grow along the Ohio River—by what financial means nobody seems to have troubled to find out. There is little doubt, however, that at least part of the money he thus invested was gained by banditry, both at Cave-in-Rock, and along a road to the ferry across the Ohio which he established at a place that still today bears his name.

This ferry, operated from a landing on property owned by Ford, at the site of present-day Ford's Ferry, Kentucky, crossed the river to a point just two and a half miles above Cave-in-Rock. Exactly when it was established is not of record, but it must have been about 1816, when the great influx of settlers began to pour into Illinois, following the close of the War of 1812.

There were other, competing, ferries up and down the river, and Ford knew that those which had the best roads running to them would get the largest part of the custom. He therefore set about providing such access to his ferry.

He had acquired "influence" in what was then Livingston—now Crittenden County. By using this political influence he managed to have a good road built and maintained from what was known as Pickering Hill to his landing, a distance of about four miles leading down across the difficult terrain of the rough descending valley, to the river.

North of the river, in Illinois, however, he possessed no such influence. The existing road there ran along the bottoms and was known as the Low Water Road, because it could be used only when the river was low, being subject to flooding at other times. At his own expense Ford constructed what was known as the Ford's Ferry High Water Road, out of the bottoms and over higher ground, some twelve miles to what was then and still is known as Potts' Hill, a rise just north of Cave-in-Rock. Having established the road, Ford advertised it by means of signboards placed at all crossroads leading to his ferry, and very soon began to enjoy the revenue from considerable traffic that used his crossing.

Thus far his efforts had represented a great amount of enterprise and investment. But Ford was avaricious. He was not long content merely to receive the fees from his ferry. There was that road to be paid for and he was impatient. He had by this time made acquaintances who had sufficient lack of scruples to help him make profits which could hardly bear scrutiny.

Potts's Hill at the northern terminus of his High Water Road was named for one Billy Potts who kept a tavern on its slopes. This Potts, with whom Ford had a close and thorough understanding, was a gruesome character. Near Potts's Tavern there was a Potts's Spring where weary travelers often stopped to refresh themselves with cool water. Both spring and tavern could tell bloody tales. A short distance east, where the Ohio bent northward and was joined by the Saline River, was a farm known as Potts's Plantation, where, it will be remembered, the Harpes murdered three men.

To complete the triangle with Ford and Potts, Bloody Jack Sturdevant at this time occupied Cave-in-Rock, and pursued his coining activities, with robbery as a collateral occupation. In the latter, if not the former, he was abetted by James Ford.

Under these arrangements a gang of robbers, known as the Ford's Ferry gang, came into being. Travelers were frequently murdered and robbed on the ferry road or at Potts's Tavern, and a fearful menace was also added to flatboat traffic down the river past Cave-in-Rock.

2.

If there could exist any doubt as to Ford's connection with Cave-in-Rock, it is effectively dispelled by a strange and romantic adventure of Dr. Charles H. Webb, referred to above, who in his reminiscences[1] related the following story:

In the year 1822, young Dr. Webb, fresh out of medical school, with a license to practice medicine but no practice, left his home in South Carolina, accompanied by his brother, to seek their fortune in what was then the West.

Being short of cash, the Webb brothers decided to work for their passage down the Ohio. From Pittsburgh they descended as far as Louisville and the falls; and beyond that they became part of the crew of a broadhorn belonging to a man named Jonathan Lumley, bound

[1] Preserved by William Courtney Watts in his *Chronicles of a Kentucky Settlement*.

for the southern markets and carrying a cargo of corn, provisions, and whiskey. There were three other boatmen on the craft, who with the Webb brothers and Lumley made a total of six.

One spring day as the boat floated down the stream, Dr. Webb, who was proficient as a flute player, was taking it easy, playing on his instrument, a fine one.

All at once the craft neared a cliff in which a cave yawned. They did not know it, but this was the dread Cave-in-Rock. Suddenly they saw a woman, on top of the bluff, waving a white cloth at them, as if to hail them.

This was an old trick of the Cave-in-Rock robbers—the siren set to lure the boats inshore—but Lumley and his crew apparently knew nothing of it, for the owner ordered his men to pull close in and ask the woman what she wanted.

As they neared the Cave itself a man stepped out and called to them, "Hey, Cap! Have you any bacon or whiskey on board?"

Lumley replied in the affirmative. The man then asked him to land, adding, "We're short on rations here, an' want to buy right smart!"

Lumley objected that he was headed for the lower Mississippi and did not want to break bulk, but the man had another argument:

"We've got a woman here an' a boy who want passage down to the mouth of the Cumberland. They've been waitin' a long time an' will pay passage."

At this Lumley landed, about two hundred yards below the Cave.

Dr. Webb and one of the boatmen were left on the craft, while his brother, with Lumley and the rest of the crew walked to the Cave and entered.

They did not return. An hour passed. Dr. Webb grew worried and asked his companion to go to the Cave and find out what was causing the delay. The man did so, and likewise failed to come back.

Another hour passed. The sun went down and clouds covered the sky, bringing swift darkness. On the boat a large dog belonging to the owner began to howl mournfully.

By this time Dr. Webb's anxiety was acute. Yet he could not leave the boat. Presently he was able to descry three men coming from the Cave in the darkness. At first he thought they were part of the crew.

They were not. With drawn pistols they boarded the boat and told Dr. Webb that if he made a sound he would be killed.

He ventured one question. What about his friends?

"They're all right," said one of the men, adding that the captain (Lumley) had sold the boat and cargo, and "that's enough for you to know."

First binding the young doctor hand and foot, they blindfolded him, took all his money and valuables—including his prized flute—lifted him into a skiff, and rowed out into the river. Shortly he felt the boat he was in collide gently with another in the stream.

A brief colloquy took place, in tones so low that he could not catch the words. Presently he was aware that one of the men was making his way toward him, where he lay blindfolded and bound, in the stern of the boat.

This man, according to Dr. Webb's recollection, seemed to have "a remnant of mercy." He whispered in the captive's ear:

"We're goin' to vi'late orders a little an' turn ye loose here in the middle of the river. An' the further ye float away from here 'fore ye make any noise, the better for ye by a damn sight. Lay low an' keep dark till mornin', make sure."

With that the man, whom Dr. Webb was unable to see because of his blindfold, loosened the captive's bonds, after which he whispered again:

"Ye kin work 'em loose when we're gone, say in about an hour, *but not sooner*, or ye may git into trouble. An' don't ye never come back here or ask any questions, or ye'll fare worse, an' do nobody any good."

Thereupon the man climbed into the other boat, and Dr. Webb could tell by the sounds that he had been left alone to drift down the current.

For an hour, as nearly as he could estimate it, he remained silent and motionless, fearing that the other boat might be close beside him, keeping watch on him. But he heard nothing "except the moaning of the night winds among the forest trees that lined each shore, the occasional barking of wolves, and the weird cry of night fowls—particularly the blood-curdling hooting of great owls."

At length he began to struggle, and after considerable effort succeeded in removing his bonds and the blindfold. He found himself in a boat without an oar or paddle, the night so pitch dark that he could barely see the dim outline of the shore.

To add to his troubles and alarm, thunder began to rumble, lightning flashes lit up the wild scene, great crashes from the skies seemed to split his eardrums, and a terrific storm burst, sending rain down in sheets, with a wind that whipped the river into waves. The boat began to ship water, and for lack of any other utensil, Dr. Webb desperately used one of his own shoes to bail.

Eventually the long and terrifying night passed. In the morning his boat drifted against the head of an island and he got ashore. There he found a cabin, the home of a man named Prior and his wife, who fed him. They told him they had often heard of the depredations of the

"Wilson gang"[2] about the Cave and assured him he was lucky to escape with his life. Prior kindly supplied him with a paddle "cut out of a clapboard," with which he could at least make some shift at navigating his boat, and told him how to reach Smithland, at the mouth of the Cumberland River, only a short distance downstream.

With some difficulty Dr. Webb managed a landing at Smithland. He was, quite naturally, terribly concerned about his brother, and although he had no money, managed to borrow a horse on which he rode to Salem, a small town northeast, in the general direction of the Cave. There he was advised to go to the farm of a Colonel Arthur Love, "a highly esteemed citizen" who lived within a few miles of the house of James Ford near Tolu. Already, in 1822, Ford was "suspected by many" of being in close connection, if not the leader of the Cave-in-Rock gang. Colonel Love[3] was expected to tell Dr. Webb how best to go about gaining information as to his brother's fate.

But Dr. Webb did not reach Love's farm. On the way, his horse, frightened by something, bolted and ran away. The doctor was thrown and seriously sprained an ankle. There he lay in the road, unable to walk, when a curious coincidence occurred.

A young woman—very attractive to his eyes—driving a buggy or other vehicle of some kind, found him, took pity on him, helped him into her equipage, and took him to her own home.

Only when he arrived there did he discover that he was in the house of James Ford himself, and that his rescuer was Cassandra, Ford's only daughter. Ford was away at the time, and the girl and Ford's wife made the young man comfortable. His realization of the perilous position he was in became more acute when he was shown the very flute that had been taken from him at the Cave—a certain proof of Ford's connection with the gang, for how else could it have reached his place?

[2] This name went clear back to Samuel Mason's early days, when he advertised "Wilson's Liquor Vault and House of Entertainment" at the Cave. Mason was long dead and the sign had been gone for a quarter of a century, but place names have a habit of clinging.

[3] This man probably was a relative, perhaps a brother of the Major William Love, who was murdered by the Harpes at Stegall's house. Major Love's widow moved to that neighborhood from her home near Knoxville, Tennessee, after her husband's death. After her own death she was buried near Marion, Kentucky, only ten miles from Tolu and a little farther from Salem. The following inscription was placed on her tombstone: "My name was Esther Love, daughter of Wm. & Nancy Calhoun of Abbeville, South Carolina, born Sept. 30, 1765. died Mar. 2, 1844. My husband Wm. Love was killed by the Harpes Aug. 1799. Blessed are the dead which die in the Lord." The fact that she moved to this country bespeaks family relationship with Colonel Arthur Love. Perhaps she lived with his family.

It required time for the sprain to heal so that Dr. Webb could travel, and it was a week after he arrived at the house before Ford himself appeared. Now, for the first time, the young doctor saw the "masterful, self-willed, dreaded, almost outlawed man."

Meantime, during Webb's stay, a special interest had grown up between him and Cassandra. When he was able to leave he returned to Salem, "which then contained a population, white and black, of about two hundred and fifty" (it is not much larger now), and hung out his shingle as a physician.

His decision to open practice there was entirely due to Cassandra, upon whom he called frequently, and whom he eventually married. After a time he at last happily located his brother, who had escaped or been released by the robbers, and was in business in St. Louis, Missouri.

Dr. Webb lived out his life in western Kentucky, and was one of the best loved men in the entire area. To the end of his days he insisted that Ford's wife and daughter, while they were "somewhat suspicious" of Ford's activities, never really knew what they were.

3.

Even before this time the Ford's Ferry Road had begun to claim its victims. At the ferry landing on the Kentucky side, in a house belonging to Ford, lived Vincent B. Simpson, who ran the ferry boat. Almost opposite, across the river, at Cedar Point, dwelt Henry C. Shouse. These two men, with Ford's sons, Philip and William, evidently were Ford's chief lieutenants, together with Potts who ran the sinister tavern at the end of the road.

Nobody knows how many travelers disappeared on that route. Long after the outlaw days the balconied, two-story, frame structure once Potts's Tavern, still stood. It was deserted and at one time was used as a stable. When it was torn down in 1938, bloodstains a hundred years old were found in one of its rooms, evidently the murder chamber. And over the years plowmen, turning the soil in what was called Potts's Old Field, have more than once uncovered moldering human bones, the relics of men killed and buried there in shallow graves.

All this time Ford, on his side of the river, represented himself as a solid citizen and an enemy of the outlaws. At times, when it was reported that robberies had grown too frequent in his personal purlieus, he sent a warning. The suspected men immediately disappeared for a time, and word was broadcast over the countryside that "Jim Ford found the robbers and ran them out of the country."

One such case ended in a peculiarly bizarre tragedy. Billy Potts's son, a venturesome youth who early joined the bandit gang, was in the act of robbing a man on the road when two farmers, who knew him, came upon him in the act. He fled, but they reported him as the robber.

Presently, as was the custom, a quiet warning came from Ford, telling young Potts to leave the country, not only for his own sake but to save others from exposure. He took the advice, and as usual people were told that James Ford had driven him away.

Years passed. Young Potts was not heard from, but in that period he managed to gather quite a roll of money through crimes of one kind or another. He also gained weight and grew a beard.

Believing he would not now be recognized he decided to pay a visit to his old home. When he reached Pickering Hill on the way down to the Kentucky terminus of the ferry, he noticed some men who said they were "resting" and getting ready to cross over into Illinois.

Young Potts recognized them as members of the bandit gang, but his appearance had so changed that when he rode along with them and crossed the ferry not one of them knew him. Presently he saw, by signs he knew only too well, that they were preparing to rob and probably murder him.

It was high time for him to reveal his identity. He did so, by signs, passwords and other proofs so indubitable that they not only believed him, but were gleeful at his return.

The outlaws were all for riding with him to his father's tavern, to celebrate the occasion, but young Potts had a different idea. He wanted to surprise the old folks, and also to make a large impression on them. Alone, therefore, he continued his journey and arrived at the tavern as night fell.

His father and mother were there, but that evening there were no other guests in the place. Neither parent recognized him, because of his beard and changed appearance, and the son, highly amused, decided not to reveal himself to them until later in the evening. Meantime, to make the surprise greater, he would show them that he had money, which would make his revelation all the happier.

Presently he drew from a pocket a large roll of money, which he displayed, as if carelessly, before he put it back, remarking that he knew he was in a safe place for the night. His mother after a time went to bed, but his father and he stayed up rather late, talking, and Billy Potts, the sinister tavern man, still did not suspect that he was conversing with his own son.

At last the young man asked for a drink of water.

"Why, sure," said Billy Potts. "Right down the hill is a spring— coldest, finest water you ever drank."

Right well the son knew that spring and its water. It was down the slope three hundred feet, and it was lined with stone. Together they walked to it, and the younger man knelt down and stooped over to drink.

With a sudden movement, the murderous tavern keeper drew a keen knife and thrust it to the hilt into the stooping back before him. The steel went in under the left shoulder blade, penetrated the heart and almost instantly caused death.

Now old Potts felt in his victim's pockets and took out the money, a considerable sum, according to one story about three thousand dollars. Next he dragged the body to his "private graveyard" in the neighboring field, dug a shallow grave, and buried it. Then, with the money, he returned to the tavern, cheerfully told his wife when she awoke at his entry, that he had "made a good haul," and went to bed, and to sleep, as if nothing had happened.

Next morning came the stunning shock. The robber gang rode up to the tavern, expecting to find young Potts and celebrate the return of the prodigal. Gleefully, old Potts began to recount how he had finished "an easy one" the previous night, by killing and robbing him.

As they listened, the outlaws, hardened as they were, showed amazement and even horror. He could not understand why they did not congratulate him and asked what was the matter.

"Why—Billy—" one of them at last blurted out, "that man you killed —was your own son—"

Mrs. Potts gave a scream. Billy Potts refused to believe that the victim of his murderous treachery could be his own son. Not until the body was exhumed was the dreadful truth proved, by a birthmark which the mother all too clearly remembered.

It crushed even the hardened ogres that the tavern keeper and his wife had become. Soon after Billy Potts and his spouse closed their hostel and left the country, never more to be heard from.

4.

This episode in the lives of the Potts family occurred in the late 1820s, perhaps about the time of the wedding of Dr. Webb and Cassandra Ford, which took place February 5, 1827.

Shortly after the marriage of his daughter, James Ford's first wife died. The outlaw chief did not relish being left with no woman in his house. He soon supplied the deficiency.

In the latter part of 1828, a farmer named Frazer came down the
river in a flatboat, in which were all his possessions, together with his
wife, Elizabeth, and their three daughters. They bore some sort of an
introduction to Ford from an associate or acquaintance upriver, and
when they arrived at his landing they presented it.

The burly householder, "masterful, self-willed, almost outlawed,"
was all smooth hospitality, especially after he looked upon Elizabeth
Frazer, and he invited the travelers to break their journey at his
home.

Elizabeth, mother of three small daughters, was a comely, capable
young woman in her late twenties, and how Ford's steel-gray eyes
roved to her bright face and pretty form can be imagined, whenever
he viewed her during that visit. His daughter had married and gone,
his wife was dead. He himself was in his late fifties, but still strong
and lustful. This girl half his age amazingly appealed to him.

Suddenly Frazer became mysteriously ill. In a few days he died.
Perhaps the cause was natural; but there were no certificates of death
and no autopsies in that day. One is unavoidably left wondering if
the death might not have been conveniently caused, perhaps by poison, for it is clear that Ford desired the farmer's pretty wife.

He hardly allowed time for decent mourning before he began pay-
ing court to Elizabeth, for he meant to have her. And have her he did.
She had no home or place to go, and she had three young daughters
to care for. These probably were the reasons why she consented to
become the second Mrs. Ford.

They were married January 15, 1829, and once more James Ford
had a woman in his bed, and a mistress for his house. Elizabeth became mother of a son by Ford in 1830. She named the baby James,
for his father.

It was her fourth child, and also his fourth, since by his first marriage
he had two sons, each about as old as his new bride, named Philip
and William, and a daughter, now Mrs. Cassandra Webb, living at
Salem, Kentucky.

Up to now James Ford, portly and prosperous, had been in the
ascendancy. But about this time some curious events took place.

The first was a suit in court which he brought in September, 1829,
against Vincent B. Simpson, his ferryman and lieutenant, to recover
money paid for a slave named Hiram, whom Simpson had sold to
him. According to the language of the lawsuit, the slave died shortly
after the sale, although Simpson had "guaranteed him to be a good
blacksmith, sound and healthy," whereas the slave was "no blacksmith
and no labourer and was labouring under a disease called hernia."

The suit seems to have been compromised out of court, but it in-

dicated a rift between Ford and his henchman. Rothert[4] surmises that
the real purpose of the suit was to prove Simpson a deceitful man; for
it was suspected that he might "blab" about some of the secret operations of his employer in connection with certain gentry across the
river, and the suit could be cited to discredit any "accusations" Simpson might make. Meantime Simpson continued to run the ferry, though
now he was closely watched.

Next, two strangely coincidental deaths occurred. On November 12,
1831, Ford's eldest son, Philip, then thirty-one years old, made his will.
Two days later he was dead.

It can be assumed that the will was made on his deathbed—one
story is that he had yellow fever. He named his father and Dr. Webb
administrators, and left his estate—he was a widower—to his father,
his brother William, and his small son Francis. Included in the property thus divided were seven slaves.

On June 1, 1832, the second son, William, twenty-eight, also made a
will. He died November 3 of that year, less than seven months after
the demise of his elder brother. Cause of death is unknown, although
cholera is suggested. The inscription on his gravestone read:

> To the memory of William M. Ford, who departed this life on the
> 3rd day of Novr. 1832, aged 28 years. Whose benevolence caused the
> widow and orphan to smile and whose firmness caused his enemies to
> tremble. He was much apprest while living and much slandered since
> dead.

Overlooking the spelling, the epitaph suggests that William Ford
shared some of his father's evil reputation. His will indicated also that
he had an eye for pretty women and a way with them, for while it
mentioned no wife, it bequeathed his estate to two boys, one seven
years old, the other seven months, naming the mother of each (neither
of them a Mrs. Ford), and adding: "Both of said children I acknowledge to be my sons." If both boys died before they reached majority,
the will went further and provided two thousand dollars for the young
daughter of still a third woman, name not given. Though the will did
not specifically name this girl as his daughter, it left the impression
that William Ford believed she was, if he was not entirely sure. In
case the girl received this sum, the residue of his estate went to
Richard Miles, his uncle and brother of his mother, James Ford's first
wife, who at one time operated a ferry across the Ohio, sufficiently far
away so there was no competition between the brothers-in-law.

[4] Otto A. Rothert, *The Outlaws of Cave-in-Rock.*

5.

James Ford's household now was completely changed. His first wife and both his elder sons were dead. His only daughter had married and moved away. In his home were only his new wife, Elizabeth, her three daughters by Frazer, and her infant son by himself.

With his two best lieutenants, his sons, gone, Ford's organization began to break up. The rift with Simpson grew wider. More and more the outlaw chief seemed to fear that his ferryman might, from motives of revenge and to save his own skin, turn state's evidence and expose Ford to escape punishment for himself.

On the Illinois side of the river lived the watcher of the ferry, Henry C. Shouse. Soon after the death of Ford's second son Shouse, acting on his own or Ford's idea, bitterly quarreled with Simpson, and challenged the other to fight, frontier style. But Shouse, a powerful man, had a reputation as a fierce and ugly rough-and-tumble fighter. Simpson prudently withdrew into his house, and Shouse thereupon returned to the Illinois side.

The enmity did not cool. Within a few days the quarrel was resumed, and this time Shouse openly accused Simpson of treachery, and of having told various persons that "someone will soon turn state's evidence, and certain robbers, counterfeiters, and murderers will then quit business for good."

Seven uneasy months passed. Then, June 30, 1833, Simpson—the ferry being idle at the time—took a skiff and rowed down to Cave-in-Rock. His business is unknown, but though Sturdevant and his "coiners" had been driven from it by the regulators in 1831, it still was a meeting place for bandits, being just two and one half miles below the Illinois landing of Ford's Ferry, whence the road led to Potts's Tavern.

Whatever his reasons for this visit, Simpson must have been drunk when he returned. A sober man would hardly have behaved as he did.

Rowing back up the river he landed at Cedar Point, and walked directly to the house of his enemy Shouse. Later testimony indicated that he carried a pistol, and his mood was anything but pacific.

He never reached the house. As he approached it, he turned aside for a moment, perhaps to glance back toward his boat which was tied at the bank. In that instant a rifle shot lashed out from an upstairs window of Shouse's place, and Simpson fell mortally wounded, a bullet hole in his back.

Men who saw the shooting took Simpson across the river to his own house. He died next day.

Soon after his death a crowd of neighbors gathered to talk with his widow. These men were law-abiding, but they also were vengeful. The general feeling was that Simpson, while perhaps guilty of participation in the crime wave on the Ferry Road, had been murdered because he was about to reveal the secrets of the gang and implicate its members and its leader.

Shouse, of course, was the chief suspect. The fatal shot came from his house. But two other men living on the Illinois side, James Mulligan and William H. J. Stevenson, were close associates of Shouse, and therefore probable accomplices.

When the hastily assembled posse crossed the river and found that all three men named had disappeared overnight, the previous suspicions hardened into certainties—in the minds of the people—and a pursuit at once was organized.

The countryside on both sides of the river, long quiescent, was aroused to action, and the Simpson murder triggered a general regulator movement, the object of which was to exterminate the Ferry Road and Cave-in-Rock robbers.

6.

That James Ford was believed by many to be involved in the gang's operations, perhaps even was the boss robber, seems evident. But he had never yet had a crime traced to him with "sufficient clearness to cause his arrest and trial." As a big landholder, and a former —if not present—magistrate, he would have to be handled carefully.

It is probable that the widowed Mrs. Simpson, grieving and bitter, supplied the unofficially assembled regulators with some scraps of pertinent information. Whatever the reason, that grim assemblage decided that Ford must die; and furthermore, that the courts could not be trusted to see to it.

Another meeting was called a few days after Simpson's death at the ferry house, and three men were named as a committee to ride to Ford's home near Tolu, and invite him to attend the gathering, to confer with the others on what testimony should be given the following day before a grand jury which was to consider the Simpson murder.

As the three rode on their errand they saw a heavy, impressive figure on horseback coming to meet them. It was Ford himself, and the encounter was at the Hurricane camp ground, near the mouth of

Hurricane Creek, and opposite the head of Hurricane Island, just a short distance above his house near Tolu.

Impassively he pulled up his horse, and listened to the committee's request. Then he said, "Gentlemen, I am now on my way to the ferry to offer my services."

He seemed to have no inkling of the dangerous public feeling against him, and with the other three rode on to the landing, arriving there just as the sun was setting.

About a dozen men were present, and it must be remembered that, regardless of what took place that night, these men were essentially law-abiding, seeking to secure peace and safety in their very rude and unpoliced community.

Mrs. Simpson was preparing supper for the men. The ferry house was a log structure of a familiar plan. It had two rooms, one a living-dining room, the other a bedroom. These were connected by an open roofed passage, called in that day a "turkey walk" and sometimes a "dog trot." In this breezeway the men gathered, conversing gravely, and waiting for the meal to be served.

James Ford found a chair, and tilted back comfortably, his broad shoulders against the log wall. When Mrs. Simpson announced that supper was ready, she explained that because of the size of her table only half the men could eat at once. Some went in, but Ford elected to take the "second table," and remained where he was in the darkness.

One imagines that he must now have felt an unspoken hostility in the crowd, for talk lagged, and one by one the men remaining in the turkey walk left it and slipped off into the night. At last the portly figure of Ford remained alone, tilted back against the wall in the gloom.

Then a candle flickered in the passageway as one of the men returned. "Here," he said, "I've got a letter I want you to read."

Ford took the letter, and still leaning back, prepared to read, while the man held the candle up, ostensibly to allow him to see the written page. But the holder stood well aside from the reader, for the lightening of Ford's figure by the candle was for a very different purpose.

All at once a long tongue of flame spurted from the darkness, and with it came the keen crack of a rifle. Ford fell crashing to the floor, his chair overturned. He was dead, shot through the heart. The bullet had passed through his body and lodged in the log wall behind him.

To this day the name of the man who held the candle and that of the man who fired the shot are unknown. That they were members of the regulator party is certain. Collusion is self-evident between the candle-holder and rifle-wielder. But these could have been any of a

dozen men, and that their act was approved by all is shown by the
fact that the secret of their identity was never revealed.

Ford's connection with the outlaws was so generally believed that
there was no investigation of the assassination by officials. The body
was that night conveyed to his home in an ox wagon, and there delivered to his widow.

At his funeral two days later only the bereaved Elizabeth, Dr. and
Cassandra Webb, the young children, two neighbors and a few slaves
were present. Presumably the "two neighbors" (unnamed) were a
country preacher, to conduct the services, and his wife.

Even in death a sinister aura seemed to brood over James Ford.
During the services a thunderstorm came up. It broke while he was
being buried, with lightning flashes and reverberations so terrifying
that the superstitious slaves felt that the devil was coming for his own.

At the very time when the coffin was being lowered into the grave
by the slaves, a particularly terrific blast of levin fire accompanied
by an ear-splitting crash of thunder so startled one of them that he lost
his grip on the lowering rope. The coffin dropped head-first, landing
in the bottom of the grave where it was wedged, slanting upward
toward the feet of the corpse within.

Then came the rain, sweeping in such blinding sheets that it was
found impossible to move the coffin. The grave was hastily filled, leaving the casket in that incongruous tilted position, after which everyone fled for shelter.

For years after the Negroes told the story of how "Jim Ford landed
in Hell head-first."

7.

While these events were taking place, a posse of regulators sent to
pursue the murderers of Simpson were hot on the trail. It led them
southeast toward Arkansas, and for a very good reason. Shouse, the
leader of the three fugitives seems to have been acquainted with a
truly terrible outlaw named John A. Murrell, who had at least two
hideaways in Arkansas, one in the northeastern part of the state,
which he called his "Garden of Eden," the other in the southeastern
corner of the state on Lake Chicot.

The fugitives did not reach either of these havens. Soon after they
crossed the border into Arkansas, they were overtaken and captured.
Brought back to Equality, Illinois, the county seat of Gallatin County
—of which Hardin County was then a part—they were lodged in jail.
A grand jury promptly indicted Shouse as the actual slayer of Simp-

son, and named Mulligan and Stevenson as accessories before and after the fact.

There were delays. Not until May, 1834, was Shouse tried. Meantime Mulligan died in prison and Stevenson managed to escape.

Judge Wyley P. Fowler, who—perhaps significantly—had been James Ford's legal counsel for several years, defended Shouse in his trial. One witness, William Sharp, signed a statement that a few days before his death Simpson told Sharp that "he intended then in a few days to take his pistol and go over to Shouse's house and settle him." But he made this avowal after the two-day trial was over and the jury had retired to consider the case.

Judge Fowler made an effort to have the statement placed in the record to show a motive of self-defense even though the jury brought in a verdict of guilty. The court overruled the motion.

The jury's verdict was that Shouse was "guilty as charged." He was sentenced to be hanged, the day of execution to be June 9, 1834.

And here occurred an interestingly mysterious episode.

During the days that Shouse lay in jail, awaiting his death, Judge Fowler spent much time with him. It began to be whispered that Shouse was dictating to his lawyer a full confession, including names of all persons associated with the robber gang of which he and Ford were leaders.

The report created surprising uneasiness in some highly reputable circles. Judge Fowler began to receive anonymous letters threatening his life if he ever made the confession public; so many and so threatening, that for safety's sake he spent that winter in Frankfort, Kentucky.

When he returned to the lower Ohio country again in the spring, he said publicly of the document that "No good could come of its publication. It would cast a shade upon the reputations of some of Livingston County's most esteemed citizens."

Note that "esteemed citizens" were, by Judge Fowler's statement, implicated in the doings of the outlaw band. Even before this time a greater list had been obtained, and only a few months later *it was published*, in the Murrell disclosures which this book will chronicle.

Judge Fowler permitted nobody to see his notes; and later, in the presence of a witness, he burned them. But when asked on one occasion whether or not the Ford's Ferry robbers were part of the vast network of Murrell outlaws, he said that the gang "at one time made some preparations" to combine with the criminal organization of the man who was called "The Great Western Land Pirate." And it was common talk that Shouse had made one or more trips to the place near Marked Tree, Arkansas, where Murrell had his "Garden of Eden," conferring with, or perhaps carrying communications to, that arch-bandit.

On June 9, near Golconda, in Pope County, Illinois, the gallows for Shouse was erected, "two heavy timbers with a crossbeam over them." It was situated at the bottom of a valley with hills rising on either side of it, making a natural amphitheater. That day those slopes were black with thousands of spectators.

Shortly before two o'clock in the afternoon the condemned man was brought to the scene, under heavy guard. He rode to the gallows sitting on his coffin, which was conveyed in an ox cart, and his hands were tied behind him.

At precisely two o'clock, the ox cart was led between the uprights of the gallows. Shouse was made to mount standing on his coffin, his legs as well as his arms were bound, and he was blindfolded.

If he made a final statement, it was not recorded. The noose hanging from the beam above was adjusted about his neck.

"Hiyah, thar!" shouted the driver of the oxen.

The two beasts shouldered forward, drawing the cart. The prisoner's toes seemed to cling for a last moment to the edge of the coffin passing out from under him, and then he was suspended, in his death struggles, strangled by the rope about his neck until he was dead.

It was the end of the Ford's Ferry gang. Cave-in-Rock ceased to be a robbers' roost, partly because the country was settling up, and partly because river traffic was being taken over by steamboats which churned up and down the stream, making the waylaying of flatboats unprofitable because so few now came.

But Cave-in-Rock's influence did not cease. The evil it spawned extended up and down the Mississippi and Ohio valleys for years to come.

XI.   *Satan's Satrap*

1.

After Samuel Mason and Wiley Harpe were gone, divers other outlaws beset the Natchez Trace and the lower Mississippi. Joseph Thompson Hare was one of them. Unlike most of the others, he was no frontiersman. He dreaded hardships and hated the wilderness.

"Let not anyone be induced to turn highwayman by reading this book and seeing the great sums of money I have robbed, for it is a desperate life, full of danger, and sooner or later ends at the gallows," he wrote in his diary-confession, which was published after he was executed in 1818.

Hare was a city hoodlum, born in Pennsylvania, who learned to be a thief in the slums of Philadelphia and New York. Just ahead of the law he signed on as a seaman on a coasting vessel, jumped ship when it docked at New Orleans, and having assessed the possibilities of the Natchez Trace, gathered a group of thugs and began to prey on that route of overland travel.

His career was short: two or three years. As a robber he was successful, taking "twelve or thirteen thousand dollars" from one company, seven thousand dollars from another, as well as smaller hauls. But he disliked murder. More than once he spared the lives of his victims and once he whipped with his bare fists a member of his own gang for trifling with the affections of a young woman—or so he claimed in his "confession."

At times he murdered, but he did so unwillingly, and it was this very unwillingness, praiseworthy as it was, that brought about his downfall. He let one drover go after taking "the man's pistols and a small sum of money." Unfortunate mercy! That very night the drover, with a posse, overtook Hare and captured him.

He went to prison for five years. But there was no reform in him. After his release he returned to the East, where in March, 1818, he robbed a mail coach.

In that holdup he got $16,900. But it was his greatest of all mistakes. Robbing a mail coach was a capital offence.[1] Two days after the holdup he was identified and arrested for the crime. Found guilty, he was hanged, September 10, 1818, at Baltimore, Maryland, leaving his confession, written while in jail, an interesting study of a man in conflict with himself.

2.

Though Hare's career on the Trace was short, it had one ramification more important than its own various crimes. It stimulated the imagination, and a desire for emulation, in the mind of a youth just growing up, whose daring and lack of scruples were so great that he would one day become a far more dangerous and dreaded outlaw than Hare had ever been.

"I have robbed more men and stolen more Negroes than Hare ever did," was one of the boasts of John A. Murrell at the height of his perilous power. Which brings us to the arch-criminal of this entire era.

In his prime, John A. Murrell had a satanic handsomeness—black eyes, black hair, graceful manners, and a kind of wicked courtliness. He dressed in the latest modes, his garments of superior cut and material; and he always wore gloves, the most expensive sort, not from mere foppishness but from another very good reason as we shall see. He had a lust for women, the more depraved the better. But he had

[1] This is probably why Mason and his robbers gave John Swaney such immunity as he carried his mail along the Natchez Trace. As a former magistrate Mason would likely be acquainted with the law.

even a more monstrous lust for blood and suffering, and a hate for humanity that was diabolic. One almost imagines there may have been a smell of sulphur on his breath.

There is disagreement about the date of Murrell's birth. Phares says, "about the year 1800."[2] The Tennessee Guidebook fixes the date specifically at 1804, and this from what we know of his life, seems about correct. There is question again on the exact place of his birth, but in all likelihood it was in a roadside tavern belonging to his parents near Columbia, Tennessee, forty miles or so south of Nashville.

It was a place of quite remarkable iniquity, that tavern. Murrell's mother, from available information, operated it as a combination inn, thieves' market, and brothel. She was dishonest, immoral—and capable.

Of his father, Murrell later had little to say: "My father was an honest man, I expect." Tradition has it that the senior Murrell, whose first name seems to have been William, was an itinerant preacher, who was at home little of the time, sometimes being gone for weeks and even months on end.

Though Murrell bore his name, there is a strong likelihood that he owed his being to some other sire than this putative father. As hostess of the tavern Mrs. Murrell, according to long tradition, was more than hospitable to some of her male guests to whom she took a fancy, or perhaps who had "the price." She must have been an expert in the secret arts of love, possessing a facile amorousness that caused men to forget everything else when she was in bed with them, for she turned this forgetfulness to her advantage, and without any scruples.

In his mother, Murrell gloried. "My mother was of the pure grit;[3] she learnt me and all her children how to steal as soon as we could walk. At ten years old I was not a bad hand."

She gloried in him, too. He was her favorite when it came to picking locks of a guest's trunks and portmanteaus, while she kept the owner entertained in his bed "until he was so exhausted an earthquake wouldn't have wakened him," as Murrell later put it.

[2] Ross Phares, *Reverend Devil*.

[3] This word, misspelled "girt" by a printer's error in Stewart's original book, has been picked up in that form by subsequent writers who followed the Stewart story. "Girt" has no meaning in this sense, but "pure grit" or "right grit" has been an underworld expression since the days of Claude Duvall.

3.

"Earthquake" was a word of special and awful significance in Murrell's boyhood. When Murrell was seven years old a tremendous earthquake, one of the greatest ever known on this continent, shook the Mississippi valley from New Madrid south, and a long distance up the Ohio valley, starting December 16, 1811, and continuing for days after.

> Over a region of country three hundred miles in length, from the mouth of the Ohio to that of the St. Francis, the ground rose and sank in great undulations, and lakes were formed, and again drained . . . The central point of the violence of this remarkable earthquake was thought to be near the Little Prairie, twenty-five or thirty miles below New Madrid . . . The vibrations were felt all over the valley of the Ohio, as far up as Pittsburgh.[4]

According to eyewitnesses the ground heaved like waves on the sea and was broken into great fissures which opened and closed. Houses were flattened and whole forests wrecked. Hills disappeared; and along the banks of the Mississippi, water, mud and sand were thrown up in huge jets higher than the tops of the wildly tossing trees; while great sections of the banks collapsed, and many islands, including two of the most dreaded because of river piracy—Wolf and Stack —were obliterated and sunk.

On both sides of the river the earth sank deeply in wide areas so that lakes were created into which the river rushed to fill the depressions; with such fury that for a time, the only time in recorded history, the Mississippi actually reversed its current and ran backward, leaving its bed drained of water for a distance of many miles. Only the scantiness of the population averted great mortality and enormous property loss.

The date of that terrifying disaster looms large in another important respect: it had a decisive effect on the history of crime in general in the South, and upon the career of John A. Murrell in particular. Yet, strangely, it was not the mighty convulsion that changed everything for the outlaw gangs. It was a clumsy, ugly little experiment of man which was destined to alter life and conditions along the river far more than the earthquake itself.

Shortly before the convulsion, the first steamboat ever to attempt to navigate the Mississippi was on its way down the Ohio from Pitts-

[4] R. M. Devens, *Our First Century, Great and Memorable Events.*

burgh, where it was built. Its captain and builder was Nicholas J. Roosevelt of the famous New York family, who for a time had been an associate of Robert Fulton, inventor of the first successful steam-driven craft.

Named the *New Orleans*, it was of only one hundred tons burden, with a stern wheel and a single smokestack. On December 15, the day before the earthquake, the little steamboat stopped where a vein of coal cropped out on the banks of the Ohio, not far above the confluence of that stream with the Mississippi, to refuel. Coal had been mined there for the use of the vessel. While loading it, men noticed that "the weather was oppressively hot; the air misty, still and dull; and though the sun was visible, like an immense and glowing ball of copper, his rays hardly shed more than a mournful twilight on the surface of the water."

After refuelling, the *New Orleans* started on downstream, bound for Natchez, and eventually for New Orleans. Exactly where it felt the full fury of the earthquake which struck next day is not certain; but it was on the Mississippi, somewhere above New Madrid.

Suddenly those on the craft saw trees begin to toss madly, high banks disappearing on either side, the river heaving in waves like a storm on the ocean. Shelter was sought behind an island, and the steamboat fortunately was so far upstream that it did not encounter the reversal of current and the temporary empty bottom which the Mississippi presented below New Madrid while it was filling the newly created lakes.[5]

A day later, after the new lakes were filled, and the Mississippi once more ran within its banks, the *New Orleans* resumed its inter-rupted voyage. As the boat chugged downstream, the crew noted the damage at towns and in the forests. Eventually the destination was safely reached.

The great earthquake of 1811 so appalled people that the passage of the first steamboat hardly excited the amazement it would ordinar-ily have created. Yet it was that primitive little craft which struck the knell of both the land and river pirates. In the wake of the *New Orleans* would follow other steamboats, until they almost monopolized traffic on the river, including passenger travel both up and down-stream. Flatboating would in a great measure disappear, and within a few years the Natchez Trace would cease to be the profitable hunt-ing ground for robbers it had been for so many bloody years, because travelers rode upstream on steamboats, saving time and avoiding hardships by so doing.

[5] One of those lakes, Reelfoot Lake, of Tennessee, is today a widely known sports fishing area. It did not exist before 1811.

4.

This end result, however, was still in the future in 1820, when Murrell, a sixteen-year-old boy, began his career as a highwayman. His own thievery precipitated him into his first great step in outlawry.

One night a man named Daniel Crenshaw[6] came to the Murrell tavern. He was "a stocky, burly, hearty fellow, with a fat face and a jolly eye"—a man of interesting background. Ostensibly he traveled through the country as a peddler, but this was only to cover up his other activities. He seems to have been, at one time, a pirate serving under Laffite, the Barataria freebooter. His highway robberies and murders he did not enumerate, but they were not few. He knew key men in the robbery ring—originally, in all probability, formed by Samuel Mason—together with their hideouts and "fences." And he had connections with Cave-in-Rock.

One of Crenshaw's specialities was "shoving the queer"—distributing counterfeit money, which at that date, around 1820, was being turned out in quantity at Cave-in-Rock by Bloody Jack Sturdevant and his crew. According to one story he even paid Murrell's mother, after a romp in bed with her, in counterfeit notes.

If so, she probably got it back. Her thieves' market took over the loot Crenshaw brought to her, and she disposed of it at a handsome profit. Perhaps he made good the counterfeit bills after a jovial laugh, for he seems to have remained one of Mrs. Murrell's favorites.

On the particular night in question young John Murrell watched his mother playing the old, old game with the "peddler." He waited in inconspicuous silence until they reached an understanding and both retired to her room for the night's regalement. When he presumed his mother had sufficient time to occupy her paramour's mind to exclusion with herself and what she had to offer him, he stole into Crenshaw's room, opened the man's trunk with a skeleton key, and took from it a fine pistol, a bolt of linen, and several other articles.

Crenshaw did not suspect he was being robbed—evidently he believed he enjoyed immunity in that house—what with his relations with its mistress. Later, Murrell said with a laugh, "I thought that was not a bad figure I made." But he had robbed his mother's lover, and she might be understandably furious at his thievery in this par-

[6] This name is also rendered Harry Crenshaw by some writers, including Coates. But Ross Phares and Paul Marshall both have it Daniel Crenshaw, which seems more probably correct, since in his list of accomplices given later Murrell gave a D. Crenshaw, but no H. Crenshaw.

ticular case. So now he was off for good. His last act was to turn his
mother's training to account—against herself. He opened her secret
money box, took from it fifty dollars, and stole away in the night,
chuckling to himself at her rage and Crenshaw's when they found
they had both been robbed while they lay in each other's arms.

Nashville was the nearest large town, and for Nashville Murrell
headed, and hung around there for a few days. Nashville had a public
square, where a few years before Andrew Jackson and the Benton
brothers fought their bloody melee. One morning while Murrell was
walking across this square, he suddenly found himself confronting—of
all persons—Daniel Crenshaw!

A moment of panic. But to the youth's amazement the man he had
robbed gave a great guffaw. Daniel Crenshaw was not even angry. On
the other hand he was actually glad to see the boy.

It is more than likely that Crenshaw and Murrell's mother discovered Murrell's thefts the morning after he departed. Being of the
underworld themselves, they perhaps saw humor in their being so
victimized, and even admired the youth for his adroitness. Mrs. Murrell perhaps gave her bedfellow of the previous night some account
of her son's skills, and Crenshaw sized him up as a good prospect to
apprentice in the line of major robbery.

A vagrant thought: Could Daniel Crenshaw—who had known
Murrell's mother for many years, transacted with her in the loot she
disposed of, and ranked as one of her favorite partners of the couch—
have been John Murrell's actual father?

Nobody will ever know, but certainly the youth far more resembled
in his mental habits and instincts the highwayman, than he did the
vague itinerant preacher, his ostensible sire, who was home so rarely.

However that may be, on that day in Nashville Crenshaw was
friendly, ready to overlook the thieving episode. Aside from any possibility of paternity, he saw in the handsome youth something tran-
scending ordinary rascality. Here might be a developing genius in
crime.

But Crenshaw wanted to see how much of the "pure grit" the boy
had in him. So he invited him to join in "gathering"—a euphemism for
stealing—four good horses, and with them started for Georgia.

We have Murrell's own words for what happened thereafter:[7]

"We got in company with a young South Carolinian just before we
reached Cumberland Mountain, and Crenshaw soon knew all about
his business. He had been to Tennessee to buy a drove of hogs, but
when he got there pork was dearer than he had calculated, and he de-

[7] Virgil A. Stewart's account in H. R. Howard's *History of Virgil A. Stewart.*

clined purchasing. We concluded he was a prize. Crenshaw winked
at me; I understood his idea. We had traveled several miles on the
mountain when we passed near a great precipice. Just before we
passed it, Crenshaw asked me for my whip, which had a pound of
lead in the butt. I handed it to him, and he rode up by the side of the
South Carolinian and gave him a blow on the side of the head. He
tumbled from the horse. We lit from our horses and fingered his
pockets; we got $1,262. Crenshaw said he knew of a place to hide
him, and gathered him under the arms, and I by his feet, and conveyed him to a deep crevice in the brow of the precipice. We tumbled him into it. Crenshaw said, 'That ought to break him up some.'
We tumbled in his saddle, and took his horse with us, which was
worth $200."

It was John Murrell's first murder, and a singularly brutal one, for
they did not even know their victim was dead when they "tumbled
him in" the abyss, to "break him up some." Perhaps he lived for a
time to linger out his last hours in agony.

But was sixteen-year-old John Murrell shocked or sickened? Far
from it. After they sold the stolen horses and divided the money, "We
frolicked for a week or more, and were the highest larks you ever saw.
We commenced sporting and gambling and lost every cent of our
money."

Crenshaw, in addition to schooling his young pupil in crime and
murder, showed him the multifarious aspects of vice. Again and again
it comes up in Murrell's recital: "I had become a considerable liber-
tine, and I spent a few months rioting in all the luxuries of forbidden
pleasure with the girls of my acquaintance." Afterward: "My stock
of cash was soon gone, and I put to my shift for more." Easy come,
easy go, and the wastrel spent his criminal gains as fast as he got
them.

Thus far his life was a reckless series of adventures, without plan
or focus. But John Murrell was no ordinary young man. He had some
qualities that might have made him notable in a legitimate walk of
life: courage, a precise mind, a seeing eye, and the ability to judge,
organize, and handle men. He attained a polished manner as by instinct, was a student whose mind grasped abstruse points of law and
theology when he had need for them, a ready and fluent speaker in
public or private. When you add to these things an intense hatred of
humanity, and a satanic instinct to do evil, you have the ingredients
for a super-criminal.

He was maturing; and as he matured he became the leader, not
the follower; the thinker, the planner, while riding with his tutor in
wickedness. One day he saw a sight that planted in his mind a seed

which would burgeon into a monstrous flowering, an incredible night-bloom of evil.

With Crenshaw one day he rode into a town in southern Alabama —the name of which he did not remember later. The two of them were astonished to find it apparently almost deserted. Business houses were closed, families locked inside their barred homes, armed men patrolled the streets.

This was about 1821. Alabama had been admitted as a state into the Union only two years before and was much disorganized as yet. Courts were most primitive or entirely lacking; police authority had not been established. In the midst of this disorder a rumor spread that the Negro slaves were planning a revolt; that Spaniards, who were bitter over the loss of this disputed territory to the United States, were fomenting the outbreak. It was enough to cause a tremor of dread among the white people of the settlement.

5.

It seems almost superfluous to discuss the evils of slavery, so well recognized and universally accepted in this country are they today. But less than a century ago, there were some millions of slaves in the United States alone, and other millions elsewhere. Nor, incidentally, is slavery entirely ended in the world. According to a recent investigator,[8] slaves are held and sold by thousands in some of the African countries, such as Abyssinia and the Sudan, and in Arabic countries like Yemen and Saudi Arabia (although the latter recently declared slavery illegal). There are, as a matter of fact, many thousands of *white* slaves—in the slave labor camps of Siberian Russia—today.

In the United States slavery has long been abolished. But prior to the Civil War it was prevalent in all the Southern states. The condition of the slaves was from tolerable to intolerable, depending on their masters and the type of labor they were assigned to perform. "House servants"—those who were immediately connected with the plantation homes—were usually well treated. "Field hands"—and this often included women and even children—who did the hard labor in the cotton, rice, tobacco or sugar cane fields, were often mistreated, especially when, as in some cases, a sadistic overseer had charge of them.

Their food was coarse and poor, their quarters the merest shacks,

[8] Sean O'Callaghan, *The Slave Trade Today*.

their clothing cheap and ugly homespun. They were kept in complete ignorance. It was against the law in many states to teach a Negro to read or write.

But the evil did not end there. The first thing a slave owner did was to break the will of a slave, by so convincing him that he had no rights of any kind, and must obey without question any order given him, at the pain of the whip, that obedience and subservience were unquestioned. One of the worst aspects of slavery was this wholesale "brainwashing" of its helpless victims, so that they became little more than robots to carry out the will of their masters.

It became second nature for the Negroes to obey white men, and they were in many ways childlike because of their ignorance and helplessness. This docility, this acceptance of white superiority, made possible some of the deviltries that Murrell later practiced.

Yet there was always the natural wish of any people for freedom, and in many parts of the South, particularly the cotton growing areas, Negroes greatly outnumbered the whites, so that a servile uprising was an ever-present fear. There had been such outbreaks—in New York, Virginia, South Carolina, Louisiana, and elsewhere—and the revolting slaves, many of them savages fresh out of the African jungles had sometimes, it must be admitted, been murderous and destructive before they were suppressed.

Most fearsome as a precedent, however, was the Negro rebellion in Haiti in which every white person on the island was massacred during the rule of the black "emperor" Dessalines, white women being universally subjected to rape until they were finally killed or died from abuse. Under Christophe, who succeeded him as "king" even *mulattoes* were slaughtered—everyone who had a trace of white blood in his or her veins—and grisly tales of torture kept coming from the island, these events being quite recent in 1821.

The fears of the white minority in some parts of the South were therefore real and understandable. It is possible to realize from the foregoing how a devil like Murrell could impose upon the black people to their own great harm.

6.

When Murrell and Crenshaw reached this particular town, white women and children were locked indoors while their men guarded them with loaded weapons. Negroes were forbidden to leave their cabins after dark. Patrols saw that these orders were obeyed. The community was simply prostrated.

To Crenshaw the situation offered no more than a rare opportunity for looting. That night he and his young companion emptied the till of the principal store, slugged and robbed two or three wayfarers, and rode on, secure in the knowledge that this "crime wave" would be blamed on the slaves, who probably would suffer for it.

But Murrell's imagination far transcended that of Crenshaw. The picture of that fear-stricken town, helpless to defend itself if the Negroes actually did make a violent uprising, remained in his mind to breed and fester.

Already the younger outlaw, far cannier than Crenshaw, perceived that the old days of easy pickings along the trail were nearing their end. He spent much of the next four or five years in the so-called "Neutral Strip"—the disputed area along the Sabine River, policed by neither the United States or Spain, nor by Mexico after the latter won independence. This area was in chaos, and robbery in it was relatively easy, but even there Murrell studied the changing status of affairs. Steamboats were now conveying most travelers, except for local journeyings; and it was becoming increasingly dangerous to murder people in neighborhoods where they lived and would be quickly missed and searched for.

And at last he came up with a new scheme: a scheme of such cruelty and horror that one can hardly help thinking of the young man with the satanically handsome face as the devil himself, or at least the devil's chief satrap.

Slave stealing was not new. A Negro, in good condition, would bring six hundred to eight hundred dollars in the market. Slaves could be kidnaped, carried to distant parts of the country, and there sold. At times even free Negroes were abducted and sold into servitude.

But stealing slaves had this difficulty: they might tell their new owners from what plantation they came, and who was their former owner. If the new owner was a man of honor this could create complications, including a determined hunt for the thieves—and slave stealing was heavily punished.

It remained for Murrell, the dark diabolist, to add a new twist to the practice—a plan which was the synthesis of cruelty and treachery, but which built up the profits and eliminated the risks in the peculiar form of crime this was.

He had now become a master of the plausible manner and facile tongue, and to prepare himself for perfection in his new form of deviltry he even went to the lengths of corresponding with some of the Abolition societies in the North, to obtain their peculiar phraseology and ideas, the more readily to delude his victims.

The so-called "Underground Railroad," a system by which slaves were helped to flee from their masters, and were transported from station to station by a network of secret routes into Canada, was in full operation by 1825, and many of the Negroes had heard of it.

For Murrell it was easy to approach a slave in an out-of-the-way place, and talk smoothly with him. By using that magic word "Underground" and representing himself as a friend to the colored people, he had little difficulty in persuading a Negro to trust him on a promise that he would be conducted to Canada or some free state where he would be at liberty.

But first—so Murrell proposed—the slave must permit himself to be sold to a new owner, for money to "cover the expense," of which he was promised a share. After that sale he would once more be picked up and carried "toward freedom."

What Murrell secretly planned was to gain complete ascendancy over his victims; and of this he felt fully capable. Once the slave trusted him completely, or feared him to the point of blind obedience, which came to the same thing, he would make repeated sales of each Negro; always holding forth the promise of eventual liberty each time he compelled his prey to go through the process of being bought, the money paid over, and then being stolen again.

Even the most ignorant, however, must at last see through this scheme and realize that the promise would never be kept. Murrell took this into consideration and watched closely. The first intimation that a poor slave suspected treachery became his death warrant. He was murdered in some remote place to silence his tongue.

The first experiment was with a Negro man named Tom, on a Tennessee plantation. Murrell and Crenshaw convinced him they were his friends, but as soon as they had him in custody, instead of heading north to carry him to freedom, they "pushed for Mississippi."

They sold Tom in that state for six hundred dollars. When they left him with his new owner, he "seemed very uneasy, and appeared to doubt our coming back for him, as we had promised." All the next day the two white scoundrels lay in a creek bottom, not far from the place where they sold him. After dark they went to an old chinaberry tree in a lane, where they were to meet him. He had been waiting for some time, and he was pathetically glad to see them.

Poor Tom! He had every reason *not* to welcome them. The men into whose hands he had fallen were monsters. They took him to the "house of a friendly speculator." How often that phrase comes up in Murrell's story! Accomplices of the outlaws, living apparently respectable lives, seemed fairly to honeycomb the country.

That night this friend of theirs reported that he had seen in a small

village nearby a placard advertising the Negro, with a description of
Murrell and Crenshaw who sold him, and mention of them as "suspicious characters."

"It was rather squally times," Murrell later recalled, "but any port
in a storm."

That night they took poor Tom down beside a creek. Now occurred
the supreme and heartless treachery. Crenshaw shot him through the
head. After that came the gruesome process which Murrell here
adopted for the first time, imitating the Harpes and Masons, and
thereafter made it a virtually invariable pattern. He "cut open the
belly and scraped out the guts, and then filled him [Tom] with sand,
and threw him into the river to feed the eels."

This accomplished they decamped to spend the money they had
received for him and plan new atrocities.

7.

When they were not on one of their prowling raids, Murrell and
Crenshaw betook themselves to one of the three then celebrated cen-
ters of sin-peddling to amuse themselves—Natchez Under the Hill, the
Swamp at New Orleans, or what was called the Pinch Gut district of
Memphis.

By this time Murrell had become a confirmed lecher. Invariably he
spent most of those sprees with "the girls" in one of the more luxurious
bagnios. His favorite resort of all was the pleasure house operated by
the woman known as Mother Surgick, in the Swamp at New Orleans.

But girls—and whiskey and cards—cost money; and soon he and
Crenshaw would be on the road again to recoup their losses sustained
in the beds of wantons, or over the tables, or at the bars.

Once, while Murrell was pleasuring himself down in Natchez Under
the Hill, where gamblers, prostitutes, and robbers preyed upon the
river men—and also sometimes on sleek gentlemen who came down
from Natchez On the Bluff for a frolic—he heard something that set
his mind working to complete an idea already latent there.

In one of the filthy alleys he joined a group of thugs who glared
venomously up at the top of the Bluff, where stood the fine homes of
the gentry, and where the likes of them were never permitted to come.
There was deep hatred between the lawless element and the "genteel"
element which despised it.

Drunk and ugly, the ruffians growled threats and talked of rich
pickings that might be had up there in the aristocratic dwellings

where the "quality" lived. Murrell pricked up his ears. Why surely! A bold foray by enough men might net enormous loot!

But the thugs in the alley confined themselves to drunken talk. Nothing came of it. The leadership was lacking—as yet.

Murrell, listening, thought of various things—including that deserted town in Alabama where the mere threat of a Negro uprising prostrated everyone with terror. And with these thoughts he began to conceive his greatest plan of fiendish enormities.

He was sensuous, yet his mind was cold and passionless in its avarice. He possessed the craft, also, to adapt himself to the mood of those he wished to use or to defraud.

By this time he was in his later twenties, a man who already had shown his ability to impress other men, make them his followers, himself their leader. Crenshaw, who began as his tutor, was now his underling. Murrell possessed incredible energy and endurance; and, what made him most dangerous, an imagination that refused to balk at any limits. By this time, also, he was developing another trait which would lead to his eventual downfall—an extraordinary egotism, accompanied by contempt for all the rest of the human race.

Yet time and thought were still required, and additional information and education, before he would arrive at the full fruition of the scheme toward which his mind was reaching with all its consummate dreadfulness.

Meantime he acquired a new accomplishment. He met "a young man who professed to be a preacher among the Methodists." The new acquaintance was named Elijah Carter, and he was about Murrell's own age.

In that time and place a man needed no divinity school training or formal ordination to set up as a preacher. Anyone with "the gift of gab" and a smattering of biblical quotations could do it. Country folk accepted a preacher, real or false, at his own value. In settled New England there was sometimes inquiry, as Stephen Burroughs, the famous Yankee jail breaker, learned to his cost.[9] But in the Southern states there was no such skepticism.

It was a period of almost constantly recurring revivals. Camp meetings were held in different parts of the country, and there was always employment for preachers at a revival. The two great evangelical rivalries were between the Methodists and the Baptists.

"Forty-gallon" Baptists and "Sprinkle-wrinkle" Methodists—as they jeeringly called each other—could turn even a funeral into a furious denominational discourse. Frequently the deceased, as a last act be-

[9] *Memoirs of Stephen Burroughs.*

fore death, requested that his funeral sermon be preached from a certain text. The preacher usually managed to twist the given text around to fit his theme, which was the excellence of his particular persuasion, together with a violent picture of the misguided and tormented souls who fried in hell-fire because they chose the "wrong" path to salvation.

Camp meetings were great occasions on the frontier, prime events both for social gatherings and for excitement in the drab life of the little settlements. From miles around families would come, to participate in the day and night meetings, camping about the central place of preachings, whence the name, "camp meeting."

For hour after hour men and women in homespun and linsey leaned forward in eager attention as the evangelists on the platform went through shoutings and contortions and rollings on the ground in the frenzies which were the vogue of the times. Sinners in the congregation foamed and fainted from sheer excitement, jerked, jumped, screamed, fell down, shouted, crawled on hands and knees, in a veritable orgy of emotional excitement.

Frontier revivalist preachers were popular according to their ability to "beller like a scrub bull in a canebrake durin' cocklebur season." Most of them were "unlarnt" and prided themselves on the fact. But most of them also were sincere according to their lights.

This fact did not prevent gentry who were far from sincere from taking advantage of the obvious opportunities offered. Traders and peddlers followed the crowds, and in the outskirts of the camp meetings barrels of whiskey would be set by liquor sellers who did a brisk business "by gourd dipper or crock."

The hysteria into which the crowds worked themselves sometimes operated in strange directions. After the meeting ended for the night, and the crop of sinners were welcomed to the "footstool of God," the excitement was hard to get out of the blood, especially if one happened to be a lusty young man with a warm-blooded girl. So frequently did the sexes assuage this spirit of overwrought emotion together in the bushes that the rising tide of illegitimate babies following great camp meetings was notorious. Wrote one witness:

There may be some who think that a camp meeting is no place for love-making; if so, they are much mistaken. When the mind becomes bewildered and confused, the moral restraints give way, and the passions are quickened and less controllable. For a mile or more around a camp ground the woods seemed to be alive with people; every tree or bush had its group or couple, while hundreds of others in pairs were seen prowling around in search of some cozy spot.[10]

[10] J. M. Keating, *History of the City of Memphis and Shelby County.*

The most sinister elements were unfragrant individuals who "assumed the cloth"—frontier style—for objects other than the conversion of souls to a higher and better spiritual life. To this class belonged Murrell's new friend, Elijah Carter. Very soon he demonstrated how easy it was, taking advantage of a ministerial guise, to "shove the queer" and commit thefts of various kinds.

Murrell was the aptest of pupils. His father—if the senior Murrell was indeed his sire—may have given him a start in pious cant, the mouthing of bible quotations, and the kind of hell-fire and damnation preaching most convincing to the crowds, and therefore most necessary for an impostor who wished to victimize members of those crowds.

To such a background of preacherly phrases and behavior, Murrell brought an eloquent tongue, a handsome presence, and exceptional cunning. Before very long he surpassed his preceptor and was the leader, Carter the lieutenant, in the fleecing of revival meetings.

"I could preach a damned fine sermon," he boasted in his later days.

XII.   *The Perfection of a Scoundrel*

1.

What Murrell required, although he perhaps did not realize it, was a chance to do some deep thinking of his profoundly vicious type, to perfect his devilish abilities, and his plans, still nebulous, which were bubbling evilly in his mind. Fate soon gave him opportunity—of a kind quite undesired by him—for just such ponderings, uninterrupted by activities, enterprises, and dangers.

It was in 1831, and he was twenty-seven years old, when luck turned against him. He stole a mare from a widow living south of Nashville. The animal was a poor nag, hardly worth the trouble, and that was bad; but Murrell was caught, and that was far worse.

He was tried in the Nashville courthouse. In after years he never liked to discuss the episode, and he hired counsel in a vain effort to avoid conviction. Fortunately for him, people had no idea that he was a murderer and a robber at that time. But horse larceny in itself was regarded with great severity on the frontier.

Murrell was found guilty, the widow appearing against him and the mare produced in evidence. He was sentenced to receive thirty-nine lashes upon his bare back, to be branded on his left thumb with the letters H.T., for "Horse Thief," to be exposed in the pillory for two hours on each of three successive days, and to serve twelve months in prison.

The first of these barbarous penalties to be inflicted was the branding. The proceedings were described by a witness:

"At the direction of Sheriff Horton, Murrell placed his hand on the railing around the Judge's bench. With a piece of rope, Horton then bound Murrell's hand to the railing. A Negro brought a tinner's stove and placed it beside the Sheriff. Horton took from the stove the branding iron, glanced at it, found it red hot, and put it on Murrell's thumb. The skin fried like meat. Horton held the iron on Murrell's hand until the smoke rose two feet. Then the iron was removed. Murrell stood the ordeal without flinching. When his hand was released, he calmly tied a handkerchief around it and went back to the Jail."

Murrell's friend, Daniel Crenshaw, also had once been branded as a horse thief. "According to tradition, Crenshaw was defiant . . . as soon as the branding was finished, and while his hand was still smoking from the effect of the hot iron, he bit the letters from his thumb with a savage wrench of his hand and spat the mangled bit of flesh at an attendant."[1]

Murrell did no such thing as that. But while he appeared calm, the calm was outward only. Inside he was a volcano of fury.

The brand on his thumb was the reason for his later habitual wearing of gloves. After his prison sentence was concluded he was never seen with his hands bare. Always they were covered by gloves, the finer the better, of doeskin, kid, or even silk. He sought out and paid for the very best that money could buy, and wore them even when he was eating or sleeping, if anyone was present to see him. His vanity could not bear the thought that someone might catch a glimpse of that shameful "H.T."

But meantime, before he went to prison, he also had a whipping to undergo. Evidently later on the same day that he was branded, he was led, stripped to the waist, to the whipping post. His demeanor as he walked with his guards was firm and grim. He was bound to the post, and the cowhide began its wicked work.

Murrell ground his teeth like a madman, but uttered no sound although with each cut of the whip a gash was opened in his back from which the blood streamed.

At the tenth stroke, however, he gasped a plea: "Give me time to rest."

1 Ross Phares, *Reverend Devil*.

The request was granted and the whipping was suspended while he regained his breath and his composure.

Then it began again. Once more, and still another time, as the lashes continued, Murrell asked to be allowed to catch his breath. Each time he was given a few minutes' respite, while he fought for control. Each time the whipping was resumed until he had received the prescribed thirty-nine lashes and his back was a bloody horror.

Except for his requests for rests, not one sound did Murrell utter during that punishment. It was thought later that because he seemed to show so little pain the lashes had been the heavier.

At the finish he hung for a time by his bound wrists from the whipping post, as limp and pallid as if he had fainted. Someone told him it was all over. At that he straightened and seemed himself again. When he went back to jail he did not even accept a helping arm.

There still remained of course the three days, two hours each day, when he had to submit to the jeers, rotten eggs and vegetables, and other filth hurled at him by the crowd as he stood helpless, head and hands fastened by the pillory board so that he could not avoid the insults and unfragrant missiles.

The branding, the whipping, and the pillory completed a hatred for the whole human race which Murrell already had been building in his soul without the justification this gave him.

There followed his year in the state penitentiary. Murrell was no ordinary prisoner. His behavior was exemplary. In that year he devoted his time, when not at prison labor, to books. He "read the scriptures and became a good judge of theology"—not, however, for the uplift of his own soul. He also spent much time in the study of criminal law, although he "had not neglected the criminal laws for many years before that time." To carry out his plans for vengeance against all mankind, he needed a thorough knowledge of the code.

In those days behind the bars he brought to completion the great scheme which he had concocted out of many unrelated events. There was the Alabama town he had seen paralyzed by fear of a slave revolt: and Murrell knew from experience the discontent of the bondsmen and how easy it was to impose on their confidence and convince them of almost anything. There were the threats he had heard at Natchez Under the Hill and the speculation on the rich loot obtainable if the houses of the "quality" were raided: but nothing happened on that occasion—there was no leader.

Now, in his corrosive bitterness, Murrell's mind seized upon these and other factors. *He* would be a leader. Not, however, of any haphazard raid. His venomous imagination embraced the entire South, envisaged a violence so widespread and daring that it transcended every other criminal scheme of which he had ever heard.

A Negro uprising of gigantic proportions—that was the way! He would set about enlisting a secret Negro army, and with it he would not only revenge himself on the world, but gain wealth such as neither he nor any of his associates in outlawry had even dreamed.

Details must be worked out: a network of aides who could be trusted to secrecy and obedience; the patient fostering of turbulence among the slaves; securing of money to buy guns and ammunition; choosing a time to strike when the blow would be most paralyzing to the country; means of collecting and making away with the money and valuable loot; dozens of other matters of personnel, policy, and logistics. Above everything his men must be trained to murder without mercy, and regardless of age or sex, when the great day arrived. Murrell even formulated a name for his secret organization: the *Mystic Clan*.

All these details he considered as if he were a general planning a vast campaign, and his inordinate egotism assured him that campaign could not fail. Meantime he was a model prisoner, careful to give no trouble, living only for the day of his release. It came at last, the end of the seemingly endless year of imprisonment.

"When they turned me loose," he later said, "I was prepared for anything; I wanted to kill all but my own grit, and one of them I will die by his side before I will desert."

2.

When he stepped out from the prison gate he was faced by present necessities before he could do anything toward setting his scheme on foot. Somehow he must get money, and he fully understood that the old days of highway robbery would yield no great profits. The steamboat almost entirely had replaced the flatboat, and since it was far easier and quite cheap to travel upstream on the big side-wheelers, the Trace was almost abandoned by wayfarers to distant points.

Murrell decided that wholesale dealings in stolen Negroes would be the safest and most profitable course for him. Enlisting his younger brother William—trained like himself in crime by their mother—he stole two fine horses which they took down into the Choctaw Nation to sell.

Arrived in Mississippi, his first crime was one of consummate ferocity. With his brother he set about winning the confidence of a slave named Clitto. They promised to take him to Texas—where slavery did not then technically exist—and if he worked for them one year, they would let him go free.

Clitto was convinced. But he had a wife and three small sons, and he wanted freedom for them, too. So he begged to be allowed to bring them along.

It was a fatal error for him. In trying to reach the great river, in order to cross it, the party became lost in a morass. They were forced to abandon their horses; and even when they reached the river they were at a loss, for a boat they expected to find at the bank was not there.

Murrell's temper was tried. The children were tired and hungry and whimpering, which annoyed him. At last Clitto "became suspicious that we were going to sell him and grew quite contrary."

The outlaw's patience came to an end. Decoying the slave out of sight he drew a pistol and shot him through the head, "then ripped open his belly and tumbled him into the river."[2]

"I returned to my company," went on the outlaw, "and told them that the Negro had fallen into the river, and that he never came up after he went under."

Evidently they discovered a boat, for they "landed fifty miles above New Orleans, and went into the country and sold our Negroes"—the woman and three children—"to a Frenchman for $1,900."

Now Murrell had some money, enough to serve as a beginning for financing his greater program of murder and pillage. But the temptation for a carouse was too great. He and his brother went down to New Orleans, bought new clothes so that they "dressed like young lords," and prepared to enjoy themselves.

The devil must have guided him, for at New Orleans he had the very chance he had been looking for, to begin his secret organization.

Tavern rooms were secured, but the brothers made their real headquarters in the Swamp, at Mother Surgick's establishment of nymphs, where they "mixed with loose characters every night." One night when Murrell was returning alone to his lodgings through a dark street, two men stepped out from an alley with cocked pistols.

"Hand over your money," they said.

With a sardonic bow and smile, Murrell gave them his pocketbook.

"I'm happy to meet with you gentlemen," he said, "as we're all in the same profession."

They stared. His satanic manner and bearing impressed them.

[2] Coates, in *The Outlaw Years*, has Murrell clubbing the children to death, and shooting their mother, also. But Murrell would hardly have sacrificed such valuable property. His own story, indeed, does not confirm this.

"Damned if I ever rob a fellow chip," said one.

Said the other, "We've had our eyes on you and the man that generally comes with you for several nights. We saw so much rigging and glittering jewelry that we concluded you must be a wealthy dandy with a surplus of cash; and determined to rid you of the burden of some of it. But if you're a robber, here's your pocketbook, and you must go with us tonight, and we'll give you an introduction to several fine fellows of the craft."

"Stop," said the first, with sudden suspicion. "Do you understand this motion?"

Murrell understood it well: a gesture of the hand with a peculiar flip of the wrist, used as a secret sign by outlaws, which had been taught him by Crenshaw. He made the proper reply.

That removed all suspicion. He received back his purse.

"Thank you for your kindness," he said, replacing it in his pocket. "I'll be delighted to go with you."

Recalling that evening later, he said, "We went to old Mother Surgick's and had a real frolic with her girls. That night was the commencement of my greatness in what the world calls villainy. The two fellows who robbed me were named Haines and Phelps; they made me known to all the speculators that visited New Orleans, and gave me the name of every fellow who would speculate that lived on the Mississippi River, and many of its tributary streams, from New Orleans up to all the large western cities."

His visit to New Orleans, with the holdup and its sequel, thus comprised a stroke of luck of which he had hardly dared dream. As if by magic he had been furnished the very foundation for which he had been looking, and which he had expected to devote years and vast effort to form: a network of confederates, already hardened criminals and well known to each other, upon whom, if he handled them properly and sufficiently impressed his qualities of leadership, he could build an invisible empire of crime the like of which no man in America had ever before conceived. Those New Orleans crooks did not know it, but a master had stepped into their secret circle.

Haines and Phelps, the two men who held him up, both became important lieutenants in his operations that ensued.

Before he left New Orleans, he demonstrated to his new associates his versatility as a robber, and also his ability as a leader.

"I had become acquainted with a Kentuckian," he later said. "He boarded at the same tavern I did, and I suspected he had a large sum of money. I felt an inclination to count it for him before I left the city; so I made my notions known to Phelps and my other new comrades, and concerted our plan. I was to get him off to the Swamp with me on a spree, and when we were returning to our lodgings, my friends were to meet us and rob us both."

The scheme worked to perfection. Murrell lured the flashy Kentuckian into the ambush. Both of their purses were taken, although Murrell's, of course, was soon returned to him, along with his share of the victim's money. From the Kentuckian they got seven hundred and five dollars, and he was "so mad that he cursed the whole city."

He did not know that his "fellow victim," Murrell, was the brains behind the robbery. There was another thing he did not know: he was lucky that he got off with his life. Not many of Murrell's victims did so.

3.

Having thus impressively proved his talents to the underworld, Murrell made a grand swing over the territory he was to regard as his special realm. Upriver from New Orleans he traveled to Cincinnati, Ohio. On the way he passed Cave-in-Rock, but he did not stop there. This was probably late in 1832, and Sturdevant's "coiners," whose product he had helped spread over the South, were routed from the Cave in 1831. James Ford, of course, was in the vicinity; but at this time Murrell was just beginning to build his organization and his dealings with Shouse, Ford's right-hand man, and perhaps with Ford himself, did not begin until later when he established his "Garden of Eden," where Shouse was reported to have visited him.

From Cincinnati, Murrell crossed over to Lexington, Kentucky, where he came to an understanding with a "speculator." On a fine horse furnished by this new associate, he rode first to Richmond, Virginia, then to Charleston, South Carolina, Savannah and Augusta, Georgia, and finally, by way of Milledgeville, Tennessee, back to his old "stamping grounds" in Williamson County, Tennessee.

He had the list of "speculators" furnished him in New Orleans, and this trip—in which he at times assumed his ministerial role at revival meetings along the way—was for the purpose of making contacts, establishing means of communication, and drawing these widely scattered criminals into his net of outlawry. He was half apologetic later over the comparative paucity of his own illegal activities on this tour.

"In that route," he said, "I only robbed eleven men; but I preached some damned fine sermons and scattered some counterfeit money among the brethren."

His procedure, as related by himself, was as follows: Tall, handsome, impressively and soberly dressed, and "well versed in the scriptures,"

Murrell frequently took the pulpit before devout congregations. Before he began his sermon, he usually pointed out a fine horse for a confederate to steal while he held the crowd spellbound.

And hold them spellbound he did. Nobody could describe hell as vividly as Murrell . . . it was almost as if he had personally inhabited the place. Was he not the very personification of Satan?

The tastes of revival attenders which in that day strongly favored a diet of fire and brimstone, the wrath of God, and the fascinating malignancy of the devil, including the torments of the damned, were so vividly satiated by Murrell's tongue that nobody noticed that a valuable animal had disappeared from the hitch-racks while the sermon was shouting along.

Sometimes the arch-outlaw devoted himself—almost for amusement it seems—to individual victims. Once he stopped at the house of a devout old farmer named Nobs. At supper that night, Murrell, according to his own account, "raised his hands in the most solemn manner, as though he was just going to open the windows of heaven and select its richest blessings for Brother Nobs, his wife, and latest posterity," and said a long prayer.

So bemused were Nobs and his wife that they not only refused to accept payment for lodgings, but eagerly got change—in good money —for a twenty dollar counterfeit bill he offered, and even "loaned" him a fine jack on his promise to meet them at a camp meeting and bring the money for the animal. Of course Nobs never saw him again, and the jack brought him four hundred dollars, which with the twenty dollar counterfeit bill he passed, he considered a fair day's work.

Returned to the Mississippi country, he used his knowledge of the law to get himself out of a "bad crack." In Tipton County, Tennessee, he induced a bright young Negro to run away with him. This man he called Tip, perhaps because of the county from which he came.

With the slave on the lower deck of a steamboat, and himself on the upper deck, Murrell started down the river for New Orleans. But though he was "dressed like a lord"—a favorite expression of his—one of the passengers recognized him and denounced him at New Orleans as a notorious Negro thief.

The captain of the boat put the slave under guard and would have arrested Murrell, had not the outlaw escaped by a daring leap from an upper deck to the New Orleans dock.

In New Orleans he had "connections." Very shortly the captain was presented with a process—drawn up by a lawyer member of Murrell's gang—summoning him before the major. There Murrell swore the boatman had detained his Negro, produced a bill of sale (forged),

and presented witnesses (his own men), who swore they were present
when the slave was sold to Murrell.

The bewildered steamboat captain was fined and sent to jail. The
Negro was turned over to Murrell. As for the man who informed
against the outlaw chief, in the arch-outlaw's words, "he soon had a
nurse that attended him day and night, until he found his way to the
bottom of the Mississippi River."

Whether Murrell himself stalked this man to his death and disposed of him by the Harpe "invention," or ordered it done by one of
his gang, he did not state.

He sold Tip in New Orleans for eight hundred dollars, since the
slave was a good body-servant, worth a high price; and within a few
nights stole him again. Then they traveled to East Feliciana Parish,
north of Baton Rouge, where Murrell once more assumed his ministerial role.

Tip appears to have been a likable young chap, very attractive to
feminine members of his own race. He took his servitude lightly—and
indeed he had little to do but keep Murrell's boots polished and see
that his garments were in perfect press—and even entered into the
spirit of his master's pretended activities.

None was more religious than Tip while Murrell was preaching in a
Methodist church, where the Negroes sat in a loft at the rear. But
his piousness did not prevent him from seducing one of the slave girls
in the congregation—a young woman belonging to a Mrs. Powers.
The love affair between the couple grew so hot that both Tip and the
girl begged Mrs. Powers to buy him so that they could be together.
Mrs. Powers appears to have been a kindly and sympathetic woman.
Through Willis Higginbotham, of the neighborhood, she bought Tip
for seven hundred dollars, and love apparently had found a way.

But Tip scarcely had time to enjoy his conquest, when once more
he was spirited away by Murrell. Perhaps he had tasted enough of
the particular sweets of his connection with Mrs. Powers' girl, for he
seemed nothing loth when called to depart.

Again, on the Arkansas River, Tip was called upon to play his
Lothario's role with a Negro woman. This time, since they were in a
poorer district, Murrell disposed of him for only five hundred dollars.

But by this time Tip knew too much about Murrell's operations.
He had become unsafe; he might talk. So, after all his dealings with
the slave Murrell delivered him into the hands of a member of his
Clan, who, to use his own words, "put him forever out of reach of all
pursuers, and they can never find him, for his carcass has fed many
a tortoise and catfish before this time; and the frogs have sung this

many a long day to the silent repose of his skeleton; and his remembrance is recorded in the book of mysteries."

This last curious statement reveals the ghastly pleasure which he seemed to obtain out of a murder. Incredible as it sounds, Murrell, in his wholesale operations with Negro slaves—of which only a few instances have been given—may have murdered, disemboweled, and "sunk in the river" more than one hundred human beings who trusted him. He would often recite details of his revolting practices with a hyena-like relish.

4.

All this time his mammoth plot of evil was stewing in his head. Thus far he had entrusted to nobody its complete details, but it was assuming such grandiose proportions that he decided to reconnoiter Latin America, envisaging possible international aspects for it.

Having sold a stolen slave in Texas, he "resolved to visit South America[3] and see if there was no opening in that country for speculation; I had also concluded that I could get some strong friends in that quarter to aid me in my designs relative to the Negro rebellion."

What country he "honored" with his presence, he did not state. It may have been Colombia or Venezuela, or one of the Central American states, which could easily be reached by a sea voyage from New Orleans or Galveston.

In any case he set up as a doctor in a small village, "having read Ewel and several other works on primitive medicine." He perhaps had a smattering of Spanish on which he rapidly improved, and he soon won the confidence and friendship of a "prominent man," and in a very short time was a "great Roman Catholic, and bowed before the cross, and attended regularly all the ceremonies of that persuasion."

By such means he met "all the best people," and so facile was he that he quickly built up a medical practice. One can imagine this arch-fiend prescribing nostrums with a smooth, demure face, and also his "bedside manner"—especially if the patient happened to be feminine and handsome, for he always was a woman's man.

But he was disappointed in his chief design: he could not interest anyone in his outlaw conspiracy. Disgusted, he robbed his benefactor's secretary of nine hundred and sixty dollars in gold, "and I could

[3] Phares speculates that Murrell only visited the Spanish part of Texas. But the outlaw's own words were "South America."

have got as much more in silver if I could have carried it"; and with this loot he slipped down to the coast and boarded a ship for the United States.

He had been gone only three months when he returned. His ship docked at New Orleans and there he immediately went to the Swamp where "I had some high fun with old Mother Surgick's girls."

Having thus refreshed himself, he called together all his associates in that city. In addition to Phelps and Haines, who once robbed him and then returned his money, there were others of their ilk named Cooper, Coris, Bolton, Harris, Doddridge, Celly, Morris, Walter, Depont, and Murrell's younger brother, William.

To them he now revealed for the first time the full outlines of his vast plot. "We sat in council for three days before we got all our plans to our notion," he said. "We then determined to undertake the rebellion at every hazard."

These men plotting with him were consummate scoundrels, every one. "I was encouraged in my new undertaking," said Murrell, "and my heart began to beat high with the hope of one day visiting my vengeance on the pomp of the Southern and Western people; and of seeing their cities and towns one common scene of devastation, smoking walls, and fragments."

He was greedy for money, but hatred and contempt for humanity were still his ruling passions. Once more he thought of the terrified and deserted Alabama village where a mere *threat* of a slave insurrection paralyzed the community. Again he remembered the mutterings of the thugs at Natchez Under the Hill. And never long absent from his mind was the reason why he wore those elegant gloves at all times—the branding, the whipping, the pillorying, the imprisonment, and the shame. His hunger for revenge against all society was like an avarice eating at his heart.

He was by now the unquestioned leader and his accomplices listened to his proposal with awe at first, then with full acceptance. He described to them how the loot not only of New Orleans and Natchez, but all the rich cities, towns, and plantations, could be taken.

Again the slaves would be his victims and cat's-paws. But not this time by being sold, and sold over, and then murdered and ripped open. Instead they were to be cozened and tricked into a giant rebellion complete with uncounted murders, rapes, arsons, and cruelties. And under the cover of that holocaust Murrell's chosen gangsters would steal through the smoke and confusion of stricken communities and rob banks, homes, and warehouses of anything their greed dictated.

It was a criminal scheme of such nightmare proportions that at first it sounds insane. But the strange thing about it is that in that day and under the conditions then existing, it could have taken place as the master-mind of Murrell conceived it—the entire Mississippi valley ablaze, men, women, and children slaughtered, and thieves carrying away money and valuables worth millions of dollars—had it not been for one little slip, an accident in which the vanity and egotism of Murrell and the cool nerve of one brave man played decisive parts.

Before his plot could reach its fruition, Murrell must perfect his invisible empire of accomplices. Furthermore, he had to convince the Negroes that they could win their freedom by revolting. This, of course, he knew full well they could never do. In the end they would be defeated and suppressed, and terrible would be the endless woe, death and misery they would suffer. But the poor dupes must not be allowed to think of this. Two or three days of wild, unbridled violence and disruption were all Murrell asked for. After that the unfortunate people he had tricked into their futile and abortive uprising could face the consequences. He and his men would be gone with the loot they had gathered; gone, he expected, far beyond the power of the government to reach or punish them.

Meantime he had to keep the entire gigantic scheme a secret. Perhaps the greatest single testimonial to Murrell's personality is the fact that with hundreds of accomplices knowing it, in many parts of the country, his scheme *did* remain completely secret—until he revealed it himself.

In that first conference in New Orleans he gave his name for the new organization to the twelve. It was to be called the Mystic Clan. There was a mumbo-jumbo ritual of admission, an oath "signed in blood," and a signal of recognition—that flip of the wrist Murrell had himself used the night he was robbed, and which was, as he said, "in use among robbers before I was born."

But he also established an inner circle. The commonality of the Clan were to be known as "Strykers" (Strikers). They would obey orders, do the dirty work, but not know the full details of the plans. The higher order, of which these twelve men were to be the nucleus, would be called the "Grand Council," with a ritual of its own, and a sign of its own—a handshake with two fingers crossed on the palm.

"We practiced ourselves to give and receive the new sign to a fraction before we parted," Murrell said later. "And in addition we invented and formed a mode of correspondence, by means of ten characters, mixed with other matter"—some sort of a code, the exact form of which has never been described.

5.

Now he bade them farewell. There was much to be done, and "every man's business being assigned to him, I started for Natchez on foot."

On foot!

But Murrell did not intend to continue in that manner. He saw no reason for buying a horse in New Orleans, since he was quite sure he could steal one within a few miles.

Luck, however, was against him. For four days he walked, his elegant boots growing inelegantly battered and worn; and in that time he had no chance to steal a horse without being caught. His experience at Nashville was burned in his mind as deeply as the brand on his thumb, and he did not wish to risk a repetition of it.

When he assumed the title and position of Grand Master of his Grand Council of the Mystic Clan, he intended to commit no more robberies himself, but delegate that sometimes dangerous activity to his subordinates. Yet here, right at the start, necessity intervened.

On the fifth day, footsore and furious, his boots all but worn out, he sat on a log to rest, when he saw a horseman approaching from the direction he himself had come. As the rider neared, Murrell could tell by his "equipage"—portmanteaus and so forth—that he was a traveler, not a resident of the immediate vicinity.

The outlaw rose, drew "an elegant rifle pistol," and ordered the man to dismount. White-faced, knowing he was helpless, the rider obeyed.

Murrell took the horse by the bridle to lead it, and with his pistol motioned for his victim to walk before him, away from the road, and down the creek into the woods. Ashen of countenance, convinced already what his fate was to be, the man did so, walking ahead in that hopeless state in which a condemned man walks to his execution.

A few hundred yards into the woods and well concealed from any passers, Murrell ordered him to stop, hitched the horse to a tree, and told his captive to undress himself. The poor fellow did so, stripping off his clothes down to his underwear, trembling and glancing piteously at his captor.

"Now turn around with your back to me," came the deathly command.

For the first time the prisoner spoke. "If you're determined to kill me," he said in a shaking voice, "at least let me have time to pray before I die."

"I've got no time to hear you pray," was the curt reply.

Forlorn and bereft, the man turned around and dropped on his knees. Murrell pitilessly shot him through the back of the head.

The victim already was undressed, which facilitated the usual horrible aftermath. "I ripped open his belly, took out his entrails, and sunk him in the creek."

Presumably Murrell removed his pretty gloves for these details, for he was nice in such matters. After he washed his hands in the water that closed over his victim, he drew the gloves on again and turned to the clothes lying on the bank. In the pockets he found four hundred and one dollars and thirteen cents in cash, and some papers which he did not examine. The pocketbook, hat, and papers were sunk in the creek.

There was one windfall, quite welcome. Murrell tried on the dead man's boots and found they "fitted him very genteely." They were brand new. He sunk his old boots in the creek "to atone for them." The victim's clothes also were "quite new cloth and of the best quality." These he stuffed into the portmanteau, and then, "mounted on as fine a horse as I ever straddled," he set forth once more for Natchez—but this time in the style so dear to his vanity.

He was heading for Tennessee, but his sexual appetites were unappeasable. For two days at Natchez he disported himself "with the girls under the hill," and at the same time conferred with thugs whom he knew, always building his criminal Clan.

From Natchez he swung east through the Choctaw country. While he was riding between Rankin and Benton, Mississippi, a tall, good-looking young man overtook him.

The newcomer's "horse was elegant, his apparel of the gayest that could be had, and his watch chain and other jewelry were of the richest and best." He was full of talk, said he was glad to fall in company with Murrell "for fear of the outlaws," and confided that he had on him the cash for the sale of twenty Negroes.

Murrell at once "concluded he was a noble prize, and longed to be counting his cash." The country was wild, hilly and broken, and he led the way down into a hollow to water the horses and get a drink.

Nothing loth, the young man followed. About four hundred yards from the road, Murrell suddenly drew his pistol and shot the other through.

Thus far, everything had gone smoothly. The victim was dead when he struck the ground, and the outlaw searched him for money. There was a large pocketbook, stuffed very full. Twenty Negroes—say five hundred dollars apiece at the least—there must be ten thousand dollars in that purse! "I thought I had a treasure indeed," Murrell later said.

But now came an astounding disappointment. The pocketbook contained no more than copies of love songs, the forms of love letters—some of the owner's own composition—and no cash! Feverishly, the robber cut off the dead man's clothes with his knife, searching for money. He found just four dollars and fifty cents. He remembered the watch and jewelry and gathered them. The chain was gold, but it was attached to an old brass watch.

"He was a puff for true," said Murrell, "and I thought all such fools ought to die as soon as possible."

At least there was the dead man's horse. The outlaw sold it, and then continued his journey to Madison County, Tennessee.

6.

There were gigantic labors ahead for him—how gigantic even he himself hardly realized. A lesser man could never have accomplished the task. But Murrell, a combination of fiend, fatalist, and genius, embarked upon it with undaunted energy.

First, he must establish an aura of respectability under which he could work with the eyes of the community upon him, yet without the community suspecting him. To this end he had a stone house built three miles from Denmark, Tennessee, a rather pretentious house for the time, which is still standing.

In that house he established a "Mrs. Murrell." The "wife"—there is little likelihood that they were formally married—was, according to one version,[4] a romantic girl named Mary McClovey, who fell in love with Murrell on one of his visits to Cincinnati, eloped with him and was "married" to him, probably according to the outlaw's notions, by a common-law status.

Another version[5] says she was a girl from one of the brothels in the Pinch Gut district of Memphis. She perhaps was one of the practitioners of the bedroom arts whom he had found especially proficient; her underworld background would be such that he could trust her with certain necessary secrets; and her bawdy house experience would make her tolerant of any "frolics" in which he might indulge with other women—a useful trait in a wife, to one of Murrell's lecherous instincts. What makes this version seem especially likely is that Murrell mentioned a man named Nolin (or Nolan) as his "brother-in-

[4] J. M. Keating, History of the City of Memphis and Shelby County, Tennessee.
[5] Robert M. Coates, The Outlaw Years.

law"—and also a member of his Clan. This man must have been a brother of his "wife," whose last name therefore would be Nolin rather than McClovey.

Whoever she was, she presided over his home, where he entertained his "friends," matured his schemes, and from which he made frequent journeys.

One such trip took him a second time through Georgia, South Carolina, Virginia, Maryland, back through the Carolinas, thence by way of Florida into Alabama and so home again in Tennessee. On this journey he renewed his contacts, and began "to establish my emissaries over the country in every direction."

On another trip he and his men overwhelmed a flatboat on the Mississippi, butchered the entire crew, threw the bodies into the river, and confiscated the boat and its cargo. This robbery and multiple murder caused a posse to attempt to invade the territory of the outlaws, without results. It was specifically mentioned in an affidavit signed later by Colonel Orville Shelby, who knew of it personally and may have led the posse.

Murrell also crossed over into Arkansas, still a territory at that time, where he established at least two and possibly more robber retreats. One of these was his famous "Garden of Eden" in northeast Arkansas. Another was on Stuart's Island in Lake Chicot in the southeastern part.

His Clan, as it grew, was to embrace all forms of crime; and even among the Strykers there were various classifications. Some were highwaymen. Later, about 1840, one of the men in this category described its workings to Sile Doty, the notorious horse thief and burglar:

> We were a band of highwaymen, and, of course, we were all mounted, and we kept the number of our horses good, by stealing one now and then. No doubt, I should have stayed among them longer, had they not been so desperate to kill. We were in couples, and were scattered all over the southern States. Our orders were to report once a month.[6]

At the time Doty knew this man, he was operating as a "fence" for stolen horses near Woodville, Virginia, but during his service under Murrell his headquarters were in Louisiana.

A second category consisted of slave stealers, and if they perhaps did not follow the master's extremities of brutality, they did kidnap Negroes, and carried them far away to sell them—for the Clan exchequer. Murrell was building his treasury.

[6] *The Life of Sile Doty, a Forgotten Autobiography.*

A third classification was that of innkeepers, householders, and mer-chants, who furnished refuges for outlaws, and acted as "fences" to dispose of stolen property. Of these, many belonged to the Grand Council, for they often were men of substance and standing.

Still another group was composed of men employed almost exclu-sively in talking to slaves and breeding discontent among them. These were the smoothest of Murrell's agents. Usually they represented themselves as emissaries of the Abolition movement in the North; and they were schooled in all the catch-phrases to use in deluding the poor Negroes into risking their lives for a rainbow promise which never could come true.

It was in 1832 that John Murrell was released from prison—with that brand on his thumb and in his heart. Within two years he wove out of disparate elements in every part of the South a crime web of incredible proportions.

Yet even as he wove it, he was spinning also the threads of his own doom. He did not see the greatest weakness of his whole gigantic organization and plan. It was himself.

XIII. *Days of Danger and Dread*

1.

On January 24, 1834, a young man named Virgil A. Stewart arrived at the home of the Reverend John Henning, a rural minister living in Madison County, Tennessee. He was warmly welcomed, for he was an old friend, just returned from the Choctaw Purchase in Mississippi.

The Hennings knew him as the son of a respected widow, Mrs. Samuel Stewart, who lived in Georgia. Previously he had owned a farm near them, which he worked with several slaves belonging to him, left to him as part of the estate of his late father. Of good appearance and address, about twenty-four years old, he was considered a coming young man who might some day achieve wealth and prominence.

In the latter part of 1832, Stewart had sold his land and servants, hoping to use the money thus obtained in gaining larger holdings in the new Choctaw Purchase, from which the Indians had just moved, and which was opened for settlement. Now he was back in Tennessee for a visit and to transact some business.

That evening about the supper table, Stewart entertained his hosts —Parson Henning, Mrs. Henning, and their son Richard, about his own age—by describing the Yalobusha country where he had been living and his life there. For a time, he told them, he managed the affairs of a merchant named Matthew Clanton, while the latter was away. Clanton, on his return, was so highly pleased with the way his store had been conducted that he wished to go into partnership with Stewart. But the young man declined, although he did accept a building lot in a small town-site laid off at the crossroads where the Clanton store stood. Eventually, he said, he hoped to build a home on that lot.

But meantime he wished to put all his resources into land, and finding it necessary to return to Tennessee to wind up some affairs, he left his own goods in the care of a certain William Vess, who was employed by Clanton as a laborer. Those names—Clanton and Vess— will reappear in dark connotations in the narrative that follows.

In the course of the conversation that night Parson Henning mentioned the fact that three days before two Negro men belonging to his son Richard and himself had disappeared. The minister had suspicions as to what happened to them.

"There's a man named John Murrell," he said, "who lives in a stone house with his wife in this neighborhood. People have begun talking about him. He has a doubtful and suspicious reputation. There was even a move to arrest him some time ago after three Negroes belonging to a neighbor named William H. Long disappeared. The Negroes were retaken and implicated this man Murrell in their disappearance. But the effort of the posse to arrest him came to nothing. Now my son and I are wondering if he had something to do with taking our Negroes off."

Stewart remembered the name, Murrell. Before he left Madison County the man had been somewhere in the vicinity. But he kept to himself and though Stewart once had seen him, it was at such a distance that he did not believe he would recognize him if he saw him again.

"One of Murrell's neighbors," went on Henning, "tells us that he's leaving on the 25th for Randolph, on the Mississippi River. If Murrell did steal the Negroes, that country around Randolph—just above Memphis—would be a good hiding place for them, and he might be heading that way to dispose of them."

Stewart nodded; it sounded reasonable. But the preacher had a proposal to make. He indicated his son.

"Richard is going to try to trail Murrell," he said. "Would you consider going with him? Two are better than one, and you might get some report of the Negroes. I'll be glad to pay you for your services and loss of time."

After a moment's thought, Stewart said, "I'll go on the hunt. But I wouldn't accept a cent from a friend like you, Parson Henning. Where will I meet you, Richard?"

"At Denmark," said the younger Henning. Both father and son thanked Stewart.

The two young men discussed plans briefly. They decided to take the trail on January 26, as that would give Murrell a chance to be ahead of them. Thereafter Stewart bade the Hennings good night, for he was to sleep at the house of another friend in the neighborhood. As they parted Richard mentioned that he had not been feeling well, but he was sure he would be ready for the ride on the day set.[1]

The morning of January 26 was bitter cold, following an ice storm, and the roads were hard-frozen and covered with sleet. Nevertheless, Stewart rode to keep his appointment at Denmark, a small town on the road to Estanaula where a toll bridge across the Hatchie River provided the only good crossing for some distance. At Denmark he waited for several hours, believing the man he was to trail had by this time gone on ahead. But Richard Henning did not appear. Later it was learned that his illness had grown worse so that he was unable to meet Stewart.

As for Stewart, after a long wait, he finally decided to go on alone. About ten o'clock that morning he rode out of Denmark toward Estanaula.

When he reached the bridge there, he asked the toll collector if he knew John Murrell.

"Why, sure," was the reply.

"Has he passed through this toll gate recently?"

"No."

This was a surprise to Stewart, but even as they talked they saw a horseman coming up the road. He was riding a fine mount, sat very erect in his saddle, and wore a heavy coat with a rolled collar, and a high-crowned beaver hat.

"That's Murrell now," said the bridge keeper.

As the horseman came up, Stewart was struck by his elegance, of garb and manner, and at the same time by a certain black-browed sternness of his face. He halted his mount and lifted his hat.

"Good day, gentlemen," he said with graceful courtesy. Then, without further words, he paid his toll and rode on across the bridge.

[1] All of the foregoing was later attested to in a sworn statement by the Reverend John Henning, signed October 10, 1835.

"You're sure that's Murrell?" asked Stewart.

"Positive," said the bridge man. "I know him well."

Stewart paid his toll, mounted, and followed. A brisk ride brought him up to the traveler who had just preceded him.

2.

It must be remembered that at this time Stewart had not the faintest inkling of the deadly ferocity of the man, or that he was the head of a great and perilous organization of crime. Had he known these things he might not have plunged into the adventure that followed, in which many times he thought he was about to experience his own death. As he overtook Murrell he thought the man might be a Negro thief, but nothing more, and not even that was proved.

"Your indulgence, sir," he said, saluting the other politely. "I was at the toll bridge when you passed, and seeing that we're taking the same road, I make bold to offer myself as a companion, to make the travel more pleasant with conversation."

Murrell shot a suspicious glance at him. "Very well, sir," he said shortly.

For a few minutes they rode silently side by side on the icy road. Then Stewart ventured, "We have disagreeable weather, sir."

"Extremely so," was Murrell's curt reply.

After a time Stewart made another effort. "This traveling and my business correspond very well."

It seemed to arouse a spark of curiosity in the other. "Pray, sir, what might your business be?"

"Horse hunting, sir."

Murrell nodded. "Yes, yes, disagreeable indeed: your comparison with travel on such a road as this is not bad. Where did your horse stray from?"

"From the Yalobusha River, in the Choctaw Purchase," said Stewart, naming the vicinity from which he had recently come.

"Where's he aiming for?"

"I'm told he was owned by a man in this part of the country somewhere. He might be heading home. But it's an uncertain business—a cross-and-pile chance."

"How far are you going?"

"I haven't decided. The roads are so bad and the weather's so extremely cold, I'm getting tired of it. And I'm quite lonesome traveling by myself. How far will you go on this road?"

"About eighteen miles, to the house of a friend," said Murrell. Then he added, "Perhaps your horse was stolen."

"No, I guess not stolen," Stewart said. And then he tried a shot at random. "Though I'd much rather some clever fellow stole him than that he should be straying."

At once he knew he had struck a responsive chord. Reference to a horse thief as a "clever fellow" caused a change in Murrell's manner.

"Are you acquainted in this part of the country?" asked the outlaw.

"I'm a stranger, sir."

"Where are you from?"

"I was born in Georgia, but moved to the Choctaw Purchase, where I've been about nine or ten months."

"How do you like that country?"

"Very well, sir."

Murrell's glance grew keen. "Is there much stealing going on in that country?"

"Not so much," said Stewart, "considering we're pretty much savages and forerunners."

The outlaw's questions had been designed to discover if his companion might know something of his character. He felt reassured when he learned that Stewart was from the Choctaw Purchase and had lived there only nine or ten months. From this time he scrutinized Stewart less closely, and even chatted in a friendly manner on various topics. Presently the conversation reverted to the subject of stealing —evidently a favorite theme with Murrell.

"This country's about to be completely overrun by a company of rogues," he said. "They're so strong that nothing can be done with them. They steal from whom they please; and if the person they take from accuses them, they jump on more of his property. It's found that the best plan is to be friendly with them."

Another shrewd glance at Stewart. At this time Murrell was still actively recruiting followers and agents for his Clan, and this young man had given more than an inkling that his attitude toward crime was tolerant if not actually friendly.

"There are two young men who moved down from middle Tennessee to Madison County, keen, shrewd fellows," the outlaw resumed in an offhand way. "The eldest brother is one of the best judges of law in the United States. He directs the banditti; and he so paves the way to all his offenses that the law can't reach him."

Stewart was intensely interested, but he spoke casually.

"Well, sir," he said, "if they have sense enough to evade the laws, let them do it. It's just as honorable for them to gain property by their superior powers as it is for a long-faced hypocrite to take advantage

of the necessities of his fellow-beings. What constitutes character, pop-
ularity, and power in the United States? Sir, it is property. Strip a man
of his property, and he's a ruined man—you see his friends forsake him.
Sir, my doctrine is, let the hardest fend off."

He felt sure of his man now, though he still had no idea of the extent of Murrell's criminality. The outlaw's next words even more
strongly confirmed his belief.

"You expressed my sentiments better than I could myself," said
the arch-bandit, "and I'm happy to fall in with company possessed of
principles so congenial to my own. I have no doubt these two brothers
are as honorable among their associates as any men on earth, but
perfect devils to their enemies. They are undaunted spirits, and can
never be found when they're not armed like men of war."

He went on to describe the cleverness of the "elder brother" in
evading the law, and how he prepared to resist a posse when he
learned an attempt was to be made to arrest him on a charge of
stealing three Negroes from a certain Long—the very William H.
Long about whom the Hennings had told Stewart!

"He (the elder brother) got several guns, made an immense quantity of cartridges and prepared his house and buildings with port-
holes, ready for an engagement," said Murrell. "He had eighteen
friends who came to his assistance."

But, he added, the posse got wind of these arrangements and the
raid did not take place.

"All who had anything to do with it have got sick of it," went on
Murrell, "and are trying to make fair weather with him. Not that they
love him, but because they dread him as they do the very devil himself—and well they may, for he's sworn vengeance against them, and
he'll execute it."

He glanced at Stewart to see how he was taking this, and must
have been satisfied by the other's expression, for he went on talking
about the "elder brother."

"He is a fellow of such smooth and genteel manners, that he's very
imposing," he said. "He rarely fails to captivate the feelings of those
whom he undertakes; and, what's more astonishing, he has succeeded in many instances where the strongest prejudice existed. And
where his revenge has been excited he never fails to effect either the
destruction of their property or character, or frequently both."

The outlaw was of course describing himself, and here the great
weakness of his character began to appear. He had astonishing vanity,
was fond of boasting, and very susceptible to flattery.

A moment later he made Stewart's ears prick up.

"There's an old Methodist minister and his son," said Murrell, "who had two very fine Negro men stolen a short time ago. This old Parson Henning and his son were officious in expressing their sentiments about him and his brother, and saying what the country ought to do with them, and all such stuff as this."

He paused, then added darkly, "I have no doubt that these two young men have got the Negroes. They live within about two miles of the old preacher, and he and his son are as much afraid of these two young men as if they were two ravenous beasts and were turned loose in the forest. If they were sure of finding their Negroes by following them, they'd sooner lose their property than fall into the hands of those dreaded men."

Young Stewart could fell his hair rise under his cap; for he himself was after those Negroes, risking the very fate the outlaw had described with such iron-shod fury. But he managed to keep his wits about him, and his next speech was smooth and placating.

"Those two young men must possess talents of the first order," he said. "And the elder brother of whom you speak must be endowed with some supernatural power, or an extraordinary capacity and practical experience."

He could see Murrell swell under this flattery, and was encouraged to proceed further:

"I'll warrant them to be devoted friends and noble spirits in the sphere where they move. And if this old preacher was their enemy, and treated them as such when they had not been hostile to him, then they are his enemies now for cause. And if they're what my imagination has made them, he'll have reason to repent in sackcloth and ashes. But, sir, my doctrine: Let the hardest fend off. By the way, of what age is this wondrous man of whom you speak?"

By this time Murrell was fairly purring. "He's about thirty, I suppose, and his brother just grown up, and as smart a fellow as the elder brother, but not half the experience."

He went on to relate some of the exploits of the "elder brother" in slave-stealing, murder, and robbery, while Stewart listened openmouthed with apparent interest and approval. Once the outlaw gave a short disquisition on the law in Negro stealing.

"This is how the law is, sir, when it is examined by a man who understands it. When a Negro escapes from his master's possession, and the master offers a reward to any man who can catch him, that advertisement amounts to the same, in virtue, as a power of attorney, to take his property and act for him to a certain extent. Since the advertisement is a commission to take the property into possession, if the holder of the property makes a breach of the trust which the advertisement confides in him, and instead of carrying the Negro to the owner, converts him to his own use—this is not stealing and the owner can only have redress in civil action. As for civil action, they [the outlaws] care nothing for that. Their funds are deposited in a bank that belongs to their Clan."

This was the first mention of that word "Clan." Stewart had assured himself that Murrell was the thief who kidnaped the Negroes, but he did not yet know where the slaves were hidden.

Now, for the first time, he received an intimation of something shadowy and sinister, far greater than he had imagined, something powerful and many-tentacled, fearful and frightening and hard to comprehend.

"This is the way," continued Murrell, "that the elder brother's ingenuity perplexes them [victims of the thieves]. He has sifted the criminal laws until they're no more in his hands than an old almanac, and he dreads them no more. He can do anything he wishes, with the many friends he has, who are willing to be subject to him and his views in all things. *There* lies his power: his great talent in governing his Clan. He is universally beloved by all his followers."

With increasing clarity Stewart saw the terrible outlines of the pit into which he was entering. But there was no escaping it now: already he knew too much. He must go ahead, as boldly as he could. So he attempted a still greater flattery:

"Such a man as that, placed in a situation to display his talents, would render the name and remembrance of an Alexander, or a Jackson, little and inconsiderable compared with this man."

It was a shrewder touch than he knew. Alexander the Great. Andrew Jackson, then President of the United States. These were mighty men even in Murrell's estimation. He flushed with pleasure.

3.

Evening drew on as they entered the valley of Poplar Creek, which ran north into the Hatchie River. The sleet storm of the previous night had clothed with silvery ice the poplars which stood thickly on either side of the road, and the setting sun touched their sparkling tops with rosy light.

Even Murrell was impressed. "This is a beautiful scene," he said, "and continues through the valley. Beyond, a good road conducts us to the house of my friend."

The last words brought a thrill of fear to Stewart. So much had he fallen under the spell of the outlaw's personality and conversation that he seemed almost to be in a dream. Now he awakened suddenly to full realization of his situation.

He was in the hands of a diabolist the like of whom he had never imagined. Had Murrell seen through his pose, and was now smoothly leading him on? The house of the bandit's friend might be the very place selected to murder and rob him. Cold terror crawled up his back and all the goblin-tales of his childhood came back to him with eerie suggestions of horror.

The sun went down and it began to grow dark. Ahead they saw an old log burning by the roadside, evidently left by former campers.

"Let's stop there and warm ourselves," said Murrell.

Stewart agreed. When they reached the fire he found that his legs were so numb and stiff with cold that he could hardly dismount. For a few minutes he stamped his feet to restore circulation, and meantime his mind was filled with desperate apprehensions.

Murrell watched him. "You appear very cold, my young friend," he said. "I fear you're frosted. You can't stand it like me—I've undergone enough to kill a horse. We'll stay here until moon-up. Ever travel much by moonlight?"

Stewart seated himself by the fire. "Not much, sir."

"Then you haven't the same love for those silver beams as an old veteran in the mysteries." The outlaw seemed frequently to throw what he considered poetic phrases into his conversation. After a pause he said, "I would suppose that you're too young to be of much experience in the *practical part,* though you're well skilled in the *theory.*"

He was evidently referring to crime, and Stewart was in an agony wondering just what lay behind his words. The next statement, in a measure, reassured him.

"You'll find many difficulties to surmount in the execution of plans you've never thought of," went on Murrell. "You'll learn to suffer privations of all kinds—privations and difficulties which, surmounted, are the glory of an old veteran and prominent actor."

In his high-flown way he seemed to be talking as if already he counted on his new acquaintance to become one of the Clan! But was this genuine, or a subtle scheme to trap Stewart? The young man dared not let himself be lulled.

Presently the moon rose, reflecting like molten silver on the sleety tops of the trees. They mounted and rode on.

At first Stewart tried to stay a little behind. "This man may smile, and murder while he smiles," he said to himself. He had a pistol, but it was under his greatcoat, and he hardly knew how he would get it into action if the other attempted some treachery.

Murrell was serene. "Come, sir, ride up. The night's cold and we have far to go. Let's pass the time as pleasantly as possible. Come up, and I'll tell you of another feat of this elder brother of whom I've been speaking."

"Yes, sir, with all my heart," said the inwardly quaking Stewart.

As he ranged his horse up alongside, the outlaw began to recount one adventure after another of the "elder brother." It was, in fact, from his own lips, as recorded by Stewart, that we have the story of his earlier career previously related. Listening to the narrative which at times made his blood run cold, the young man at last came gradually to believe that not only had he succeeded in hiding his real aim, but that the arch-criminal believed he was of his own kind.

Taking courage, he said, "It would be a source of the highest pleasure to me to see and become acquainted with this wondrous man. My fancy makes him a princely fellow. Perhaps I've been too extravagant in my conceptions; but I know he must be a great man and possessed of unrivaled mental power."

"That is his character, sir," said Murrell, very smugly.

"I confess that what I've heard of this man has excited my admiration," Stewart went on, and then he added, as if by afterthought, "Perhaps it's because we are congenial spirits."

He had decided long since that Murrell was speaking of himself when he recited the adventures of the remarkable "elder brother," and this was a plain effort to induce the man to avow his identity. But the outlaw did not at once rise to this bait. Instead he said they were nearing his friend's house and asked if Stewart would continue as far as Randolph.

"It's likely that I will, sir," said the young man. "And if I weren't rather scarce of change, I'd continue my journey over into Arkansas— cold as it is—since I'm so near it. I've heard much of that country, and I think the land and people would suit my designs and inclinations very much."

Stewart's mind was racing, and he had reasons for making such a statement. Though he had quite a little money on his person, he spoke of being "rather scarce of change," to suggest that he was not worth robbing. Furthermore, during the ride he had come to suspect that Henning's missing Negroes might be held at the "friend's house" they were now approaching. If so, Murrell's journey would end there, and Stewart thus offered a reason why he would be going on. He did not wish to remain in this perilous company longer than necessary.

The moment was critical. He almost held his breath as he awaited the reply. When it came it was surprisingly reassuring, in one way. In another, it was additionally alarming.

Said the arch-bandit, "I'd be very glad if you'd go over into Arkansas with me. I'll let you have money if you run out of it; and I'll show you the country. I have thousands of friends over there—it won't cost us a cent if we stay six months. And I'll carry you where you can bring away a better horse than the one you're hunting for. I'll learn you a few tricks if you go with me. A man with as keen an eye as yours should never spend his time hunting for a strayed horse."

The words were friendly: but Stewart realized that by his reference to Arkansas he had bound himself to Murrell's company in such a way that, since the outlaw had declared himself, it would be the height of danger to attempt to escape from him unless some exceptional opportunity presented itself; one which, in his present state, he could not even imagine. He rode along with a curious feeling mingled of dread and despair.

It was midnight when they reached the house of Murrell's friend and knocked for admittance. The place was eerily still. An old man presently opened the door, "silent as death."

When he entered the cabin Stewart's first act was a hasty glance around. He feared he might see Henning's Negroes. If so they almost surely would show they knew him, since they had seen him often at the Henning place.

But the slaves were not in the house, and he felt a temporary sensation of relief from immediate peril.

Until late that night Murrell and the old man sat before the fireplace, talking in subdued voices of their secret affairs. But Stewart, pleading weariness, asked where he should sleep and retired, fully dressed and with his pistol handy. For hours he lay awake, fearful that he might yet be stalked and set upon as he slept.

He considered also the strong possibility that the missing Negroes were somewhere else on the place, and he might encounter them in the morning, and by them be exposed. So greatly did the peril of his situation stimulate his wakeful and bewildered imagination, that it was not until nearly morning that exhaustion overcame him, and he slept fitfully.

XIV.   *The Monstrous Plot Revealed*

1.

At earliest dawn he was up. A quick walk outside the house gave him
a chance to look into the barn and other outbuildings so that if the
Negroes were there he could warn them not to show recognition of
him. They were not to be seen.

When he returned to the house Murrell was up, telling his host to
get the horses ready. A crude and hasty breakfast, and they were away
before the sun had risen over the horizon.

Strangely, neither of the men had thus far introduced himself.
Stewart, of course, knew Murrell's identity. But the outlaw had spent
most of the previous day probing to discover his companion's inner
motives and background, and either did not think it worth the trouble,
or neglected to ask his name.

Now, however, shortly after their start, Murrell said, "Well, my
young friend, I believe I've not yet been so inquisitive as to ask your
name, we've been so engaged in other conversations."

Stewart dared not give his real name. Though they had never met
before, the bandit almost surely had heard of him, and his association

with the Hennings, especially during the period he lived in Madison County before moving to the Choctaw Purchase.

"I seldom have a name," he replied, with a sidelong glance. "But you can call me Adam Hues at present."

I seldom have a name. That remark, whether spoken by accident or design, convinced Murrell that Stewart was a shifty, perhaps a hunted character. To the outlaw the name Adam Hues was fine, since at that very moment he had five men by the name of Hues who were members of his secret Clan.

"Well, Mr. Hues," said Murrell, "what say you of the trip to Arkansas this morning?"

"I think I'll go," said Stewart, who really had little other choice under the circumstances.

"Go? Yes, you must go!" Murrell now had fully accepted him. "I'll make a man of you."

"That's what I want, sir."

The bandit leered confidentially. "There are some of the handsomest girls over there you ever saw. I'm in town when I'm there."

Stewart returned the grin. "Nothing to object to, sir. I'm quite partial to handsome ladies."

"Well, then, go with me to Arkansas, and I'll put you right in town; and they're as plump as ever came, sir." A wink and another leer. Murrell now felt sure of the young man.

"I'll go, sir," said Stewart.

"We can strike a breeze worth telling over there."

"I don't doubt it, sir."

Fully at his ease now, Murrell embarked on further tales of "this elder brother." Some of them were bloodcurdling, in particular that of the man who "betrayed" the outlaw to the steamboat captain and "soon had a nurse to attend him by day and by night, until he found his way to the bottom of the Mississippi River." It was a telling description of the gang's pitiless and remorseless pursuit of its enemies, and Stewart, who somehow had managed to worm himself much further into Murrell's confidence than he had planned or desired, realized that if he were unmasked there would be no mercy for him. He continued riding in a kind of horror, hardly knowing what to do, or how he could ever extricate himself from this terrible position.

Presently he experienced a new and more immediate apprehension. They were approaching a small town called Wesley. Stewart remembered suddenly that he had acquaintances there. What if one of them familiarly greeted him? Since he had told Murrell he was an entire stranger in the country, it would be a fatal embarrassment for him.

Fear made him think fast. As they entered the town he handed his flask to Murrell.

"Do us both a favor," he said. "Take this to the tavern and get it filled with brandy—*good* brandy. Meantime, I'll stop at the first store and write some advertisements for my stray horse, and perhaps see if the animal has been seen hereabouts."

To Murrell, the suggestion was perfectly natural. Taking the empty flask he galloped on ahead to the tavern down the street.

The store which Stewart entered was kept by one of the friends he feared might unwittingly expose him. But when he asked for the man he found he was away for the day.

Now he confronted a second problem: how to get word to his other two friends, both of whom were at the tavern—*to which Murrell had just ridden before him!*

He lingered at the store, and presently, to his relief, saw the outlaw leave the tavern with the flask in his hand. Murrell had been unable to get the brandy he desired—he had a nice taste in liquors of all kinds—so he went to another dram shop for it.

Stewart hurried to the tavern and quickly warned the two men there whom he knew. One of them was Colonel William H. Bayliss. The colonel not only promised to help him if he were attacked, but loaned the young man a pistol.[1] Very soon after that Murrell was back in the tavern, his flask now filled with the brandy he preferred.

"Hues," he said jovially, "let's have a glass before we resume our journey."

They did so, and in a few minutes once more mounted and rode on.

2.

Hardly a mile out of town, Murrell said suddenly, "We'll ride a little from the road, eat some cold victuals, and take a little more of the God Bless Us."

Stewart's heart gave a leap of fear. Was this an excuse to get him off the road and kill him, as Murrell had killed others about whom he boasted? He could do nothing, however, but follow.

Fifty yards into the woods, he asked, "Why are you leaving the road so far?"

[1] In view of the efforts made later to discredit Stewart's account, Colonel William H. Bayliss on October 20, 1835, signed a statement confirming this conversation, including Stewart's explanation as to what he was doing in Murrell's company, and his revelation of Murrell's character, together with the loan of the pistol; also that Stewart in due time returned the borrowed weapon.

Murrell gave a foxy grin. "That old Methodist Henning, knowing me to be a particular friend of those two young men I've been speaking of, I shouldn't be surprised if his son was in pursuit of me. If so, I'd much prefer his being before, rather than behind—if he's been fool enough to undertake the adventure. I'd know better how to handle him."

A hundred yards or so, when they were out of sight of the road, they stopped, tethered their horses, and Murrell took cold bread and bacon from his portmanteau. Sitting on a log they ate, and took swallows from the brandy flask which was set on the log between them.

Fearful every moment, Stewart was sparing in his drinking. But Murrell drank heartily.

He hardly knew how, yet the young man evidently had succeeded in winning the bandit's friendship. Perhaps it was the fact that Stewart was educated, a relief from the chaw-bacon backwoods hoodlums with whom Murrell habitually associated. Perhaps it was some pleasing trait of his appearance or manner. In any case he had impressed the outlaw so strongly that he was eager to gain this young man as a recruit for his Clan.

The curious part of it was that Stewart really had made no overtures, except to respond to the other's statements in a manner that demonstrated his intelligence and tact. It was Murrell who, actually, had gone from step to step in reaching a confidential standing, on his own volition, bemusing himself as it were. This of course in no way made Stewart's peril less if he were found out. He was not yet, nor was he ever, fully confident of his position, so that every new scene and new word brought him new apprehension in the days that followed.

Murrell, meantime, feeling he knew his man, grew boldly confidential.

"Well, Hues," he said after several pulls at the brandy flask, "did you ever hear of those devils, Murrells, up in Madison County, in this state?"

Stewart shook his head. "I'm an entire stranger to them."

The outlaw swelled with importance. "My name, sir, is John Murrell," he said. "And I am that *elder brother* I've been telling you about!"

Stewart did his best to play the part of a young man dazzled and enormously impressed.

"Is it possible?" he exclaimed, as if awed out of all countenance. "Have I the pleasure of standing before the illustrious personage of whom I have heard so many noble feats, and whose dexterity and skill are unrivaled by any the world has ever produced before him? Is it a dream, or is it a reality? I can scarcely believe that this is a man in real life who stands before me. My imagination would make you the genius of some master spirit of ancient days, who is sent as a guide to protect and defend me before all who may oppose. Sir, under so able a guide and preceptor, I have nothing to fear; but I will look back to the hour of our meeting as the fortunate era in which my importance and victories were to commence."

It was overdone, fulsome. But Murrell's vanity only further expanded under it. With almost fatuous pride he gazed at Stewart.

"Sir," he said, "I pledge you my head that I'll give you all the instructions my long experience will enable me to; and I flatter myself that I'll never be ashamed of so intelligent a pupil. Sir, I am the leader of a noble band of valiant and lordly bandits; I will give you our plans and strength hereafter. I'll introduce you among my fellows, and give you their names and addresses before we part—but we mustn't be parted longer than you can arrange your business. I'll make you a splendid fellow, and put you on the high road to fortune."

He paused, and then in his half-drunken mood went further, with a promise that perhaps exceeded what he first intended.

"You shall be admitted to the Grand Council of our Clan; for I consider you a young man of splendid abilities. Sir, these are my feelings and sentiments towards you."

One cannot help wondering at Murrell's complete captivation. He had not tested Stewart in the slightest degree, yet he put full confidence in him. The only possible explanation is the prodigious vainglory that possessed him. His conversations reveal strong indications of paranoia: feelings of persecution followed by delusions of grandeur. Those who opposed his lawbreaking were "villains," and "malicious individuals," who "persecuted him," and on whom he constantly sought to be "revenged." On the other hand he himself was "lordly," and "a prominent actor," with "talents and acquirements of the first order," and "universally beloved by his followers," whom he described as "noble and valiant."

In short, Stewart's continued flattery and affectation of astonishment and admiration, were exactly what most appealed to the outlaw's swollen egotism.

They finished eating, and after replacing the flask and what was left of the provisions in Murrell's portmanteau, they mounted and continued their ride. A little farther along the road the outlaw said:

"I'm going now to the place whither I sent that old Methodist's Negroes, in charge of a friend."

He added that he had been delayed, and the time already had passed when he promised to meet his colleague, and he was afraid that the man would become alarmed and not wait for him.

"I shall have to insist on your consenting to travel all night," he went on. "My delay was caused by the following circumstances: At about the time I made arrangements for leaving Madison County, I was told by a friend (by the way, a most estimable man, and one, too, who stands before the public entirely above suspicion), that old Henning and his son suspected me of being a participant in the abduction of their Negroes—that they had spies to watch my movements—and were intending to follow me. A keen perception of the old fellow's [Henning's]; and if he'd known how to hold his tongue, he might have given me some trouble. But I always have men to manage the case of such gentry as he and his son."

The outlaw allowed himself another leer, then continued, "Upon being informed of their intention, I wrote Dick Henning a letter, from the village of Denmark, which ran in substance as follows: 'Sir, I have been told you accuse me of being concerned in stealing your and your father's Negroes. If it be true—I can whip you from the point of a dagger to the anchor of a ship. But, sir, if I have been misinformed by malicious individuals, I wish you to receive this as a letter of friendship. I am about leaving for Randolph, and shall be pleased to have your company—that you may be satisfied that my business is honest." [2]

The land pirate laughed exultingly. "I could take Dick Henning by my side, and steal and sell every Negro he and his father own, and receive the money for them, and he shall know nothing of the transaction."

He described the trickery by which he could accomplish this: inducing the slaves to run away, having them met by an accomplice, and disposing of his interest in them to a "friend" who would count out the money before Henning's face. He considered this a capital bit of humor. Then he added more seriously:

"It was never my intention, Hues, to disturb my immediate neighbors until they commenced their sharpshooting at me. They may now look out for breakers. Their long prayers and Methodist coats shall be no protection against my sworn vengeance."

"Vengeance" has been a familiar self-justification for criminals before and after Murrell. They say they commit a crime to "revenge" themselves on someone who has "wronged" them—perhaps by rightfully suspecting them of their felonies, as the Hennings suspected Murrell.

[2] A statement signed October 11, 1835, by Richard G. Henning, attested that Murrell actually did send him this letter at the time stated, and that everything else Stewart wrote concerning him (Henning) was true.

Stewart recognized this sophistry, but he replied: "Your revenge is just! Above all things I should glory in contributing to the downfall of such mistaken beings!"

The outlaw smirked, his vanity and desire to be admired pleased by Stewart's outburst. He regarded the young man as his willing and dazzled disciple, and now allowed himself the luxury of patronizing him a bit.

"Hues," he said, "how do you suppose I understood your disposition so quick, and drew you out on the subject of speculation, so that I could get your sentiments in so short a time?"

Stewart expressed himself as mystified.

"Why," boasted Murrell, "I hadn't been in company with you more than two hours before I knew you as well as if I'd made you, and could have trusted my life in your hands. A little practice is all you want, and you can look into the very heart and thoughts of a man. Begin by telling of some act of villainy, and notice his answers and countenance as you go on with your story. If you discover him to lean a little, you advance a little; but if he recedes, you withdraw and commence some other subject."

3.

Having thus preened himself on his "mastery" of men, he began once more to boast, and in the next brief period he astonishingly revealed the full enormity of his plot to Stewart, who was a virtual stranger, and who was, had he known it, his actual enemy.

"This may seem bold to you, Hues," he began, "but that is what I glory in. All the crimes I've committed have been of the most daring; and I've been successful in all my attempts as yet. I'm confident that I'll be victorious in this matter; and I'll have the pleasure and honor of seeing and knowing that *by my management* I have glutted the earth with more human gore, and destroyed more property, than any robber who has ever lived in America or in the known world."

He spoke impressively, as if this were a goal of achievement more desirable to him than any other. Then he went on:

"I look upon the American people as my common enemy. They have disgraced me, and they can do no more. My life is nothing to me, and it shall be spent as their devoted enemy. My Clan is strong, brave, experienced, and rapidly increasing. I shouldn't be surprised if we were two thousand strong by the 25th of December, 1835. At least half of my Grand Council are men of high standing, many of them in honorable and lucrative offices. Should anything leak out by chance, these men could crush it at once by ridiculing the idea. They'd soon make it a humbug, a cock-and-bull story, and everything would be accounted for to the satisfaction of the community."

This was a safeguard Stewart could well understand; and it showed him the cunning of the master criminal who rode beside him.

Next Murrell, sure of his listener, revealed the heart of his plan: a Negro uprising of terrible proportions. All up and down the river his agents were busy at this time secretly stirring the slaves to fury against their masters, so he said. They would be armed, he added, and on a date already decided—December 25, 1835—they would all rise at once and murder every white person in the country, except only members of Murrell's Clan. These would be protected by a "mystic sign," and would direct the slaves in their raiding.

Christmas Day, the outlaw chief explained, was chosen as the time for the blow, because white vigilance would be less alert in the celebrations of that season, when by custom the slaves were allowed to mingle together for jollifications, their duties suspended.

He went on to say gloatingly that cities like New Orleans, Natchez, Memphis and other places would be devastated and burned. All white men, children, and "old or ugly" women would be slaughtered. The pretty women would be carried away—as an added incentive Murrell promised them to the Negroes to gratify their lusts. Meantime in the desperate confusion and wreckage, with fires sweeping towns and cities, the members of the Mystic Clan would flit here and there, looting, robbing, carrying off everything valuable. The "take," he said, would be so enormous it was beyond computation.

"But how will you provide the Negroes with arms?" gasped Stewart.

"We have considerable money in our treasuries to purchase guns and ammunition to fit out the Negro companies that are to attack cities and banks," replied the arch-bandit. "And we'll manage to get possession of different arsenals and supply ourselves from every other source. From each house we enter we'll take weapons and supplies. As for the Negroes who scour the country settlements, they'll not need many guns until they can get them from the houses they destroy. An axe, a club, or a knife will do to murder a family late at night when all are sleeping. There can be little defense possible the first night, and all will be confusion and alarm for the first day or two, until the white men can rally."

"What then?"

A cruel, mocking laugh from Murrell. "Why—we'll just let the Negroes fight out their own war. The poor fools don't know it's hopeless for them. The military will come and the citizens who survive the first massacre will gather, and the Negroes will be defeated, hunted down, and made to pay for their temerity."

He looked relishingly at Stewart. "But before that *we'll* all be gone. I have ships that will be waiting at New Orleans to bear away our loot—to some island or country where we'll not be bothered and where we can enjoy it to the full. We'll be the richest men in the world!"

Stewart was so stunned by the monstrous revelation that it must have shown on his face had it not been that night had fallen and darkness surrounded them. Murrell showed no signs of suffering from the bitter cold or fatigue; but the young man not only was numbed and weary in his body, but overwhelmed in his mind. He needed time to think.

They took a bypath around Randolph, since the outlaw seemed to wish to avoid the town, and houses were few along the lonely trail. But now Stewart begged that they stop and warm themselves. At first Murrell demurred, but finally he agreed, and they rode up to a lonely cabin and asked for quarters for the night.

It was a miserable hovel. As soon as they restored circulation before the blazing fireplace, they went to their beds, a few quilts or blankets spread on corn husks on the floor. Stewart later recorded that these beds were "cold, dreary and comfortless."

XV.   *Murrell's "Garden of Eden"*

1.

As he lay sleepless that night, Virgil Stewart thought with a new horror how he had, by a series of seemingly unavoidable moves, so involved himself in a web of deadly danger that it would be all but impossible for him to escape.

The start had been simple enough: no more than a friendly effort to find the missing Negroes for Parson Henning. But by degrees he learned, first, the true depth of the deviltry of Murrell, through the outlaw's own lips. And then he was made privy to a nightmare plot in all its details by a man so pitiless that the mere thought of arousing suspicion in him was terrible.

Murrell, it was certain, would stop at nothing if he discovered that Stewart was other than what he pretended to be, a slavish and admiring follower "of the pure grit." The young man had now come into possession of so many of the secrets of the master-bandit that his death, probably in some shocking and barbarous manner, was certain if his real character were discovered.

He considered Murrell: "An individual whose whole history appeared but a continued series of basest deceptions and the darkest deeds of villainy and crime." He considered the atrocious scheme itself. Sleeping families would be slaughtered in the night. Property would be destroyed and looted wholesale. He thought of the fate destined for the "young and pretty women," ladies both delicate and accomplished, who would be "charged with death, ravishment, and prostitution, in all their hideous, torturing and humiliating forms."

Ten thousand human lives and millions in treasure were Murrell's ghastly goals. Somehow that plot *must* be exposed before the fatal hour—the day already set, December 25, 1835, less than two years away.

But how? He alone was in possession of these facts, and unless some stroke of fortune occurred, such as he could not at this present time imagine, he would never escape to reveal them to the world.

Even if he made his escape from the immediate clutches of the outlaw there were other considerations. Would people ever believe the fantastic story he would tell them? What would the world say if he returned and recounted such a confused phantasmagoria of death and destruction? Even if in some manner he succeeded in capturing the arch-outlaw himself, and accused him before a court of justice, would his accusations be accepted?

Murrell had boasted of the influential citizens in his Clan who would "make a humbug and a cock-and-bull story" of such an exposure —unless it was accompanied by indisputable evidence. That evidence Stewart did not now possess. It would be his unsupported word against Murrell's *if* he managed to capture the bandit chief. Too well he knew public skepticism to expect that a story as wild as he must tell would be credited.

Another doubt: Could he capture Murrell if he tried? The man was as intensely watchful as a wild beast, always armed, deadly with his weapons, without the slightest scruple against dealing death. For a single man to attempt to take him would be foolhardy and might destroy the only hope of exposing him and his Clan.

Lastly, it was borne in on Stewart that he did not *dare* go back to Madison County at present. Even if he gave Murrell the slip and disappeared, unless he left some satisfactory explanation he would be tracked down no matter where he went, and slain without mercy by Murrell's agents. Once more the outlaw's chilling phrase concerning another man who turned against him, returned to mind: "He soon had a nurse that attended him day and night, until he found his way to the bottom of the Mississippi River."

Stewart knew that, like it or not, he *had* to go ahead.

2.

When they set out again next morning the weather had moderated, and Murrell seemed to be in high good humor. During the short ride that brought them to the Mississippi shore, he continued to regale Stewart with the story of his ferocious life, including some of the episodes previously recorded in this narrative and others as well, running the gamut from burglary and fraud in his guise as a camp-meeting preacher, to horse theft, Negro stealing, robbery, and murder.

But now they found their way barred. The Mississippi was "booming," to use the river men's phrase, and the lowlands were so deeply flooded that the trace Murrell intended to follow was submerged. The check made the outlaw impatient, but he knew the country well and by retracing his course a few miles came to another route, over higher ground, which he said would come to the river "at the foot of Chickasaw Bluff, above the Shelby plantation, and then on down until they reached the private crossing place of the Clan."

Rather late in the day they came down on the environs of the plantation of Colonel Orville Shelby, a member of a notable Southern family which produced such men as General Isaac Shelby, a hero of the Battle of King's Mountain and first governor of Kentucky, and (later on) General Joseph Orville Shelby, a famous Confederate cavalry commander.

Murrell knew Shelby's uncompromising attitude toward all law-breakers, and his activities at the time not long before, when the outlaws overwhelmed a flatboat on the river, murdered its crew, and sequestered the boat and its cargo among the swamps on the Arkansas side. He had no wish to encounter the doughty colonel and carefully avoided the house. But when he found some of the planter's slaves working on the river bank, though they were in full sight of the house, he could not resist the temptation to impress Stewart with his "tact in producing disaffection" among the Negroes.

This certainly must not have been difficult to do, especially among the class of slaves called "field hands" upon whom fell all the hardest and most disagreeable labor. They would not have been human had they not been willing to lend an ear to any proposal that would better their condition, particularly the hope of freedom. So when the plausible white man began to talk to them he very quickly succeeded "in stirring them into excitement and a spirit of rebellion," and they promised to go with him to a "free state" any time he called for them.

Murrell plumed himself on this "success" and having thus demonstrated his "power" to his young friend, led on to a place about four miles below the Shelby plantation where night overtook them. As yet they had found no way to cross the swollen and dangerous river. But a house stood overlooking its broad course.

"I know that place," said Murrell. "It belongs to John Champion. We'll ask to spend the night."

At Champion's they were received with the usual cordial hospitality of the country, and that evening Murrell—who now called himself "Merrill"—sounded out their host on the subject of "speculation." Stewart was forced to listen to some of the stories of the "elder brother" which he already had heard. But Champion was far from dazzled by the "brilliant" achievements of the hero of his guest's stories, and showed the reverse of approval of the exploits described.

Watching him, Stewart felt he was an honest man. In his present desperate situation he very much needed a person in whom he could confide, and their host might be such a person. But how could he talk with Champion without Murrell's knowledge?

When they arose next morning, Champion told them that while he himself had no boat, they might find one at Matthew Erwin's, just below his place on the river; and if that failed, he was quite sure they could be accommodated at the house of Parson Hargus, who lived still lower down.

But the high water had created such a morass ahead that it would be almost impossible to travel farther with horses. Murrell asked Champion if he and Stewart might leave their mounts in his stable, while they continued down the river on foot, hoping to find a skiff which would get them across the Mississippi.

"I can see Champion is no friend to speculators," he confided privately to Stewart. "For this reason I pretended to know nothing about the people on the other side of the river."

Such a judgment from the chief devil himself confirmed Stewart's decision to interview their host privately. So he devised an expedient. When, after breakfast, they set forth on foot, he purposely left his gloves behind him in the house.

Within a few hundred yards he halted.

"What's the matter?" asked Murrell impatiently.

"I forgot my gloves," apologized Stewart. "Will you wait here while I hurry back for them?"

Murrell scowled, then nodded. While the younger man hastened back to the house, the outlaw seated himself on a log to await his return.

Champion greeted Stewart at the house. Now came another moment of doubt and fear. Stewart asked himself if he dared trust his life to this man whom he had never seen until the night before. In spite of Champion's apparent distaste for "speculation," there existed the possibility that he might be one of Murrell's secret agents and his whole attitude was a pretense. Or, if he was not a direct associate of the bandit's, Champion might betray him for pay.

Nevertheless, he felt it was his only chance. Hurriedly he stammered out the story of his adventure, his situation, the identity of Murrell, how he became involved with him, and his own real name.

"Will you help me if I need you?" he asked anxiously.

Champion nodded promptly and gravely. "You can depend on me. I believe I can get together fifty honest men as a guard. Matthew Erwin and Parson Hargus, whom you'll meet down below, are both reliable and trustworthy. You can confide in them. I'll hold your horses here. If Murrell returns for them alone, I'll consider that sufficient evidence that you've been killed or detained, and have him arrested."

He then gave Stewart a loaded pistol, and the young man took his missing gloves and returned to the outlaw waiting on the log with a somewhat lighter heart. He now carried three pistols—his own, the one given him by Colonel Bayliss, and Champion's. Fortunately, the "thick Bolivar overcoat" he was wearing concealed the weapons.

Murrell rose from his log and led the way as they began crossing the sloughs toward Erwin's house. It was difficult traveling, and unpleasant, with many stretches of deep water about which must be found detours in the deep mire and mud, thick growths of shore trees and brush to be penetrated, danger every minute of making a misstep into a quagmire or slipping into an icy plunge in muddy water.

Three miles of this, and when at last they reached firm ground on the other side of the swamp, and saw Erwin's house, the morning was far gone. Matthew Erwin received them politely and they had their noonday meal at his house. But to Murrell's intense disappointment, he had not a skiff available to cross the river.

The nearest possible boat, he told them, was at the house of Parson Hargus. But between the Erwin place and that of the parson the overflowing river had created a wide lake which could not be crossed without a craft of some kind. They could only wait until some boat came down the river.

Here was another delay—and each delay increased Stewart's tension. No telling when he might make a fatal slip and expose himself to the bandit's deadly wrath. But he remembered that Champion had said Erwin was a true man.

Patiently he listened while Murrell talked to their host. The outlaw

was at his best, with, as Stewart afterward recalled, "a manly address and captivating demeanor." His few leading statements, designed to learn if Erwin had any leanings toward "speculation," satisfied not only the bandit, but Stewart that the man was an upright
citizen. Thereupon, Murrell changed his line of conversation and represented himself as a slave trader. Since this was a legal occupation,
and Erwin in need of more hands, the two agreed upon the delivery of
three Negro men within three weeks, at a price of six hundred dollars
apiece. Stewart well knew the kind of merchandise that would be delivered—stolen slaves, who would be re-stolen, and re-sold, and finally
murdered in the bandit's revolting way.

They spent the night, perforce, at the Erwin house. One member
of the household was a young woman, who was not hard to look upon.
We do not know her name, and she may have been a daughter of a
younger sister of Erwin's. But we do know that she was blond, and
a widow, and not averse to a handsome young gentleman's company.

Stewart paid some smiling attentions to her that night, about which
Murrell slyly joked with him later. But the young man had something
in his mind beyond merely flirting with a pretty girl. He had a half-
formulated plan in which she, and his quite open attentions to her,
might later play a most important part, although she perhaps would
never know of her own role.

One of the more remarkable things that Stewart did in this period
of constant strain and peril, was to keep a sort of a journal of events
and conversations. He could not, of course, write a diary in the regular manner, for it might be discovered, with dread consequences.

But he carried in his pocket a "blank book"—a sort of notebook—
on which, whenever he had a chance, he put down a record of statements, places, and especially names: names of men both good and
criminal. These he hid in an ingenious manner. Instead of a hat, like
Murrell, he was wearing a winter cap which had an inner lining. By
making a slit in this lining he could slip pieces of paper into it, carefully numbering and dating each to preserve their chronology, so
that he literally "traveled with his information on his head."

Since he could make no notations on paper while riding with Murrell, he took a needle from his "housewife"[1] and with this homely little
implement he managed somehow to scratch proper names, places,
and significant incidents wherever he could find a surface to do so—
on his boot-legs, saddle-skirts, portmanteau, even his fingernails.

---

[1] A little package of effects for repairing clothes which almost every traveler in
those days carried, including needles, pins, spools of thread, and bits of cloth for
patching.

By these aids to his memory he was later able to write an enlarged
account on the secret bits of paper he placed in the crown of his cap.
It was, of course, a highly dangerous expedient; but by it he was enabled to keep a journal which was to be of enormous interest and
value.

3.

Next afternoon, January 20, a small trading boat stopped at Erwin's
yard for fuel. They made arrangements to ride this craft across the
lake to Hargus's landing.

Before they left, however, Stewart, catching a moment alone with
Erwin, hastily told him what Murrell was, his own business with him,
and begged for his help when he needed it. Erwin was struck silent
by this revelation. But after a moment's thought he promised the help
whenever he was asked for it.

Across the lake, Parson Hargus received the strangers in the kindly
manner of the times, having no inkling of their true identity. But
another disappointment awaited them.

"I'm sorry," said Hargus to their inquiry, "but I've loaned my good
boat. All I have here is an old canoe. It's out there on the bank, and
you're welcome to it, but it hasn't been used for a long time, and I'm
afraid it's in bad shape. Go and look at it, and if you can use it, by all
means take it."

They examined the craft. It was a dugout of the pirogue type, old,
half-rotted, and evidently unseaworthy. But Murrell was in a fever to
get across the river, and they went to work on it.

Before they finished putting the canoe in any sort of condition for
navigation night fell again, and they had to sleep at the friendly
frontier home. Parson Hargus, a God-fearing farmer-preacher, was
much impressed by Murrell. One can imagine the evening supper
table, with the outlaw lifting his hands and giving a long and sonorous
blessing before they ate, this being a frequent practice of his to throw
off suspicion. He had full command of all that type of religious
rhetoric which passed for piety on the frontier.

One can also imagine how shocked and surprised Parson Hargus
must have been when later, some time during that stay, Stewart got
him alone and told him the same story he had told to Champion and
Erwin. This must have been at the very end of their visit, and as before the young man compelled belief. Hargus promised support if he
could give it.

That night a storm came up, and when they rose at dawn a violent gale, accompanied by a heavy snowfall, was lashing the river. Bitterly disappointed, Murrell agreed that it was best to wait for fairer weather. The patched-up dugout was at best a frail craft of doubtful safety, and it could never live in that river, which was so buffeted by winds and waves.

All that day and the following night the tempest continued. Murrell grew edgy, and his rage and impatience increased as the bad weather continued with no letup. At times—when not in hearing of Parson Hargus—he would "break out in a stream of terrible oaths."

"The devil has ceased to cut the cards for me," he said once to Stewart. At another time, "That damned old preacher's [Henning's] Negroes have cost me more trouble and perplexity than any I've ever before stolen."

But when Parson Hargus was about, he quickly changed his demeanor. Stewart recorded: "In the midst of all his excitement, he never once so far forgot himself as to let fall one imprudent word in the presence of his landlord. On the contrary, his conversation was studiously turned on those subjects which he deemed most consistent with his [Hargus's] feelings. He dwelt with peculiar emphasis on the great advantages of a moral and religious education, and the happy effects of a general diffusion of religious intelligence."

These conversations must have been before Stewart told their host the true nature of Murrell. If not, the parson dissembled most skillfully, for the outlaw did not dream his true character was known.

When he was alone with Stewart, Murrell became more and more like a volcano of fury ready to erupt. His mind kept harking back to the Negroes he had stolen from the Hennings, and he wondered wrathfully what steps "Young Henning" might be taking toward recovering them.

"I'd just like to meet Dick Henning over in Arkansas," he said, hungrily as a wolf slavering for blood. "I'd give five hundred dollars for the chance to punish his damned officiousness."

He mulled this over with internal mutterings, then all at once the volcano burst forth, and spewed its lava on Stewart.

"You know, Hues," he said furiously, "I'm not satisfied with stealing the preacher's Negroes. I'm going to make him smart for making so free with my name and my brother's. When I give the word, some of my friends, headed by one of the most prominent members of my Clan, Eli Chandlor, will wait upon Parson Henning, take him from his house, and give him two hundred and fifty lashes."

He gave Stewart a grim glance. "I know suspicion will at once attach to me, so I'll spend that night at a hotel at Jackson, and make myself very prominent so that fifty persons can swear I was there at the time of the whipping. I have no fear of Chandlor carrying out the job, he's a second Caesar." A gloating chuckle. "What a joke! It would bring a laugh from the gravest: that an individual should first lose his property, and afterward be punished by the thief for complaining!"

Two hundred and fifty lashes! It amounted almost to a sentence of death, for a man could die under such punishment. Stewart was so alarmed by this new danger which threatened his friend that he had to struggle to keep a smooth countenance. Yet he did so, and even managed a little laugh to suit his companion's suggestion of cruel humor.

For the third time that night they slept at the Hargus house. When the morning of February 1 dawned, the sky was still dark with rolling clouds. Waves continued to roll high and threatening on the river and snow yet flew, though not as thickly as before. The wind had fallen somewhat and Murrell decided they should try to cross.

A foolish risk. Very soon they saw how impossible it was. The leaky old dugout was almost swamped before they got back to Hargus's landing; the whole adventure might have ended then and there for both Murrell and Stewart in the swirling waters of the Mississippi.

But luck turned at last. The boat Parson Hargus had loaned was brought back. He allowed his guests to use it, and sent his son with them to bring it back. In this boat, larger and more seaworthy, they at last succeeded in crossing the Mississippi, landing at a point opposite the mouth of what was called Old River, which ran into the Mississippi at the Chickasaw Bend.

4.

A word here about the geography of the strange and mysterious place called the "Garden of Eden," by Murrell, to which Virgil Stewart was being conducted. His account makes it difficult to locate because he was confused in directions, but I have a valuable letter from W. M. Hackett, of Little Rock, Arkansas, who has studied the matter and knows as much about it as any one. Mr. Hackett writes:

> In eastern Arkansas the Tyronza River begins near the Missouri state line and meanders through Mississippi County, crossing into Crittenden County (a corner) and on into Cross County, where it joins the St. Francis River about a half a mile from Parkin.
>
> This river loops around the present town of Tyronza, Arkansas. The Murrell so-called "Garden of Eden" was between the Tyronza River and

Little River (a local river so named) in that then very swampy country, not too far from Marked Tree, Arkansas.

I do not know that the exact place could be pin-pointed, except for the approximate locale. Little River, Mack's Bayou, and the Tyronza are certainly its outer borders.

Legend has it, that pine trees were transplanted at the cabins of members of the gang, being a marker, where members could know that help or friends were. Marked Tree was one of those spots and later a town grew there bearing still the unique name. That was in a new country, in a day of not too many written records, as you know.

It is also legend that they (the Murrell Clan) had also a spot at Plum Point on the Mississippi near Helena, and they did also operate some on the White River. But the "Garden" was in Mississippi County, where it is given above.

Legend has it that they even had a member in the Legislature in Little Rock and so kept tab on when it would "get hot" for them.

The newspapers of the day, especially the Arkansas *Gazette* and the Arkansas *Advocate* had much about them in the papers.

John Patterson, allegedly the first white child born in Arkansas, was alleged to be a member also. He was born near Marianna, Arkansas. He possibly was not the first white child, though it has been stated.

The Murrell gang had wide ramifications and did steal Negroes, horses, etc., and rob and plunder. They did steal Negroes in one locale and resell them in another place, the same with horses. When it got too hot they would just cut them open (the Negroes), fill them with mud and sink them in some slough or bayou to get rid of the evidence.

As thus located by Mr. Hackett, the "Garden of Eden" would be in southeastern Mississippi County, Arkansas, about ten or twelve miles from the nearest present bend of the Mississippi River. Marked Tree, the town, is in Poinsett County, west of the triangle located by Mr. Hackett. It must be remembered that the Mississippi has frequently changed its stream bed since the days of Murrell, so these distances can only be approximate. The country has also changed greatly in the intervening years, much of the heavy morass having been drained and put to agricultural use.

One Murrell stronghold not mentioned by Mr. Hackett was in the present Lake Chicot, an abandoned channel of the Mississippi, in Chicot County, at the extreme southeast corner of Arkansas. Near the upper end of Lake Chicot is Stuart's Island, on which stood one of Murrell's "council houses," similar to that in the "Garden of Eden." After Murrell's final arrest and conviction, a posse of indignant citizens attacked the stronghold of Stuart's Island and burned it to the ground.

A friend of mine, Colonel Ken Croswell, now living near and doing business in Los Angeles, spent his boyhood in that section of Arkansas. He has told me how old-timers would point out where Murrell's "castle" stood, and the country was then and still is full of legends concerning the arch-bandit. But in more recent times the site is so obliterated that it cannot be identified.

As a footnote, John Patterson, of Arkansas, was not included in the roster of names given by Murrell to Stewart later, although of course that list was by no means complete. There were, however, on the list two Pattersons, both of Kentucky.

John Patterson, who died near Marianna, Arkansas, in 1886, used to say of himself, "raised in the wilds of Arkansas, uncultivated as a poke stalk, unlettered as a savage; birthplace caved in when I was young; father was shot from ambush while asleep at home." He said nothing of his connection, if any, with Murrell.

5.

But to return to Stewart's adventures:

Carrying their portmanteaus and led by Murrell, the two left the Hargus boat to return across the river, and struck out in a northwest course afoot through the great swamp. Progress was difficult because of dense growths of cane, together with frequent intervals of turbid water too deep and wide to cross, which had been created by the flooding of the Mississippi.

After a time they skirted a "considerable lake" until they came at last to a bayou, on the opposite shore of which squatted a small cabin. Murrell gave a halloo, and presently a man appeared, entered a boat and rowed over to them.

"A friend of mine," said Murrell, with pride in his empire.

They did not linger once they were set across the bayou but headed west "along the borders of what appeared to be an extensive tract of overflowed country." All at once they saw in a clearing ahead a small open hut—a "half-cabin," or lean-to—with blue smoke curling from the chimney, showing that the place was tenanted.

Again Stewart's fears rose. What if Henning's Negroes were here!

For some time the danger that he might come suddenly upon them and be recognized had been out of his mind. But now it returned with terrifying force. He was sure that they had been brought across the river. Perhaps they were in that very shack!

"Sensations of indescribable horror" seized upon him, as, preceded by Murrell, he "advanced with almost trembling step towards the door of the hut."

He managed to cock the two pistols which he carried in the pockets of his overcoat, the third being in his inner coat; and he tried to muffle his face by holding his handkerchief at his mouth. Thus, keeping somewhat behind Murrell, so that he could at least shoot down that great scoundrel before he himself was murdered, he entered the fearsome hovel.

Within it he saw dark faces—Negroes. But a quick look brought him immediate relief. These were not the Henning slaves. With the two Negroes in the shanty were three white men. All five, black and white, were eating together by the fire in the fireplace.

Murrell spoke to one of the white men, calling him Rainhart,[2] and asked how "things were moving." After a few words between them he said to Rainhart, "I'll see you tomorrow at the Council House."

From that shanty Murrell and Stewart walked again until they came to another lake beside which a skiff was moored. This they entered and rowed out across the water; then along the opposite shore for nearly an hour before they found a place where the ground was sufficiently raised above the drowned lands to permit them to disembark.

Here they turned through the cane and ragged woods in a direction more northerly—as near as Stewart later could remember—and in a short distance reached a second bayou. On its bank stood "a small filthy cabin which proved (to be) the wretched abode of a white man and his family."

Each time they approached a different cabin Stewart experienced again the fear that he might encounter the old parson's Negroes. But the man of this house, a shiftless "poor white," with his wife and two children, "who sat in drowsy silence by the fire," were the only inmates of the foul and gloomy habitation.

6.

In spite of its unprepossessing appearance, Murrell felt quite at home in this cabin. He spoke to its inmates in the familiar manner of long acquaintance, and once more borrowed a craft—a dugout canoe. In this they again found difficulty in reaching a landing place, paddling nearly an hour as they explored before they set foot ashore in a heavy growth of cane.

By this time Stewart was completely confused as to where he had

[2] No Rainhart was listed in Murrell's roster later given to Stewart. Perhaps this man was a Stryker, too unimportant to be included in that roll.

been, but even in this tangle Murrell seemed to know exactly where he was going. After toiling through the canebrake for a considerable distance, he and Stewart came upon a shack "constructed of boards and exhibiting anything but the appearance of comfort."

In it sat three Negroes, "alone and cheerless, in filthy attire, and with subdued and downcast countenances, bespeaking rather the melancholy pensiveness of desponding criminals than the cheerful hilarity of freemen."

Stewart felt pity for these wretched beings. He knew how they must have been tricked, betrayed, and what would be their probable bloody end. But he could do nothing for them.

"Where's your boss?" asked Murrell.

"Ain't seen him several days," one of the Negroes replied.

His voice sounded hopeless. Probably he already sensed the disappointment of his dreams of liberty, and even guessed what his fate might be.

Without another word, Murrell turned on his heel and led Stewart away. A few hundred yards more through the cane and the outlaw halted. He pointed to where a large tree at some distance rose above the surrounding growth.

"Do you see yon lofty cottonwood that towers so majestically over all the other trees?" he asked, in the grandiloquent manner he sometimes affected.

"Yes," said Stewart.

"That tree," said Murrell, "stands in the Garden of Eden, and we have but a quarter of a mile to travel before we set foot in that happy spot, where many a noble plot has been concerted."

In a few minutes they reached the shore of a lake, and Stewart saw that an island rose in its middle, on which stood the giant cottonwood to which Murrell had called his attention. Toward this, in a dugout canoe which the outlaw found in a spot evidently familiar, they paddled.

Their landing was on a point of the island. The thickly matted cane of its borders, and the high trees with choking undergrowth of its interior, gave it an unpleasantly gloomy appearance.

Following Murrell, Stewart made his way by a footpath to the center of the island. There stood a solitary cabin.

Stewart was struck with astonishment. He knew he was looking at the "Grand Council House" of Murrell's "Mystic Clan." It was the capital of the outlaw's "Invisible Empire," the place where he and his "Grand Council"—protected in truth by the almost impenetrable swamps and wilderness which surrounded it—plotted a scheme more alarming, extensive, and potentially destructive than any criminals had ever dreamed before.

The Garden of Eden? Stewart had been prepared for something far more magnificent. The very squalor of the place, which differed in no respect as to its exterior from any other weather-beaten log cabin—save that it was perhaps slightly larger—acted as a further depression for his spirits.

XVI.   *Downfall of a Monster*

1.

Virgil Stewart never claimed to be heroic. He had involved himself in an adventure the terrors of which he had not even dreamed, and from which he could not now retreat. His only hope was to keep his wits about him, make no mistakes, and perhaps find some unforeseen chance to extricate himself alive and carry word to law-abiding people of this nightmare outlaw plot.

As they approached the ill-omened "Council House," ugly and stained, in the tangle of woods and underbrush that was uncared for and wild, he was again filled with apprehensive doubts.

Had he really succeeded in his imposture with Murrell? Or was the outlaw amusing himself with him, playing a cruel cat-and-mouse game, only to murder him in the end as an example of the Clan's "vengeance"? If so, this would be the place of all places for his execution—in Murrell's central headquarters, before the eyes of Murrell's closest accomplices, and possibly with cruelties that only a mind like Murrell's could invent and delight in. As he himself put it he was "nerved to meet an occasion to which he felt well-nigh unequal."

Murrell pushed open the door, and ushered him inside. Within, Stewart saw eleven men, some in the rough garb of the frontier, others as well dressed as Murrell himself—and every man of them, without exception, glaring at him savagely and suspiciously.

The arch-bandit seemed grimly amused at their bristling hostility which brought them to their feet from whatever sitting or lounging positions they occupied, their hands reaching as if by instinct for guns or knives.

After looking at them with his wolf's half-grin, he took Stewart by the hand and said, "Here, my brave Counsellors, this is a Counsellor of my own making, and I'm not ashamed of my workmanship. Let Mr. Hues be examined by whom he may."

Surprise replaced hostility, but did not erase suspicion. The eleven scoundrels approached Stewart, looking at him narrowly, and asked him some questions, to which he replied adroitly, sticking to the story he had previously told Murrell.

Then they conferred together darkly, shooting glances at him as if to surprise in him any sign of weakness or duplicity. At length one of them said to Murrell:

"All right, if he wants to be in the Council, let him state his opinion of the Negro war, and of our faith and principle."

Murrell nodded at Stewart to speak. The young man, though suffering from a quite normal terror of these people, was possessed of considerable moral courage. He began, with this scant warning, what literally might be a speech for life.

For the time and area he possessed a better than fair education, and he knew the impression that fine words and evidences of learning made on these crude people. So he delivered an address, which he later recorded, and which was attuned to his purpose:

"Gentlemen of the Mystic Conspiracy: My youth and inexperience must plead the cause of any deficiency I may betray before this worthy and enlightened congregation. I am better qualified to acquiesce in the measures and sentiments of others than to advance anything of my own. So recently have I been honored with the secrets of this august Conspiracy, that I am unable to offer anything original. I have received all my ideas from our honorable Dictator; and I should feel myself guilty of presumption were I to offer any amendments to his present deep and well-arranged plans and purposes. Your schemes, under the guidance of our experienced leader, appear to me practicable and praiseworthy."

These flattering expressions toward Murrell caused the outlaw to swell visibly. Stewart turned now to winning the other members of the Council:

"My opinion of the faith and principles of this lordly band may be expressed in few words; and as I have been honored by the instruction and confidence of our gallant Leader, to be whose creature is my highest aspiration, I flatter myself of its correctness. I consider the members of this Fraternity to be absolved from duty or obligation to all men save their Commander. We find ourselves placed in the world surrounded with everything needful for our comfort and enjoyment; and shall we stand supinely by and see others enjoy those things to which we have an equal right, because an established order of things, which we neither believe in or respect, forbids our participation in them?

"Be it our boast that we are lords of our own wills, and while we live let us riot in all the pompous luxuries which the spoils of our enemies afford. We are told in history that Rome lost her liberty by the conspiracy of three Romans, on an island of the River Rhenus. And why may not the conspiracy of four hundred Americans in this morass of the Mississippi River glean the southern and western banks, destroy their cities, and slaughter our enemies? Have we no Antony to scatter firebrands of rebellion; no Lepidus to open his coffers of gold; no Augustus to lead us in battle? Such a conclusion would be an impeachment of our gallant Chieftain."

There was more of the same. It was not a brilliant effort, being pompous, labored, and verbose. But young Stewart had correctly judged his audience. It was exactly the kind of a speech to impress these listeners. "Fine language," a parade of classical knowledge, banalities keyed to their own interests and self-justifications—the rogues were enthralled.

When he finished they applauded and gathered about to shake hands with him. Thereafter he went through the solemn and somewhat ridiculous mummery of initiation into the two orders of the Clan —lengthy and supposedly dreadful oaths, secret signs, and passwords. He was installed in the lower order, the Strykers, which did most of the dangerous work—the robberies, horse thefts, transporting stolen Negroes, shoving counterfeit money, and so on—numbering, he was told, about three hundred members.

Then he took the higher order of the Grand Council, which contained about forty members in all, the officers for directing the traffic of crime under Murrell. The "Counsellors" took great pains and a kind of childish pride in drilling the new initiate into these "mysteries" until he "could equal the most skillful."

2.

Stewart was now a full-fledged member of the Mystic Clan. And by so becoming his danger was increased because everyone in the Clan would be doubly desirous to close his mouth if he were suspected of being a spy in its ranks. Furthermore, he was now known to several members of the Clan, who would be able to recognize him in the future even if he escaped from the immediate toils he was in. He was introduced to all present and not until later did he fully realize how greatly "honored" he was.

There were five whose names he remembered—the spelling in some cases slightly confused—and he was to learn that all of these were members of the innermost circle, the group subsequently described by Murrell as "transient members who travel from place to place." These five were James Haines, Perry Doddridge, Samuel Roberson, Lloyd and Sperlock (probably Skerlock).

Haines and Doddridge in fact were of the original New Orleans group, together with Phelps who was, Stewart learned later, unhappily in jail at the time of this meeting.

These were the real hatchet men of the organization, who carried out the most important and secret orders and sometimes went on murderous errands. Their homes were anywhere, but they came like vultures to this roost at the call of their leader.

For the rest of the session which consisted of reports on distribution of counterfeit money, new "speculations," what members of the Clan were in prison and needed assistance, how many proselytes were candidates for admission, Stewart sat silent, attracting as little attention to himself as possible, but all ears.

Flames, dancing in the fireplace, lit up the dark interior and revealed to him a bizarre spectacle: the harsh faces of the criminal leaders, the crude furniture, the barrel of whiskey on the table. It was later reported that there was a trap door at one corner, leading down into a lightless, wet and muddy hole, without exit save through the trap door itself. A man thrown in there might never again see daylight. But Stewart appears not to have taken note of this feature of the "Council House," if indeed it existed.

Once Murrell asked sharply what had happened to the Negroes he "sent down" from the Henning place. The man named Lloyd explained that the slaves had arrived some days before, badly frosted. Because of the delay in the chief's arrival, the Council had decided to "push them and make sales as early as possible." The Negroes had therefore been sent south to be marketed. He named the man in charge of this shipment.

One worry at least was eliminated for Stewart. He would not in this area stumble upon the stolen slaves and risk identification by them.

There was food, and plenty of "chawing terbaccy," and the inevitable whiskey, drunk neat by the dipperful from the barrel. After the men had eaten the meeting broke up and the various members dispersed to scattered quarters in huts erected on high points of land about the morass, to reconvene for a fuller session of the Grand Council scheduled for the next day.

Murrell and Stewart returned to their dugout canoe and paddled for several miles along the cane-choked channels of the flooded swamp, toward the place of a member of the Grand Council, named Jehu Barney, with whom the robber chief had business.

Once they passed a small shack on the bank of a bayou. Near it four Negroes were at work, cutting wood for one of the woodyards on the river where steamboats were supplied with fuel, which were conducted by some members of the Clan as a pretense of honest occupation.

"See those Negroes?" asked Murrell.

"Yes, sir," said Stewart.

"Those fellows have been stolen and sold several times already," said the outlaw with his devil's grin. "And they're still in reserve for a future market. We'll sell them again as soon as the excitement regarding them subsides."

Stewart inwardly wondered if these were not the very slaves destined to be "sold"—and then taken away—to Erwin who had been their kind host on the far bank of the Mississippi.

Some distance farther on they saw a large flatboat, drawn up on the bank for repair work of some kind.

"That boat belongs to me," said Murrell. "I'm going to use it to convey Negroes to some point below New Orleans. There's a route through that bayou country which members of our Clan know, a quick and secret way over to the Sabine River and into Texas, where there's a brisk market for slaves even though the laws of Mexico forbid it. I've already made arrangements for forty or fifty prime Negroes with that in view."

Later, Stewart was to learn that this was the very flatboat that had been attacked by Murrell's gang, its crew murdered, and the boat and cargo confiscated by the Clan, causing Colonel Shelby and a posse to attempt action, though fruitlessly.

It was evening when they finally reached the wretched log cabin of Jehu Barney, where Murrell said they would spend the night.

Barney seemed to be an especially unsavory member of the outlaw horde, and Stewart mistrusted him on sight. He decided that, weary as he was, he would not allow himself to go to sleep that night.

Throughout the evening, while the three of them sat before the fire, he listened to Murrell laying plans with Barney to re-steal the Negroes he had promised to deliver to Erwin. The arch-outlaw would himself deliver them—the four Stewart had seen chopping wood, sure enough —and get his money, six hundred dollars apiece or twenty-four hundred dollars. The Negroes would be instructed to appear at a certain point on the river bank the following night, where Barney would meet them with a boat and take them away again to a hiding place.

Stewart could only wonder at the hypnotized docility of the slaves who would allow themselves to be so handled. He decided that fear must play a large part in their behavior. They knew they would be murdered, one by one, if they failed to obey.

3.

Stewart need not have feared that he would fall asleep that night. There was enough on his mind to keep him awake while his companions snored.

Somehow he must get away from Murrell. He had seen enough and heard enough from the arch-criminal to convince him that there was brewing a scheme so fantastic as to be almost crazy; yet just crazy enough that it might succeed in bringing death and suffering to thousands.

He had learned the extent of the Clan; that it had members in all the states of the South; and that many of those members were of respectable standing, and lived in the very parts of the country where he was known, so that he would be in constant danger from them.

Furthermore, he now knew that Parson Henning's Negroes were so far away that present pursuit of them was useless. In any case he had a far greater, more urgent, matter to deal with than those two lost slaves.

Murrell intended to return to the Council House next day and had stated that a far larger gathering of the Grand Council would be held, at which vitally important matters would be discussed. Some members were coming from distant places.

Distant places! They might be from localities where Stewart had lived, perhaps they were men who knew him well, whom he had considered friends or at least acquaintances of everyday relationship.

Thus far, by great good fortune, he had escaped recognition; but he could hardly afford to run this added risk.

When they rose next morning, February 2, an idea suggested itself to him. It just might work . . . if he had enough finesse to use it.

While they breakfasted on bacon and corn pone, he said as casually as possible to Murrell, "I believe, sir, that I'll leave you today."

"What?" cried Murrell, astounded. "So soon? There's some things of big importance before the Council today, on which I'd promised myself the pleasure of hearing your views. Besides"—a crafty and insinuating leer—"what about those plump and pretty Arkansas girls? I haven't shown them to you yet. And I promise you they'll give you the merriest time you ever saw."

Stewart gave him a grin. "Well, as to that—" he hesitated, and tried to look self-conscious and embarrassed. "To tell the truth," he went on, "it's a lady I'm interested in right now. You remember that yellow-haired girl at Erwin's? She's a widow, and acted really friendly—"

Now Murrell thought he comprehended. "I see. Well—"

"As for my advice, it wouldn't be of much importance anyway," continued Stewart. "I'm too new at it to advance anything of value as yet. Anything you say to the Council will get my full approval, and I'll be proud to adopt it as my own policy."

As always, Murrell succumbed to flattery. To him the desire of a young man to get to a girl, who not only "acted real friendly," but was a widow—suggesting shadowy possibilities—was exactly what he would expect. Perhaps, also, the land pirate's evil sense of humor was tickled by the thought that Erwin, who was to be his victim, would end up not only by being defrauded in the matter of the slaves, but also would find that the prettiest member of his household had been seduced by a member of Murrell's following.

"I'll wait for you at Erwin's," said Stewart. "It may take me a day or two to get my—er—business there accomplished to my taste."

Murrell's knowing grin widened. "Good enough," he said. "I'll see you to the other side of the river."

Jehu Barney's cabin stood on the shore of the Mississippi itself, and the robber chief insisted on accompanying Stewart across in a boat, landing him some distance from Erwin's, then rowing back alone to the Arkansas side.

Free for the first time of the outlaw's dread presence, Stewart walked to Erwin's. It was the master of the place, not the girl, whom he really was impatient to see.

Above everything Stewart wanted to catch Murrell in an act of crime, because he foresaw how hard it would be to convince the world of all he had seen, without such evidence. Members of the Clan who as yet stood unimpeached in their communities, would discredit him and bring his motives into question; and he, young, without any great influence or standing, would fail in the very purpose for which he had risked his life.

There was an even greater personal peril. It would be the policy of the Clan to assassinate him. How he could escape when some four hundred murderous men, few of whom he knew, were scattered over the country so that he could hardly travel through it without encountering some of them, he hardly dared ask himself.

His only hope was that if he could place the head, the central brain, of the far-flung reptile organization where orders could not proceed from it, there might be enough confusion so that a concerted plan to destroy him could not be made before he had time to expose the whole incredible plot.

Fortunately, Erwin was at home when he arrived. The planter listened closely to his account of the visit to the Grand Council, the general layout of the morass, the members of the Clan he had seen, and other details, including the scheme behind the Negro transaction. After studying the matter, Erwin agreed to Stewart's proposal: to have a guard warned and ready so that when Murrell delivered the slaves he would at once be arrested. The slaves themselves would furnish the names of their former masters, and these would give the evidence on which the outlaw would be convicted.

4.

When Murrell arrived at the Erwin place next day, February 3, he did not have the Negroes with him. But he carefully went over matters with Erwin, stating the time and place where the slaves would be delivered.

On this day he appeared to be in a hurry. "Let's go to Champion's," he said to Stewart. "We'll get our horses and be on our way."

Early that evening they reached John Champion's house across the marsh. There they slept, and next morning mounted and once more rode together, heading back this time toward Madison County, where Murrell lived with his "wife" from the Memphis stews, and whence Virgil Stewart had started on his strange and eerie adventure.[1]

---

[1] John Champion, Colonel Orville Shelby, and Matthew Erwin later signed sworn statements, the first dated Tipton County, Tennessee, October 18, 1835, the second also Tipton County, October 19, 1835, and the third Shelby County, Tennessee, October 20, 1835. In these statements the three men each verified absolutely all assertions made by Stewart as to his visits with them, his conversations, and the

As they rode along, Murrell still appeared to feel that he had run into bad luck with the Henning Negroes—as if some wild instinct warned him that somewhere peril lurked for him as the result of that abduction. He did not, however, for one instant suspect that the fresh-faced young man by his side was the nemesis that would pursue him to the finish. Stewart, as if sympathizing with him, for the first time asked directly what market the Negroes had gone to.

"They've sent my two [Henning's], with three others, and seven horses [stolen], down the river in one of those small trading boats," said Murrell. "They intend, if they can, to go through the Choctaw Pass to the Yazoo market, and they have with them $10,000 in counterfeit money." He paused, then said fretfully, "That last, I fear, may upset the whole matter. I'm not pleased with the arrangement. The fellows they've sent are only Strykers, and that's too much to put into their hands at one time. Damned if I'm not fearful they'll think themselves rich when they sell, and leave us behind in the lurch. Though Lloyd says there's no danger in them," he added, as if to reassure himself. "He told them to sell and mizzel."[2]

Presently, however, he seemed to recover his good humor, and after teasing Stewart about the "yellow-haired widow," began to boast of more of his own rascally adventures, including how he first gained the idea of the Negro war, "as the sure road to an inexhaustible fortune to all who engaged in the expedition," by his visit to the town in Alabama which was prostrated by fear of a slave uprising.

Once he laughed as he told how he posed as a preacher in the home of an "old Baptist," whose wife was sick. "The old man got his bible and hymn book and invited me to go to duty. I used the books, and then prayed like hell for the recovery of the old lady."

Meantime his confederates were robbing the place.

He grew more serious. "I've been going from one place to another, directing and managing; but now I have others as good as myself to manage. This fellow Phelps, that I told you of before, he's a noble chap among the Negroes. He knows how to excite them as well as any person. But he'll not do for a robber, as he can't kill a man unless he's received an injury from him first."

---

business he said he was on in accompanying Murrell. Colonel Shelby further stated that he found that his Negroes had been tampered with, and that he conferred with Champion and Erwin on the subject, adding that he had previous knowledge of the Murrell Clan in Arkansas, its capture of a flatboat and the massacre of its crew, and the Barneys on the Clan list stole two slaves from him the previous fall, but returned them when suspicion turned too strongly on them.

[2] In other words decamp, an underworld expression.

He looked at Stewart, as if deploring such a weakness in an outlaw, then went on, "He's in jail now at Vicksburg, and I fear he'll hang. I went to see him not long since, but he's so strictly watched that nothing can be done. He's been in the habit of stopping men on the highway, and robbing them, and letting them go on. But that will never do for a robber. After I rob a man he'll never give evidence. There's but one safe plan in the business, and that is to kill. If I couldn't afford to kill a man, I wouldn't rob him."

Murrell let this sink in. "I've often told Phelps," he added, "that he'd be caught before he knew it. I could raise men enough to go and tear down the Vicksburg jail and take Phelps by force. But that would endanger all our other plans."

So Phelps, though a loyal lieutenant, would be left to rot in prison, or more likely to die on the gallows, so that nothing might interfere with Murrell's maniacal schemes.

Later Stewart ventured—experimentally, to see how the outlaw would take it—that he intended to go down to the Yalobusha country "on business." The other ruminated a moment, then said:

"I've frequently had enough money to settle myself in wealth; but I've spent it as freely as water in carrying out my designs. The last five years of my life have been passed in the same way I've been telling you, Hues. I've been from home the best part of that time, and have let few chances escape me when I could rob, that I didn't do it."

To Stewart's relief he did not object to the Yalobusha journey, though he had other plans for the young man.

"It would take me a week yet, Hues," he said, "to tell you all my scrapes of that kind. You must come and stay at my house the week before I start with those Negroes to Erwin, and I'll have time to tell you all your ups and downs for the last five years. I want you to go on that trip with me. You can manage your business in the Choctaw Purchase in two weeks, and get to my home in Madison County. You'll make more on that trip than all your concerns in the [Choctaw] Nation are worth, so you'd better give away what you have there rather than be confined to it."

But going on "that trip" was the last thing Stewart desired. Even now they were approaching the village of Wesley, where he was known. About two miles before they reached the town, a trace turned off toward the south, and here Stewart reined up his horse.

"I'm taking this trail," he said. "It leads to the main road to the Choctaw Purchase where I must be as soon as possible."

Upon this he insisted, in spite of Murrell's protests.

"I'll take care of my business down there in a hurry," he promised, "and will be back to join you."

"If that's your determination," said the outlaw reluctantly, "I'll go on alone. Those Negroes I promised Erwin will be ready for delivery by the time you return."

But he seemed unwilling to part from Stewart, and lingered for some time where the trails separated.

"I'm not half done talking," he said, "but I'll quit telling you what I've done, and tell you what I'm going to do. I have about forty Negroes now engaged that are waiting for me to run them; and the best part of it is that they're almost all the property of my enemies." He gloated for a moment, then went on, "I have a great many friends who have got to be overseers—one named Nolin,[3] is my brother-in-law's brother, who is overseeing in Alabama for a man who is from home. Nolin has decoyed six likely Negroes for me. I'll have a Stryker drive them down to the Mississippi swamps for me. I have eight more engaged in Alabama. The rest of the forty I'll get in my own country. You recollect that boat I showed you on the bayou? That boat I'll fill with Negroes for my own benefit."

"There's a fellow named Bundels, or Buns, or some such name," said Stewart. "A Negro trader, who, I think, is as hard to cheat as any man I've seen—"

"Oh, I know who you're thinking of," broke in Murrell, who saw another chance to boast. "His name is Byrn. He does pass down through your country sometimes, and a great sharper he is; he can cheat you to death. But in spite of him I handled the cash that one of his Negroes sold for."

He gave a self-satisfied grin.

Stewart, who had asked the question, knew R. H. Byrn well—a resident of Madison County and a friend of the Hennings. He also knew that Byrn had lost a slave and deliberately used this expedient to learn if Murrell stole him.

---

[3] Or Nolan. This man, to whom Murrell referred as his "brother-in-law's brother" brings up an interesting question of relationships. The brother-in-law must have been named also Nolin (or Nolan). But where was the connection? At least it seems that this effectively disposes of the version that Murrell's "wife" was named Mary McClovey. Could it have been Murrell's sister who was married to one of the Nolins? Apparently not, for the sister seems still to have been known as Elizabeth Murrell when she was arrested for larceny, convicted, and pardoned from a prison term on payment of a nominal fine, a few months after this. That would leave only the outlaw's "wife" through whom to trace relationship to the Nolins. And if her maiden name was Nolin (or Nolan), the theory of Coates that she was from the Memphis stews is greatly strengthened, for the man to whom Murrell here referred, E. Nolin, was a great scoundrel and a member of the Clan, and there were besides two Nolins, members of the Clan, living in Tennessee, very likely, as in the case of their sister, products of the criminal Pinch Gut district of Memphis. Crime seems to run in families.

5.

For days and nights on end young Stewart had been listening to the boasting of the outlaw until it became almost insufferable. He could hardly abide it any longer, and he was eager to part company with him. But there remained one vital piece of information he wanted.

"You've never given me a list of your friends," he said.

"Oh, yes, yes," replied Murrell. "Have you any paper with you? We must have that to write the names on before we part."

Stewart groped in his pocket for the blank book. So many of its leaves had been torn out for the notes he now carried in the crown of his cap that only four and one half pages remained.

"That's too little to contain all the names of the Clan," said Murrell. "Wait till you get back to Madison County, and I'll give you a complete roster, with the residence of each."

But Stewart *had* to have those names.

"Give me all the paper will hold," he said, "and confine yourself to the principal figures in the different parts of the country."

"Well," said Murrell, after a moment, "but since you've got so little paper, I'll omit the Christian names."

"Maybe an initial to prevent confusion?" suggested Stewart.

The outlaw assented, and amazingly, there and then, as they sat in their saddles, he gave from memory a list by states, of four hundred and fifty-two names which Stewart scribbled down on his pages, and which today is still preserved. For the interest of antiquarians, and making allowance for probable mistakes in spelling and initials here and there, here is the list:

TENNESSEE: 2 Murrells, S. Wethers, D. Crenshaw, M. Dickson, V. Chisim, K. Dickson, L. Anderson, P. Johnson, J. Nuckels, L. Bateman, J. Taylor, E. Chandlor, 4 Maroneys, 2 Littlepages, J. Hardin, Squire Wilbern, Y. Pearson, G. Wiers, 5 Lathoms, A. Smith, 6 Hueses, S. Spiers, 2 Byrdsongs, Colonel Jarot, 2 Nolins, Capt. Ruffin, Ja. Hosskins, W. Crenshaw, J. Goaldin, R. Tims, D. Ahart, 2 Busbeys, L. More, J. Eas, W. Howel, B. Sims, Z. Gorin, 3 Boaltons, G. Sparkes, S. Larit, R. Parew, K. Deron—a total of 61.

MISSISSIPPI: G. Parker, S. Williams, R. Horton, W. Presley, C. Hopes, G. Corkle, B. Johnson, D. Rooker, L. Cooper, C. Barton, 5 Willeys, J. Hess, 2 Willsons, Capt. Moris, G. Tucker, 3 Glenns, 2 Harlins, Bloodworth, J. Durham, R. Forrow, S. Cook, G. Goodman, Stantton,

Clanin, C. Hickman, W. Thomas, Wm. Nawls, D. Marlow, Capt. Medford, 3 Hunters, 2 Gilberts, A. Brown, 4 Yarbers—a total of 47.

ARKANSAS: S. Pucket, W. Ray, J. Simmons, L. Good, B. Norton, J. Smith, P. Billing, A. Hooper, C. Jimerson, 6 Serrils, 3 Bunches, 4 Dartes, 2 Barneys, G. Aker, 4 Tuckers, 2 Loyds, 3 Spurlocks, 3 Joneses, L. Martin, S. Coulter, H. Petit, W. Henderson, 2 Nowlins, 3 Hortons—a total of 46.

KENTUCKY: 3 Forrows, 4 Wards, 2 Foresytes, D. Clayton, R. Williamson, H. Haly, H. Potter, D. Mugit, 2 Pattersons, S. Goin, Q. Brantley, L. Pots, 4 Reeses, 2 Carters—a total of 25.

MISSOURI: 4 Whites, 2 Herins, 6 Milers, G. Poap, R. Coward, D. Corkle, E. Boalin, W. Aker, 2 Garlins, S. Falcon, H. Warrin, 2 Moaseways, 3 Johnsons, Col. S. W. Foreman—a total of 27.

ALABAMA: H. Write, J. Homes, G. Sheridon, E. Nolin, 3 Parmers, 2 Glascocks, G. Hammons, R. Cunagen, H. Chance, D. Belfer, W. Hickel, P. Miles, O. More, B. Corhoon, S. Baley, 4 Sorils, 3 Martins, H. Hancock, Capt. Boin, Squire Malone—a total of 28.

GEORGIA: H. Moris, D. Harris, 2 Rameys, 4 Cullins, W. Johnson, S. Gambel, 2 Crenshaws, 4 Peakes, 2 Heffis, D. Coalmon, 4 Reves, 6 Rosses, Capt. Ashley, Squire Denson, 2 Lenits—a total of 33.

SOUTH CAROLINA: 3 Foats, 4 Williamses, O. Russet, S. Pinkney, 6 Woods, H. Black, G. Holler, 3 Franklins, W. Simpson, E. Owin, 2 Hookers, 3 Piles, W. King, N. Parsons, F. Watters, M. Ware, G. Gravit, B. Henry, 2 Robersons—a total of 35.

NORTH CAROLINA: A. Fentres, 2 Micklejohns, D. Harrilson, M. Coopwood, R. Huiston, 4 Solomons, J. Hackney, S. Stogdon, 3 Perrys, 4 Gilferds, W. Pariners, 3 Hacks, J. Secel, D. Barnet, S. Bulkes, M. Johnson, B. Kelit, V. Miles, J. Haris, L. Smith, K. Farmer—a total of 32.

VIRGINIA: R. Garison, A. Beloach, J. Kerkmon, 3 Merits, W. Carnes, D. Hawks, P. Hume, F. Henderson, J. Ferines, G. Derom, S. Walker, 4 Mathises, L. Wiseman, S. Washborn, E. Cockburn, W. Milbern—a total of 21.

MARYLAND: W. Gwins, H. Brown, F. Smith, G. Dotherd, S. Strawn, 3 Morgans, D. Hayes, 4 Hobees, H. McGleton, S. McWrite, J. Wilkit, 2 Fishers, M. Hains, C. Paron, G. McWatters, A. Cuthbut, W. Leemon, S. Winston, D. Read, M. O'Conel, T. Goodin—a total of 27.

FLORIDA: E. Carmeter, W. Hargeret, S. Whipel, A. Sterling, B. Stafford, L. McGuint, G. Flush, C. Winkle, 2 McGillits, E. Foshew, J. Beark, J. Preston, 3 Baggets—a total of 16.

LOUISIANA: C. Deport, J. Bevley, J. Johnson, A. Pelkin, A. Rhone, T. McNut, H. Pelton, W. Bryant, 4 Hunts, 2 Baleys, S. Roberson, J. Sims, G. Murry, R. Miler, C. Henderson, 2 Derris, D. Willis, P. Read, S. McCarty, W. Moss, D. Cotton, F. Parker, L. Duncan, M. Bluren, S. Muret, G. Pase, T. Ray—a total of 32.

TRANSIENT MEMBERS WHO TRAVEL FROM PLACE TO PLACE: 2 Hains, S. Coper, G. Boalton, R. Haris, P. Doddrige, H. Helley, C. Moris, 3 Rinens, L. Tailor, 2 Jones, H. Sparkes, 3 Levits, G. Hunter, G. Tucker, S. Skerlock, Soril Phelps—a total of 22.

It must be remembered that Stewart was writing rapidly and had little time to ask for exact spellings, even if the outlaw knew them. Therefore misspellings of some names are probable. For example Hues might sometimes be Hughes; Boalton could be Bolton; Howel, Howell; Pots, Potts (Billy Potts, perhaps?); Haris, Harris; Moris, Morris; Miler, Miller; Baley, Bailey, and so on. One of the names in Arkansas, Darte, should have been spelled Dark. We know that Colonel Jarot of Tennessee spelled his name Jarrott.

Great efforts later were made to discredit this list, to which Stewart swore, as an invention of his mind. But some of the names in the catalog included persons well known in their communities, whom Stewart, who had lived only in Georgia in his youth, in Tennessee for a time, and in Mississippi for a few months, could not possibly have known, except through someone else—Murrell, undoubtedly.

The weight of the list is shown by the fact that it contained two persons who could write Colonel before their names, five who were Captains, and three who were Squires.

Family ties seem to run through it. For example, the name Crenshaw occurs in Tennessee and Georgia, and the "D. Crenshaw" must have been Daniel Crenshaw himself, Murrell's first tutor in crime. We find Nolins in Tennessee and Alabama. The Alabama Nolin was the overseer who was "decoying" Negroes for Murrell, and all of them were perhaps related to his "wife" from the Pinch Gut district. Names like Forrow, Roberson, Haines, Skerlock, and others are repeated in different states.

The two Murrells of Tennessee were, of course, the outlaw chief and his brother William. One of the six "Hueses" was Stewart himself!

On that list was Eli Chandlor who was to take Parson Henning out and give him a terrible whipping, described by Murrell as "a second Caesar." In the Mississippi roster was Captain Isham Medford, who later was to be whipped and confess many Clan secrets. G. Tucker, in the same state, would one day threaten Stewart's life. The Glenns of Mississippi also would appear in subsequent events. The D. Cotton of Louisiana was the "Doctor" Cotton who was one day to hang, with others, for his confessed share in the conspiracy. George Aker, of Arkansas, would later come hunting Stewart to murder him.

Already Stewart had in person met some of the "Transient Members"—those closest to Murrell's councils: Samuel Roberson of Louisiana, S. Skerlock, James Haines, Perry Doddridge, one of the Lloyds and Jehu Barney. He knew that Soril Phelps of that same inner group was at the moment lying in the Vicksburg jail, with a probable hanging sentence awaiting him.

All in all, the list Stewart took down from Murrell's lips, partial as it was, sounds authentic; and there were yet other names of the Clan, not given on it because of the lack of writing space, that were destined to play a part in events later.

Murrell was half apologetic for the paucity of his roster. "There aren't near all the names on this list, but there's no more paper to write on. Hues, I want you to be with me at New Orleans, on the night the Negroes commence their ravages. I intend to head the company myself that attacks that city. I feel an ambition to demolish the city which was defended from the British army by the great General Jackson."

So at last they parted, and Murrell rode away, a darkly impressive figure superbly sitting his fine horse.

6.

Stewart rode a short way down the side-trail, then waited until he was sure Murrell had gone far enough ahead for safety, before he in turn rode into Wesley, where he returned the pistol he had borrowed from Colonel Bayliss. That night he spent at the house of a friend, and the next day, February 6, proceeding cautiously, arrived after dark at the home of the Reverend John Henning without attracting any special attention.

There he related his story. Very quietly, the same night, a group of men who were known to be trustworthy, were brought in and the circumstances revealed to them. They were all for immediate action.

"They determined," Stewart later wrote, "never again to trust so fearful and dangerous an enemy beyond their reach. He was now in their power and they were resolved to make sure of him."

But this in part defeated Stewart's purpose. He wanted to arrest Murrell in the act of delivering stolen Negroes to Erwin. But his objections were overruled, the posse was impatient.

Early next morning, February 7, a band of six men, all well armed, rode up to Murrell's house. The posse consisted of Stewart, Richard G. Henning, David Henning (probably a relative), George Hicks, R. H. Byrn, and William H. Long. At least three of these had suffered from Murrell's depredations—Richard Henning, Byrn and Long. Apparently Stewart lingered outside when the others entered the house, in order that the outlaw would gain no instant knowledge of why the posse was calling on him.

For once Murrell was taken completely by surprise. Though on a previous occasion he had summoned his men and planned a deadly ambush when threatened by just such a raid as this, on this day he seemed to have no inkling of an action against him, and surrendered meekly and with some questions in his mind.

"Who went with you to Arkansas?" the leader of the posse (probably Richard Henning) asked.

"A young man by the name of Hues," said Murrell, sullenly.

"Had you ever seen him before he went with you to Arkansas?"

"Never, until I saw him at the bridge at Estanaula, on my way to Arkansas," the prisoner replied.

He was then confronted by Stewart. At the sight of him, "the countenance of the arch-demon fell, and for the first time in his life, his self-possession and wonted firmness forsook him."

He knew now why he was arrested. The things he had revealed to this accuser!

Though he felt that the consequences were appalling, something else went even deeper into Murrell's heart. The thought that he, who prided himself on seeing through others and imposing on them, had been so cozened by a mere youth whom he had imagined he had captivated and bedazzled, wounded him where it hurt the most—in his enormously swollen conceit. For a time he was stunned, like a bruised snake.

But on the way to Jackson, the county seat, where he was to be held for court, he began to recover some of his equanimity.

"Who is this man Hues?" he asked one of his guards. "Does he have many acquaintances in this country?"

The guard, anxious to hear what he would say, replied, "He's a stranger."

"Well, he'd better remain a stranger," growled Murrell. "I have friends. I'd much rather be in my condition than his."

At Jackson he was not at first placed in a jail, but lodged in a tavern, where he was watched by armed men.

Inevitably, a curious crowd gathered to see the prisoner, and since Stewart no longer felt the need of an assumed name, he was referred to freely by his real name. It was thus that Murrell discovered that he did not even know the young man by his true name, and his astonishment and chagrin grew greater. "His spirits, which a little before had seemed to revive, now sunk, and Murrell, though a mystic chief, found himself involved in a mystery he could not unfold."[4]

[4] In view of later efforts to discredit Stewart as a "disgruntled member of Murrell's gang who turned traitor," a very important statement was signed by the guards who captured the outlaw and took him to Jackson. It was sworn to by all of them, October 10, 1835, in Madison County, Tennessee, and it verified all the circumstances of Murrell's arrest, including the questions and answers above quoted, by which the guards were satisfied from Murrell's own statements that he had never known Stewart before their recent journey together, and did not even know his right name until after his arrest. The signatories, Richard G. Henning, David M. Henning, George Hicks, R. H. Byrn, and William H. Long, all were men of the highest standing and probity.

XVII.   *Trial and Ordeal*

1.

In his testimony before the committing court, Stewart told only of the abduction and subsequent disposition of Parson Henning's two slaves, as related to him by Murrell. He did not at that time reveal the full scope and nature of the man's organization, or the dark and desperate plot against the entire country.

This he felt would be too incredible for belief, unless the public mind was in some manner prepared to receive it. Murrell's confederates "in high places" would at once discredit the story as "fantastic," and he feared it would so be regarded by most people.

There was danger, also, that if he told the story of the Mystic Clan and its ramifications, its very incredibility might create an impression that Murrell was being persecuted by a weaver of wild tales. For the sake of strengthening his testimony he therefore withheld, for the present, his greater secret, even though it meant daily peril for himself.

The outlaw chief had named a date—December 25, 1835—for the Clan's prepared uprising of the Negroes. It was now only February of

1834. With almost two years ahead, he hoped he might be able to present to the world the full desperation of the scheme in such a manner that it would be accepted and prepared against.

On Stewart's testimony Murrell was held for trial the next July, before the district court. This time he was not taken to a tavern, but to the jail, where he was committed February 8, 1834.

Stewart and his friends believed they should try to obtain stronger evidence for the final trial. If they could find, for example, the lost Negroes, it would be a telling point against the outlaw.

For this reason, though he knew he was exposing himself to "bloodthirsty and subtle enemies," and "saw before him but one dark and cheerless prospect of uncertainty and danger, perhaps of death and disgrace," Virgil Stewart rode south with Richard Henning toward the Yazoo country in Mississippi, where Murrell had said the Strykers were to take the slaves, "if they could cross the Choctaw Pass," where the water sometimes was very low.

Their route took them through the Choctaw Purchase, and the very neighborhood where Stewart had his home and personal property, which he had left in care of Matthew Clanton and William Vess. Clanton seemed glad to see him, welcoming him as an old friend, and at this point Stewart made a grave mistake.

The supposedly upright Clanton—who at one time for a short period sat as a judge in Tennessee—was secretly a member of Murrell's Clan. Not knowing this, Stewart confided to him the whole story of the plot, including the names of some of Clanton's own friends who were listed by Murrell as his accomplices. The storekeeper showed great astonishment—and the astonishment probably was real, together with alarm that Stewart possessed such information. But he assured the young man he would keep the matter secret.

Thinking he had a friend to back him, when in reality he had a treacherous enemy, Stewart then rode on with Henning to the Yazoo country. They found no trace of the Negroes. At the time Murrell's boat was supposed to cross the Choctaw Pass, water conditions were wrong for navigation. They concluded, therefore, that the slaves were taken somewhere else, perhaps over into Louisiana.[1]

The young men separated, Henning going to Vicksburg for further inquiries, while Stewart visited Thomas Hudnold, named by Murrell as one of his victims, and from him obtained an affidavit telling of Murrell's criminal activities, and a promise to testify against him if called upon at the trial. He also obtained an affidavit from Willis Hig-

[1] Subsequently the abducted Negroes were actually found—and recovered—in Avoyelles Parish, Louisiana.

ginbotham, describing how Higginbotham had purchased the Negro youth Tip, for a "widow woman" named Mrs. Powers, who was moved by her slave girl's pleas that she wanted Tip for a husband; and how Mrs. Powers lost Tip through the theft by Murrell, and also her seven hundred dollars, "which broke her."

2.

For the present, Stewart had done all he could do. Now he returned to his sadly neglected affairs in Yalobusha County, Mississippi. Hardly had he arrived there, taking lodgings as before with William Vess, when he learned not only that everyone in the neighborhood knew of Murrell's arrest, but that a story was current of the exposure of the outlaw conspiracy, which he had never publicly told. In addition, he discovered that efforts were being made to blacken his own character, as if to discredit him.

It does not seem to have occurred to Stewart at this time that the information about Murrell and the conspiracy could have been bruited about by Clanton. He thought too highly of the man, who had promised complete secrecy.[2]

Bewildered, he returned to Tennessee. There he found the same story in circulation. At the same time he began to receive anonymous threats of "vengeance" should he reveal the names believed to be in his possession.

With deepening apprehension he rode back to Mississippi, feeling that he was "exposed to the united vengeance of a whole confederacy of exasperated and blood-hungry ruffians." He was right; although he did not know it, word already had gone out that he must be killed and the damning papers he carried destroyed.

Fortunately he traveled south with extreme caution, taking unusual routes, speaking to few, spacing his rides sometimes days apart. It took him much longer than such a journey would ordinarily require, but at last he reached his destination without serious incident.

Both Clanton and Vess seemed startled by his arrival. Why? Because the two knew of the Clan's order to murder him, and his return from Tennessee was so slow that they assumed he was put safely out of the way—when suddenly he appeared before them.

Stewart thought nothing of their strange surprise. On Clanton's sug-

[2] He might have noticed a name *Clanin* on his list of Murrell's accomplices in Mississippi, had he dreamed that this was a mispronunciation and misspelling of Clanton. But no such thought occurred to him.

gestion he continued to lodge with Vess, a shiftless fellow, "a mechanic
though a very lazy and indolent man." Vess had done some work for
both Clanton and Stewart. The latter did not know how closely Clanton and Vess were working in a more sinister direction now.

Soon after taking his old lodgings Stewart, in going through his effects, found that some articles had been stolen. He asked Vess about
it, but both Vess and his wife declared they had not opened his chest,
nor had anyone else except Clanton, who had done so on one occasion
"to get a powder flask." Since Clanton had Stewart's permission to do
this the young man said nothing of the theft for fear of throwing suspicion on the man he believed was his friend.

A few days later a ruffian named George Tucker—one of those on
Murrell's list—while apparently drunk became very abusive and threatened Stewart's life. Stewart was a member of the local regulators,
which had been formed in absence of other law enforcement. He
went before this body and lodged accusations. Strangely—as he
thought at the time—Clanton refused to attend the meeting.

The regulators called on Tucker, took him into custody, tried him,
and dealt with him "according to the law"—presumably whipped him
—and ordered him to leave the country. He obeyed.

A second case did not go so smoothly. The regulators seemed mysteriously to increase in numbers, and when a man named Glenn—also
on Murrell's roster—was questioned in connection with a crime, he was
quickly acquitted and freed. Stewart now believed that the added
members of the body probably all were associates in the great conspiracy, and withdrew from the regulators.

He began to fear everyone. Returning late one night from a land
surveying trip, he drank a cup of coffee at the Vess house and became
violently ill. Afraid that he had been poisoned, he took warm draughts
of water to cause him to vomit. But all that night he felt great debility
and spasmodic symptoms.

Next morning he was sufficiently recovered to ride, and returned
to the area of public lands which were offered for sale, to take the
numbers of plots on which he hoped in the future to make bids.

As he rode back to the settlement late that afternoon, a mounted
stranger cantered up from behind and ranged alongside of him.

3.

The man was bearded, dirty and grim. He was armed with two
holstered pistols and a large "buoyer" (bowie) knife. Stewart at once
saw that he was dangerous.

After the usual greetings of strangers, the man asked, "Say, do ye know anybody in the country around Troy—like a family, name of Glenn?"

Troy was a new town in eastern Yalobusha County, and there were three Glenns on the Murrell list—one of whom had been questioned, though acquitted, by the regulators. Stewart made a noncommittal reply.

"Well, then," pursued the stranger, "are ye acquainted with a man by the name of V. A. Stewart?"

Now fully alert, the young man replied cautiously. "Yes, sir, just as well as I'd want to be with all such fellows."

"Ye don't like him much?"

"I've seen people I liked as well."

The ruffian considered for a moment. Then, "Any pertic'lar objection to this feller Stewart?"

"Yes, many," said Stewart, convinced that he was dealing with a member of the Clan.

"I'd like to hear 'em, becuz I don't like him much myself."

"Oh, he's too smart," said Stewart. "Interferes with things that don't concern him. He had no right to take the advantage he did of a man by the name of Murrell."

A sudden, sharp look from the stranger. "Do ye understand this?" He gave his hand a flirt, the sign of the Strykers.

Stewart replied with the prescribed signal.

"Oh, yes," said the stranger. "You're up to it. Glad to see ye, sir; what's yer name?"

He offered his hand. Stewart gave him the grip of the Grand Council—a shake with two fingers crossed on the palm.

"I've got several names," said he. "But when I wish to be smart, or successful in a speculation, I go by the name of Tom Goodin. I see you're a master of mystic signs—what's your name, sir?"

"My name is George Aker, sir." Stewart well knew that name. "G. Aker" was a member of the Arkansas list of the Clan. "I'm on a mission from the Council to stop the wind of Stewart," went on the ruffian. "Kin ye help me?"

"Yes, sir," replied Stewart coolly. And he added, "I didn't know there'd been a meeting on the subject."

"We collected an' consulted on plans to deestroy the rascal," Aker said. "We've got him in a close box—why, he's livin' with his enemies! We'll give him hell afore we quit him. The plan is to git Murrell out'n prison; an' after that git a charge ag'inst Stewart that'll ruin his character. When court sits, Murrell will appear for trial, which'll convince the world that he's innocent of the charge. Even if Stewart appears ag'inst him, nobody'll believe him, for we'll prove him one of the biggest rascals a-livin'. Murrell's shore to be acquitted."

The Arkansawyer paused to give Stewart a wink and a laugh. Then he went on: "But we ain't intendin' to let Stewart live to testify. We'll disgrace him—an' kill him, too. Got it all fixed—the fellow he's with is a friend of the Clan, an' we've promised him a thousand dollars to raise a charge ag'inst Stewart. He's a big fish—anything he says will be believed. I'm told he's a confidential friend of Stewart's, an' they've done business for each other. It'd be easy for him to make an accusation, but he won't agree to do it until Stewart's killed. We hired an old man an' his wife to poison him for a hundred dollars, but they ain't done it for some reason, an' we're tired of waitin'. So they made up two hundred dollars for me to kill the traitor. If I don't git a chance at him, we intend to bring men from Arkansaw to swear he passed counterfeit money on 'em, an' arrest him an' take him back with 'em. Once we have him in the morass, *we'll give him hell!* We'll give him something to *keep him busy* besides actin' as a spy!"

Stewart had heard his own death sentence pronounced. But he did not panic. Instead, he said, in his best conspiratorial manner:

"I know the man—all his habits, where he walks, and where he sleeps, just as well as he does. And I'm not in the least suspected by any person; so you see I can fix him."

Aker grinned through his tangle of whiskers. "I'll split with ye—give ye a hundred dollars to help me git his scalp." Then he added a piece of information which to Stewart, at least, was startling: "I expect the company that went to git Murrell out of jail done so more'n a week ago."

Murrell out of jail! Perhaps the arch-criminal already was on the loose again! To Stewart it came as a severe shock.

"Whar do ye live, Goodin?" Aker asked.

"I'm like a stray dog, sir. I have neither home nor master, and stay longest where the speculations are best."

"Think ye kin kill Stewart tonight, an' meet me tomorrow an' let me hear the news?"

"I'll meet you in the morning," said Stewart, and mentioned a place on the road to Glenn's. When they parted Aker actually gave him a hundred dollars in advance—for committing his own murder!

Stewart was now convinced that Mrs. Vess had tried to murder him by poison. But there was something even more alarming. Aker's words returned to him: "He's a big fish—anything he says will be believed. I'm told he's a confidential friend of Stewart's, and they've done business for each other."

That could only mean *Matthew Clanton*.

Now he knew where the story came from that he possessed the Clan roster—from his supposed friend, the man he had trusted with his secret. He was in the midst of enemies; he began to think that perhaps everyone he knew here was a member of the Clan, watching him, ready to strike.

That night he did not sleep at Vess's. Instead he went to the house of George N. Saunders, who had a good reputation in the community. Saunders was, to be sure, known to be a friend of Clanton's; but then Stewart himself had counted Clanton as his friend. He seemed to have nowhere else to turn.

Next morning he rose early to meet Aker. This time he was armed, as he had not been the night before.

But though he waited for hours at the appointed place, Aker did not appear. Stewart at length departed, unpleasantly convinced that somehow Aker—perhaps through the Glenns—had learned his real identity and disappeared for fear of being denounced and arrested.

To cap all this, when he returned to the settlement he received a letter from a friend in Tennessee. Aker had been all too correct in his prediction.

Murrell had escaped from prison.

4.

With the arch-demon loose to plan the movements of his Clan, certainly with the assassination of Stewart as one of his prime objectives, the situation had grown very much more serious.

Stewart visited Clanton, who had circulated a rumor that in the few weeks the young man operated his store, while Clanton was away—he had done so "in an unsatisfactory manner"—with a strong hint that he had been dishonest. Stewart "cautioned" his treacherous acquaintance against making slanderous remarks, and in order not to be obligated to him in any way, returned to Clanton the deed for the building lot once given him by that worthy.

But now he had reached a state of some despair. After thinking things over with a mind greatly perturbed, he appointed Saunders as his agent in place of Clanton—a confidence misplaced as events proved—and started north toward Tennessee, riding carefully as before by a roundabout route. He planned to go to Lexington, Kentucky, to prepare and have printed Murrell's confessions, because he felt his only resource was to get before the world the nature of the great conspiracy.

In due time he reached the Henning home, where at last he could feel safe for the night. Next day he rode east toward Randolph, where he intended to take a steamboat up the Mississippi, and then up the Ohio to Louisville, Kentucky, from which it was only a short stage ride to Lexington.

A few miles along the road to Randolph, he heard a horse galloping behind him. Stewart drew his mount to a halt and turned, pistol drawn, expecting to defend his life. But the lathered horse pursuing him was ridden by his friend, Richard Henning.

"News! News!" Henning cried. "They've caught Murrell again! He was captured at Florence, Alabama, and they're bringing him back to Jackson for trial!"

It was a most accidental turn that led to the outlaw's recapture. He was traveling in a grain wagon, and had stepped out to have a bite of food at a tavern when someone—there is no record of his identity—recognized him and called officers. A few miles down the road the grain wagon was overtaken and Murrell surrendered when he saw the pistols looking his way.

To Stewart the news was in some sort a relief. With Murrell behind the bars, he reasoned, the Clan might hesitate for the time being to murder the state's most important witness, since this would be, in a manner, a confession of guilt on the part of Murrell, and would arouse public indignation as it had not yet been aroused.

In an instant he changed his plans and returned with Henning to his home to await the day of the trial. During the weeks following, in spite of his reasoning that the Clan would go slow in acting against him, he spent most of his time indoors; and when he went abroad he was well armed and accompanied by two or more of his friends.

When Murrell, heavily manacled and guarded, was brought back to Jackson, Stewart was shown a letter which was found in the outlaw's possession at the time of his arrest. This, later read in evidence against Murrell during his trial, gave a key to Clanton's mysterious conduct, and revealed some other matters of high importance.

The letter—according to a true copy attested to by H. W. McCorry, clerk of the district court of Madison County, September 29, 1835—read strangely, as follows:

> This day personally appeared before us &c Jahu [Jehu] Barney, James Tucker, Thomas Dark, Joseph Dark, Wm. Lloyd &c, who being sworn in due form of law, did depose and say, that they were present and saw————Stewart of Yellow Busha [Yalobusha] in the evening of the first day of February last, in company with John Murrell at the house of Jahu Barney, over the Mississippi River; and that the said Stewart, informing us, that he was in pursuit of John Murrell, for stealing two Negro men from Preacher Henning and his son Richard, in

Madison County, near Denmark; and that he had told Murrell his name was Hues, and he wished us to call him Hues in Murrell's hearing—we also recollect to have heard him, the said Stewart, say distinctly that he was to get five hundred dollars for finding the said Negroes, & causing Murrell to be convicted for stealing them—But he did not say, who was to give him this reward—But he held the obligation of several rich men for that amount, &cc.

The above is a *copy* given to me, by one who heard him say it, in the presence of you all. You will therefore please to send me the names of all, that will testify these facts in writing—also send me the names of all and every man that will certify these witnesses to be men of truth &cc.

J. † † MURRELL

But above all things, arrest him, the said witness, for passing the six twenty dollar bills—You will have to go out in Yellow Busha, in Yellow Busha County, near the centre, for him, and undoubtedly, this matter will be worth your attention—for if it be one or two or three hundred dollars, the gentleman to whom he passed it can present it before a magistrate and take a judgment for that amount; and his little provision store acc's &cc. is worth that much money.

I shall conclude with a claim on you for your strictest attention. My distressed wife will probably call on you, and if she does, you may answer all her requests without reserve.

Yours &cc.   J. † † ‡ ‡ MURRELL

Dear wife, I am in tolerable health, and I hope this will find you all well; I am of opinion that the business, that I was endeavoring to effect, will be done, in the course of this week—On last night there was a man committed, which is no little PITY. † †

The first paragraph was signed by Murrell with two crosses between his initial and name. The second part of the letter was signed with two single crosses and two double crosses between initial and name. The message to his wife was signed only by two crosses. Whether this cabalistic method of signature had a code meaning has never been determined.

But the document itself is easily interpreted. The first paragraph is simply a form of affidavit which Murrell wished to have signed and attested by his friends before a notary. When captured it was neither dated, signed, nor attested, though it was in Murrell's handwriting.

Its object was to make it appear that Stewart was hired to capture Murrell, which might throw prejudice against his testimony because of the alleged monetary interest of five hundred dollars for convicting the outlaw. As we have seen, it was sworn by Reverend John Henning and his son that though they offered to pay Stewart for his time and trouble—no five hundred dollars, however—he refused absolutely to accept one penny from such good friends.

All the men suggested in the Murrell manuscript as possible attestors—Barney, Tucker, the two Darks, and Lloyd—were members of the Arkansas branch of the Clan, included in the list given by Murrell to Stewart, although on that list the name Dark was spelled Darte by a natural error of hearing the name rapidly given as the young man wrote.

The second paragraph of the manuscript, after the affidavit form, was one of instructions to the Clan, to see that the instrument was signed, and for the gathering of witnesses—members of the Clan—to swear to it and to the "truth" of the men who did so swear. Interestingly, Stewart saw none of these men at Jehu Barney's house, he and Murrell, with Barney himself, being the only persons present that night.

The third paragraph (after the first signature) was a direction for a false charge of circulating counterfeit money to be lodged against Stewart—to the length of using this perjured testimony to foreclose on his small property. As Aker already had unwittingly informed Stewart, this was the plan whereby he would be carried over to Arkansas under "arrest," where in the "morass" they would "give him hell"—torture him—before killing him. The mention of the "six twenty dollar bills" evidently referred to spurious paper Murrell knew was in the hands of his accomplices.

There was also the injunction that if his "distressed wife" called on these people, they should "answer all her requests without reserve." Since the Pinch Gut girl had been admitted to his cell during his imprisonment at Jackson, before his escape, she evidently carried Murrell's secret orders to his men.

The final paragraph, after the second signature, which was directed to his wife—who evidently was to see that this information reached the proper hands—included a cryptic sentence. "I am of the opinion that the business I was endeavoring to effect will be done in the course of this week." That business, without much question, was to have been the assassination of Stewart by Aker; and it failed only because Stewart was able, by the mystic signs, to convince Aker that he was somebody other than he was. It will be remembered that Aker told Stewart that Murrell probably already had escaped from prison when the two had their colloquy.

The man "committed, which is no little PITY," was unnamed, but he must have been one of Murrell's upper echelon of lieutenants upon whom the outlaw chief had depended for an important role in all the activities outlined in his instructions.

Thus the whole conspiracy of murder, and failing that, of character destruction—by Clanton and others—was revealed by the letter which, fortunately, Murrell had no chance to post before his arrest.

5.

At last, late in July, the great outlaw was brought to trial. With Judge Haskell presiding, a jury was impaneled, and the case began before a crowd which packed the Jackson courtroom to utmost capacity. Murrell had obtained eminent counsel to defend him. Chief of his legal battery was Milton Brown, who later went to Congress and gained for himself a paragraph in history by introducing in that body the resolution whereby Texas was annexed to the United States. He was assisted by Colonel John Read of Jackson, and another lawyer named Harris. Attorney General Alexander B. Bradford prosecuted, assisted by Major A. L. Martin. Throughout, Stewart was the chief witness for the state.

From the Choctaw Purchase now came a flood of accusations, some charging Stewart with outright theft. These depositions were presented by the defense attorneys. They were met by character witnesses for Stewart and by persons who had personal knowledge of the property involved and who could testify that the witness being attacked acquired it in an honest and legal manner.

In spite of the attacks upon him by the defense Stewart told his story clearly and calmly to the judge and jury. Milton Brown used every trick in his power to shake him. For two full days he put the witness through the most severe cross-examination, trying in every possible way to trip him and make him contradict himself—all without the slightest success.

At the conclusion of the trial, in his summation before the jury, Brown stretched the latitude allowed a lawyer almost beyond the point where he might be cited for contempt of court, and furiously lashed Stewart's character without a scintilla of evidence to back his statements: accusing the young man of being a fraud, a secret friend of Murrell's, a member of the outlaw gang who had become disgruntled and turned to treachery, a thief and a villain.

Stewart was understandably very angry. He said to his friends after adjournment of court on the last night, "I'll give him [Brown] a Stanbery reproof for that!"[3] But his friends dissuaded him. They argued

[3] By this he referred to the drubbing Congressman Stanbery received not long before at the hands of General Sam Houston for libelous remarks he made on the floor of Congress.

that it would only harm the case against Murrell if Murrell's attorney were attacked. Stewart bowed to their judgment: but those accusations by Brown, groundless though they were, remained to haunt him throughout his life.

When the case was committed into its hands, the jury took very little time for deliberation. Murrell was told to rise as the jury returned from the jury room and took its place in the jury box.

"Gentlemen of the jury, have you arrived at a verdict?" asked Judge Haskell.

"We have," replied the foreman.

"What is it?" asked the judge.

"We find the defendant, John A. Murrell, guilty of Negro stealing as charged."

"And so say you, all of you?"

Every juryman replied in the affirmative.

The man who reduced villainy to a system and carried on a cruel and brutal war against the entire human family, which he plotted to increase to proportions of unspeakable horror, had come to the end of his career.

6.

In one respect Murrell was lucky. He might have been convicted, had the evidence been a little more comprehensive, of murder, many times over, and sent to the gallows.

Nevertheless, the arch-criminal's face went ashy white when he stood before the judge's bench and heard himself sentenced to ten years at hard labor in the state penitentiary.

He had reason for that pallor. In his day a penal institution was regarded strictly as what its name implied—a place of punishment. "Do-gooders," amateur or professional, with schemes to "rehabilitate" prisoners were conspicuously scarce; and if there had been any such they would have been regarded as exponents of nonsense, if not enemies of the commonwealth.

Just what happened to Murrell during his prison term we have no way of knowing. But Stephen Burroughs, a notorious criminal and escape artist in the latter part of the eighteenth century, left a vivid and at times bloodcurdling picture of treatment in prisons at that time.[4]

Burroughs, convicted of passing counterfeit money, was sentenced

[4] *Memoirs of the Notorious Stephen Burroughs of New Hampshire.*

to three years in prison. He tried to escape, received ten lashes with a whip, and was chained in his cell. Wrote he:

> They in the first place made fast a ring around my leg, about six inches wide and an inch thick. This was connected with a chain weighing about thirty-six pounds and ten feet in length. The other end of the chain was fastened to the timber composing our floor, with a staple driven in with a sledge, which made the whole jail tremble. After I was fixed in this manner, the deformed Vulcan [a blacksmith] and his grisley Cyclops [journeyman blacksmith] left me to my own reflections, inwardly exulting at their mighty power in making a poor soul secure from enjoying the cold comfort of better times.

His leg iron so tortured him that it took the skin off and wore a living sore in his flesh. In desperation he set fire to his cell, preferring to die in the flames rather than live in these conditions. Other prisoners aroused the guards with their cries for help and Burroughs was rescued with the rest.

Next day he was taken into the courtyard, "tied to the grates," stripped naked, and given twenty lashes. Then he was placed in a different cell, and confined in the following manner: A large iron ring was welded about each leg, the rings connected by an iron bar which in turn was bolted to the floor. An iron belt was welded about his waist and this, too, was bolted to the floor. His wrists were confined by iron handcuffs.

In this condition, hardly able to move, he was left without fire in a cold winter month, with little clothing, a pitiful allowance of straw to sleep on, and was starved until a relative left two dollars to buy him food. Through the intervention of an uncle he was relieved of his terrible iron bonds after thirty-two days. He was by then emaciated almost to a skeleton, with uncut beard, uncombed hair, a sore on his leg from which he never recovered, and he had "more the appearance of some savage beast of the forest than anything appertaining to the human species."

Though well educated—at Dartmouth College—Burroughs by his own confession was guilty of numerous crimes. He passed counterfeit money, for which he was convicted; he was charged with the rape (of a statutory nature, he claimed) of three young girls, two of them in his charge as pupils in a school of which he was master, and convicted in two of the instances; was charged with thievery and lay in jail for it; impersonated a minister, without ordination, for the sake of the easy life it gave him; was exposed, and joined a confidence man who defrauded people by claiming to be able to transmute copper into silver, and who also was a "coiner"; and performed other acts, criminal or shady.

Yet it is hard not to feel sorry for him. After the rigor of his bonds was eased, he still contemplated escape. Now came a curious episode illustrative of the penal systems of the times.

One of Burroughs' fellow prisoners was a man named Hinds, who "was committed for adultery with the wife of one Wallace," the woman also being held in prison. With surprising laxity the head jailer allowed this man and the woman to have liberty in an alley between the cell houses, "for a criminal connection." There, in the hearing, if not in full view, of the other prisoners, the couple disported themselves for an hour each day at the very activity for which they had been committed, after which they were returned to their respective cells.

Burroughs learned later that Hinds was an informer, who was given "as compensation, liberty to be alone with his Miss one hour in the course of every day." It was Hinds who revealed the next escape attempt, in which a man named Norton, charged with murder, was Burroughs' accomplice. Burroughs once more was bolted to the floor.

Shortly after this he, with some other prisoners, was removed to another prison: Castle Island, in Boston Harbor. Though the island was occupied by an old fort and guarded by troops, Burroughs managed to lead an escape by himself and seven others.

He was quickly recaptured while hiding in a barn. This time he and the seven were sentenced to one hundred lashes each with a cat-o'-nine-tails. They were "punished with great severity, the flesh flying off at every stroke." Burroughs, held by irons to the whipping post, felt "the blood stream at every stroke, so that my shoes were filled by the time I was taken down." He was in a state of collapse, from which it took him three months to recover.[5]

All of this took place during a three-year sentence. Eventually Burroughs was freed and lived out his life, writing his memoirs which were published in 1811.

There is no record that I have been able to obtain of the circumstances of Murrell's imprisonment. But it must have been severe. He

[5] Worse brutalities than this were not uncommon, even in the military and naval services. John Preble in his fine book *Culloden* records that in the British army marching against the Highlanders of Scotland in the rising of 1745, men "received anything from the minimum of twenty-five strokes to the maximum of three thousand," with a whip, "the nine-tailed cat with knots of precise size." In the navy men were whipped for slight infractions of discipline, even for being the last down from the mast when they were furling or unfurling sails. For striking an officer, a seaman was "flogged through the fleet," being taken through the entire flotilla, flogged before each ship to a dolorous tune on the file and rattle of the drums, until at the end he was usually dead, the flesh literally beaten from his back until the organs of his body could be seen through the gaps in his ribs.

left the penitentiary a broken man. One thing he did acquire—a trade. Among the various occupations to which prisoners were put at the penitentiary was that of blacksmithing. John Murrell, who had never done one useful thing in all his life, learned enough blacksmithing to be able to operate a small shop for the short time he lived after he obtained his freedom.

XVIII.   *To Break the Mystic Clan*

1.

Murrell was in prison, but the Mystic Clan still existed—without a leader now, but with a brooding purpose which was a threat to the entire country. Stewart faced the question of how to avert this threat, and in so doing he faced alone his days of greatest peril.

There were men—many men—who would do almost anything to prevent publication of the roster he held. Shortly after Murrell's sentence to prison, one such man (name not given) approached Stewart suggesting "in the most artful and insinuating manner" that the Clan might be willing to "advance a large amount of money" to have it burned. He rejected this feeler and never knew how large the amount "to be advanced" might have been.

His one great ambition now was to get his disclosures into the hands of a publisher, and since his chief fear was assassination, he stayed secluded in the home of Colonel Thomas Loftin, a good friend of his, where he devoted himself to putting his experiences on paper, in order to furnish a graphic account to go with the list of names.

At last, September 28, 1834, he left Colonel Loftin's hospitable house, planning to ride by circuitous routes, keeping his identity secret, toward Lexington, Kentucky. On the first day of his journey nothing eventful occurred, and he hoped he had escaped the notice of the prowling emissaries of the Clan.

That night he put up at a country house. To his surprise and alarm, four men shortly arrived on horseback, and told the proprietor they wished to spend the night there. All were strangers to Stewart, but he noticed that they studied his appearance most carefully, and asked him questions as to what part of the country he intended to travel, what road he would take, if he intended to cross the Tennessee River, and if so by what ferry.

Questions were natural in a land where rustic curiosity pried as far as possible into the business of others. But to Stewart these men seemed dangerous. He believed they were desperadoes of the Clan, and though they were not sure he was the man they were hunting, they strongly believed he was, and were trying to make certain.

He endeavored to throw them off by saying that he had business in the vicinity and would be there for several days. Later, when he thought he was alone with his host, he asked, "Which is the nearest road to Patterson's Ferry, and how far is it?" This was a crossing of the Tennessee River on the direct route to Columbia, Tennessee, where he planned to turn north toward Lexington by way of Nashville.

His host replied, giving him the information. Stewart retired to his bed, not dreaming that a member of the Clan—as he learned later—had secreted himself to overhear this revealing conversation.

At daybreak next morning the four ugly strangers left. Stewart remained to eat breakfast with his host and family, then mounted his horse and rode eastward toward Patterson's Ferry. The following night he spent at the house of a man named Gilbert, and remained there until the morning of October 2, when again he journeyed on.

In all this time he had seen nothing more of the four men, and he began to think that his fears were without cause, that they were no more than ordinary curious travelers.

But as he progressed along this road, the country grew more wild and desolate, and at length he became uneasy. After a time he took his pistol from his portmanteau, looked to its priming, and then put it in a side pocket of his coat for easier availability.

2.

Two hours passed after he took this precaution, and by that time he was within about eight miles of the ferry. All at once, from behind a copse of bushes ahead, three armed men stepped into the road.

Instinctively Stewart put his hand into his pocket and gripped his pistol. But he did not draw it.

There was a shout from one of the men. "Dismount!"

Stewart reined his horse to a halt. The three were dirty, dangerous, deadly. The rogue who had given the command stood at his right with a shotgun. The one on the left held a long rifle. Just ahead, with his back to a tree, the third ruffian was aiming at him a heavy-barreled horse pistol.

A single glance and Stewart recognized the man on the right—he who had shouted the order and was obviously the leader—as one of the four who had been with him at the farmer's house three evenings before. The other two he had not previously seen, but he was sure all three were assassins.

Their triangular formation—one on either side, the other directly in front, indicated that they meant to take him alive if possible, and failing that, to kill him. Too well Stewart knew what would be his fate if they took him alive—torture at the hands of the Clan. He preferred immediate death.

Yet for a moment he sat silent and motionless on his horse, his hand on the butt of the pistol in his pocket.

The head ruffian grew impatient. "Are ye goin' to dismount or not?" he asked in a menacing growl.

"No!" answered Stewart.

The fellow leveled his shotgun. But Stewart had expected the move. Out came his pistol and he fired it directly into the assassin's face.

The man pitched forward. As he fell, his piece was automatically discharged, but its load of buckshot harmlessly tore up the ground under the horse's belly.

The two sudden reports of the pistol and the shotgun caused Stewart's horse to give a convulsive leap. It saved his life, for in that instant the man with the rifle fired, and the jump of the animal made him miss even at that short distance.

For the moment only the man in front had a loaded weapon. He sighted his pistol grimly for a close and fatal shot.

In desperation Stewart flung his own empty weapon. It struck the ruffian in the face, half stunning him, and though he pulled his trigger the horse pistol misfired.

Meantime the man on the right, wounded apparently in the top of the head by Stewart's pistol shot, but not fatally hurt, scrambled to his feet. Both he and the assassin on the left, having wasted their shots, clubbed their guns.

Stewart felt a heavy blow across the chest from the rifle, and an even heavier blow on his back from the shotgun.

The two blows almost counterbalanced each other, or he very probably would have been hurled out of his saddle. As it was, stunned and dazed, he fell forward on his horse's neck. The terrified animal leaped ahead, out of immediate reach of the men who beset him.

Somehow Stewart clung to the back of his galloping horse as it drew away from the three unmounted assailants. Presently he straightened in his saddle, though weak and dizzy from the blow on the back of his neck and head, which he feared might have fractured a neck vertebra, and also from that on his chest where he felt as if some of his ribs were broken.

In his pain, hardly knowing what he was doing, he swung his horse from the road into the thick woods. As he did so he lifted his left arm as a support for his throbbing head.

From behind came the report of a firearm, and a buckshot struck his uplifted arm, inflicting a painful wound but fortunately breaking no bones.

This, he later judged, must have come from the horse pistol of the assassin who had been directly in front of him. The weapon had misfired when the trigger was first pulled, but its owner could have reprimed it quickly, and since it was the only loaded gun among the three, it only could have been the one fired.

Down a gully in the woods he continued his flight, half fainting in the saddle, until he supposed that he had put at least three miles between himself and his assailants. He dared not return to the road, for fear that another party of the same desperate gang might be ambushed ahead. Incredible luck had enabled him to escape the first trap. It could hardly be counted upon to carry him through a second.

3.

Nausea overcame him. He did not know whether he was being pursued, but he felt he could not ride much farther.

When presently he came to a small stream, he halted his horse, slid from the animal's back, tethered it in a thicket where it could not be seen easily, and dragged himself to the water to drink.

Somewhat refreshed, he managed to regain his feet and walk some distance away from his horse, so that if his pursuers found it, they might not discover him. There, in great pain, he lay down under some bushes.

The long day dragged on. Each sound he heard caused him to start with fear. But at last the sun sank, leaving the forest in darkness.

Half delirious, Stewart slept little that night. "He frequently found himself crawling through the brush and thicket as if under a horrible dream; his feelings were wild and desolate."

Morning came. He was feverish, his neck much swollen and his wounded arm very stiff and sore. But his situation was even worse than his physical condition. How many of the Clan were on his trail, or where he might encounter them, he did not know. But he felt it would be almost certain death to continue his journey to Lexington; and an effort to return to Madison County might be equally fatal.

Late in the afternoon he gained strength to mount again. By this time his mind was made up. He must get out of the country, and by some route which his merciless pursuers would not expect.

He was faint from hunger and wound-sickness, and covered with blood. It occurred to him that his bloody garments themselves would call attention to him; so after about an hour he stopped near a creek, cleansed himself, bound up his arm, and changed his clothes.

Once more he mounted, and took a southerly route, intending to go to Mobile, and from there to some port of Europe, to hide from his enemies with whom his fevered mind seemed to people the entire country about him.

About sunset he passed an isolated farmhouse, but avoided it. Without food, in agony, he rode by unfrequented paths until nearly midnight, when he dismounted, unsaddled his horse, watered it, and hobbled it to graze, while he lay down on the ground without fire or covering. The weather was not cold, but a thick dew fell and during the night he contracted a heavy cold, the racking cough of which added to the misery of his other ills.

Early, the morning of October 4, he was again in the saddle, heading for the Mississippi state line. About eight o'clock he stopped at a farmhouse and asked if he could feed his horse and get a bite to eat. But the farmer stared, made excuses, and began to ask his name, destination, and other questions. Stewart believed the man might be a member of the Clan and rode on.

Shortly before noon he reached another house. There he did obtain food—the first he had tasted in two days—and provender for his horse.

His host seemed kindly and hospitable enough, but Stewart discouraged conversation, said nothing of his ailments, and soon rode away, his fever growing worse, his wounds more inflamed and painful.

In this secretive manner he continued south, stopping where nights overtook him, once at a house in the Chickasaw country, which he later remembered belonged to an old Indian. Days later he reached Columbus, Mississippi, on the Tombigbee River, more than two hundred and fifty miles from his original starting place.

He was by this time in a state of extreme mental and physical torment. But he knew the Mississippi River was west of him, and once more he changed his mind, deciding to reach it and travel by steamboat to New Orleans.

His weakness was growing. He could no longer ride faster than a walk. Finally he fell fainting from his saddle.

A wagon driver found him lying in the road. He managed to get Stewart into the wagon and caught his horse for him. In the jolting vehicle the wounded man regained consciousness, and after a time he felt strong enough to thank the kindly man who had picked him up.

The wagoner, it developed, was taking a different route from that which Stewart wished to follow. So he mounted his horse again, and they parted at a crossroads, with Stewart's renewed thanks.

Shortly after, the hunted fugitive had his first stroke of luck: he met a friend.

4.

In his journal, which was published early in 1835, Stewart concealed the name of this friend, for fear of incurring against him the wrath of the Clan. For sake of identification he called him Watson.

In reality the man's name was Augustus Q. Walton, a Tennessean on a business trip from Memphis. He recognized Stewart; and at once was gravely concerned for him. Though he was heading for Tennessee, he turned and took the wounded man to the nearest house, where he remained with him, caring for him, until the next day.

In those hours Stewart told him the full state of his situation, and entrusted to him something for which he had several times risked his life—the entire manuscript of his experiences with Murrell, the roster of names, and two thousand dollars in cash, almost all the money he possessed, to cover the cost of its printing.

Walton was in haste to return to Tennessee, but so impressed was he by Stewart's story and the gravity of his responsibility, that he promised to see to it. He also advised Stewart where he could find a trustworthy man who would shelter him until he was strong enough to proceed, and promised to meet him as soon as possible at Natchez.

The man thus recommended was James Moore, a planter. Next day, after a ride of ten miles, Stewart reached his home. There he remained for several days, and there he received from Moore and his family the best treatment they knew how to give for his wounds and illness. It was not until the latter part of October that Stewart left his hospitable home and turned his horse's head toward Natchez.[1]

Meeting Walton and lodging with Moore were the turning points in Stewart's fortunes. From this time his affairs mended. He met Walton as agreed, traveled by steamboat to Cincinnati, Ohio, finished work on his manuscript—including his latest adventures—and published his journal, with the roster of names as a pamphlet entitled *A History of the Detection, Conviction and Designs of John A. Murrell, the Great Western Land Pirate*. There was more to the title which ran to great length in the fashion of the day, and the interesting thing concerning the book is that it referred to Virgil A. Stewart throughout in the third person, and set forth as its author Augustus Q. Walton.

Why this expedient in publication was adopted is hard to understand at this late date. Possibly it was because Stewart was ill much of the time, so that Walton did considerable of the work on the manuscript and also dealt with the printers; and also because Stewart was then and later quite secretive for very good reasons about his whereabouts.

Whatever the reasons for the method employed, Stewart at once mailed copies of the eighty-four-page pamphlet to all the principal military and civil officers of the South, and to any persons of prominence whom he could trust.

Quite naturally it created a sensation. It was republished in New Orleans, and later went through various editions, rewritten by other authors some of whom made a penny-dreadful of it.

It was, of course, immediately controversial. While it alarmed many and caused numbers of men to flee from the country,[2] others attempted to brazen it out and discredit it.

[1] A signed statement by James Moore, dated Madison County, Mississippi, December 27, 1835, verifies Stewart's visit; his lodging with him while wounded and sick at his house in the latter part of October, 1834; how Stewart told him he planned to go to Europe, possibly France, to escape the Murrell gangsters who were hunting him; and also that he had placed his papers in the hands of a friend to be made public.

[2] It was at this period that Texas, then still a Mexican province, acquired a considerable accession of undesirable persons, particularly in the Sabine region. It was at this time also that numbers fled north into Illinois and Iowa, then thinly populated, while still others went west, to the Rocky Mountain country as renegades.

In Mississippi, Matthew Clanton (probably Murrell's "Clanin") and Colonel Jarrott (listed in Murrell's roster under the spelling "Jarot") aided by white-haired, venerable-looking George N. Saunders—who was at that very time acting as Stewart's agent—issued statements and swore to falsehoods about the young man.

But Saunders, who until this time had been reckoned a very respectable old man, now was revealed as having a far from reputable past.

Swore Colonel Orville Shelby:

> From his general character here, I should say he was a base man; and whatever he might say or swear to, not entitled to credit.

Swore fifteen Tennessee citizens, their names still of record:

> We are well acquainted with George N. Saunders, and from our knowledge of him and his character, we would not believe him upon oath in a court of justice.

Stated Judge J. Tipton, of Tennessee:

> I am acquainted with George N. Saunders, now of Mississippi; and he is not worth the notice of any man, much less the public.

At the same time friends of Stewart, who had known him throughout his life, came forward in numbers to attest to his honesty and integrity and the truth of his assertions.

Meantime the deadline for the uprising of the slaves, which Murrell had set for December 25, 1835, was still far ahead. The Mystic Clan, deprived of its leader, lay quiescent. Many people began to think the whole tale was fantastic.

They were wrong. The uprising had not been called off. Fearful proofs of it were soon to be forthcoming.

5.

Had John A. Murrell not stolen Parson Henning's Negroes, which he himself, by some inner instinct, felt was the unluckiest act of his life, he would have kept his organization taut, everything arranged so that his coup of savagery and bloodshed, with its overtones of robbery, rape, and murder, would have erupted stunningly on Christmas Day, 1835.

How far would it have progressed? There had been several servile rebellions, of which the most recent was the Nat Turner uprising in Virginia, August 21, 1831. Nat Turner, a Negro preacher, having convinced himself and some of his fellow slaves that he was a divine instrument to lead them out of bondage, got together sixty or seventy of them that fatal night, near Southampton, Virginia, and set out to attack the plantations. For two days and nights death and destruction raged, and fifty-five white men, women, and children were murdered "in the most horrible forms" to quote a description of the time.

By then the militia mustered, the slaves were captured, and the leaders, including Nat Turner, were hanged. The outbreak, however, exercised a profound influence on the South's attitude toward slavery. Virginia, for example, which had emancipation motions for consideration in the legislature of 1831–32, turned from that instead to far more stringent slave laws.

New Orleans also had a slave insurrection in January, 1811, when a frenzied mob of Negroes in the Parish of St. John the Baptist burned five plantations and killed some white people before militia under Major Hilton met them. The Negro "army" was defeated, many of its members killed or hanged, and the others returned to servitude worse than before.

Other revolts had occurred here and there, in each case speedily put down. But Murrell did not reckon on sixty or seventy Negroes— or even five hundred—in his calculations. He plotted to inflame thousands with rum, hatred, lust, and perhaps a gaudy dream of a Negro nation like Haiti, which would appropriate the white man's constructive works, and the white men's loveliest women in a wide area.

Would he have succeeded? Of course not. What Murrell did not understand was the Negroes themselves.

There are always violent and easily influenced individuals in any race group. But in every one of the previous slave rebellions the great mass of the Negroes refused to participate. Partly this was because many of them were wise enough to see that a revolt of this kind could never accomplish the purpose for which it was aimed. They patiently abided the time when freedom would surely come through an aroused conscience of the nation, as it did. Partly, also, it was because many of the slaves were well treated. In some homes they were almost members of the family. They had affections and loyalties they would not violate. Partly also it must have been that many of the more intelligent Negroes saw through the pretensions of the smooth white criminals who were attempting to organize them into a tool for their own purposes.

Nevertheless there would have been vast trouble and death and misery inflicted even by the comparative minority that Murrell would have been able to muster. It might have taken months before the saturnalia of slaughter, sex, and arson was entirely ended and the last diehards hunted down.

In this scheme the Negroes were to be the dupes and victims. On them would fall the final retribution; and when the troops marched and the hangmen finished their work, many innocent persons would suffer with those guilty, and as a race they would be in a condition far worse than before. It is not too much to suggest that the horrors of an uprising on so great a scale as Murrell proposed might have created a reaction even in the North, which would have delayed emancipation by perhaps decades.

But Murrell cared nothing about the Negroes. To him they were only cat's-paws in his giant scheme of looting; and he planned to be far away in the ships he had arranged to meet him at New Orleans before the final day of retribution. He expected then to be richer in goods, valuables, and money than any other pirate ever dreamed to be.

Now, however, with Murrell in a prison cell, the Mystic Clan was like a great many-tentacled monster deprived of its head. It writhed and twisted away into its hiding places, and for a time lay as if in truth it was dead for all time.

Murrell's idea, however, remained alive. It so appealed to some of the Clan that they could not drop it.

In the end, some of the old Murrell followers resolved to attempt the "Negro war" anyway. And in their planning, they hit upon a scheme which had the advantage of surprise.

The South had been warned by Stewart to be alert on Christmas Day, 1835. What if the outbreak started six months *ahead* of that date —on July 4? The South would hardly be expecting that.

The Fourth of July, like Christmas, was a holiday for the slaves, when they were not required to work, and were permitted to mingle together in large groups. The plotters decided upon that date.

But the new scheme had two fatal defects: Murrell was no longer present to direct it; and it did not provide enough time to fully perfect the organization and indoctrinate slaves who might be sufficiently rebellious to participate in it. The men who now were in charge were mere bunglers compared to the criminal genius who first proposed the plan.

XIX. *Tragic Denouement*

1.

Toward the end of June, 1835, Mrs. Reuben Latham, wife of an important cotton planter living at Beattie's Bluff, on the Big Black River, in Madison County, Mississippi,[1] overheard one of her Negro servant girls make a strange remark.

"I wish to God it was over an' done with," said the girl to another of the servants. "I'm tired of waitin' on white folks, an' I want to be my own mistress the balance of my days, an' clean up my own house."

The wish was humanly natural, but Mrs. Latham could not help wondering about the opening remark, "I wish to God it was over an' done with." *What* was to be over and done with?

Shortly after, perhaps next day, she stepped out on her upstairs balcony and heard the voice of the same girl below her. Since this particular servant was a nursemaid to Mrs. Latham's grandchildren who lived at the house, she listened closely to what was said.

[1] Not to be confused with Madison County, Tennessee, in which Murrell and Stewart came to their showdown.

The girl was talking to a Negro man belonging to a neighbor named Landfair—who, incidentally, had no business being there in the first place. Her voice came up to her mistress on the balcony above:

"But ain't it a pity to kill such a purty little baby as this?"

The man's deeper voice replied, "Yes, it is. But it's gotta be done, an' it will be doin' it a big favor, 'cause it'll go to heaven an' escape all the troubles of this here world."

But the girl rebelled. "Go on, kill all you-all wants," she answered. "Won't nobody touch this lamb here. I won't let 'em!"

And the man said, "Won't be no never-could about it. Us got to kill 'em all!"

Now thoroughly alarmed, Mrs. Latham stepped back into the house. She called her son, who confronted the girl with the story.

Remember that this young Negress had already protested against the plan suggested by the man, and had declared that she would protect the child in her care. This was the great flaw in Murrell's plan. There were countless like her who would have no part in the violence he proposed. The great mass of Negroes were too essentially humane, too law-abiding—even when the laws were unjust—to join such an uprising.[2] Even had Murrell been present, he could never have summoned a general revolt of the colored people as he had envisaged, although it is certain that with the comparative few whom he could arm and lead he might have caused enormous harm.

But to return to Mrs. Latham's nursemaid: as soon as the girl knew she had been overheard, she immediately and willingly told all she knew about the conversation, stating that the Negro man had said there would be a rising of the black people *soon*, and that then they would kill all the whites.

The word was quickly spread by the Lathams. A meeting of citizens was held June 27 at Livingston, then county seat of Madison County, an investigating committee appointed, and patrols set up. Three days later William P. Johnson, a planter, confirmed the report that there was talk of a rising among the Negroes—how soon he did not know.

At that a committee of safety was organized. It acted promptly and with great severity—for now Virgil Stewart's warning was at last remembered and assumed a grim reality.

An old Negro man belonging to Johnson was brought before the

[2] This point was forcibly illustrated at the time of John Brown's raid on Harper's Ferry, October 16–18, 1859. In that quixotic foray Brown intended to seize the arsenal with its arms and raise a force of slaves to win liberation by conquest. But *not one slave willingly joined his so-called "army of liberation."* Furthermore, during the Civil War thousands of Negroes willingly and loyally followed their masters through danger and hardship as the Confederate armies battled the North.

committee, refused to tell anything, and was laid upon a table where he was lashed with a blacksnake whip. At once he broke and babbled all he knew—that the black people were going to rise on a certain day and kill all the whites, and that he was involved in the plot. He did not know the exact day, but he said a Negro named Peter, belonging to Ruel Blake, who lived in Livingston, had given him the information, which included a plan to rob a store belonging to William M. Ryce for the several kegs of powder it contained. He implicated no white man, but did name another slave, belonging to Captain Thomas Hudnold—who, it will be remembered, had been victimized by Murrell, and signed an affidavit which helped convict that master criminal. Hudnold's slave, learning he had been denounced, escaped temporarily by taking to the swamps. Later he was captured.

Ruel Blake's slave, Peter, was taken into custody. Under a severe lashing he showed remarkable manhood. He refused to talk, even when he was flogged unmercifully.

"You can whip me till you kill me," he moaned, "but I'll never tell."

At length they ceased the punishment and locked him up with Johnson's man. Among all those implicated, white and black, Ruel Blake's Peter stands out for courage and loyalty. He died confessing nothing, and it was not until later that they found he had taken the whip and even the noose of the gallows to protect his master, Ruel Blake. It was steadfastness worthy of a much better cause.

Thus far no white man had been named by the Negroes "examined," and it was believed at first that the conspiracy was confined to the slaves of a few plantations, fomented by Negro preachers—who had always been blamed for previous conspiracies in the past, whether rightly or wrongly. If the conspiracy was so limited, it was believed there could be little organization or system in its plans.

But now the investigation widened. Several slaves believed to be ringleaders were arrested in the vicinity of Beattie's Bluff. After "two days of patient and scrutinizing examination"—no doubt with the whip —these men all admitted they were in the conspiracy.

Every right-minded person must deplore whipping, and it is true that almost any kind of a confession could be extorted by flogging. But the sinister thing in these cases was that although each Negro was "examined" separately, neither knowing nor suspecting that any other was in custody, *each told the same story*. Not only did they implicate themselves and each other, but several white men.

This last gave new importance to the whole matter, and men began to study over Stewart's warning in his book published some time before. Stewart had said the day set was Christmas Day, 1835; and this was only July. It took some time for the idea to penetrate that the *white* conspirators had advanced the deadline by six months, hoping thus to catch the populace unprepared.

One slave's testimony suffices to illustrate the general tenor of the rest. As Captain Jesse Mabry recorded it:

"The Negroes were going to rise and kill all the whites on the 4th [of July] and they had a number of white men at their head: some of them he knew by name, others he only knew when he saw them. He mentioned the following white men as actively engaged in the business: Ruel Blake, Drs. Cotton and Saunders, and many more, but could not call their names; and that he had seen several others. He also gave the names of several slaves as ringleaders in the business, who were understood to be captains under those white men. He said that one belonged to his master, by the name of Weaver (a preacher), and one belonged to Mr. Riley, named Russell (a preacher also), and a carpenter, Sam. Joe (the witness) stated that the insurrection was to commence the 4th of July; that the slaves of each plantation were to commence with axes, hoes, &c., and to massacre all the white men at home, and were then to make their way to Beattie's Bluff, where they were to break into the storehouses and get all the arms and ammunition that were in that place, and then proceed to Livingston, where they would obtain reinforcements from different plantations; and from thence they were to go to Vernon and sack that place, recruiting as they went; and by that time they calculated they would be strong enough to bear down any and every opposition that could be brought against them from there to Natchez; and that, after killing all the citizens of that place [Natchez], and plundering the banks &c., they were to retire to a place called the Devil's Punch Bowl—here they were to make a stand, and that no force could be brought that could injure them."

Another Negro, by the name of Jim, a very sensible, fine-looking fellow, identified a white man named Dunaven (Donovan) as one of the inciters, and also a certain Moss and his sons, who furnished the Negroes with whiskey, and whose home was headquarters for the "bad white men" when in the neighborhood. He independently verified the story of the rising and final retreat to the Devil's Punch Bowl, and added one other detail:

"Jim further stated that it was their intention to slay all the whites, except some of the most beautiful women, whom they intended to keep as wives; said that these white men had told them that they might do so, and that he already picked one out for himself; and that he and his wife already had a quarrel in consequence of his having told her his intention."

For all the simple ingenuousness of the statement that he had "picked out" a white woman, and quarreled over her with his wife, this testimony was significant. White women as part of the bribe! It was exactly the plan Murrell had revealed to Stewart; and it was exactly the sort of thing that drove husbands, fathers, and sweethearts of Southern women wild with rage.

There is no question that a wave of hysterical fury swept over the white people. But this is scarcely to be wondered at, considering the ominous portents. Wrote a contemporary writer:

The County [Madison] is settled principally in large plantations, and on many of them there is no white man but an overseer, most of the large planters being absent at the north; and on a number only the families of the absent—being at least 50 Negroes to one white man in the neighborhood of Livingston and Beattie's Bluff, where the scene of desolation was to commence. Having no arms for their defence but their fowling pieces; no organized militia in the county; what would the ordinary array of arms avail, opposed to the stealthy marauder of the night—the demon of firebrand and dagger—and no place of security as a retreat for their families. Intense excitement was pervading the whole community at this time and was increasing every hour.

On June 30 the Negroes who had admitted or had been identified as ringleaders of the uprising, were led out and hanged to some trees beside the Big Black River. These included Peter, Ruel Blake's brave and loyal slave; an old Negro belonging to William P. Johnson; one belonging to Captain Thomas Hudnold; Joe and Weaver (the preacher) belonging to Captain Stansberry; Sam, belonging to Captain Mabry; Russell (a preacher); Jim, belonging to William Saunders (he who had "picked out" a white wife already); Bachus, belonging to a man named Leggett; and a man belonging to Landfair, presumably the one who had talked to the nursemaid at the Lathams'.

This was a total of ten in all; but the lynching of a few obscure and unknown Negroes was not considered sufficient to halt the conspiracy, now perilously near. *White* ringleaders must be apprehended.

Mounted posses scoured the country. "Doc" Joshua Cotton, and William Saunders,[3] "steam doctors"—practitioners of a form of treatment of that period—were arrested. Cotton was a reputed swindler. It was learned that he left Memphis, Tennessee, "soon after the conviction of the celebrated Murrell," and crossed from Louisiana to Livingston, Mississippi, to set up his establishment near there. When he left Memphis he was accompanied by a wife and child *who were never*

[3] Cotton was on Murrell's list as "D. Cotton." Saunders was perhaps related to George N. Saunders, Stewart's treacherous "friend."

after seen or heard from. Since his arrival at Livingston he had married another woman; and his partner, Saunders, during the inquisition, accused him of planning to "get rid" of this second wife also.

2.

Now the committee of safety faced a problem. Testimony of slaves, under the law of the state, could not be accepted as evidence in the courts. Having discovered so much, however, the alarmed and angry citizens decided to proceed in an extralegal manner, "to arrest the progress of the impending danger, to give the parties implicated something like a trial, if not formal, at least substantial."

One hundred and fifty men from Madison and Hinds counties assembled and passed resolutions giving their full support to the power of the committee of safety. Dr. M. D. Mitchell was elected chairman of the committee and William Royce secretary. Other members were Hardin D. Runnels, Thomas Hudnold, Israel Spencer, Sack P. Gee, Nelson L. Taylor, Robert Hodge, Sr., John Simmons, James Grafton, Charles Smith, D. W. Haley, Captain Jesse Mabry, and William Wade, all prominent men in the district.

Lynch law thus went into full effect. "Something like a trial" was hardly a legal court proceeding, and executions performed under its authority were little better, if any, than mob actions. Nevertheless the people were tremendously excited and aroused, and one of them cited the old Roman axiom *"salus populi est suprema lex,"* and on this basis, that the "safety of the people was the supreme law," the citizens bound themselves to carry out any order of the committee of safety, after investing that body with authority to punish all persons it found guilty.

The committee moved swiftly against the white instigators, who were considered far worse and more dangerous than the Negro conspirators. First to be tried was Cotton. His partner, Saunders, had been released and tried to get out of the country, but was rearrested and returned to Livingston.

Saunders became the chief witness against Cotton, and was the first specifically to name Murrell's Mystic Clan, as being behind the conspiracy. He admitted that he knew of the plot, but protested that he had no part in it himself. Cotton, however, he told the committee, had used his business as a front for Negro stealing at first, and later for drawing Negroes into the conspiracy. He told of Cotton's shady past, the disappearance of his wife and children under circumstances never explained, and his reputation as a swindler and a "fence" for stolen goods.

Saunders further implicated Ruel Blake and Andrew Boyd—the latter supposed to be Cotton's brother under an alias—as co-conspirators and specifically referred to their organization as the Clan.

A Negro, brought into a room in which Cotton stood with a number of other men, unhesitatingly pointed him out as the person who, on pretext of hunting horses, approached him and tried to enlist him in the conspiracy—which the slave refused to join.

After that, when the guard took Cotton out of the room so that the committee could deliberate, he exclaimed, "It's all over with me! All I wish is that the committee will have me decently buried and not suffer me to hang long after I'm dead."

"Great God!" exclaimed a bystander with horror. "You don't know that you'll be convicted, Cotton!"

"The testimony is so strong against me," he said despondently, "that they must convict me—they can't avoid it." He then sent a request to the committee, saying that if they would not have him hanged immediately, he would tell them all he knew about the conspiracy.

The request for a reprieve was denied, since the committee was satisfied of his guilt. Thereupon Cotton, with no promise of clemency, made the following extraordinary confession, to which he swore as being the truth and signed:

I, Joshua Cotton, acknowledge my guilt, and I was one of the principal men in bringing about the conspiracy. I am one of the Murrell Clan, a member of what we called the Grand Council. I counselled with them twice: once near Columbus this spring; and another time on an island in the Mississippi River [perhaps the island where the "Garden of Eden" stood in the morass, or even Stuart's Island on Lake Chicot, Arkansas].

Our object in undertaking to excite the Negroes to rebellion was not for the purpose of liberating them, but for plunder. I was trying to carry out Murrell's plan as laid down [that is, explained] in Stewart's pamphlet. [Ruel] Blake's boy, Peter, had his duty assigned to him which was to let such Negroes into the secret as he could trust, generally the most daring scoundrels; the Negroes on most of the large plantations knew of it; and from the exposure of our plans in said pamphlet [Stewart's], we expected the citizens would be on their guard at the time mentioned, being the 25th of December next; and we determined to take them by surprise and try it on the night of the 4th of July, and it would have been tried tonight, perhaps may yet, but for the detection of our plans.

All the names I now recollect (in the immediate country around) who are deeply concerned are Andrew Boyd, Albe Dean, William Saunders; two Rawsons of Hinds County, who have a list of all the names of the men belonging to the Murrell Clan in this state, being

about 150, and the names of all who are connected with me in this con-
spiracy, being 51; John and William Earl, near Vicksburg, in Warren
County; Ruel Blake of Madison County. I have heard Blake say he
would make his Negroes help, and he was equal in command to me.
Lunsford Barnes, of this county; James Leach, near Woodville, in
Wilkinson County; Thomas Anderson, below Clinton, in Hinds County;
John Rogers, near Benton, Yazoo County; Lee Smith of Hinds County;
and John Ivy in Vernon. There are arms and ammunition deposited in
Hinds County, near Raymond. (Signed) Joshua Cotton, July 4, 1835.

After receiving this confession, the committee voted to hang Cotton
within the hour, thinking that if news of his execution was circulated
throughout the area before night, it might frighten his accomplices
from the undertaking.

Surprisingly, Cotton, under the gallows—which had been especially
erected since the Negroes were hanged from the trees—endorsed this
action.

"It's nothing more than I deserve," he said. In answer, when someone asked if he really thought there would be danger that night, he
replied, "I do, if they don't hear I was hung."

His last words were, "Take care of yourselves tonight and tomorrow night." With that he swung off into eternity.

3.

He did not die alone. With him under the gallows stood William
Saunders, in spite of his turning "state's evidence." He was so deeply
implicated by his own statements and those of others that he was
condemned to be hanged with his partner. The fact that he was an
ex-convict from the Tennessee penitentiary (where he may have met
and talked with Murrell) and had a general bad character did not
help him.

So two corpses dangled on the gallows July 4, the very day when
the slaves were supposedly primed to break out in the night.

Patrols armed to the teeth kept watch throughout the country during
those night hours. All white women and children were locked in their
homes with armed guards to protect them.

Nothing happened. All remained quiet. It was believed that the
execution of ten Negroes and two white leaders had cowed the conspirators.

Actually, so badly organized and so precipitate had been the plot
of Cotton and others, that it is to be doubted that any very widespread revolt could have been mounted that night, even had the

scheme not been discovered. Which raises again the question of how many Negroes really would have participated even had Murrell remained on the scene and had full time to perfect his machinations. Many of them certainly would not. Perhaps even at maximum preparation Murrell might have seen his conspiracy fall far short of his dream of unbridled destruction and looting.

But the committee of safety was not through. One after another the men named by Cotton or Saunders were ordered arrested and brought before the now dreaded tribunal: Albe Dean, Angus L. Donovan, Ruel Blake, Lee Smith, William Benson, Lunsford Barnes, William and John Earl, James Leach, Thomas Anderson, John Rogers, John Ivy, and "Old Man" Moss and his sons, the latter named only by a Negro witness.

Some of these escaped. Andrew Boyd "said to be Cotton's brother" was arrested but for some reason released. He took refuge in a swamp near Livingston. A posse started after him with "track dogs," and followed him until it grew so dark they could no longer see their way. When morning came and the chase was resumed they found he had escaped by getting on a horse he found in the woods. Where he went nobody ever knew, but he never reappeared in that country. "He left a large family dependent on charity for subsistence," the old record states.

What happened to Moss and his sons, accused of furnishing a rendezvous for the Clan, is not of record. Perhaps they made a quick exit when they first heard of the discovery of the conspiracy.

Others were not so fortunate, though in some cases mercy was shown to the prisoners brought in. For example, William Benson, who had been working for Ruel Blake and was quoted as saying "The Negroes ought to free themselves, there being at least twenty Negroes to one white man," was adjudged by the committee, "A great fool, little above an idiot," and they did not punish him, but ordered him to leave the country forthwith, which he did.

Lunsford Barnes, accused by Cotton of complicity in the conspiracy, was only a youth, very ignorant and uneducated. In view of his previous good record, and not being fully satisfied of his guilt, the committee ordered him also to leave the state on pain of punishment if he disobeyed. He obeyed very promptly.

But no clemency was given to any of the others who were captured. Angus L. Donovan, a ne'er-do-well, who had deserted his wife in Maysville, Kentucky, attempted after the first disclosures to circulate among the Negroes and persuade them to keep quiet if questioned. He was arrested in actual conversation on this subject with the two frightened maids on the Latham plantation who first told of the plot.

It was shown that Donovan first came to Mississippi "ostensibly as an emissary of those deluded fanatics in the North, the Abolitionists, to create rebellion," but finding that he had been anticipated by "a band of cutthroats and robbers who were engaged in the same work" (the Murrell Clan) he joined the conspiracy to get a share of the anticipated spoils. He was sentenced to hang.

Albe Dean, a shifty character who "pretended to make a living by making washing machines," and who was specifically named by Cotton as "deeply engaged in the conspiracy and a member of the Murrell Clan," also was sentenced to be executed. Dean and Donovan were hanged together on the same gallows on which Cotton and Saunders died, the date being July 8.

Ruel Blake's case was somewhat different. In spite of the testimony against him the committee found it difficult to believe he was guilty. He was a man of substance, a slave owner himself, and it seemed strange that he would advocate a rebellion of slaves.

But investigation showed that he had a shady background. By his own account he was a seafaring man in his youth, taking to ships in Connecticut where he was born. Vague hints he dropped before the conspiracy was known gave some people the impression that he had been at one time a pirate. He was cold in manner, "with a forbidding countenance," so that he had few friends among the white people. As a gunwright he did a good business, but "had been detected in several attempts to swindle fellow citizens, who, if they exposed his rascality, were ever after objects of his deadly hatred."

One of the first Negroes brought to Livingston for questioning was his own slave, Peter. This was before it was suspected that any but Negroes were in the plot, and according to custom Blake was given the right to whip his own servant to make him tell what he knew. But he applied the whip so lightly that the committee asked him to turn it over to someone with a stronger arm. This he did unwillingly, then became very excited as the whipping went on, and even tried to interfere, hitting and knocking down the man who was conducting the "examination." Bystanders pulled him away and told him to "run or the gentleman he had so grossly insulted would kill him if he should see him."

At that Blake mounted a horse and fled from Livingston, first riding to Vicksburg, and from there to Natchez. Later he returned to Vicksburg, passing himself off as an "Indiana boatman."

This was before the disclosures that white men were at the bottom of the trouble. When the full story of the conspiracy came out, Blake was so deeply implicated that a five hundred dollar reward was offered for him. He was discovered at Vicksburg and arrested. Under a heavy guard he was returned to Livingston July 8—the same day that Dean and Donovan were hanged.

The confessions of Cotton and other whites, as well as the Negroes, so convinced the committee of his guilt that he was sentenced to die. On July 10, in the presence of a large throng of people, he was conveyed to the gallows. In his final statement he insisted he was innocent, that his life was sworn away; but he added that the committee could not have done otherwise than condemn him with the evidence before it. Then the noose took his life.

Lee Smith, a member of the Clan from Tennessee (perhaps the "A." Smith of Murrell's list), attempted to resist arrest but was overpowered by the posse. A number of guns and pistols, together with a large quantity of ammunition, were found stored at his place. Though Cotton had directly implicated him, his character had been reputed good up to that time, and the committee decided to let him go with an order to get out of the state. He did so, but later returned for some reason. Thereupon he was "waited upon" by a group of angry citizens of Hinds County and lynched.

The last whose deaths are of formal record were the brothers, William and John Earl, living near Vicksburg. They were brought to Livingston July 18. When he heard that he had been named as a conspirator by Cotton, William Earl made a full confession before a justice of peace, in which he disclosed more completely the Clan's plot.

Andrew Boyd, he said, had notified him about June 12 that the "Negro war" would start July 4. Cotton and Saunders were to be captains in Madison County, and a man named Lofton in the Yazoo Swamp. He and his brother helped talk Negroes into the conspiracy and he named others who were involved:

"Samuels, William Donley, and Lofton said George Rawson would join them. All of us were sworn to stick to our own company. We all calculated to take Madison County; and by that time we expected to have a force to visit the large plantations in the river counties, and by the time we reached Natchez we could take any place. We held out the idea to the Negroes that they should be free; but we intended they should work for *us*. Spies were to go ahead on all occasions."

There was more to the confession, and at the end he gave the sign of the Clan (probably that of the Strykers), to prove he was a member.

He was locked up for the night in a sort of a shed. In the morning when they came for him he was dead: dangling from a rung of a ladder carelessly left in the room, from which he had hanged himself by a noose improvised from his handkerchief.

John Earl, when he heard of his brother's suicide, said he was glad; that William had made him a rascal, and if they had been released he feared William would have killed him for something he divulged.

He went on to say that he knew Andrew Boyd, and belonged to the "Domestic Lodge" (Strykers), knowing the chief men in the conspiracy. Arms caches were to be provided in the Yazoo Swamp and at the Old Agency in Hinds County, Mississippi, and near Baton Rouge, Louisiana. These disclosures show the extent of the plot. Territory directly involved, within John Earl's personal knowledge, extended in two states, up and down the river more than two hundred miles, and in breadth covered some sixty or seventy miles. And Earl was only a Stryker.

A delegation from the committee of safety at Vicksburg came for him, and he was turned over to them. They returned him to their own county, Warren, and there hanged him.

Punishments of other men, specifically named, like Lofton, William Donley, Scruggs, the two Rawsons, John Rogers, John Ivy, and others, are not of record. They may have been lynched without the ceremony of a "trial," or they may have escaped.

Over in Attala County, Captain Isham Medford, named by Murrell as a member of his Clan, was taken by a posse and flogged. Following the whipping, and on being assured he would receive no further punishment, he stated that the Clan had stolen many Negroes and horses, which they generally disposed of in Arkansas, Texas, or along the lower Red River in Louisiana. He furnished the names of many persons at whose houses the gang could call in moving this stolen property from place to place, *and among those named was Matthew Clanton,* Virgil Stewart's treacherous "friend," now listed openly as a member of the Clan of "counterfeiters and thieves which had so long infested the country."

By this time the fury of the populace had subsided. Men were sick of lynchings and it appears that Clanton was not punished, and even attempted to regain some part of his reputation by writing letters of denial of those charges.

The committee of safety at Livingston "adjourned *sine die.*"

It was the death blow of the Mystic Clan. Without Murrell's leadership it mismanaged things in an almost ludicrously blundering fashion.

Now, from all over the South, rogues fled in every direction. Part of these "absconded" to Texas; which was then in revolt against Mexico, and in the following spring of 1836 won its independence under the leadership of General Sam Houston.

Dr. C. L. Sonnichsen has recorded that life along the Sabine River, already a refuge for desperadoes and fugitives from justice, became astonishingly worse after the breakup of the great Murrell conspiracy. Wrote Dr. Sonnichsen:

> This was an incredible but all-too-real plot to turn the whole south-western portion of the then United States over to a gang of freed slaves and unscrupulous hoodlums. It was no outlaw's pipe dream either. Murrell had the men and the means to carry out his nefarious plans. His organization was enormous. Before he could organize his big strike, however, his luck ran out. In 1834 he was apprehended and sent to prison, and before the next year was finished his gang was scattered.
>
> This was a good thing for the rest of the country, but it was hard on Texas. Murrell's men concentrated on the border as soon as their former haunts became unsafe.[4]

Other members of the Mystic Clan headed north. The outbreak of outlawry which took place along the upper Mississippi about 1844–45 very probably had its roots in the Murrell conspiracy. Some of the Murrell names even appeared in the annals of that crime wave, although of course almost all the ex-Clansmen adopted aliases.

But never, after the events around Livingston, Mississippi, did there exist a threat to an entire section of the nation such as John Murrell so diabolically planned.

It has become a sort of fashion among some writers dealing with affairs long past to describe the whole Murrell story as false, or a sheer creation of legend and rumor. Burton Rascoe, after reciting some of the "legends" concerning Murrell, thus dismisses him:

> It is quite possible that he (Murrell) was invented entire, except for the name—which may have been that of a minor outlaw—by one of the anonymous rewrite men on the original *National Police Gazette,* before Richard Fox acquired it. Certainly the activities of the Murrell gang were luridly described in those early issues, and there one finds what is probably the source of many of the Murrell legends that have passed into folklore and have been accepted as authentic by historians as credulous as Mark Twain.[5]

It will be remembered that many persons, even at the time of the occurrences, denounced Stewart and questioned his motives and the truth of his assertions. The statements made against him by Murrell's attorney, Milton Brown, although unsupported by any evidence, were believed by some. Writing in 1860, J. F. H. Claiborne, the Mississippi historian, said:

[4] C. L. Sonnichsen, *Ten Texas Feuds.*

[5] Burton Rascoe, *Belle Starr, the Bandit Queen.*

The whole story was a fabrication. Murrell was simply a thief and counterfeiter, and Stewart was his subordinate, who, having quarreled with him, devised this plan to avenge and enrich himself. The whole "plot" and its tragical consequences, may now be regarded as one of the most extraordinary and lamentable hallucinations of our times.

I suggest that neither Mr. Rascoe nor Mr. Claiborne had fully studied the record. What about the sworn testimony of persons of repute who were involved in the events at the time and had personal knowledge of them? And what of the confessions of men who were convicted of complicity, when they stood at the foot of the gallows? It may be well to summarize a few of these corroborative statements.

1. A written statement by the Reverend John Henning, verifying all details of his friendship with Stewart, the episode of the stolen slaves, and how Stewart undertook to hunt for them *refusing any recompense* because of his friendship for the Hennings.

2. A sworn statement by Thomas Hudnold, dated August 3, 1835, and given to Stewart, relating to Negro stealing and fraud practiced on him by Murrell.

3. A sworn affidavit by the Reverend John E. Higginbotham, signed September 12, 1835, describing another of Murrell's slave operations, and given to Stewart for the prosecution of Murrell.

4. A signed statement by Colonel William H. Bayliss, dated October 20, 1835, confirming his conversation at Wesley, Tennessee, with Stewart, including the latter's explanation of what he was doing in Murrell's company and revelation of Murrell's character; and also his loan of a pistol to Stewart, which was later duly returned.

5. A statement signed October 11, 1835, by Richard G. Henning, attesting that Murrell sent him the threatening letter described by Stewart, and stating that everything Stewart wrote about him (Henning) was true.

6. Sworn statements by John Champion, Matthew Erwin, and Colonel Orville Shelby, completely and absolutely verifying every detail of the statements Stewart made concerning them, his conversations and revelations concerning Murrell, and going further to add facts of their own knowledge about the Clan.

7. A sworn statement, after Murrell's arrest, signed by his captors and guards, David M. Henning, Richard G. Henning, George Hicks, R. H. Byrn, and William H. Long, certifying that Murrell stated of his own volition in their presence that he had never met Stewart before their journey together, and that he did not even know his real name, calling him Hues, until it was revealed to him after his arrest.

This gets rid of the story that Stewart was the arch-outlaw's "subordinate."

8. Murrell's own letter to his Clan, describing Stewart as a "detective" pursuing him, and saying nothing whatever about any relationship between them prior to that, a sufficient proof in itself that there was none, since otherwise he would have used it to discredit Stewart's tesimony.

9. A confession by Captain Isham Medford, sworn before John B. Murray, justice of peace in Attala County, Mississippi, July 5, 1835, and witnessed by Squire James C. Bole, Allen Collins, Everett L. Ford, James S. Bains, A. J. Patterson, Job Taylor, A. Hays, William McAllister, and J. M. Taylor, describing operations of the Clan of which he was a member (and named on Murrell's list), and describing Matthew Clanton as one of the important members of that body. In his statement summing up this case, Squire Bole wrote: "That V. A. Stewart has rendered important services to his country, is a fact which no honest man will deny."

10. A letter from Dr. D. O. Williams, published in the Clinton, Mississippi, *Gazette,* describing the rendezvous of the Clan, giving some of the very names Stewart listed as members of it, and telling of the recovery of Parson Henning's Negroes in Avoyelles Parish, Louisiana, where a planter who had bought them, on finding they had been stolen, willingly and gladly returned them.

11. A letter to Virgil A. Stewart from Attorney General Alexander B. Bradford, stating that he prosecuted Murrell, that the man had a fair and impartial trial, and that Stewart himself had undergone and sustained a most rigid cross-examination; and further referring to the high character given Stewart by prominent men who knew him, including Colonel Thomas Loftin, and Squire Alexander Patton.

12. A resolution of gratitude to Stewart for the many dangers he underwent in bringing Murrell to justice, and raising a subscription for him (amount not stated) as a reward, dated Jackson, Tennessee, September 29, 1834, signed by thirty-nine citizens headed by Sheriff Mathias Deberry.

13. An affidavit by James Moore, dated Madison County, Mississippi, telling of lodging Stewart while the latter was wounded and sick, at his home; and of Stewart's telling him how he was pursued and attacked by Murrell gangsters, and his plan to leave the country, and go to Europe, probably to France, to escape them; and also of his having put his papers into the hands of a friend (Walton) to be made public.

14. Affidavits of Colonel Orville Shelby and others, including Judge

J. Tipton, stating the bad character of George N. Saunders and Matthew Clanton, who were Stewart's chief defamers.

15. A resolution signed by forty-three citizens of Carroll County, Mississippi, August 8, 1834, condemning Matthew Clanton, and voting gratitude and friendship to Stewart.

16. A letter from Sheriff M. Deberry of Madison County, Tennessee, testifying as to the exact truth of the circumstances of Murrell's apprehension and trial as described by Stewart in his pamphlet.

17. Affidavit sworn to by thirty-five prominent men, including three attorneys, two physicians, four squires, one colonel, and one major, in Jackson County, Georgia, from which Stewart moved to Tennessee after spending his young manhood there, testifying to his respectable and honorable character.

18. Recorded proceedings of the committee of safety at Livingston, Mississippi, in June and July, 1835, describing the discovery of the surprise date of July 4 of that year, set for the onset of the conspiracy, which before Murrell's capture and conviction was to have been Christmas Day of the same year; and describing the capture and punishment of both colored and white ringleaders—among the latter being several named in Murrell's list as given to Stewart.

19. Letter written by Squire James C. Bole, of Franklin, Mississippi, describing the punishment and confession of Captain Isham Medford, agreeing perfectly with the affidavit previously sworn by witnesses, but giving still further particulars of Medford's revelations concerning the Clan and its membership.

20. Statement of policy by the committee of safety at Livingston, Mississippi, in which the reason for its actions is given in the following words:

> The question may arise, why was not the civil authority appealed to? and which the Committee are free to declare, is always greatly to be preferred, when its powers are competent to restrain the evil. The civil authority was inadequate to this end in Madison County; for there is no jail in that county sufficient to contain more than six or eight prisoners, and even those very insecurely; and whenever prisoners would have been dispatched to any other county, a guard would have been required which would have left many families defenceless; and it was unknown at what moment this protection might be required; besides, immediate example, without hope of law's evasion or delay seemed, as in truth it was, indispensable to safety.
>
> Already had many of the slaves marked out the victims of their lust or revenge; and no time to convince them of the fatal results of their rash enterprise was to be lost. If they had been permitted to commence it, horrid their momentary triumph would have been. That the plot was headed by a daring band of villainous white men, there now re-

mains no doubt, and the desperate evil required a prompt and efficient remedy, to the extent of the one resorted to by the citizens of Madison County, and carried into effect by this Committee.

21. The confession, signed and sworn to by Joshua Cotton before his execution, that he was one of the principal men in the conspiracy, a member of the Grand Council of the Murrell Clan, fully verifying the plot of the "Negro war" as being that of Murrell "as laid down [that is, described] in Stewart's pamphlet," which the members of the Clan planned to put in effect by launching in July 4, rather than waiting for the date set by the imprisoned chief outlaw; and giving the names of some members of the Clan, stating there were one hundred and fifty in Mississippi alone.

22. The confession of William Saunders of his knowledge of the conspiracy, his membership in the Clan, and his part in fomenting the proposed uprising of the slaves.

23. The confession of Albe Dean as to his membership in the Clan and his knowledge of and participation in the conspiracy.

24. Confessions of four Negroes as to the conspiracy and the white men involved in it, together with promises made to them and the plans explained to them by members of the Murrell Clan.

25. Confession of A. L. Donovan that he had gone among the Negroes to foment rebellion as a paid emissary of the Abolitionists, discovered the conspiracy was ahead of him and thereupon joined it, to get his share of the plunder.

26. Confession of William Earl, giving details of the organization of the conspiracy, its plan of operation, some of its "captains," and giving the sign of the Clan to prove his membership.

27. Confession of John Earl, confirming William Earl's statements and furnishing additional details, including the far-reaching system of arsenals to be set up by the Clan.

The reality of the conspiracy and the wide activities of Murrell and his Clan are amply attested by this array of evidence given by men—some of them confessed members of the Clan itself—either at the time or immediately after the arrest and conviction of Murrell and the nipping of the plot.

Bear in mind that this testimony was not given years later, but *at the time and on the spot*. The major points made by the large numbers and wide variety of witnesses agree throughout.

As for Virgil Stewart's character, the only statements made against it were by Milton Brown (Murrell's paid attorney, without evidence to back his accusations), Colonel Jarrott (named a Clan member by Murrell as "Jarot"), Matthew Clanton (named as a Clan member by Cap-

tain Medford), and George N. Saunders whose character for veracity
was impugned by men of standing who knew him, and who in all
probability was a member of the Clan, although this last has never
been shown.

On the contrary the testimony as to Stewart's honesty and veracity
is overwhelming, not only in the sworn statements corroborating his
account, but in the men who came forward in each of the three communities where he had lived—forty-one reputable citizens in Tennessee, thirty-five in Georgia, and forty-three in Mississippi—to attest to
his probity and good character.

What about the names of the Clan roster? One must allow for misspellings, as previously pointed out. Allowance also must be made for
the tendency of men engaged in criminal activities to assume aliases.
It is also to be remembered that Murrell gave these names from
memory and Stewart scrawled them on paper held probably on his
portmanteau. Chances for error in spelling and pronunciation were
great.

But several of the names recorded by Stewart later checked out—
Chandlor, Crenshaw, Tucker, Jarrott, Aker, Lloyd, Barney, Nolin,
Glenn, and Cotton among others.

Cooper was a name listed, and an Edward Cooper was a notorious
counterfeiter at the time. There were a Haines, a Harris, and a Boyd
in the upper Mississippi crime wave later on.

Without attempting to say that the names on the Clan list were all
correct, I believe that they were given to Stewart by Murrell as he
published them, and if all were not really involved, some of them
assuredly were. It should be recalled that Murrell, as he himself said,
did not furnish a complete list, and many were on his roster whom
he did not name because of the hurried nature of the occasion. For
example, reciting from memory, he named only forty-seven in Mississippi, while Cotton—whom he listed as in Louisiana, and later was
at Memphis, Tennessee—in his confession at the gallows said there
were one hundred and fifty members of the Clan in the state, of
whom fifty-one were directly connected with his own operations.

No, Murrell was not "invented"—nor was his conspiracy which came
to naught a "fabrication."

4.

When John A. Murrell went to prison he stepped off the stage of
history. But before leaving him it is interesting to learn his end. This
has been the subject of unceasing legend, wild stories, and many
errors.

Some of these legends were gathered by Janice Clark, in the form of an article in the Crosset, Arkansas, *News-Observer*. One story she recorded was that after he served his prison sentence Murrell returned to Arkansas, setting up a new rendezvous at Montgomery Point, near the mouth of the White River. He gathered about him some of his old gangsters and a few new recruits. Later he moved to Stuart Island on Lake Chicot, an old ox-bow channel of the Mississippi, where he resumed his career of robbery and murder.

Each time he made a "strike" he buried the cash and jewels in pots at scattered places. At the end of the summer of these activities his men demanded a division of the year's take. Murrell then—according to this legend—produced a blackened iron kettle filled with supposedly golden coins.

He distributed small valuables, such as watches, gold chains, and enameled snuff boxes to his men, then counted out to each one share of the coins, keeping two shares for himself as the leader. Thereafter he passed around a jug of whiskey for them to celebrate with.

Unfortunately for him—the legend continues—one of the gang, a man named Rudd, was suspicious. By cutting with a knife he discovered that all his share of the coins were spurious—lead dipped in a film of gold.

When this was revealed to the other men, they promptly gathered about Murrell and murdered him. But in doing so they committed a grievous error—with their dead leader they also buried the secret of where all those pots of *real* gold were hidden.

This, according to the legend, may have been fourteen or fifteen years after his release from prison, and since then digging for Murrell's gold has been a frequent activity for some residents of the territory.

Colonel Kenneth Croswell, U. S. Marine Corps (Ret.), now living near and doing business in Los Angeles, grew up as a boy in that very area. He remembers the frequent Murrell stories told by the old-timers and quite probably took part in one or more "Murrell treasure hunts." It is through him and his wife, Mrs. Daphne Croswell, that I have gained a considerable fund of legends concerning Murrell, through their research and Mr. Croswell's personal recollections.

One farmer (unnamed) was reported to have become suddenly rich, so that he sold his property and left the country—presumably with Murrell gold, although this never was proved.

Another farmer, George C. White, plowed up a pot of money in his field, only to discover that the five hundred dollars in gold coins it contained was all counterfeit pieces "like those Murrell used to pay his men." The son of this man, Carrol White, remembered as a boy seeing the coins.

Still another man, according to Janice Clark, succeeded in coming out of the Murrell gang with some money. He was David Agee, a spy and informer for the band. Agee hid his treasure. Just before his death, January 5, 1867, he suffered a stroke which made him speechless and helpless. He tried by signs to describe where he placed the loot, but failed. And, adds Miss Clark, "Several generations of boys and men have dug all through the area hoping to find a pot of Murrell's treasure."

These legends may concern days prior to Murrell's imprisonment, because it is fairly certain that one of his headquarters prior to that time was on Stuart Island in Lake Chicot. This house was attacked and burned down by citizens of the surrounding country shortly after his arrest and conviction.

It is certain that Murrell did not die in the manner set forth in the legend quoted, but the story is interesting as an example of the way in which folklore embellishes historic episodes, almost always including that little touch about "buried treasure," so dear to romantic (and perhaps acquisitive) hearts.

Fred Allsop in his *Folklore of Romantic Arkansas* notes a story that the Murrell stronghold contained a trap door and a pit beneath it where victims were thrown to die "a lingering death by starvation." He also relates a story he brands as "improbable" that Murrell had at his "Garden of Eden" an underground passage five hundred yards long running from the Tyronza River, "as an outlet for stolen property and captured slaves." He adds, "The story of the passageway is so widely told that there must have been some sort of tunnel, used for evil purposes."

Interesting as relating to the name of the town Marked Tree, is the statement in the Allsop collection that "Murrell Clan's path extended diagonally from New York to Texas . . . Along the whole route lone pines were planted at intervals from five to twenty miles. Near each pine stood a cabin of logs, crude and homely, but to the bandits— friendly."

The extent of this route may be doubted, but the pines as a sign of hospitality to the Clan is probable.

Mark Twain, writing in 1883, left his record of the arch-bandit's career as it was told then. His comment is not lacking interest:

> There is a tradition that Island 37 [in the Mississippi, above Memphis, Tennessee] was one of the principal abiding places of the once celebrated "Murel's Gang" [Mark Twain's spelling]. This was a colossal combination of robbers, horse-thieves, Negro-stealers and counterfeiters, engaged in business along the river some fifty or sixty years ago. While our journey across the country toward St. Louis was in progress we had no end of Jesse James and his history; for he had just been as-

sassinated by an agent of the Governor of Missouri, and was in consequence occupying a good deal of space in the newspapers. Cheap histories of him were for sale by train boys. According to these, he was the most marvelous creature of his kind that ever existed. It was a mistake. Murel [sic] was his equal in boldness, treachery, and in general and comprehensive vileness and shamelessness; and very much his superior in some larger aspects. James was a retail rascal; Murel, wholesale. James' modest genius dreamed of no loftier flight than the planning of raids upon cars, coaches, and country banks. Murel projected Negro insurrections and the capture of New Orleans; and furthermore, on occasion, this Murel could go into a pulpit and edify the congregation. What are James and his half-dozen vulgar rascals compared with this stately old-time criminal, with his sermons, his meditated insurrections and city captures, and his majestic following of ten hundred men, sworn to do his evil will![6]

By far the wildest story of Murrell's end was given by Burton Rascoe:

"Some say he [Murrell] was cast by his followers into his own dungeon and left there to starve to death and rot without benefit of quicklime. Some say he was hanged by a citizens' posse in Arkansas."

5.

No such thing occurred to John A. Murrell.

He served out his sentence and was released, broken in health and apparently, through the rigors of prison treatment or disease—he had tuberculosis and probably syphilis—practically an imbecile.

I have a letter from Dr. James W. Patton, Director of the Southern Historical Collection of the University of North Carolina, which says:

Murrell at the end of his sentence in the Tennessee State Penitentiary settled in or near Pikeville in Bledsoe County [Tennessee], and worked at the trade of blacksmith—or so the accounts say. He died of tuberculosis within a relatively short time and was buried in Bledsoe County.

Dr. Patton also mentions a tradition—for which he does not vouch—that "Some time after Murrell's death his body was exhumed for some purpose; and was found to be in a state of petrifaction; and was sent to the old University of Nashville Medical School where it remained until the building was eventually destroyed by fire."

Dr. Dan M. Robison, State Librarian and Archivist at Nashville, Tennessee, to whom Dr. Patton referred me if I wished to run down this tradition—which, as I say, he only mentioned in passing and by

[6] Mark Twain, *Life on the Mississippi.*

no means gave it weight—cleared up that part of the story. No record of such an exhibition as that of Murrell's body can be found, Dr. Robison wrote me. Furthermore, there is no record that any building of the University of Nashville Medical School was ever burned.

Paul Marshall, in an article, "John A. Murrell and Daniel Crenshaw," in the *Tennessee Historical Magazine* for April, 1920, says of Murrell: "He went to Pikeville and died in that part of the state."

Robert M. Coates, in his *The Outlaw Years*, says:

> Long before his sentence ended, the man's [Murrell's] mind cracked. When at last the prison doors opened and he emerged again it was as an invalid and practically an imbecile. His wife had gone; his lands had been claimed; his brother had vanished. He, too, in his turn disappeared: his final outcome—his death, his place of burial—unknown.

Ross Phares, in *Reverend Devil*, concludes "Apparently no one knows what became of him (Murrell)."

But I think we can provide an answer to this apparent puzzle. I have a letter written to me from Nashville, January 24, 1954, by Mrs. Margaret B. Hollinshead, former State Historian of the D.A.R. in Tennessee, in which she says:

> John A. Murrell died in Bledsoe County, Tennessee. He was, I think, pardoned by our Governor but do not know.[7] However these facts are well known throughout the county: a most respectable citizen, Mr. John Billingsley, brought Murrell to Pikeville, our county seat, built him a blacksmith shop and through his influence Murrell was enabled to make a living. He joined a church—Smyrna, I think—anyway he was buried in the cemetery there. Some men disinterred the corpse, cut off the head, and carried it around the country, exhibiting it at .25 cts. a look, until it became "so noisome"—my informant's word—it was buried again, I do not know where. The room in which the infamous robber, murderer and horse thief died used to be pointed out—and when I was a little girl, in the seventies of the 1800's, his blacksmith shop was still in use. Several of Mr. Billingsley's descendants married kin of mine and also I knew well some of his daughters. I am [in 1953] nearly 79 years old.

The taking up of the head for exhibition was perhaps the foundation for the tradition to which Dr. Patton referred, in which the entire body was exhumed and exhibited.

This, I think, should be the final word. Like Micajah Harpe, Wiley Harpe, Samuel Mason, and James May before him, John Murrell's ghastly head was the last of him that men saw upon this earth.

---

[7] Murrell was, as a matter of fact, pardoned about four months before the end of his sentence, possibly because of his ill health.

XX.   *Crime and the Prophet's City*

1.

Already, before the final breakup of Murrell's Mystic Clan, a new factor was appearing on the American scene—the railroad—which, by largely supplanting other forms of transportation would eventually make the old-style crimes of the frontier obsolete. But before this advent there occurred an outbreak of lawlessness in the upper Mississippi valley, which because of the prominence of the persons involved, and the peculiar connection of a religious sect with it, deserves to be studied.

Those who observe the Mormon people today, industrious, frugal, prosperous, and law-abiding, may find difficulty in envisaging the vicissitudes through which this sect passed in its earliest days. Beset by violence and bloodshed, rent by schisms and internal jealousies, driven from place to place, hated and execrated—and returning that hatred and execration with interest—it had little resemblance to the present respected religious body.

In the year 1845 those tenets and policies which have since given the sect its constructive powers and stability were still in the process of formation. It would require the murder of Joseph Smith, giving the Mormons a "martyr"; the heroic march across the plains and through the mountains; the brave and patient struggle to make a sagebrush desert blossom and grow fruitful; the united labor of building cities, towns and industries; and the record, in later years, of respect for law and its enforcement, to bring Mormonism to its present dignity.

In 1845 the Mormon capital was not in Utah, but at Nauvoo, on the banks of the Mississippi River, in Hancock County, Illinois. Already members of the sect had twice been expelled: first from Kirtland, Ohio, after their leaders, Joseph Smith, Jr., and Sidney Rigdon, were tarred and feathered by a mob which accused them of fraud in the failure of a bank they had started; and then from western Missouri, where there was violence and bloodshed on both sides.

This latter episode ended when Governor Lilburn W. Boggs, of Missouri, as civil war broke out between the Mormon "Host of Israel" and the Gentiles (non-Mormons) in which some small "battles" were fought and some murders committed, ordered out the state militia with the words: "The Mormons must be treated as enemies and must be exterminated or driven from the state, if necessary, for the public good."

The Mormons surrendered to a military force commanded by the famous General Alexander Doniphan, a hero of the Mexican War. Joseph Smith and some of his leaders were sentenced to die before a firing squad for "treason," but Doniphan's clear thinking and courage prevented the executions. Thereafter Smith and the other Mormons fled with such of their property as they could transport, to Illinois.

Later Lilburn Boggs was shot and seriously wounded by an assassin who fired at him from the darkness of night outside his house in Independence, Missouri, while the victim was reading by the light of a candle. Boggs recovered. The assailant was, by his own later statement, Porter Rockwell, Joseph Smith's personal gunman, who became leader of the notorious "Danites."

A word about the Danites. Their name was derived from Genesis 49:17: "Dan shall be a serpent by the way, an adder in the path that biteth the horse's heels so that his rider shall fall backward." It was a secret organization of reprisal, and though its existence has been denied by some Mormon writers, the historical citations of it are too numerous and specific to be refuted.

When the Mormons, in their exodus, appeared in Illinois, they were welcomed as having "fled from a slave state for their principles," and received a grant of land along the Mississippi, in northwestern Hancock County, across the river from, but only ten miles below, Fort Madison, Iowa. They named their new town Nauvoo, and under the usual hive-like industry of the Mormons it rapidly grew and flourished, until with a population of more than twenty thousand it actually was the largest city in Illinois, in that day.

But even on this new site the Mormons quickly aroused public resentment. A major reason for this was the theocratic government by Joseph Smith, repugant to a people with democratic beliefs. When Prophet Smith commanded, the Mormons *voted as a unit,* delivering a solid block of several thousand ballots which could not only control the county, but perhaps even the state elections.

With this as a bargaining wedge, Smith induced the state legislature to give Nauvoo a city charter unparalleled in the history of the United States. The city was empowered to pass its own laws; have its own courts with exclusive jurisdiction in cases arising under city ordinances (which quickly included almost all forms of law in the jurisdiction elsewhere of state courts); and establish its own militia, called the Nauvoo Legion, independent of all officers in the state except its own "lieutenant general," Joseph Smith, himself, thus forming a private army for the prophet.[1]

That charter had much to do with Nauvoo's later misfortunes. It was *too* favorable. Under it, Joseph Smith made his city practically independent not only of the state, but of the entire nation. He had personal monopolies on many forms of commercial enterprise, and he ruled as an autocrat, not always wisely. His word was law to the faithful until he encountered trouble in the top echelon of his own church and made some political blunders which brought him into conflict with the outside world.

Joseph Smith, Jr., was a man of strange contradictions. The portrait of him usually seen is a profile view showing a portly figure in a gorgeous uniform—which he designed for himself, complete with sword and plumed hat. His face is singular for a sloping forehead, a chin that retreats almost into the high collar of his coat, pursed lips, heavy-lidded arrogant eyes, and an oddly hooked nose. Compared with the evident force and mental power of his successor, Brigham Young, as shown by portraits of the latter, he seems almost inadequate.

He was, according to contemporary testimony, given to strong drink and over-fond of the ladies—this last leading to his celebrated "revelation" sanctioning polygamy. His writings, in their original form, revealed a surprising illiteracy. He was fierce and unrelenting in his hatreds, and was called a charlatan and blasphemer for his claims

[1] As an interesting sidelight, a member of the Illinois state legislature named Abraham Lincoln, later to be President of the United States, was among those who voted for this remarkable document.

that he had converse with Almighty God, who "directed" his movements, good or bad.

Yet this man was a dreamer, a zealot, a tremendous personality who had that ability seen in few men, to win the faith, belief, even the idolatry of other men, not only the ignorant and credulous, but the educated and worldly-wise as well.

The Mormons were fanatical and tactless. Bluntly and openly they declared that all forms of worship except their own were "works of the Devil." This went down hard with fervent Methodists, Baptists, and other devout church people of the frontier. They took their religion seriously. Though a modern generation may look with tolerance upon rival sects, in that day denunciation of a man's beliefs was fighting talk.

The Reverend Peter Cartwright, celebrated Methodist circuit rider, an honest, though perhaps not unprejudiced, critic, in addition to calling the Mormon religion "un-Christian," bitterly assailed the Mormons as follows:

"The Mormons stole stock, plundered and burned houses and barns, and there is no doubt they murdered some of the best citizens of the county, and owing to perjured evidence at their command, redress was impossible."[2]

This attitude was typical of many preachers in the more orthodox churches. It must be said it had some justification, except that the Reverend Mr. Cartwright lumped together *all* Mormons, when he should have charged these depredations against only a few, and these mostly no more than *so-called* Mormons.

There was public excitement, of course, at the reports that polygamy was practiced by the Mormons, which at first was denied, but later was made public under sensational circumstances. The first great resentments, however, were based on a general belief that much crime originated in Nauvoo, and that the Mormons were guilty of this *by doctrine.*

2.

Let us look at this last charge.

Long before the Mormons built their city, the upper Mississippi valley "was unusually infested with reckless and bloodstained men," to use the words of Governor Thomas Ford of Illinois. Especially was this true of southeastern Iowa and northeastern Missouri, and the is-

[2] *Autobiography of Peter Cartwright,* edited by W. P. Strickland.

lands and groves along the Mississippi near Davenport, Iowa, and Rock Island, Illinois, as well as the woods and hollows near Nauvoo itself.

Some of these outlaws were without much doubt fugitives from the Murrell gang which had been broken up in the South a few years before. One of them, Granville Young, in fact made a statement that he was a member of the "united banditti" (the Murrell Clan); and names on the Murrell roster keep cropping up in the annals of crime on the Upper Mississippi, although some of these may have been borne, by coincidence, by other persons not members of the original Clan.

But Murrell fugitives were a minority compared to other criminals, equally bad, who fled from justice in the East, and also "natives" of the country whose naturally evil tendencies made them willing accomplices. Lacking all scruples, these outlaws, of all stripes, were quick to see the unusual opportunity for them in the peculiar conditions then prevailing in Nauvoo.

The Mormons had been gathered from all parts of the United States except the South, and large numbers came from England, Ireland, Wales, and other foreign lands, where Mormon missionaries had labored. Many, perhaps most, of the new converts were from the poorer, more illiterate classes of society. They were in large measure strangers to each other, undergoing new and in some cases frightening experiences; the whole world seemed to be against them. To them the name Mormon was the one great cohesive force, and these bewildered children of adversity instinctively clung to all who bore that name.

For the criminals it was easy to impose on the confidence of these people and insinuate themselves into their disorganized society. They went through the forms of conversion and baptism as a cloak for their depredations *outside* Nauvoo. This had been cautiously stated by a Mormon historian, George Q. Cannon, as follows:

There were a number of bad men in those days, who, professing to be Latter Day Saints, were guilty of many evil practices. Not content with doing wrong themselves, they tried to lead others to engage with them by telling them that Joseph [Smith] knew all about their acts, and that he had given them authority to steal. They endeavored to screen themselves by using the names of Joseph and Hyrum and other leading men. They said it was not wrong to take anything from a Gentile; the prophet Isaiah had said that Zion should suck the milk of the Gentiles; and Micah had said that the gain of the Gentiles was to be consecrated to the Lord and their substance to the Lord of the whole earth. When, therefore, they stole property from men who did not belong to the church, they said they were "consecrating" or that they were "milking the Gentiles," and justified themselves for so doing, and called it perfectly right.[3]

Thus in Nauvoo, where the vast majority were honest and devout followers of their faith, there grew up an evil core of scoundrels. Some of these outlaws remained with the Mormons when they later made their great hegira to the West. One of them, described as "one of the most notorious rascals unhung," came to ghastly fame as a slayer in Utah, under the dread name of Bill Hickman, the Destroying Angel. Another was Return Jackson Redden, better known as Jack Redden, a member of a family of robbers, one of whom served in prison, who became a Danite like Hickman, and dealt out death on the frontier. Others were Isaac C. Haight, a participant in the dreadful Mountain Meadows massacre, and John D. Lee, executed by a firing squad for his part in that atrocity, who, like the others was a Danite from Illinois. Another of the Danites, who went to Utah in the hegira, and could be called an outlaw because of his murders, was Porter Rockwell. But Rockwell seems strangely of a better grade than the others. He killed, but from fanaticism, never for gain and never, apparently, from mere blood lust.

Outside of Nauvoo, outlaws operating in the area made a frequent practice of seeking safety in the Mormon capital, when "times got squally," as was the expression of the day. The honest Mormons, considering themselves persecuted and bitterly resentful of their enemies, quite naturally defended anyone who called himself a Mormon, in the naïve belief that if he was a member of the faith, he must be falsely accused. The result of this shielding of criminals by a harried people was that where few were guilty, all suffered.

3.

Each month the tension grew, until it built up to the tragic and almost inevitable result. The church began to be plagued by schisms, and by those who became disillusioned and "apostasized." Splitting off of fragments from the main body of the Latter Day Saints was a source of woe. Sidney Rigdon took off a company to Pennsylvania which became known as Rigdonites. Others who broke away at various times were called Gladdenites, Strangites, Brewsterites, Cutlerites, and so forth, depending on the names of their leaders. The strongest rival Mormon sect today is the Reorganized Church of Latter Day

[3] George Q. Cannon, *The Life of Joseph Smith, The Prophet.*

Saints—called Josephites—with headquarters at Independence, Missouri.

The great rock of disruption was the "Revelation Concerning Celestial Marriage"—that is, polygamy—which Joseph Smith "received" July 12, 1843, and dictated to his secretary, William Clayton.

William Law—who had a young and attractive wife—denounced the doctrine and with his brother and others defied it. They thereupon did the worst thing they could do to Joseph Smith under the circumstances: they started a rival newspaper to his own official journal, called it the *Expositor,* and in it printed an exposé of the prophet.

The *Expositor* had a short life—it published just one issue. But that issue was controversial enough to last most newspapers for a century. It "contained the statements of sixteen women that Joseph Smith or other Mormon leaders had attempted to seduce them under the plea of heavenly permission to do so." It also charged various eminent men with "bigamy, adultery, larceny, counterfeiting, etc."

The furore created in Nauvoo can be imagined. Smith was furious. His newspaper, the *Nauvoo Neighbor,* replied by charging the dissenters with the same crimes, and "sustained many of the charges by publication of numerous affidavits."

But the prophet held the whip hand in Nauvoo. Under his orders a mob stormed the *Expositor* office, pied its type, broke up the printing press with sledge hammers, and burned its paper and all other combustible property.

The Laws and their fellow apostates fled to Carthage, the county seat, and there procured warrants against Smith and others for rioting and destruction of property.

Now came a clash of authority. Nauvoo refused to allow the warrants to be served. Governor Ford called out the militia. After some delays and negotiations Joseph Smith surrendered, with his brother Hyrum, John Taylor, and Willard Richards. They were taken to Carthage and confined on the second floor of the stone jail.

That was June 27, 1834. Late in the afternoon of the same day a mob marched on the jail, dispersed the guard, and rushed upstairs. In a dreadful manifestation of mass fury they broke down the door of the room where the prisoners were confined.

Hyrum Smith was shot dead. Taylor fell, severely wounded, although he eventually recovered. Joseph Smith attempted to leap from the window, but was shot and fell to the ground below. To make sure that he was dead, the assailants propped him up against a well-curb and fired four additional bullets into his body.

It was a sickening deed: brutal murder in its worst form. In committing those murders the mob unwittingly performed a great service for the future of the Mormon church, by providing it with a "martyr," and solidifying its tenets and leadership.

Thereafter there were raids and counter-raids. Nauvoo captured Carthage and Nauvoo itself was stormed. A deathblow came when on January 21, 1845, the Illinois legislature repealed the city's unique charter, reducing it to the status of other cities in the state.

At last, in 1846, Brigham Young, the truly great organizer and leader of the Mormons—whatever his critics may say of his morals and conduct—led his people away on their tragic *via dolorosa* to the "promised land" in the Great Basin west of the Rocky Mountains.

We are not, however, interested in this book in the subsequent history of the Mormon church, and the foregoing has been outlined only to show the disorganized and confused background against which operated a powerful and dangerous league of ruffians and scoundrels.

4.

There had been several robberies in the country around Nauvoo, before and after the death of Joseph Smith; and the conscienceless nature of the bandits operating under the cloak of Mormonism is never more clearly indicated than by the fact that some of their victims were *Mormons*—supposedly fellow members of the faith.

As an example, in the fall of 1844 three men, introducing themselves as Mormon preachers, stopped for several nights at the house of "a man of the Mormon faith near Pekin, on the Illinois River." They preached in the neighborhood, and one of them induced the old man to exchange gold for a hundred dollar bill, stating that "Brigham Young wants the gold to buy materials in Nauvoo that can't be got any other way."

Having by this means discovered where the Mormon kept his money —nearly two thousand dollars—they left with profuse thanks for his hospitality. But a few nights later they returned, entered his home, and robbed him of his money, including the hundred dollar bill he had so kindly exchanged for them. Then they disappeared.

Later, by the statement of Granville Young, one of the robbers, it was revealed that the three thieves were Return Jackson Redden, William Louther, and Young himself. Redden, Young and Louther were all self-styled "Mormons." When he told the story, the bandit gleefully recounted that the bill they "exchanged" was counterfeit!

Another sincere Mormon who was to have been a victim was a certain Beach, a merchant near Nauvoo itself. This robbery was planned by Amos Hodges, Robert Birch (also known as Robert Harris[4] and Blecher), and William Fox, alias Sutton. All three masqueraded as "Mormons," Hodges even bearing the title of elder in the church.

But Beach was warned by Brigham Young, who somehow learned of the plot, and the robbers were put to flight by men who guarded the store. Later Amos Hodges told the story that he had gone to Brigham Young and asked his permission to rob Beach, and the Mormon leader then notified the intended victim of the proposed robbery! What makes this story sound incredible is that no effort was made to apprehend or prosecute Hodges, and one feels certain that had the Mormon head known the man was an accessory to a crime against a Mormon, he would have had Amos Hodges in jail.

Other victims may have been Mormons, including an old man named Mulford and his wife, living near the Rock River in Ogle County, Illinois. Birch and Fox committed this crime and escaped with four hundred dollars in loot.

But the most dreadful of the crimes occurred in the period after the death of Joseph Smith, while Brigham Young was struggling to reorganize his people and at the same time combat the forces set in motion against him both within and without. It must be described in some detail here, for it brings into the picture a curious individual named Edward Bonney.

5.

On April 25, 1845, an elderly German named John Miller, with his wife, their daughter and her husband, a young man named Leicy (or Leiza) arrived in Lee County, Iowa, and took a cabin twelve miles north of Nauvoo and about three and a half miles from West Point. They had emigrated from Ohio, were looking for land, and it was rumored that they had with them about five thousand dollars in cash to purchase acreage. Although these people proposed to settle in the neighborhood of Nauvoo, they probably were not Mormons— certainly the neighborhood was not.

A few days after their arrival two strangers appeared in the vicinity, and presently stopped at the Miller house.

"We're lookin' for an ox that's lost," they said. "Seen anything of him?" They thereupon went into a description of the beast. No stray ox had been seen by the Millers or any of their neighbors.

---

[4] An "R. Haris"—or Harris—was listed as one of Murrell's "Transient Members," the inner circle of the Murrell Clan.

That night the "ox hunters" stayed at a cabin about a quarter of a mile from the Miller place. Perhaps they might have lodged with the Millers, but the cabin was overcrowded. It had but one room, and a third couple (name not recorded) had moved in.

Next day the two men returned and asked the old German to change a bank note for them, "so they could pay for their lodgings." This was the same ruse used when the old Mormon was robbed, to find where the money was kept. Miller, however, did not accommodate them, suspecting that the note was counterfeit, for there was considerable bogus currency in the country at the time. The men went away.

That night, May 10, the Miller household, suspecting no danger, retired early. The cabin evidently had little furniture for all three couples slept on the floor. We even know the locations where their beds were spread. The mysterious unnamed couple laid their blankets on the north side of the room. On either side of them slept the other couples, Miller and his wife in the northwest corner, Leicy and his wife in the northeast corner.

About midnight their slumber was suddenly interrupted by three men who burst into the cabin, armed with clubs, pistols, and knives. One of the three carried a "dark lantern"—a primitive affair with a single opening which could be closed to conceal the light of the candle within. Quickly the lantern carrier flashed his light about and located the beds in which Miller and Leicy lay with their wives. The terror of these poor people, wakened so suddenly from deep sleep, can be imagined as the robbers sprang forward and began with diabolic fury to batter the heads of the two prostrate men.

Half stunned by the blows, the old German, Miller, struggled to his feet. An assailant buried the blade of a bowie knife in his chest.

In spite of this terrible wound, and already dying, Miller managed to push the ruffian out of the cabin door, plunging out after him. There, outside the building, the bandit closed with him for another deadly thrust with the knife, which finished the old man.

Meantime Leicy, grappling with his attacker, wrestled him to the ground. Lacking any weapons, he tried to choke the ruffian with his hands, but the man with the dark lantern, crouching over the struggling pair, repeatedly stabbed Leicy in the back and head with his knife.

At length Leicy, severely wounded and covered with blood, broke away, rose to his feet, and ran for the door. As he reached it a pistol shot brought him down, the ball penetrating his body through the intestinal cavity.

Throughout this furious struggle, while the shrieks of Mrs. Miller and Mrs. Leicy, the curses of the bandits, the groans and cries of their victims, the sounds of blows and the pistol shot made a tumult of noise in the room, the third man lay in his bed with his woman, pulling the covers over their heads, and making no effort to defend their hosts.

Why? Note that although this unknown couple lay on the floor *between* the beds of the Miller and Leicy couples, not a blow was struck at them. It must be supposed that the unnamed stranger and his consort were in league with the bandits, perhaps sent to the house as spies. Their identity has never been ascertained, for they left the house and disappeared soon after the murderers were gone.

Miller and Leicy, by their hard fight, prevented the bandits from getting the loot they were after—if indeed the rumored money was in the place. Because of noise and the pistol shot and the fear that someone might come to investigate, all three assailants leaped out into the darkness and ran away, leaving their victims lying in their blood.

Just at daybreak Sheriff James L. Estes arrived from West Point, summoned by some of the neighbors. A bloody scene of violence greeted his eyes.

Miller, the stouthearted old German, lay outstretched and dead on a sloping place a few feet from the cabin door, his head downhill, his blood covering the ground for several feet where it had run down from his body.

Leicy had been dragged into the cabin by the women. He was still alive but it could be seen that his condition was hopeless. His skull was fractured, there were several stab wounds in his body, and the pistol ball, which was extracted from where it flattened on a bone after passing through the body cavity, had produced severe internal hemorrhage. It seemed that his death was a matter of minutes or hours; yet he lived, though in great agony, long enough to identify his murderers.

Groups of citizens scoured the country about for any trace of the killers. A cloth cap, trimmed with fur, and without a visor, was found. Sheriff Estes followed the trail of the outlaws until he lost it a few miles from Nauvoo, where they were apparently heading.

6.

It was at this point that Edward Bonney stepped into the picture.

Just who he was, or what was his occupation, is obscure; but he lived in Montrose, a small town across the river from Nauvoo and knew many of the residents of the latter city well.

By avocation he appears to have been an amateur detective—one of that peculiar breed of men who delight in unraveling mysteries of crime. He was destined to play a large part in the events that ensued, and though he certainly received money rewards for some of the arrests he brought about, his real interest seems to have been in the chase itself—the matching of his wits with outlaws, hunting them down, capturing them, and seeing them convicted of their crimes.

Bonney, to judge by his statements, was anti-Mormon; yet he was able to make a distinction between sincere Mormons and those who used the name for evil purposes. He was dogged and courageous, at times quick-witted and clever; and he had a gift for winning and keeping the confidence of law-abiding men in all stations of life—farmers, storekeepers, law officers, and up the scale to heads of important banks, judges, and the governors of two states. With these qualities he combined a surpassing memory for names and faces, and a sort of bloodhound instinct that kept him on a trail, once he took it, until he reached its end.

As a friend of Sheriff Estes, possessing that officer's confidence, Bonney made an investigation and interviewed the witnesses—the two women and the dying Leicy—the morning after the attack. To him the fur-trimmed cap was the solitary clue to the case.

He noted that the trail of the criminals had headed for Nauvoo, and next day he crossed the Mississippi and began making inquiries in that city. His first discovery was important: a young man named William Hodges had been wearing a hat for the last two days, although previously he had always worn a cap—a cap which answered exactly to the description of the one found at the murder scene.

He learned further that William Hodges' brother Stephen, on the morning of May 11, after the murder, had been seen with a splash of blood on his shirt, which he made haste to conceal and changed the garment.

As a final piece of circumstantial evidence, on the afternoon of May 10, William and Stephen Hodges, and a man known as Thomas Brown, had been seen rowing in a skiff up the river in the direction toward the place where the attack occurred. "Thomas Brown" later was found to be an alias of a very notorious criminal named Robert Birch.

One feels that Bonney may have suspected the Hodges brothers for some reason, before he went to Nauvoo and made these inquiries. In any case he went directly to Colonel Stephen Markham, who headed the Nauvoo police force, for assistance in making an arrest.

Here arises an incident that refutes the wild story that the Mormon authorities were hand-in-glove with the outlaws. William and Stephen Hodges lived in Nauvoo with their brother Amos. All three were "Mormons." But Colonel Markham, a Mormon himself, as soon as Bonney presented his evidence, took a guard—also of Mormons—and arrested all three Hodges in their house. The suspect "Tom Brown" was not found.

The three Hodges at once appealed to Brigham Young, the head of the Mormon church. Young at first refused to allow Iowa officers to take the men out of Nauvoo.

Much was made, at the time, by non-Mormons, of the difficulties surrounding the getting of the prisoners out of the Mormon city for trial. The facts are that as soon as Brigham Young was shown a legal indictment, he immediately ordered his own police to deliver William and Stephen Hodges to the authorities. Since there was no evidence implicating Amos Hodges, he was released.

Sheriff Estes hurried the prisoners to West Point. Several persons living in the Miller neighborhood identified them as the suspicious acting "ox hunters" who hung around the area for a few days before the murder, and who tried to pass off a bill at the Miller house. The fur-trimmed cap was identified as belonging to William Hodges. A witness testified as to the bloodstained shirt of Stephen Hodges.

There was other testimony, but the conclusive evidence was given by Leicy. Although his wounds were mortal and he was rapidly sinking he seemed to cling to life by an effort of will. To him the sheriff brought the two Hodges, together with several other men, chosen because they resembled the brothers in general build.

These were seated in a circle about the bed of the dying man.

"Do you recognize any of these men?" the sheriff asked.

Slowly Leicy's gaze turned to the features of each of them. Then he pointed to Stephen Hodges.

"That is the man who stabbed me with the bowie knife," he said.

A moment later he again pointed, this time at William Hodges. "That is the man who shot me."

He was very certain, although the only light by which he saw them the night of the murder was that shed by the dark lantern. Nevertheless it must be remembered that he knew the men from their previous visit to the cabin as "ox-hunters," and would therefore have been able to recognize them even by the dim light.

Shortly after this identification of his murderers, Leicy died.

At the trial, which was held at West Point, several persons testified that the Hodges were in Nauvoo on the night of the murder. Among these were four whose names must be remembered as this account continues: John Long; Aaron Long, his brother; William Fox, alias "the Judge," alias Sutton; Robert Birch, alias R. H. Blecher, alias Robert Harris, who actually was the mysterious "Tom Brown" for whom the search had been made.

The testimony of these alibi witnesses differed so greatly and in many instances was so directly conflicting, that the effort to swear the Hodges out of the case failed. On the other hand, the dying

statement of Leicy, the murdered man, was so convincing that the
jury brought in a verdict of murder in the first degree. The Hodges
brothers were sentenced to die on the gallows.

Next came another in the mysterious series of events. When the
fate of the brothers was known, Erwin Hodges, a fourth member of the
family and also a "Mormon," who lived some distance from the city,
appeared in Nauvoo and demanded an interview with Brigham Young.
Evidently he expected the Mormon leader to save his brothers, perhaps by force, for he said very threateningly prior to the interview,
"If my brothers aren't released, there will be some other Mormons to
keep them company."

Nobody knows what was said between him and Brigham Young.
But at nine o'clock that same night Erwin Hodges was found in a
back street of Nauvoo, stabbed to death. Years later, in a death confession before he was executed by a firing squad for his participation
in the Mountain Meadows massacre, John D. Lee said that Erwin
Hodges was killed because he made the statement that the robbery
and murder of Miller and Leicy were committed on Brigham Young's
orders. Said Lee, "No man under suspicion was permitted to escape."

Brigham Young's "bodyguard," the Danites, undoubtedly "took care"
of Erwin Hodges when they heard him make such a charge against
their chief. The charge itself I consider preposterous, in view of Brigham Young's action in promptly turning the guilty men over to the
authorities. In view of the multitude of troubles and problems which
then beset him, in trying to organize his people after the death of
Joseph Smith, while at the same time seeking to appease public feeling
against his city, the Mormon leader was not such a fool as to order a
petty robbery and murder in the very neighborhood of Nauvoo, even
had he been so disposed, which I do not believe he was.

Stephen and William Hodges were publicly executed at West Point
July 15. They denied their guilt to the last, but not one of the hundreds of spectators who saw them swung off into eternity believed
them innocent.

Thus, largely through the efforts of Edward Bonney, two members
of the criminal gang masquerading as "Mormons" received punishment. But their fellow outlaws still were ferociously aggressive.

Even before the Hodges brothers were hanged a new crime had
been committed by them, of a nature so brutal, and involving a person
so prominent and revered, that it became a turning point in the war
against the bandits on the upper Mississippi. At least one of the men
that murdered Miller and Leicy was involved in this second murder,
which took the life of a man universally beloved, and whose name is
today borne by an important, populous and beautiful city.

XXI. The Murder of Colonel Davenport

1.

A long limestone island, at the confluence of the Mississippi and Rock rivers, lying between the Illinois and Iowa shores, was called Rock Island, and for it a town on the Illinois side was named.

Upon this island, facing across the main channel of the Mississippi toward the Iowa side, stood what for that day was an elegant and impressive mansion. Of two stories, painted white, with a portico, wide chimneys, and two spacious wings, it formed a considerable landmark in a country where the usual dwelling at the time was a log cabin.

The mansion was the home of Colonel George Davenport, who gave his name to the present city of Davenport, Iowa. In July of 1845, Colonel Davenport was a fine-looking gentleman with snow-white hair, and a benevolent, patriarchal manner. He was admired and revered by the people up and down the river, for his generosity, his invariable courtesy, and his rather impressive record.

Born in England, he came to America in his youth, became a citizen of the United States, and entered the army in which he served from

1806 to 1816, fighting against the British in the War of 1812, and in various campaigns against hostile Indians.

Near the end of his service he brought a detachment of soldiers to build a fort on Rock Island—at that time in the heart of the Sauk and Fox Indian country—which he named Fort Armstrong, in honor of John Armstrong, Madison's Secretary of War.

Having completed this assignment in a few months, he resigned in 1816 from the army, to enter the Indian fur trade. At his trading post near the fort, he first traded independently, then for a time as a representative of the American Fur Company, headed by that somewhat piratical genius, John Jacob Astor.

He was given a free hand by Astor, and by his fair dealings with the Sauk and Fox tribe he became very influential with them. Though he acted as quartermaster of the troops during the Black Hawk War of 1832, he later played an important part in the negotiations that brought an end to that conflict.

In the beginning Colonel Davenport dwelt in a log cabin, like any other frontiersman. But when Fort Armstrong was abandoned in 1836, he built his fine mansion. Already he had become interested in land, and he laid out the town-site that became the City of Davenport across the river from his home. In 1845, much respected and liked, and reputed to be wealthy, the old colonel was living in some splendor—for the times—in his mansion, with his family and servants.

In honor of the Fourth of July, 1845, the small city of Rock Island, Illinois, planned a patriotic celebration, to which the entire Davenport household was invited. At the last minute, however, because of an indisposition, Colonel Davenport decided not to go, though he told his people by all means to attend and enjoy the parade, sports, frontier oratory, and feasting that were usual events on such programs.

Some members of his family were reluctant to leave him alone, because they knew of the presence of shifty characters on the numerous wild islands both above and below Rock Island. But the white-haired colonel laughed at their fears. It was broad daylight, he pointed out, they would all be back before night, and he scoffed at the idea that anyone would molest the house or himself at such a time—especially since he did not imagine that anyone could possibly be aware that he alone would be there.

What Colonel Davenport did not know was that a man whom he had befriended, who for a time lived at his home, and who was supposed to be devoted to him, was a secret spy for a gang of bandits; and that this treacherous spy had reported to his confederates that the mansion would be empty that day, almost as soon as the family and servants themselves knew they would be gone.

Nor did the colonel know that his last-minute decision to remain home would be a surprise to the outlaws—a surprise that would bring anguish and death upon himself.

2.

At about four o'clock that afternoon of July 4, Benjamin Cole and Frazier Wilson, of the neighboring village of Moline, with another man and a boy, were enjoying a holiday fishing expedition along the island. As their skiff drifted past the bluff on which the Davenport mansion stood, they heard a faint cry.

Cole later said that he distinctly heard the words, "Murder! Help! For God's sake!"

His companions at first thought the cries were given by some prankster as a Fourth of July trick; but Cole insisted on landing. They therefore brought the boat to the shore and went up to the house. At the gate a large bulldog barked at them, and Cole spent some minutes coaxing the animal before it would allow them to enter. That bulldog would become one of the mysteries in the case.

Cole knocked at the front door. There was no answer. He cautiously opened the door, which was unlocked; and entered, followed by the others.

At once they saw blood, splashed and spattered "in every direction," in the hall. Cole hurried to the rear of the house and looked out. Nobody was in sight. As he returned to the foot of the stairs leading to the apartments above, they all heard a weak, despairing call for help.

Up the steps they rushed, noticing that the stairs themselves were stained with blood. Above they were horrified by a ghastly sight.

Outstretched on a bed, which was saturated with his blood, lay the best-known man in the country about—Colonel Davenport. He was white and suffering, and it was evident he was in a dying condition.

"Why didn't you come sooner?" he feebly moaned.

"I came as soon as I could," replied Cole sympathetically. "What can I do for you?"

"Get a doctor—get Dr. Brown," begged the old man. "He's at a picnic down at the other end of this island."

Cole ran to fetch the physician who came at once. As Dr. Brown was making his examination, Cole sent some of his party across the river for additional help.

Dr. Brown administered first aid, binding up a wound in the old colonel's left thigh, through which a pistol ball had passed, severing a large vein or artery. The hemorrhage was very heavy and he had difficulty stopping the flow of blood.

Soon two other physicians, Dr. P. Gregg and Dr. Witherwax, arrived followed by a crowd of curious persons from the mainland.

"The colonel was sinking fast from exhaustion, in great agony, and cold from head to foot," Dr. Gregg later said. "I examined the wound, and found that there had been a profuse flow of blood. The blood was *everywhere*. The house looked like a butcher's shambles—blood in the sitting room, in the hall, and along up the stairs; and in the closet by the safe was a pool of blood; and in the room below there was the same. On the door case of the closet containing the safe was the mark of a bloody hand. The left leg of his pantaloons and the bed clothes were saturated with blood. I observed contusions on his left arm and side, and he appeared as if he had been bruised or beaten."

The dying man begged to see his family, which already had been summoned by a messenger, and was on its way across the river to be at his side. As soon as his household arrived, he mustered strength to tell what happened to him.

"I have been robbed and murdered," he said with faltering breath to his two sons, George L. and Bailey Davenport. "I was sitting in the front room . . . when I heard a noise . . . in the back part of the house . . . but I fancied it was someone . . . at the well for water."

A pause, as if gathering strength, then:

"I heard the noise again . . . got up to see what it was . . . I was at once attacked by three or more men . . ."

Another halt in the weak voice, before he went on:

"One of them . . . shot me. I tried . . . to get my cane . . . All of them jumped on me . . . bound me . . . blindfolded me . . . They dragged me up the stairs by my shirt collar . . ."

He seemed to search his recollection for a moment.

"I saw three . . . but I think there were more . . ." he said. He did not say why he thought there were more assailants, but later it was shown that his supposition was correct. He continued:

"They made me . . . open the safe . . . took all the money in it . . . threw me on . . . the bed . . . beat me . . . nearly choked me to death . . . to make me tell where more money was hidden . . ."

He told them there was no more money, but the bandits would not believe him. They had miscalculated in one respect: Colonel Davenport kept most of his wealth in banks rather than about the house. Nevertheless, as he gasped on:

"They told me they would . . . burn the house . . . and me in it . . . if I didn't tell them . . . The one who shot me opposed it . . .

They choked me again . . . revived me by . . . throwing water in my face . . . choked me . . . and beat me until . . . I fainted . . ."

Afterwards he managed to moan out a description of the three ruffians he had seen. The man who shot him was "small and slim and wore a cloth cap." One of the others was "short, thick-set, square-built." The third was "a large, middling sized, tall man." He even attempted to give some description of their features, though without much clarity, before he lapsed into unconsciousness.

They had bound him with hickory bark strips and blindfolded him with a red silk handkerchief. But he managed to gnaw through the bonds on his hands and thus removed the handkerchief from his face by the time he was found.

An oddity was that he did not mention having heard the dog prior to the attack on him. Remember that a large bulldog disputed with Cole his entrance into the front gate, barking at them until it was coaxed to be quiet. Where was the animal when the bandits made their foray, and why did it not bark at them? The only supposition could be that someone *whom the dog knew* was with the outlaw party, and was able to make the dog think that all was well so that it gave no alarm.

Downstairs, Cole and Wilson found boot tracks beneath one of the windows. Wilson followed them to a slough, where the marks of a boat which had been drawn up and concealed were discovered. The craft was gone—the men had left in it. Wilson said there were "three or four distinctly different tracks, one that of a large square-toed boot, another of a small boot with a fine heel. It seemed as if the persons who made them were going rapidly, the heels struck hard, making a deep impression."

The bandits were gone. With them they took about seven hundred dollars in cash, together with Colonel Davenport's gold watch and chain, a fine double-barreled shotgun, and a pistol.

That night, at about nine o'clock, Colonel Davenport died.

3.

Edward Bonney had been trying to trace down "Thomas Brown" —the mysterious third man named in the indictment for the Miller-Leicy murders. He was spurred somewhat by a five hundred dollar reward offered by Lee County; but again the sheer zest of the adventure seems to have been his most impelling motive.

He was in the office of Sheriff Estes, the afternoon of July 8, when the shocking news of the murder of Colonel Davenport, which oc-

curred four days before, was received there. Because of the savage
brutality of the crime and the prominence of the victim, rewards were
offered for the capture of the guilty persons—two hundred dollars for
each at first, the amount later increased. A handbill gave the description of the three men which the dying old colonel had supplied.

Reading those descriptions over, Bonney was struck by a familiar
sound to them. He thought back on the list of witnesses who tried to
save the Hodges brothers by falsely swearing they were in Nauvoo
the night of the Miller-Leicy murders, and two seemed to fit: John
and Aaron Long. A third could have been "Judge" Fox.

John Long was "short, thick-set, square-built." Aaron Long was
"middling sized and tall." Fox was "small and slim," which could describe the little man who shot the colonel and also account for the
"small boot with a fine heel" which left tracks seen by Frazier Wilson.

Bonney had been about to give up the hunt for "Thomas Brown,"
but now he took a new interest. Obtaining a letter from Sheriff Estes
to secure the cooperation of authorities, he boarded a steamboat north
for Rock Island—traveling at his own expense. There he first went
over the Davenport mansion and its grounds without finding anything
new; then conferred with some leading men of Rock Island, who were
extremely anxious to bring the murderers to justice. One suspect had
been arrested thus far, a man named Bird; but he proved his innocence
and was freed. The local citizens were therefore glad to talk to anyone who might be of assistance.

In that conference Joseph Knox, an attorney, read a letter from another lawyer, Aaron L. Miller, living in Rockford, Illinois, in the northern part of the state, which brought a new name into the case.

The description of one of the Davenport murderers, wrote Lawyer
Miller, "resembles the appearance of the notorious Birch, one of the
most daring and desperate members of the gang." Birch, the letter
went on, was perhaps thirty years old (he could have been older),
"a well-made, broad-breasted man, of a light complexion, large blue
eyes, and light auburn hair; when fashionably dressed he seems rather
slightly built. He is very loquacious, and can play the bar-room dandy
to perfection."

To Bonney the most interesting part of the information was at the
end: Birch was known also under the names of Harris, Blecher, and
Brown. And he sometimes called himself Haines.[1] Birch was one of
those who tried to swear to an alibi for the Hodges brothers. It now
seemed to Bonney that he must be the third of the Miller-Leicy mur-

[1] Remember the "R. Haris" and "2 Hains" of Murrell's inner circle.

derers; and reasonably probable that the same man was involved in the Davenport murder.

Returning to Montrose, Bonney learned almost at once that the Long brothers, together with two other men, had been seen about the place of Old Grant Redden, another so-called "Mormon," who lived with his two sons, Return Jackson (Jack) and William Harrison Redden—both of whom had bad reputations—on appropriately named Devil's Creek, about five miles from Montrose. It was whispered that Old Man Redden kept there a regular rendezvous for outlaws.

The two men most often seen with the Long brothers, Bonney was informed, were William Fox, usually called Judge; and Birch of the many aliases, including Blecher, Harris, Haines, and Brown.

These four, Bonney considered, might well be involved in the Davenport murder. The dying colonel saw only three, but he said "I think there were more"—a fourth or perhaps even a fifth robber. Was this lead correct, or was Bonney on the wrong trail?

4.

Bonney knew he was a marked man: he was well known as one of the chief figures in sending the Hodges brothers to the gallows.

Yet he had a plausible way about him, and the nature of the frontier and its poeple enabled him frequently to sink into a curious kind of obscurity. Perhaps he resorted at times to some sort of disguise. At any rate he was able more than once to converse with outlaws and bandits on terms which won from them the most astonishing confidences.

The brutality of the murder of Colonel Davenport, its shocking boldness, and most of all the prominence and wide public respect the victim possessed, made this crime a sort of defiance of all law-abiding society. The criminals seemed sure of themselves—too sure. Edward Bonney set about to find the guilty parties and bring them before the bar of justice. They did not know it, but the murderers and all their associates could not have brought upon their track a more determined and resourceful nemesis.

He began at once to set his plans at work. Very soon after his return to Montrose he stopped a posse of angry men from descending on Old Grant Redden's place and wrecking it. His reasons were two-fold: the mob action would have spoiled his immediate chances of catching the men he was after; and his intervention—which he was careful to make a matter of public knowledge—might cause the Reddens and their associates to believe that he was secretly on their side, a powerful advantage for him.

Bonney's occupation—when he was not playing the sleuth—seems to have had to do with horses, either as a livery stable keeper or as a dealer; and this in itself provided him with contacts of value at times, for horse-trading was a tricky profession, and horse thieves were abundant.

One day he fell into conversation with a certain John Baker, who had "a splendid span of horses he wanted to sell cheap"—pretty good evidence that they were stolen. Bonney was affable with this man. Opportunity arising, he confidentially mentioned the names of Fox, the Longs, and others. The following extraordinary conversation ensued:

"You're acquainted with Fox?" asked Baker.

"Well acquainted with all of them," replied Bonney.

"Where are the boys now?"

"Don't know. Haven't seen any of them for some time."

"I haven't seen Fox and the Longs, either, in several months," said Baker. "Since last winter I've been in upper Missouri."

"Are you acquainted with the Reddens?" Bonney asked.

"Only by reputation. I've heard the boys speak of them."

"You might learn where some of our fellows are by going to Old Man Redden's," suggested Bonney. "He lives only four or five miles distant—but don't mention my name. I'm not personally acquainted with him and he might think something's wrong."

"Never fear. I know how to satisfy him that I'm all right." And Baker rode away."

Next day he was back in Montrose.

"What luck?" asked Bonney when they met.

"First rate."

"See any of the boys?"

"No, but I heard about them."

"What did you hear?"

"Why, damn it all, man," said Baker in a low whisper, *"they're the ones who killed old Colonel Davenport!"*

"How do you know that?" Bonney feigned surprise.

"Old Redden told me himself!"

Bonney glanced quickly about, as if to see if anyone could overhear them. "Keep a tight mouth about it," he said, "or the boys will get into trouble. What did the old man say?"

"Fox, the two Longs, and Birch went from Redden's place to rob the colonel," said Baker. "When they returned with the booty they buried the watch and money in Redden's wheat field. There they stayed until they learned that Davenport had died—then they put off, to somewhere in Missouri, Old Redden didn't know where."

Shortly after this, presumably having disposed of his horses—perhaps with Bonney's assistance—Baker left town.

5.

Bonney now knew to a certainty the names of the men he was after, also that they had participated in other crimes. But other crimes had no bearing on this case; indirect testimony was not competent in court; and Colonel Davenport was dead, his descriptions insufficient to convict.

Summing things up, Bonney thought that to put the best face on it, obtaining the arrest and conviction of the murderers, with all their protection, hiding places, widespread connections, and resources—legal as well as illegal—seemed almost impossible. He felt discouraged, in a mood to give up the whole matter, when a letter came to him from Joseph Knox of Rock Island, with an earnest appeal:

> Our anxiety for the speedy arrest of these wretches is so great, that we feel inclined to sacrifice time, money, comfort, anything and everything, to effect the object. We cluster all our hopes around your plans and efforts. Don't let us be disappointed. Heaven send you prosperity and success.

The letter added some new information: Birch was known to stop at times with a man named Bennett in the Mississippi bottoms near Lyons, Clinton County, Iowa, not far above Rock Island. He was the leader of the bandits, sometimes called by them "Captain." The letter also gave minute descriptions of three new suspects: James Veasey; John Killgore, alias Big Davis; and "Sutton"—whose real name, Bonney knew, was William Fox.

Appealed to thus personally, he once more considered the case. He remembered that three identifiable objects had been taken from the Davenport house—a shotgun, a pistol, and the colonel's gold watch. If any of these were found in the possession of a suspect, it would be strong evidence against him.

But Bonney had natural misgivings:

"I felt most heartily willing to aid the authorities of Rock Island to the extent of my ability," he later wrote, "yet to assume the responsibility of conducting an enterprise of this magnitude was a task [difficult] to undertake. The threats made by the Banditti against me individually, in consequence of the part I had already taken in the arrest and prosecution of the Hodges, convinced me that danger must attend the undertaking."

There was this difference between Edward Bonney and that other frontier detective, Virgil Stewart. Stewart was led into his adventure by degrees, hardly realizing it, until he was so deeply involved that he had to go on. Bonney, knowing full well his peril in the beginning, now deliberately decided to take his risks.

These were assuredly great. He was personally known by the very men he was to hunt—the two Longs, Fox, and Birch, all of whom had appeared as witnesses for the defense of the Hodges, where he had been the chief witness for the prosecution. If he encountered any of them he must be prepared instantly to defend his life, or else be provided with some excuse so plausible that it would convince these deadly and suspicious men that he was no enemy of theirs.

Furthermore, should he succeed in gaining the confidence of the gang and then fail to capture and convict their leaders, he would be remorselessly hunted down and killed, to stop his tongue. In other words, what he must do had only one possible solution: success. And success seemed long odds away.

Yet he undertook the assignment. He possessed a sense of civic responsibility and the rewards offered may have inclined him somewhat; but more important, the excitement of the man hunt was irresistible. And now he suddenly conceived a plan both new and daring, which he believed would enable him to penetrate the innermost circles of the criminal gang and learn its secrets.

XXII.   *"A Damned Good Article"*

1.

On August 11, Bonney once more conferred with the citizens' committee of Rock Island. First he asked for, and received, a pledge that his family would be protected and supported, and his children educated, if he were killed. Then he obtained legal documents giving him authority to act in behalf of the State of Illinois. Finally, he revealed his plan.

It was sufficiently bold and novel. What he proposed to do was to seek entrance in the underworld as a *counterfeiter*. To do so, he must have "bogus" sufficiently real in appearance that it would impress even experts in this illegal enterprise. Bonney felt confident he could fool the sharpest eye with his bills—for he would take with him *genuine bank notes and pass them off as spurious.*

He explained that he did not need many; and he wanted them blank—that is, not signed by officers of the bank, which would validate them. This last point was a subtle one. Not only were the notes worthless without the signatures, but their lack of those signatures would provide him needed time with the excuse that he must "complete his transactions"—for he would say that he must take them to the most skillful forgers to affix the requisite names.

At first they listened to him with open-mouthed amazement. Then they became convinced it just might work. Judge Wilson, an official of the Miner's Bank, of Dubuque, Iowa, went upriver with him to that city and helped him obtain the bills from the bank there.

2.

With his printed bank notes, lacking only the signatures to make them cashable, Bonney boarded the steamboat *War Eagle* at Dubuque, bound downriver for St. Louis, where he hoped he might find a clue to where the outlaws were hidden in Missouri.

As he stood on the hurricane deck of the steamboat, watching the passing shores, a small young man, with dark hair, addressed him by name. Surprised, Bonney turned to him.

"My name is Granville Young," said the stranger. "I was sick last winter in Loomis's Tavern at Nauvoo, and saw you occasionally in the bar room."

Loomis's place had the reputation of being a hangout for some of the furtive gentry, and Bonney now remembered that he had heard mention of a Granville Young—as a suspected member of the river gang—while he was hunting for "Tom Brown" (or Birch). But why had this man addressed him? He decided that here was an opportunity to try out his stratagem.

"Why, certainly, I remember you, Mr. Young," he said heartily. "Suppose we go into the saloon for a social glass."

"Agreed," replied the other.

At the bar, as they touched glasses, Bonney asked, as if carelessly, "What kind of speculation are you in nowadays?"

"Nothing in particular." The word "speculation" was, of course, as we have seen, thieves' slang, and Young glanced at him suspiciously.

"I'm not mistaken am I, for taking you as one of the right stripe?" pursued Bonney.

Again a bit of underworld argot: "right stripe" meant a fellow criminal, or one willing to commit crime, in the sense of Murrell's "right grit."

Young grinned. "If you mean the kind of fellow that likes a glass now and then, I'm of the right stripe—let's have another."

Obviously he was on his guard. Bonney was sure the other had ticketed him as the prosecutor of the Hodges brothers. But he tried a new tack.

"I've heard you mentioned as one of our sort of boys," he said. "I'd like to show you a little matter that's worth looking into."

Drawing Young into a corner, he went on, "Look at these bills on the Miner's Bank at Dubuque, and see if you can tell them from genuine."

His interest now awakened, Young took the notes and gave them a very close examination.

"That's a *damned good article*," he said finally. "How much of it have you got?"

"Only enough with me for a sample; but I can get fifteen thousand dollars' worth in Cincinnati."

Young considered. "They're very good, but I think the paper's a little thinner than that used by the bank."

The bills, of course, were genuine; but Bonney encouraged this criticism, to convince Young that they were counterfeit.

"Not much," he said, as if defending his "bogus." "By use, you know, they'll collect dirt and become rough, when they'll seem about as thick as genuine note paper."

Young nodded. "It's really a splendid imitation. How much do you ask per dollar for it?"

"I don't know, until I figure up the expense of making it."

"It's worth the highest price."

"How much do you usually pay?"

"Fifteen to twenty-five dollars a hundred," said Young. "When it's new, if good like this, it's worth twenty-five. I'll give you that and find a market for all you can raise."

Bonney demurred. "I don't think I can afford to let it go for twenty-five a hundred. It's cost me a pile of money to get it up, and it's about as good as the genuine bills right out of the bank."

"True, it is."

"I think I ought to have half the face of it."

So they haggled, and Bonney's pretense of greed was the last necessary factor in fully convincing Young that he was a rascal. There could be no immediate transaction in the "bogus" in any case for the bills were still unsigned. Presently Young said he was temporarily without money. Bonney loaned him five dollars to pay for drinks and meals to Nauvoo, which was his destination.

"You're a damned good fellow," said Young. "I was a little afraid of you at first."

"No more than proper," said Bonney. "We must all be careful."

He knew that one more point must be cleared: Young was thinking of the Hodges case, and his connection with it. So after a time he skillfully dropped the hint that a man who was in his particular "spec-

ulation" must have all sorts of dodges from which to operate: besides
which the Hodges brothers were "gone ducks" as soon as Brigham
Young surrendered them to the Iowa authorities.

This made sense to the outlaw, and before they reached Rock Island, he and Bonney were quite intimate, so that he spoke freely.
After a time he mentioned the robbery of an "old Mormon" by himself, Jack Redden, and a man named Louther. Bonney knew of the
case, and this cleared up one more mystery, but he seemed to ignore
it.

"What do you think of Redden?" he asked.

"I don't like him," said Young. "He's not honorable among his
friends. I've been on a good many snaps [jobs] with Jack. He always
manages to get the money into his own hands and holds onto it like
the cholera to a nigger. I have several good sights [prospects] which
I intend to raise [rob] as soon as I can get the right kind of boys to
help me."

"I'd like to go in with you," said Bonney, "but I've got to get back
to Cincinnati to have some more of my bogus printed and properly
signed for circulation."

Young nodded, and began to go over some of the men who might
help. Jack Redden he at once discounted. "He's cheated me enough
already." He mentioned two men at Dubuque, one opposite the Fever
River in Iowa, and three or four near Galena—all "damned cowards."

"Then there's Aaron Long," he went on, "but he won't do anything
without the Judge."

Long and "Judge Fox!" Two of the men Bonney knew were in the
Davenport murder and robbery!

It required an effort of will to conceal his heightened interest as
Young continued, "So you see the boys are all lying on their oars. I
wouldn't give a damn for such partners."

3.

More discussion. It developed that John Long was with Fox "out
of the country," but Aaron Long was at the house of his father, Owen
Long, about three miles from Galena, Illinois.

"What about Old Grant Redden and William H. Redden?" asked
Bonney.

"I always stop with them," said Young. "Old Redden always keeps
the boys when they want to stop with him. Harrison (evidently William H. Redden went by his middle name) is more honorable in his
dealings with the boys than Jack is."

"I suppose the old man and Harrison know all about the business?"

"Yes, they understand everything that's going on."

Bonney had worked the conversation around to the question he wanted most of all to ask.

"Some of the boys made a good raise lately from Colonel Davenport," he suggested cautiously. "They were smart enough not to get caught. I have no idea myself who they were."

"Oh, I know all about that," said Young, eager now to impress this new "friend." "Judge Fox, Birch, John and Aaron Long are the ones who robbed Colonel Davenport."

"I was told that Davenport spoke only of three men."

"He only saw three. Aaron stood sentry outside while John, with Fox and Birch, did the work in the house."

"Did you know anything about it before it happened?"

"Yes." Young swelled, proud of his knowledge of the inner workings of the gang. "I'd been in Fort Madison, selling two horses I'd raised near Hennepin, when I ran across them. They said they were going up to Rock Island to rake down an old man, and expected to raise thirty or forty thousand dollars. I proposed to go with them for the sight, but they refused, saying their company was made up. I insisted, as I'd been with them in a good many hard scrapes where we got little or nothing. But they wouldn't admit me. So I left."

This admission was sufficient to involve Granville Young as an accessory to the murder, a hanging offense. Bonney kept him talking by showing admiring interest.

The outlaw related what he considered an amusing experience of his own. He was trying to rob a store in Dubuque when the owner entered unexpectedly and set up a cry of "Stop thief! Stop thief!"

"I left very suddenly," said Young, with a laugh, "and ran down the alley. Near the river was a house kept by some girls of the right sort, with whom I was well acquainted. When I burst into the house, the merchant was but a few steps behind me. I cried to the girls to hide me.

"'Here,' said Big Maria, 'squat in the corner.' She straddled me and threw her skirt over me, and there I sat, between her legs, the skirt around me, when the next instant the merchant entered puffing. Maria very innocently told him that a man had just come in and passed out the back door. Away went the merchant, snuffing and wheezing like a locomotive, and I saw no more of him."

Bonney joined in the outlaw's hearty laugh. "There's nothing like a woman to help a man out of a scrape," said Young. "She's quicker witted than a man, and has more self-command in a tight place.

Who'd have thought of looking for a man between her legs, under her dress? The first raise I make I'll remember Big Maria."

Once more Bonney led up to the subject of the murder.

"How did the boys learn Colonel Davenport had money?"

"The man who got up the sight lives near Rock Island," said Young. "He was well acquainted with Colonel Davenport—lived with him, worked for him, knew all about the situation of the house. About two weeks before the boys made the raise he went to Davenport's place, spent the afternoon, and took supper with the family, under pretense of a friendly visit, but really to spy. He found that the money was kept in a chamber; and that the whole family was going on July 4th to the Rock Island celebration." He paused. "To tell the truth, when the boys found the old man in the house it was a nasty surprise for them— they'd expected to find it empty."

Young did not know the name of the informer, but now Bonney had something new to think over. In addition to Fox, Birch, and the Longs, there was another, perhaps greater scoundrel—the informer. While accepting the old man's friendship and hospitality this man plotted the crime, even to the day when the whole family was supposed to be absent. This might answer another question: the strange behavior of the bulldog at the place. If a former member of the household came to the animal, patted his head and gave him a piece of meat, it would explain why there was no barking as the four robbers entered through the back way.

One last disclosure was made by Granville Young:

"I'm a native of Virginia, and have been a member of the united banditti (the Murrell gang) for seven years. I left my home with some stolen horses and the law behind me, but got through to Kentucky and over into Indiana where I sold them without suspicion."

Here, then, was another connection with the Southern network of criminals where John A. Murrell once reigned supreme.

4.

The *War Eagle* stopped several hours at Rock Island for lading, and Bonney slipped ashore to confer with his friends. They gave him some new information.

In what was called Robber's Camp, in the bluffs overlooking the river south of Rock Island, had been found two coats, spattered with blood, and a pair of bloody kid gloves. The coats were believed to belong to the Long brothers, and the gloves to Robert Birch.

Bonney described what he had thus far learned. When he came to the activities of the man who visited the mansion as a friend but who was really a traitor, George L. Davenport, son of the murdered old colonel, gave a sharp exclamation.

"That," he said, with bitter rage, "was John Baxter! It had to be! The filthy, treacherous, ungrateful bastard! My father was good to that man—aided him when he came sniveling for help, and never expected even thanks for it! John Baxter's crime ought to be printed on his front, in letters as black as his heart!"

He would have gone out at once and searched for Baxter, but Bonney and the others persuaded him to wait. The man, who did not dream he was suspected, should not be disturbed while the search for the others continued.

Thereafter Bonney returned to the *War Eagle* and chatted with Granville Young until the steamboat reached Nauvoo, where Young disembarked to go to the hideout at Old Redden's while Bonney continued on down to St. Louis. Before they parted, however, the outlaw "recommended" to him a livery stable man named Thomas Reynolds in the Missouri city, who was of "the right stripe."

At St. Louis Bonney went to the State Bank of Missouri, and with the help of some letters from influential men in Rock Island, obtained a few unsigned bank notes from that institution, fearing that the Dubuque bank was too far away to impress people so far south. With these in his wallet, he casually encountered Reynolds, and introduced himself as "Mr. Brown." Why he should have selected that name, which was one of the aliases of Robert Birch, is not clear. But after that he used it frequently. Eventually it was to cause him some serious trouble.

The livery stable man was cautious. At first he denied knowing Granville Young, Tom Brown of Nauvoo, or anyone by the name of Long or Birch. But at last he asked where Bonney lived.

"No particular place," was the answer. "Wherever business calls me."

Reynolds studied him, then: "I think I understand your business."

"That's sufficient. The public street's no place for confidential conversation."

They drove in a carriage out into the country, where Bonney produced his bank bills. Reynolds examined them closely. Like Granville Young he was impressed by their "genuine appearance."

"This is very good," he said at last. "How much have you got like it?"

"Only a few samples here," said Bonney. "But I'll soon have plenty. When I return here, I'd like to leave a few thousand."

Reynolds, fully convinced, agreed to "help."

"When I first met you," he said, "I thought I'd best be a little careful.

It's squally times around here." A pause. "I'm well acquainted with the names you mentioned, but I was at first afraid you were a spy."

Reynolds then described his operation as a "fence" for stolen horses —a form of thievery by this time become a regular and widely disseminated business.[1] He did not know where "the boys" were at the time. He supplied one bit of interesting information. Fox and John Long had been at his place and left some horses, but there was one they would not leave.

"She's the finest race mare I ever saw in my life," said the stableman. "Fox said he wouldn't take a thousand dollars for her."

At the moment this did not seem of much importance. But that mare was to play an important role in the final breakup of the gang.

5.

When he left St. Louis Bonney was much disappointed. The outlaws seemed to have melted in thin air. Thinking matters over he believed there was only one recourse left, and that was to introduce himself into the very nests of the outlaw murderers.

He was aware of the extreme danger in this. If he was suspected the best he could hope for was a quick death. Yet his instinct was all for following his quarry to the last gasp, even if he must gamble his life under new and perhaps unexpected perils.

One of the men mentioned by Granville Young was John Birch, father of Robert Birch. He was supposed to live in Clark County, Illinois, about nine miles southwest of Marshall. As his first move Bonney traveled across Illinois to that vicinity and called upon the sheriff, William P. Bennett.

"Around here," said the sheriff, "Birch is known as 'Old Coon.' "

Bonney, knowing that an old coon was an animal regarded as exceptionally wily, remarked that the senior Birch probably deserved the sobriquet.

"He sure does," agreed Bennett. "We've set many a trap for him, but he's outwitted us all."

"Do you know his son?"

---

[1] There were regular depots, where the receivers altered the appearance of stolen animals by docking their tails, cropping their manes, and so on, before disposing of them. The astonishing Sile Doty in his autobiography named confederates of this kind in or near forty towns and cities, from Vermont to New Orleans, and from Virginia to the Mississippi River, including parts of Canada. And Doty named only places he *personally* visited in his thievery. There were many more. Reynolds belonged to this nefarious network.

"Robert Birch? Yes. But he doesn't dare show himself here."

"I'm inclined to think he may be hidden somewhere around his father's house," said Bonney.

"Well," said the sheriff, "if Robert's hidden there, a stranger coming in might excite suspicion and cause him to go away. His pappy, Old Coon, is one of the most cunning and cautious men in the country. He's said to be well educated, but he feigns ignorance—will never sign his name in any business transaction—says he can't write."

"Maybe authorities somewhere are watching for that signature."[2]

"Could be," agreed the sheriff. But he warned Bonney very seriously not to go to the Birch place alone. "It would be a very dangerous risk," he said.

Bonney, however, fully realizing that this advice probably was judicious, was determined to call on Old Coon, believing he could pass himself off as one of the gang. At that the sheriff reluctantly agreed to guide him.

By a narrow and crooked trail through exceedingly dense forest, they rode to within a mile of the place, where Bennett concealed himself in a thicket, promising to wait until Bonney returned.

With no little apprehension—as he confessed later—Bonney rode on by a "blind path" until he reached a partly cultivated clearing. In the middle of this "stood a miserable log cabin in a very dilapidated condition, almost crumbling to the ground."

Tethering his horse at the edge of the woods, he cautiously approached the house on foot. The door stood open. Just inside, near the foot of a primitive bed sat an old man, whose appearance was "wretched and poverty stricken." He seemed senile, for an old woman and a young girl about sixteen "were in the act of adjusting some portions of his dress" when Bonney entered.

They seemed startled when he appeared. But after a moment the girl placed a stool for him to sit and offered him water in a gourd dipper. The "wretched old man" was Old Coon Birch himself, as dangerous and cunning a criminal as there was in the country.

He it was who broke the silence. "Ye live in this part of the country?"

"No," said Bonney.

"Whar do ye, then?"

---

[2] Bonney might have hit close to the mark here. "Old Coon's" son used as aliases two names of Murrell's Clansmen, Haines and Harris. Either one of these quite possibly was the *real* name of John Birch. He would under such circumstances be understandably shy about putting his handwriting on paper where it might be compared to something he previously wrote, thus connecting him with a crime or crimes in his past.

"No particular place. I travel, and speculate, and so on."

"Ye want to see me?"

"One of your friends asked me to call on you, if I ever passed this way."

"Who?"

"Granville Young."

"How big a man is this hyar Granville Young?" came the instant suspicious question.

"A small man, with dark hair," answered Bonney confidently.

Old Coon seemed to relax somewhat. "Ye know Owen Long?"

"Only by description," said Bonney. "I never saw him, but I know the boys."

"Ye do? Aaron an' John?"

"Yes."

"They're Owen Long's sons. Owen an' me was raised together in old North Caroliny. I've knowed him since he was a boy. A right smart old man, an' has two smart boys."[3]

"They know how to take care of themselves," said Bonney.

"Well, they shore do!"

"I left my horse at the edge of the clearing," Bonney said. "Let me step out and look after him." He gave the old man a wink.

At once Old Coon followed him outside. "Well, what is it, stranger?" he said, all appearance of senility disappearing, as soon as they were out of hearing of the cabin.

"The boys say you're of the right stripe, so I suppose I can tell you my business?"

"It never hurts nobody."

"Look at these bank notes," said Bonney.

Suddenly keen, Old Coon took them and gave them the thorough examination of an expert.

"They're a small sample of my work," said Bonney. "I've got a lot of it to fill up and sign. I'm now on my way to Cincinnati after it, and when I get back I'll want to dispose of it. Can you help me?"

"Yes, I'll take a right smart of it myself," the old rascal said at once. "A heap of the boys stops with me, and I know who'll buy it. If you can sell it fair, I'll get rid of a power of it."

Now the old man grew quite friendly, and it might have been noticed that far fewer of the frontier solecisms appeared in his speech.

---

[3] Murrell's list named in the Carolinas an "Owin" and a "Haris." Could there have been a connection with the men in the north, allowing for the liberal usages of aliases, including last names for first names, and so on?

He told Bonney that he was perfectly safe because the clerk of the court at Marshall was a friend of the gang's.

"They can't hurt Old Coon while he's there," he boasted. "If the sheriff gets a writ against me, the clerk lets me know soon enough to skedaddle." He grinned evilly, then, "You know Robert Birch? He's my son. Smart fellow. Know him?"

"I've heard the boys mention his name, but never saw him."

"A smart fellow," repeated Old Coon pridefully. "He's traveled eight years. Got heaps of money. Never gets caught. I had three boys —him and his brother John, and Tim. We left our homes in old Caroliny together. John, poor fellow! They hung him in Texas—just strung him up by the neck without judge or jury, hung him like a dog. But they don't catch Robert!"

In this connection, it will be remembered that after Murrell's conviction and the exposure of the slave insurrection plot in July, 1835, many members of the Mystic Clan fled to Texas, where some of them were dealt with summarily.[4]

As Old Coon and Bonney turned back toward the house a youth, slovenly but dangerous-looking, came from the forest carrying a rifle. He glared at Bonney with suspicion until he saw how friendly Old Coon was with the visitor. This was Tim Birch, youngest of Old Coon's sons. Probably he had been watching this visitor, perhaps over the sights of his rifle, ready to pull the trigger, until he saw the growing warmth between his father and the stranger.

Talk ensued, some of it quite free. Old Coon urged Bonney—who, strangely, again gave his name as Tom Brown—to "join up" with his son Robert. He was apparently unaware that the name just given him was one of his own son's numerous aliases. Bonney agreed to do so at the first opportunity.

The old woman and the girl now entered into the conversation. "They were at least equal in wickedness to any of the members of the other sex," recalled Bonney, "and appeared much worse, for, as woman in her purity seems surpassingly lovely, so in her degradation she seems more debased."

"Old Mother Birch" furiously cursed a neighbor named Miller.

---

[4] Orthodox law enforcement often lagged behind the need to punish troublesome offenders. Where officials were helpless and jails were far away, the citizens had to work together as vigilantes. They made their own laws on the spot, caught horse thieves and other outlaws, and hanged them to the nearest cottonwood. Sometimes they imposed overly severe penalties or executed the wrong men; but usually they were fair, and their activities discouraged crime. The work of the vigilance committees was a form of social action against bad men and a step toward the setting up of statutory courts—Wayne Gard, *Frontier Justice.*

"I'd shoot him, an' chop him up into mince-meat," she declared. "He tried to have my Tim prosecuted just for stealin' a miserable little colt, not worth thirty dollars. I ain't sure but what he might have had somethin' to do with gettin' John hung in Texas."

They pressed Bonney to stay the night; but he had no desire to remain in that filthy cabin. Besides, he was now sure that Robert Birch was nowhere in the vicinity.

So he pleaded his necessity to get to Cincinnati and complete his "counterfeiting job," and left. Later he said, that as he walked across the clearing to his horse, his back fairly tingled as he wondered if even now he might receive in it a rifle ball from the malignant youth, Tim Birch.

But he mounted in safety and rode away. Sheriff Bennett had gone on when he reached the thicket, thinking Bonney would remain at the Birch place.

XXIII.   *Fox and Hound*

1.

His first visit to an outlaw's nest was so disappointing that Bonney might not have been blamed for giving up the whole search there and then. But one thing held him to it. Colonel George Davenport, a man who had done much for the state and its people, had been murdered most cruelly in broad daylight. The men who performed that act had been shown by Bonney's investigation to be the leaders of the entire ring of outlaws in the country. Duty forced him to continue.

Now, suddenly, shortly after he left Marshall, Bonney learned of a startling development. William (Judge) Fox had been arrested with a man named Shack Phips, for horse stealing. A judge at Bowling Green, Indiana, put them both under bail—eight hundred dollars for Fox, and four hundred dollars for Phips. In each case the father of the prisoner raised the money for the bail and they were released.

But this was eight days before Bonney heard of it. Where would Fox be now?

The outlaw might, of course, jump bond and disappear. But considering the matter Bonney thought Fox might still be hanging around, for two reasons: First, his father had put up eight hundred dollars for him, and it seemed likely the outlaw would try somehow to avoid the penalty and get the bail money back. Second—and perhaps even more important—the description of the stolen horses, now being held at Bowling Green, convinced Bonney that one of them was that "splendid racing mare" on which, Reynolds had told him, Fox set such great store. Assuredly the man would want to get that animal back.

Bonney had no idea where Fox might be, but he learned that Shack Phips, a hang-dog character in his middle twenties, had married a girl who was a cousin of John and Aaron Long, and was living with his mother-in-law, Widow Long, relict of Owen Long's brother, not many miles from Bowling Green.

He resolved to visit this branch of the Long family, although once again he was gravely warned against what he proposed to do. By now, however, his whole connection with the case, if various members of the gang compared notes as they were sure to do sooner or later, was already a death warrant for himself. He *had* to get them before they got him, and his situation was so desperate that only by continued effrontery and good luck could he win and survive.

Through the Indiana woods therefore, "by a way exceedingly devious," he rode until a stranger showed him where Old Mother Long's place was. Although this was only a few miles from Terre Haute, the country at that time was exceedingly primitive and his description is interesting:

"Following the direction of my informant through the forest, thick with tangled underbrush and nearly impenetrable, I presently emerged from a dense thicket and found myself but a few rods distant from a miserable log cabin, about fourteen feet square, with an open porch or stoop; the whole covered with rough clapboards, laid on loose, and confined with small logs placed at equal distances apart on the roof.

"The furniture consisted of crippled chairs, half a dozen three-legged stools; two miserable beds, the bedsteads of which were made of rough poles with the bark still on; a table made of a slab of timber roughly hewn; an old rickety cupboard; a half a dozen broken plates, as many knives and forks without handles, and a few tin cups."

Bonney tethered his horse and walked to the house, where he found two women: "Old Mother Long, a meagre specimen of humanity, poorly clad and besmeared with dirt, and the wife of Shack Phips, a female about twenty years of age, of rather delicate features, but

whose appearance was little, if any, superior to the old mother of the
house."

"Where's Shack Phips?" was Bonney's opening question.

The younger woman looked at him sharply. "Does Phips owe you
anything?"

"No," he said.

"Do you live about here?"

"No."

"Are you acquainted with Phips?"

"No, I've never seen him, but I'm well acquainted with some of
his friends."

Now the old woman intervened. "Do you know Judge Fox?"

"Yes. He's an intimate friend of mine."

"Is he?" she said. "Why Fox was here only a few days ago."

"He was?" Bonney's voice was eager. "I'm sorry I missed him. I've
been looking for him for a month." Which was literally true, though
not in the sense Old Mother Long interpreted it.

"You want to see Shack real bad?" now asked the young wife.

"Yes, I do."

"Well, I reckon I can holler him up."

The slatternly girl stepped out of the house, climbed up on a gate-
post and began the curious, far-carrying "Whoo-ee, whoo-ee, whoo-ee-
yah," well known to hog callers.

Soon there was an answering yell. Then Phips, who had been hiding
in the bush since the visitor appeared, came to the house.

He was at first very suspicious. But his wife and mother explained
that the newcomer was "one of the boys," and "of the right stripe."
With that Phips began to complain of being ill-treated, of never having
done a dishonest act in his life, and of having been arrested for a
horse he "bought," which they said was stolen.

2.

At this point Bonney heard a roll of thunder, and noticed heavy
clouds boiling up from the west, indicating a coming storm.

"Can I put my horse under the shed?" he asked. "Phips, why don't
you come along?"

Outside, he turned on Phips as if half-angry.

"Shack," he said, "it's all damned nonsense to talk this kind of stuff
to me. You can tell it to the folks around here, but I understand such
matters. I came here to see if those horses taken from Fox can be got
away from Bowling Green. Fox and I are old friends. I heard he got

into a scrape, but when I came to Bowling Green I found he had given bail and left. Now, if we can get those horses away before the owners call for them, they can't convict Fox. He can come back, stand trial, and get back the eight hundred dollars for his bond. If the horses stay where they are until the owners come for them, you know Fox will lose his bail, for he can't stand trial with such evidence against him—it would send him to the penitentiary for sure. If you'll stand by me, I think we can get them away."

Shack Phip's long-jawed countenance bore an expression both of hope and fear. He was under bond also, and both Bonney's irritated manner, and the proposed plan, carried conviction.

"How kin we do it?" he asked.

"Easy," said Bonney. "You get someone to go and swear the horses are my property; and I'll claim them and take them away. When the true owners come all they can say is that some rascal got all their horses and run with them, and I have no fear they'll catch me or the horses if I can get fifteen miles start of them." He paused. "If we get the horses away, we must leave the race mare where Fox can get her. I'm told the Judge wouldn't take a thousand dollars for her— she's said to be the fastest quarter nag in the whole United States."

Mention of that mare clinched Phip's confidence. He was all eagerness and discussed getting witnesses. He himself was afraid to go near Bowling Green. "People up there had as lief hang me up to a tree without trial as any other way," he whined. But in the end he said he would fetch Old Coon and Tim Birch as witnesses.

The thunderstorm was threateningly near and after Bonney took care of his horse the two started back to the cabin. Now Phips talked freely. It developed that Fox had been accompanied by John Long and Birch when he came to the Phips place with the stolen horses a few days before. Phips went with them to Bowling Green, and when he and Fox were caught the other two escaped.

He knew Fox and John Long, but had never seen Birch before.

"What do you think of Birch?" casually queried Bonney.

"Smart. But too much of a dude to suit me. Had a fine gold watch and chain. Liked to show it around an' play with the chain."

A gold watch and chain! In an instant Bonney was sure they must have been taken from Colonel Davenport—a priceless piece of evidence if found on Birch's person.

But he soon had something else to think about. As they reached the cabin three men, carrying rifles, came up. They were bearded, filthy, and their clothing was in the last stage of disreputability. Bonney was sure they were outlaws, though he recognized none of them.

Now the threatening storm broke. They were forced to seek shelter in the cabin.

A blinding bolt of lightning was followed by a clap of thunder, and with a heavy gust of wind, rain darkened the landscape. Bonney realized he must spend the night there; and as it turned out, it continued to thunder, rain and blow throughout most of that night.

There was a supper of sorts—hog jowl and hominy. When it came time to retire Bonney shared some quilts on the floor in a corner of the room with one of the dirty, bearded strangers as a bedfellow. The other two strangers occupied one of the beds with Phips, while the two women slept in the other bed.

Except for the flickering blaze from a few dying embers in the fireplace, there was no light in the house. Stealthily, Bonney placed his pistols and bowie knife where he could lay his hand on them, covering them with his coat and vest. Then, without divesting himself of any of his other clothing he lay down with his unwelcome sleeping companion.

Not once in those dark hours did he so much as nap. He knew that if his identity was suspected these enemies, without giving him an inkling of their plans, would attack him before morning.

In all his life Bonney never forgot that night. "The vivid lightning streamed forth in one continued blaze, succeeded by incessant crashes of terrific thunder, and the rain fell in torrents. The grim features of the ruffians, visible by the vivid lightning streaming through the crevices in the walls of the shattered fabric, served to complete a picture of fearful interest to me. The thoughts and reflections which crowded my mind, as I lay amid those ruffians, made a singular and ineffaceable impression."

3.

Dawn at last—a bright and glorious morning after the stormy night. The three bearded ruffians rose and left: evidently there was no suspicion of him, nor did he ever discover who they were.

Breakfast was a continuation of last night's supper. As they finished it, a sound like the long and quavering cry of a wild turkey came from the neighboring forest.

"There, Shack, damn you, you can start," said Phips' "gentle and affectionate" wife.

"Who's that?" asked Bonney.

"Hiram Long, whistling for his grub," replied Phips, starting away with a tin plate filled with food.

Bonney gathered that Hiram Long was a son of Old Mother Long. He was therefore a cousin of Aaron and John Long, and was "hiding out" from the law, so that he did not dare show himself even at his mother's cabin.

In about an hour Shack returned. "I told Hiram about your plan," he announced. "He says he'll talk with you. But you've got to meet him in the woods."

He gave Bonney directions: "Go up past the stable yonder to the corner of the fence, turn left into the woods, an' whistle. Hiram will answer."

Carrying his portmanteau, Bonney followed the directions. The whistles were exchanged. He found, sitting on a log in a dense thicket, "a small, well formed, and remarkably good looking young man of twenty-two or three years of age. His complexion was fair as that of a woman; his forehead prominent and high; while his full, clear, dark hazel eyes, and dark auburn hair made up one of the finest countenances I have ever seen."

But this handsome young man was a hardened outlaw. Hiram Long, "from his manner of living, constantly in fear of pursuit and arrest for criminal offenses, had caught a sort of suspicious watchfulness, and was startled by every noise. His quick eye, darting in every direction, seemed to catch every motion, and his practiced ear took in the slightest crackling of brush or rustling of leaves."

Bonney went through the old rigmarole of showing his "bogus rag currency." Long eagerly asked for some of it when it was completed and signed—the market for counterfeit currency seemed unlimited in this country. Then he informed Bonney that Fox was at the home of his father, John Fox.

This was quite near and Bonney made a proposal: it would take too long to get Old Coon or others to swear to his ownership of the stolen horses. He would go boldly, claim the animals as his own property, and trusting to his nerve, perhaps get them without further trouble.

"I reckon not," demurred the young outlaw.

"I can try it anyway. If they refuse, we'll send for Old Coon."

To this Hiram agreed. He also undertook to notify Fox.

Now Bonney was in a sweat to get away. Back at the cabin he had a few more words with Shack, and received a startling piece of information.

"The sheriff of Owen County," said Phips, "is one of our friends, a man of the right stripe. He always lets the boys know if thar's somethin' afoot. If he'd knowed of the posse comin' to arrest Fox an' me, he'd of give us timely advice."

Bowling Green was in Clay County, and Owen County was just east of it. Nevertheless this was unpleasant news to Bonney, though he knew there were many corrupt officers in the country. It made him decide to act independently and take nobody into his more secret plans. So, "bidding farewell to Shack's interesting family," he rode off toward Bowling Green, reaching it before nightfall.

4.

At Bowling Green he found a serious complication. Unexpectedly, the actual owner of two of the stolen horses was there before him, with a witness to prove his title.

Bonney's whole plan hung on those horses. If they were claimed by anyone but himself, his hope of capturing Fox was gone. After brief consideration Bonney decided to take the direct way, hunt up the two men, take them into his confidence, and try to enlist them in his effort.

He found them at a hotel—two honest, substantial citizens from Belleville, Illinois. At first they listened with skepticism and suspicion, but eventually with conviction as he told them his story without any reservations, including his scheme for trapping Fox, whom he wanted for the murder of Colonel Davenport rather than for horse theft.

"I have only to get the horses away from Bowling Green to accomplish my plan and give me a clear track to Fox," he pleaded.

The two men consulted, then agreed to his proposition, which was that he assume temporarily the character of the owner—with the Belleville men as his witnesses—pay the charges on the animals, take them out of town and there deliver the two belonging to the real owner to him, to take home. The race mare, whose owner he did not know, he intended to convey to Terre Haute and leave her with the authorities until the owner could be found—though he still intended to use her as bait for his trap.

But Fox had a lawyer in Bowling Green, a man named Williamson, "a shrewd, cunning man, and a fine lawyer"—although none too ethical in his methods. This man must not be allowed to suspect a snare was laid for his client.

Bonney therefore sent a message to the lawyer, asking him to call at a certain hotel, "as soon as his business would permit." He was in the bar room when, soon after, a well-dressed man entered and said:

"My name is Williamson. Who is it that wishes to see me?"

"I'm the man, sir," said Bonney. "Can we get a private room?"

The lawyer gave him a searching look. "Yes. Step upstairs."

When they were seated in the room Williamson asked permission to use, Bonney began, very cautiously, "I'm informed, sir, that you defended my friend William Fox."

"I did, sir."

"Can I talk with you confidentially?"

"You can—but stop a moment."

Williamson got up, looked through the closets, shut the doors carefully, and returned to his chair.

Clapping his hand on the lawyer's knee Bonney said, "Mr. Williamson, I'm a friend of Fox. I heard of his arrest and the detention of these horses, and I'm here to get them away. I've already succeeded in proving the horses are my property, have them in my possession, and am about to leave town with them. You can inform Fox that he can come back now, attend court, and save his bail. Everything's arranged. I'll be off in a few minutes with the horses."

An expression of amazement came over the lawyer's face.

"By God, that's a good one!" he exclaimed. "It's the best trick I ever knew! Be careful you're not suspected before you get away. I wouldn't have this miscarry for five hundred dollars."

He went on to say he had written Thomas Reynolds, the horse thief's receiver in St. Louis, asking him to send a man to claim the horses—a noted jockey named Myers.

"When Myers gets here, you can tell him that Jack Brown's saved him the trouble," said Bonney. (He here changed the "Tom" Brown to "Jack," because he feared Williamson might know Birch, who used the first alias.)

The lawyer was fully convinced. Bonney took the horses out of town, turned the two over to the Belleville men, and conveyed the racing mare to Terre Haute, some twenty miles away, where he left her with a deputy sheriff named Hickox to be claimed by her owner, believed to be in Missouri.

From Terre Haute, he took a stagecoach for Indianapolis, for the next step in his plan. He needed somebody on whom he could rely, to assist in what he had in mind, and he hoped to obtain the help of a highly regarded officer, whom he knew, Thomas B. Johnson, former U.S. marshal of Iowa.

5.

On that seventy-five mile stage ride, he received a nasty scare.

One of his fellow passengers was "a very gentlemanly looking man, by the name of Adair, son of the late Governor Adair of Kentucky."

The coach stopped at a way point, to allow its riders to take break-fast at an inn, and during this meal Adair remarked in the hearing of the other passengers who were at the same table, "A man has passed through Terre Haute in pursuit of the murderers of Colonel George Davenport, of Rock Island. From his success in tracking them thus far, the probability is that he eventually will secure their arrest. The pursuit has been conducted in a very secret manner and but few know of it."

He was a typical expansive know-it-all, who wanted to astonish his listeners with his "inside" information on a topic very much in the public attention just then. But to Bonney this sort of dissemination of information might be fatal. He was alarmed and at the same time not a little irritated. However, he answered calmly.

"If such is the case, sir," said he, "great caution should be used by all who are in the secret, as the murderers may hear the news and make good their escape."

"Very true," replied Adair.

"But isn't there some mistake about this?" pursued Bonney. "I've previously heard several similar reports."

"No," said Adair blandly, "it's no mistake. I have it from Mr. Hickox, deputy sheriff at Terre Haute, who has seen and conversed with the man in pursuit."

"Does Mr. Hickox make the matter public to anybody and every-body?" asked Bonney in an icy tone.

"No, he told me in confidence." Adair was comfortably smug.

"Sir," said Bonney sternly, "aren't you aware that you're abusing that confidence? If Mr. Hickox is in possession of such information, *he* is censurable for making a confidant of anyone, and *you*, sir, are equally censurable for betraying that confidence!"

"What do you mean sir?" Adair was angered. "You are very free for a stranger! Do you intend an insult?"

"I mean just what I say," replied Bonney levelly. "That Hickox is singularly imprudent, and that you are equally so."

His tone took some of the wind out of Adair's sails, and he said, in a more conciliatory voice, "This is the first time I've mentioned it anywhere, and it can do no harm here."

"How do you know sir," came Bonney's swift counter, "but some of the murderers or their friends may be present?"

"What! Here? By no means! These are all gentlemen!"

"Are you acquainted with all present?"

"No," said Adair. "Nor do I need to be. I know that they are all gentlemen."

"Are you aware," continued Bonney relentlessly, "that either of these

murderers might take passage on a stagecoach, mingle with gentlemen, and appear in every respect as much like a gentleman as yourself?"

"What! A murderer? No sir!"

"Certainly he might," said Bonney. "However, sir, allow me to inform you that *I* am the man spoken of by Mr. Hickox. It became necessary to disclose my business to him, as I was in need of his services,
but he has no good apology for disclosing the secret."

Poor Adair was aghast. "Is it possible? Are you the gentleman he
spoke of? I had no idea there was anyone present who had any
knowledge of the matter."

"Either of the murderers might have been here as well as myself,
and in making this matter public, you not only render the arrest of
the murderers almost impossible, but you endanger my life."

Now Adair was concerned and contrite. "I acknowledge the wrong,
and beg pardon. I was imprudent, but did not consider the consequences which might result. I'll be more cautious! I've learned a valuable lesson, and rest assured that I'll not mention it hereafter."

The apology was accepted, and the other passengers pledged themselves to keep the secret. So the matter passed off smoothly.

On his arrival at Indianapolis, Bonney's first business was to consult
Thomas B. Johnson, who agreed to assist him.

6.

Bonney believed he knew how to capture Fox—but how to get Long
and Birch?

The ruse of the horses might lure Fox to a place where he could be
seized. But that left the others free—and forewarned. Study the matter as he might, Bonney was unable to think how he could learn the
whereabouts of the other murderers, unless—an idea suddenly came to
him—he might find out *from Fox himself.*

But how to win the confidence of a man like Fox? From all he had
learned, the outlaw not only was exceptionally keen and cunning,
but very dangerous. Furthermore he had seen Bonney at the trial of the
Hodges brothers, and would undoubtedly recognize him.

A possibility suggested itself: what if he were arrested *with* the
criminal? Would Fox accept him then? Bonney had been on this trail
too long to leave any expedient untried.

Having made his decision, and leaving Johnson at Centerville, near
which place in Wayne County, Indiana, John Fox, the robber's
father, lived, he rode boldly to the latter's habitation. He found the
place "decent enough," and the elder Fox "appeared to be a grade

above the parents of other outlaws previously met, both in his manners and his education."

"No," John Fox said to him in response to his query, "my son isn't home."

"When will he be back?"

"I don't know."

"I'm anxious to see him," said Bonney, "but I have to go on to Cincinnati. Here, I'll leave him a note."

He wrote a communication to William Fox, telling of his conversation with Williamson, the lawyer, his "success" in getting the incriminating horses away, and adding that he must leave Centerville for Cincinnati early next day.

He signed the note *Thomas Brown*. At Bowling Green he had given the name Jack Brown, and he knew that Thomas Brown was an alias of Birch. This, he hoped, would arouse Fox's interest.

"If the Judge will come by wagon to town," he said to the elder Fox in parting, "I'll come back with him here and stay until time to catch the stage tomorrow."

Returning to Centerville, he found Johnson, the former marshal there, and with him held a conference with David Gentry, sheriff, and Thomas Noble, clerk of the Wayne County court. Then he went to his hotel.

Long hours passed. Johnson and Gentry had their instructions—to be ready for arrest if signaled, but not to arouse suspicion if they received a different sign.

About ten o'clock that night a slim young man with curious cat-like eyes rode into town and up to the hotel, leading a saddled horse. He was William Fox, alias the Judge.

"Is a man named Brown stopping here?" he asked.

At that very moment Bonney was standing outside under a street lamp. He stepped at once into the darkness.

"You might go down to the stage station to see if Mr. Brown's gone," suggested the landlord, with whom Bonney already had talked.

Fox tied his horses at the hitchrack and walked to the station. At once Bonney held another hasty consultation with the tavern man.

"Go after that man," he said. "Tell him his man is here in the tavern." Then he went up to his room.

7.

Bonney knew he was near the critical test of his abilities and daring. In the next few minutes he would either succeed in an imposture he had planned—or be dead. Fox would certainly shoot his way out if he suspected a trap, and Bonney would be his first target.

He threw himself upon the bed, pretending to be dozing, when the door opened and Fox entered. With a yawn, Bonney sat up. The lighted candle beside his bed revealed his face.

Quick and wild as the creature that bore his name, Fox leaped backward. Then he halted, as if deciding whether to shoot or flee.

"This is not Mr. Brown!" he exclaimed.

"Not exactly."

"Aren't you Bonney?"

"That's me—when I'm home. On the road I'm Brown," said Bonney. The outlaw's hand was in his pocket, a pistol in his hand.

"You didn't expect to see me here, did you?" was Bonney's next question, with a grin.

"No." The outlaw was on his guard and tense, his hand still on his pistol. "What are you doing here?"

"I talked with Reynolds at St. Louis," said Bonney more calmly than he felt. "It enabled me to recover your horses. Williamson said he'd write you about it, next mail."

"He did!" Fox obviously was astonished. Then, "Bonney, you're the last man from whom I'd expect such a favor—or any favor."

But in the air, unvoiced, hung the question: *Why* this favor?

Bonney allowed Fox's curiosity to build up.

"When I first entered this room and recognized you," said the outlaw at last, "I thought I was trapped. But everything must be all right —or how would you know of Williamson and the horses?"

The tension was still near the breaking point. A sudden movement by Bonney would have brought that cocked pistol out of the outlaw's pocket. But he spoke with deliberation.

"I thought that would convince you," he said. And then he coolly supplied Fox with the answer to his unspoken query. "This is my business," he said.

As before, he produced the sheets of bank notes. Fox examined them with a searching and critical eye, his hand still on his pistol.

"First rate! he said at last.

"Better were never made," said Bonney.

"Where were they got up?"

"In Cincinnati."

"How much have you?"

"Sixty thousand dollars—only a sample with me, however. Would you want some when I come back?"

"I don't like to traffic in this stuff," said Fox. "It's pretty risky."

"Not with an article like this."

"Perhaps not." But the outlaw was still tense and suspicious, his hand still on his gun. Suddenly he asked, point-blank, "Bonney—you had a lot to do with the arrest and trial of the Hodges, didn't you?"

There it lay, in the open. One blunder by Bonney would mean the end of all he had worked for and his own life as well. But he spoke as calmly as if the other had asked him the time of day.

"Certainly I did. They had committed a murder. I'm against that under all circumstances. There are ways enough to get money without killing. I've no doubt you're as much opposed to murder as I am."

"Very true," nodded Fox. "I am." But the pistol was still ready.

"If I hadn't thought so, I'd not have turned a hand to get you out of the Bowling Green difficulty. I say: if I take a man's horse, he can buy another; if I take his money, he can get more; but if I kill a man, he's lost to his friends and the world."

"Those are my sentiments," said the murderer, speaking as virtuously as if he did not at that moment have the death of Colonel Davenport and perhaps others on his head.

"Anything else in the way of speculation, I'm for," concluded Bonney. "Now you understand me."

It was a strange conversation; and the strangest part of it was that Bonney managed to convince Fox, as he had convinced other outlaws. The "bogus," of course, had a large share in this; but his manner and something in his personality also had much to do with it.

Fox slowly relaxed. The hand came out of his pistol pocket. In the end he invited Bonney to ride with him to his father's.

As they passed out of the hotel Bonney saw Johnson and Gentry, with some other men lounging about in apparent carelessness—a posse. He made the agreed gesture that it was not time now to make the arrest.

His plans had changed. While Fox was getting the horses he managed to speak with Johnson and asked him to bring the posse to John Fox's house and arrest both himself and William Fox on some trumped-up charge. By so doing he hoped to capture any evidence that might be at the elder Fox's place.

The horses were brought and Bonney mounted and rode away with his dangerous companion.

8.

That night Bonney occupied the same bed with the outlaw at the elder Fox's home.

"I was kindly received by the family and treated with courtesy," he later said. "Had Fox been anything but a cold-blooded murderer, I should have regretted the part I was playing."

Momentarily he expected the arrival of Johnson and the posse, but they did not appear. As the hours lengthened his tension grew, and he became much concerned. But when he was urged to stay until next day he constrained himself to consent.

Still Johnson did not come. Later Bonney found that this was due to a misunderstanding in the hurried directions he gave while waiting for Fox and the horses.

During that long day he watched for anything that might connect Fox with the Davenport murder—the shotgun, perhaps, or the pistol, or even the watch, although he was fairly sure the last was in the possession of Birch. He saw nothing that would help him.

But in those hours he gleaned some highly interesting information from Fox. The man had been a robber for eleven years. He had stolen more than fifty horses, and robbed many homes and stores, as well as holding up a stagecoach near Rockford, Illinois.

"I've got thousands of dollars," he boasted, "without once being seen in a neighborhood where I made the raise."

But he had been arrested twice—the Bowling Green affair was the second time. The first was at Bellevue, Iowa. There his companion was shot and killed. He was arrested, but, "They could prove little or nothing against me. So they tied me up to a tree and whipped me nearly to death, and then let me go. Some of them will have to pay for it one of these days."

Next he informed Bonney that John Long and Birch, at this very time, were in Ohio, with a man named Norton B. Royce, "to make a raise." That "raise" was, incidentally, to result in the deaths of two men.

Inevitably the talk got around to the racing mare, which Bonney said was well hidden.

"I suppose I'll have to get your order for her," Fox said.

"You can't get her with an order," said Bonney.

"Why not?" Fox was surprised.

"I always look out for breakers. Someone might forge an order. She's too valuable to lose."

"Only *you* can get her?"

"Anyone I direct there can get her."

"How?"

Bonney's mind was working fast. The mare, of course, was at Terre Haute, but on the spur of the moment he invented a fictitious farm on the Wabash River, "with underground stables," and a fictitious person named Morrison.

"Inquire of him for a horse left by a Mr. Brown," he went on, rapidly improvising. "He'll ask if you have an order from Brown, and you answer, No. He'll ask how you expect to get the horse then? You say, By giving the proper sign. He'll say, What sign? You must then cross your wrists and repeat the words Robinson Crusoe, whereupon he'll turn the horse over to you."

It was an utterly ridiculous rigmarole, concocted on the spur of the moment. But its very ridiculousness convinced Fox.

The outlaw stared for a moment, then burst into laughter.

"Well," he said, "that's the damnedest sign and watchword I ever heard of. Bonney, you're an *old one!*"

From this they passed to other matters. Fox described John Long as "bold and desperate," but said Birch was "too self-conceited."

"I believe Birch would murder his best friend for two hundred dollars," he added, and gave a long catalogue of the man's crimes.

So the interminable day passed, and still no posse. That night, once more, Bonney slept with Fox. Next morning early they saddled the horses to return to Centerville, from whence the outlaw intended to ride to the fictitious place of "Morrison," on the Wabash "about twenty miles north of Terre Haute," to get his beloved race mare.

The chances for catching Fox were waning. But when they reached the hotel Bonney, to his relief, saw Johnson and the sheriff. Fox excused himself "to see an old chum," and there was a hurried conference with Johnson.

"Arrest Fox on a feigned charge of stealing a race horse in Missouri, and myself on a charge of counterfeiting," he said.

The outlaw returned to the hotel, and he and Bonney took a private room and ordered "refreshments." As they sat drinking and talking, the door suddenly flew open, and Johnson rushed in, leading a dozen men.

"There are the men! Arrest them!" he cried.

"What's the meaning of this?" exclaimed Bonney.

For answer, they seized him and Fox, and searched them. On Fox they found no weapon, only about fifty dollars in money. But on Bonney they found "a pair of rifle pistols, a bowie knife, a dirk cane, the blank bank notes, and some three hundred dollars in currency."

They were taken to the jail. Fox was to be transported to Indianapolis. Bonney expected to be released, but now encountered a strange misfortune.

When his property was returned to him, Noble, the court clerk said to him, "I've had your money examined. The blank sheets can't be considered counterfeit, since they've never been signed. But we found a ten dollar bill that was pronounced counterfeit by the cashier of the bank."

Bonney gave a start of genuine astonishment and consternation. To be sure, counterfeit currency was common at the time, and he might have acquired this bill accidentally. But he kept wondering if it had been slipped in on him for the purpose of incriminating him. It was to cause him trouble.

Meantime, however, "Judge" Fox was at last in custody, though on a trumped-up charge. Bonney still had to catch Long and Birch.

XXIV.   *Three on the Gallows*

1.

If Bonney expected Fox to "crack" after his arrest and perhaps make a confession, he was disappointed. The outlaw admitted nothing, either then or later.

But now that the head of the gang was in prison, the capture of the others proved unexpectedly easy.

Even before Fox's arrest, a crime of singular horror was committed at Xenia, Ohio, not far east of Dayton. A store was broken into there. Two clerks, who had sleeping accommodations above the salesroom, were murdered when they awoke and in startled alarm began to make inquiries. When the robbery was completed the building was set on fire, and the slain clerks burned with it. The amount of money obtained was never known, but it was not large.

This undoubtedly was the "raise" which Fox had told Bonney was to be made by Birch and John Long, with the help of a man named Royce. One of the pieces of information Fox let fall was where Royce could be found, and Bonney, released from jail on bond, went directly to Ohio.

He found Norton B. Royce, and used his well-worn trick of the "bogus" to introduce himself. Once they were on terms of understanding, Bonney made a startling proposition: that they rob a bank!

"Small raises in the country are poor business," he said. "If this plot succeeds it will make four or five men rich."

Royce listened eagerly—eighty thousand dollars was the promised loot!

Bonney went on, "To carry out the plan will require four or five resolute, skillful and energetic men."

Royce, now avid for his share of such a robbery, suggested as "trustworthy men"—John Long and Robert Birch. They were, he said, traveling under the names of Henderson and Blecher.

Exactly what Bonney had been hoping for!

He enlarged on his plan, to tunnel under the wall of the bank, and "seize all the boxes containing specie and bank notes."

So enthusiastic was Royce, that he forthwith made all arrangements whereby Bonney was to meet Long and Birch and outline his scheme to them. He named the date, three days in advance; and the place, the Railroad House, a hotel at Sandusky, Ohio.

Birch and Long met that appointment: but Bonney did not. He remained at Perrysburg, south of Toledo, where he had Royce placed under arrest. The man was heavily armed and had one counterfeit bill on him, but eventually he was released for lack of direct evidence that he had been involved in the crime at Xenia.

Meantime Birch, who had been betting heavily on horses at a racing meet held at Little Sandusky, went with John Long to the Railroad House. They were standing at the bar when police, acting on Bonney's information, entered.

Upon seeing them Birch's first act was to tear from his vest a gold watch and chain he wore and throw it inside the bar.

The watch was recovered by the officers. It was the one taken from the murdered Colonel Davenport!

The two outlaws, held at the courthouse, refused to talk until presently Bonney arrived.

"What murder are they holding us for?" Long asked him.

"For the murder of Colonel Davenport, at Rock Island," was the reply.

"Rock Island!" exclaimed the outlaw. "I thought we were being charged with the Xenia murder, in Ohio."

Bonney, who as yet had nothing to connect them with the Xenia crime, made no answer.

After a time Long suggested that Bonney might make "a good bit of money" by letting them escape.

"No use, Long," was the reply.

"What are you going to do with us?"

"Take you to Rock Island."

"To be hung, I suppose?"

"Yes, if you're convicted by a jury."

Long began to threaten. "I've got friends along the road. By God you'll lose your own life before you get me there!"

"I'll run that risk," said Bonney shortly.

Later Birch again tried a bribe saying he "could raise ten thousand dollars."

Bonney shook his head.

In returning the men to Rock Island, Bonney was assisted by Sheriff A. Thrift, of Knox County, Ohio, who took turns with him standing guard over the prisoners. The journey was made by a variety of forms of travel.

After first having "properly ironed" the two captured outlaws—confining them by both hands and feet—they were transported by stagecoach from Lower Sandusky to Detroit. At Detroit they took the railroad, the prisoners watched carefully, as far as Marshall, Michigan. Here the officers and their charges transferred once more to a private stagecoach, which carried them to St. Joseph, Michigan, on the shores of Lake Michigan. At St. Joseph they boarded the lake steamboat *Champion,* bound for Chicago. A heavy gale compelled the ship to remain in port at St. Joseph for one full day, an anxious period for Bonney, but one during which the local authorities gave full assistance in guarding the two outlaws. Then came the passage to Chicago over the lake, after which the journey once more was resumed by private stagecoach to Rock Island, where the prisoners were safely lodged.

The reason for the frequent changes of means of travel was to throw off the friends of the bandits who might try to take them away from the officers by force. But the journey, even with these frequent changes, was not without incident.

On the cruise across the lake in the *Champion,* Birch complained of being seasick. He was allowed to go on deck, since he could not escape except by jumping overboard, manacled as he was.

But Birch had a different idea. Presently there were cries on deck, and Bonney leaped up the companionway to find the outlaw smugly smiling. He had managed to slip into the captain's office, took from it Bonney's portmanteau, and threw it overboard.

"I reckon there goes your evidence," he said defiantly.

He was mistaken. The portmanteau contained some of the articles taken from him and Long when they were arrested, but the really vital evidence—the watch, watch-chain, and seal taken from Colonel Davenport—was in Bonney's pockets.

The grin of triumph quickly faded when the outlaw was so informed.

Later, there was a moment of excitement when, in the nighttime, near Little Rock, in northern Illinois, a gang of mounted men rode threateningly up to the stagecoach in which the prisoners were being conducted.

Both Birch and Long, of course, were in irons. "Those are my friends," said Birch. "They've come to rescue us."

Bonney drew his two pistols. "If they try it, I'll shoot you both."

"But you wouldn't kill us!" protested Long, horrified. "We're ironed and can't do anything! We'd not be to blame!"

"None of your friends will try to rescue you, without some sign from you," said Bonney grimly. "If you want to reach Rock Island alive, give no signal that will interfere with me while I'm in discharge of my duty."

No signal was given. The night riders disappeared. The journey continued on until Rock Island—and the jail—were reached.

2.

Bonney remembered Fox's description of Birch as "not to be depended on," and he believed this man might be the possible weak link in the outlaw chain.

Sure enough, on September 28, two days after he was lodged in the Rock Island jail, Birch sent word that he wanted to make a confession. With other witnesses Bonney listened to Birch's story, which was taken down by a stenographer. Later the outlaw made a second confession, to Sheriff Estes, which differed in minor particulars from the first, but the substance of both was as follows:

"The first council for arranging the robbery of Colonel Davenport was held in Joseph Smith's old council chamber in Nauvoo.[1]

"Fox, John and Aaron Long, Jack Redden, [Amos] Hodges, O. P. Rockwell, John Ray, William Louther, myself and several others

[1] Probably the "council chamber" in the Mansion House. It must be remembered that Joseph Smith was dead, and after his death the Mansion House was devoted to other purposes, at one time being a boarding house. Birch's reference to the council chamber is important only because it fixes the plot as originating in Nauvoo.

whose names I don't now recollect were present. I told the boys that
I was opposed to robbing Davenport, as I had been at Rock Island
. . . for the purpose of ascertaining whether Davenport kept any
considerable amount of money by him. I became satisfied by good
authority, that if we should attempt to rob him we should not raise
more than one thousand or fifteen hundred dollars, as I was informed he kept his money in banks . . . The boys disagreed with me.
Fox said Baxter had lived with Davenport, and knew all about his
circumstances, and had told him they would get as much as thirty
or forty thousand dollars. They all thought Baxter knew better about
Davenport's circumstances than I did, and thought it best to rake the
old fellow down . . .

"When we left Old Redden's to go up and rake down old Davenport, we met with [Granville] Young . . . Young wanted to go with
us . . . I did not like his looks, and said to the boys I would not have
him with us . . . Young did not accompany us . . .

"Aaron Long took no part in the murder of Colonel Davenport, he
being left out of doors to keep watch.

"I was present when Colonel Davenport was murdered . . . John
Long was the man who shot Davenport, but the shot was accidental.
There was some defect in the lock of the pistol, and when John cocked
it, it went off, hitting the old man in the knee or thigh. We did not
choke and abuse the old man, as represented, but frequently wet his
face with cold water, as he bled profusely, and fainted several times
from loss of blood. We wanted to keep him alive, to make him tell
where the money was."

In his confession to Estes, Birch contradicted himself about Long's
being the actual murderer. This variation ran as follows:

"Fox and John Long entered the house of Colonel Davenport
through a back window, and commenced searching the house for
money, leaving Aaron outside of the door to keep watch. As they
were passing through a back hall, and about to enter the parlor, Colonel Davenport came into the room from another door. Fox turned to
fly, when John Long cried to him:

"'Take him, Chunky!'

"Fox turning, drew a pistol, and said to Davenport:

"'Stand, sir!'

"At this instant the pistol went off accidentally, and shot Davenport
through the thigh."

This conflict in stories created some doubts at first. Colonel Davenport, on his deathbed, said the man who shot him was "small and slim
and wore a cloth cap." One of the others was "short, thick-set, square-
built."

The first description fitted Fox, but the nickname "Chunky" seemed more appropriate for John Long who was "short, thick-set, and square-built." Colonel Davenport may have been confused as to who actually fired the shot, and Robert Birch might have forgotten.

In the final event, as it turned out, John Long confessed that he was the one who fired that mortal shot; which settled the matter.

This was Edward Bonney's moment of triumph. Almost single-handed he had obtained the evidence which would convict the men who slew that fine old patriarch, Colonel Davenport. Birch had named them, and included others in the crime ring, involving them in hitherto unsolved crimes. His testimony about John Baxter, as the informer, was so direct as to be unanswerable.

It was time to send out the dragnet for others in the plot.

3·

But just at this time—on the very day that Birch made his confession—Bonney received a piece of disheartening information.

William (Judge) Fox had escaped!

The gang chief had eluded the custody of Thomas B. Johnson, the former U.S. marshal, whom Bonney trusted implicitly, eight days before on September 16.

"Upon full examination of the facts connected with this escape," said Bonney with understandable bitterness, "I am satisfied in my own mind that Johnson was bribed by Fox. To say the least of it, he was guilty of gross neglect and culpable misconduct. He violated every pledge he made me, relative to the manner of keeping Fox. He never confined him in jail, as he was instructed to do, but kept him from the time of his arrival at Indianapolis, until he effected his escape, a period of eight days, in an upper room of Browning's Hotel, and placed no other irons on him than a pair of light handcuffs."

Whatever the underlying reasons, or manner of the escape, Fox was gone, a heavy disappointment to Bonney who had risked his life and used his most cunning stratagems to catch the outlaw chief.

Meantime, however, Sheriff Estes of Lee County, Iowa, descended on Old Grant Redden's place on Devil Creek. There he found Old Redden, his son William Harrison Redden, and Granville Young. The three were arrested and at once taken to Rock Island.

An effort was also made to capture Return Jackson Redden, as an accessory to the Davenport murder, but failed because of "the intervention of his Danite friends" in Nauvoo. Redden was himself a Danite, and by February, 1847, had three wives, his No. 3 spouse being a girl sixteen years old. He went with the Mormons to Utah, where he was closely associated with Porter Rockwell and Bill Hickman in the troubled affairs of that territory for the next several years. He lived to be an old man.

The trials of the outlaws began in Rock Island October 6, 1845. First to face the court and jury were John and Aaron Long and Granville Young. The cases of the two Reddens, Birch, and Baxter were postponed, the latter having been arrested in Rock Island.

Witnesses told of finding Colonel Davenport, hearing his dying story, and other circumstances. One interesting bit of information came from a man named David Kirkpatrick, who was in jail for debt where the prisoners were held.

"I overheard several conversations between John Long and Granville Young before Aaron Long was arrested. They said Jack Redden would 'shout' [confess]. Young said, 'We shall all be hanged.' John Long said he was afraid that cowardly Birch would play the devil with them. Young said, 'If Jack Redden is caught he will squeal like a pig.'"

Bonney, as a witness, refused to tell how he worked his way into the confidence of the gang and obtained the arrests, on the ground that there were others still at large and yet to be arrested.

The most important piece of evidence was Birch's sworn confession. With only one hour's delay the jury brought in a verdict of "Guilty" against John Long, Aaron Long, and Granville Young. The condemned men were sentenced to be hanged on the nineteenth day of October, ten days later.

It was afterward told how "John Long, true to the last to his daring character, upon hearing his condemnation, bowed gracefully to the judge, and thanked him, as if receiving a favor."

4.

The outlaws had been bewildered by the unerring pursuit and arrest of their members. Now learning that the alias "Thomas Brown," under which at various times they had known their fellow gangster Robert Birch, had been assumed on different occasions by Edward Bonney, they struck back, using that very name against him for his disadvantage.

First Silas Haight, of Keokuk, Iowa, an agent of the Treasury Department, and therefore supposed to be on the side of the law, visited the prisoners in the Rock Island jail.[2] Instead of attempting to obtain

2 Silas Haight probably was a brother or other close relative of Isaac C. Haight who later was so prominent in the history of the Mormons in Utah, and was eventually excommunicated by that church for his part in the Mountain Meadows

their confessions, he coached them on what they were to say, especially on accusations they were to make against Bonney, "even on the scaffold." Then he went before a grand jury at Fort Madison, Iowa, and through perjured statements made by William A. Hickman and Dr. A. B. Williams, succeeded in having four indictments brought against Bonney.

Three of the indictments were for alleged counterfeiting. The fourth was a charge that it was Bonney, under the name of "Thomas Brown," who actually committed the murders of Miller and Leicy, for which the Hodges brothers were hung.

The strategy of these actions was clever. It will be remembered that at the time of the Miller-Leicy murders, the third member of the trio who did the killing was known as "Thomas Brown" (in reality Robert Birch). Now, the fact that Bonney had at various times assumed this alias to gain his entry into the outlaw ring, was turned menacingly against him. If he were arrested on that charge he must be held in close confinement, without bail, and could not therefore be active against outlaws still at large.

The counterfeiting charges were believed to be good since several persons could swear they had seen Bonney display "bogus" bank notes—in reality his genuine notes, which he used to entrap criminals.

As soon as he heard of the charges, Bonney at once went to Sheriff Estes in Iowa and surrendered. Estes naturally knew he was innocent and refused to put him in prison, though later, at his own request he was held for a time in confinement in Springfield, Illinois, while awaiting his trial.

In the meantime, the charges against him which necessitated his remaining in the nominal custody of Sheriff Estes prevented Bonney from witnessing the execution of the three condemned prisoners.

5.

The hangings took place as scheduled, on October 19, and a contemporary account of the event is grimly interesting.

Each of the three men, standing on the scaffold, addressed the great crowd, which in the fashion of the times had gathered to see them executed. Both Aaron Long and Granville Young protested their in-

---

Massacre. The William A. Hickman who associated with him in these perjuries was the same Bill Hickman who later called himself "Chief of the Danites," and left a sensational autobiography entitled *Brigham's Destroying Angel.* The third member of this trio, Dr. A. B. Williams, was found to be the operator of a printing press for making counterfeit money in Nauvoo.

nocence of the crime: with some technical validity, for Aaron Long
was not in the house when Colonel Davenport was murdered, and
Granville Young was not even in the vicinity, being no more than
an accessory before the fact.

John Long, however, was of different metal. "Doubtless to make
himself the hero of the day, he confessed his guilt [of the actual
murder of Colonel Davenport] and exulted in his criminal career."
After that he asserted that his brother Aaron and Granville Young
were innocent. Next came the sensational part of his speech.

"He charged Bonney with being chief of the gang, and guilty of
murder and various other crimes, and called him by name, expecting, in accordance with his arrangement with Haight, that an officer
would come with a writ for Bonney's arrest."

But Bonney was not present in the crowd. He was in Iowa, where
he had surrendered to Sheriff Estes.

Evidently much disappointed by lack of an action at his words—
which he had agreed with Haight should be the signal for intervention—Long next spoke as if appealing to his friends for rescue: "I've
always been true to you, and my dying request is that all who call
yourselves my friends will make an entry port of Bonney's heart."

The sheriff told him the time for his harangue had expired.

"But so sanguine were his hopes of rescue, or of executive interference, that after his gallows cap was drawn over his face, he raised
it, and looked off in the direction from which he expected the approach of the messenger. Alas, for the doomed murderer, he looked
in vain. An expression of singular despair gathered over his countenance as the cap again fell, and shut out to him the bright and beautiful world forever."

The nooses were adjusted. The trap fell. All three men plummeted
down.

And here occurred a horror.

John Long and Granville Young seemed to die at once, their necks
broken by the hangman's knot. But Aaron Long's rope snapped.

Down plunged the condemned man to the ground. Dazed by the
fall, he was seized by officers and hustled once more up on the scaffold.

While a new rope was being prepared, the cap was removed from
his face and head, allowing him to look at the bodies of his brother and
their accomplice, now swaying dead in the air, and at the crowd
which stared up at him with morbid curiosity.

A clergyman in attendance said to him:

"You see before you the dead bodies of your brother and Young.
They have gone and you must soon follow. You have no hope of escape. If you are guilty, confess your guilt to God!"

Shaken both physically and mentally, Aaron Long, in a trembling voice, acknowledged his participation in the murder, with his brother, Fox and Birch.

A moment later he, too, died as he dropped down through the trap and the noose cut short his life.

Of the three thus executed, two without question were guilty, if not of the immediate act of murder, at least of participation in it as direct accomplices. But the fate of Granville Young seems hard.

He was, at worst, an accessory *before* the fact only because he knew of the plot and did not reveal it to the authorities. But he had no personal part in the murder or robbery. His lawyer made a special plea for him on this point, but the jury voted him guilty with the others. Perhaps it was felt that his long record of other crimes justified the death penalty.

6.

A man far more guilty of the Davenport murder, the treacherous John Baxter, who planned the robbery and furnished the gang with its information, made a confession and asked to be allowed to turn state's evidence. He was found guilty of conspiracy and sentenced to hang, but his sentence later was commuted to life imprisonment.

Incidentally, the question of whether or not he was in the vicinity of the Davenport house when the murder occurred was never settled, probably because Bonney was not present at his particular trial. Who it was that soothed the bulldog in the yard to permit the murderers to enter remains to this day a mystery. But Baxter is the most likely possibility.

William Harrison Redden, who pleaded guilty to being accessory *after* the fact, received only one year in prison, three weeks of it to be in solitary confinement.

Old Grant Redden, at least as guilty as his son and perhaps more so than Granville Young, was released "for want of evidence," and thereupon "made tracks on the Mormon trail for the valley of Salt Lake," where presumably he lived out his life in the shadow of his notorious son, Return Jackson Redden.

Robert Birch, alias Thomas Brown, alias Blecher, alias R. Harris, alias Haines, must have actually commanded the financial resources of which he boasted when he offered Bonney ten thousand dollars to let him go. He obtained a change of venue, then a delay in his trial, and finally, in March, 1847—with outside help or through bribery—escaped from jail at Knoxville, Illinois, and disappeared.

The two worst members of the gang, Fox and Birch, thus evaded punishment. But the country had grown too hot for them, and they left that area forever.

Meantime, through information and evidence furnished by Bonney, lesser members of the gang were swept in by officers. Men like Norton Royce, accomplice of Birch and John Long; Shack Phips, the associate of Fox; three individuals named Bridge, Oliver, and McDole, and others were arrested, and most of them went to prison for greater or lesser terms.

Hiram Long, whom Bonney interviewed in the forest, evidently escaped to Kentucky with Fox and perhaps there met Birch.

Bill Hickman and Dr. Williams eluded arrests by fleeing westward to Utah, and Silas Haight was dismissed from government service, and perhaps followed them.

In his confession Baxter stated that after the stolen Davenport money was taken up from its first hiding place in Old Grant Redden's wheat field, it was reburied by Fox on a bluff on the Des Moines River, south of Redden's place. He gave directions for finding it as told him by Fox. They sound like some old piratical direction to buried treasure:

> At the point where Fox left Birch, to go and bury the money, he made the figure 72, on a large black walnut tree. Seventy-two yards from this tree in a northeast direction is a small black walnut tree with a cross cut in the bark with a bowie knife; fourteen yards from this small tree, due north, is a large stone; midway between the tree and the stone is the spot where the money was buried.

Bonney searched for the place. He discovered on the river bluff a large tree with the "72" carved on it, then the small tree with the cross. The stone was due north as described. Next he discovered evidence of digging, and using a shovel to excavate he actually found three American half dollars, and two Spanish "quarters" (probably pesetas), but nothing else. The rest had been removed, probably by Fox after his escape from Johnson.

The pistol and shotgun taken in the robbery were recovered by the colonel's son, George L. Davenport, and the watch and chain were captured at Birch's arrest. But the money was gone; and more important, so was the life of the fine old colonel.

7.

Judge Brown, who presided at the trial of the Longs and Young, one day received a letter worth quoting:

To the Honorable Judge: If I should use the word honor in connection with a name that is as black in the eyes of the world as the devil himself. You damned old stack of carrion. I find in looking over the news that you have passed sentence on two innocent men, Aaron Long and Granville Young: and I cannot say that John Long was guilty of the crime for which he was hung. True, he was in the crew who killed Davenport; yet, *he* did not kill him. I am the man who shot Davenport; and beware, sir! since things have gone as they have. I'll be damned if you don't share the same fate as the Colonel. The pistol that closed the scene with him, will have the honor of conveying a bullet through your infernal, old empty skull. You cut a figure on a judge's seat. Just take that seat again, and I may be damned if it won't be the last seat you will ever take. I carry a six-barrel revolver next my heart, and I carry her henceforth for your special benefit—together with the hell bound jury. You may inform the gentlemen, for well I know them; and if their blood don't atone for the execution of my friends—the Longs and Young—may I be damned. So, look out; for by the time this letter reaches you, I will be close behind.

I am the commander of a company which will, for one blast from my bugle, be at my side; they are true to their cause, and never pull a trigger but what she counts. And this man, Bonney, will come up missing when least expected. I knew where the chap was on the 19th of October [the day Young and the Longs were executed]; he knew it best to be absent on that day; and well the pup knows me, and intimately, too. You can inform him that he will see me again and only *once* more; then I am inclined to think his eyesight will fail.

And now to the citizens of Rock Island: Your rights can never be protected while such a judge is permitted to sit upon the bench; but I shall soon put you to the trouble of selecting another one.

The letter was unsigned, but it certainly was written by William (Judge) Fox, his last braggadocio. His claim that he fired the shot that killed Davenport was to throw doubt on the justice of the convictions of the others. It was a false claim, because in his death speech John Long stated flatly that he was the guilty one. The envelope was postmarked Columbia, Adair County, Kentucky.

Adair County! A locality with terrible events in its records. It was in Adair County, near Columbia, that the Harpes murdered Johnny Trabue. Not far away they slew Dooley. Close to Russell Springs, at one time a part of the county, dwelt "Old Man" Roberts, said to be the father of two of the Harpe women, who sometimes gave hospitality to them and their ghoulish consorts. In the same general area Samuel Mason lived for a time before entering on his career as a criminal leader along the Ohio River. In Adair County John Leiper, who mortally wounded Micajah Harpe, lived before moving north where the final hunt for the outlaw took place. Later, in the days following the Civil War, this same area would be a favorite lurking ground for outlaws and in the county seat of Adair County, Columbia, the bank would be robbed, and R. A. C. Martin, cashier, killed by the two James and three Younger brothers.

From this county, at that time still wild, Fox wrote his threats to Judge Brown. But he never made good on them. Instead, he disappeared from view, as did Birch, Hiram Long, and others who had once defied the laws in the upper Mississippi country. Where did they go? Fox and Birch were self-styled Mormons. Perhaps they fled west to Utah. Or they might have gone down into Texas, where one hopes the ever-ready regulators in that still somewhat turbulent state took care of them.

8.

What of Edward Bonney who sent five of the outlaw gang to the gallows, put several in prison, and caused the others to flee from the upper Mississippi valley?

He presumably received various bounty moneys, but these sums totaled no more than a thousand dollars, and he must have been out of pocket more than he could have received in his six months of traveling, riding steamboats and stagecoaches, hiring or purchasing horses, and maintaining himself.

He stood trial on the various charges brought against him by the gang, and was acquitted. But when a new charge of counterfeiting was brought in Illinois, he voluntarily went to Springfield, conferred with Governor Ford, and then surrendered to the U.S. marshal, insisting on remaining in prison for some weeks, refusing bail.

When his case was called for trial, December 29, 1846, he was cleared and his vindication was so complete that ten of his jurors signed a communication to the Secretary of the Treasury, requesting the dismissal of Haight, which accordingly was done.

Governor Thomas Ford wrote and signed a certificate stating that he attended Bonney's trial, heard the evidence, and "was fully persuaded . . . that the prosecution was put on foot, as far as Haight and the other witnesses against Bonney were concerned, to be revenged on him for ferreting out and bringing to punishment the murderers of Colonel Davenport. And for the further object of stopping Bonney from pursuing the residue of said murderers, then yet at large."

Bonney's health was wrecked by his long pursuit under every condition of hardship, inclement weather, weariness, danger and unwholesome food; and he was accused of many deceits and illegal acts by his enemies. But he acted as he thought the necessities of the situation demanded. Wrote he:

> I believe that the circumstances justified the deceit I adopted [to capture the criminals], I felt compelled to meet the gang with their own weapons, and had I followed the stern tenets of a high morality, the scaffold and jail would have been without their just appendages.

Poorer in health and wealth, it is nevertheless pretty sure that he obtained a mighty satisfaction from his exploits. His great reward, and the sole reason why he undertook his perilous adventures, was the successful conclusion of his hunt for the outlaws. He was, without question, a bloodhound of a man, who would follow a trail to the death, and even relished the problems and perils of the pursuit, provided he brought his criminal quarry at last to justice. There are, and fortunately always will be, such men on the side of the law.

Some years later he wrote a book, *The Banditti of the Prairies,* describing his experiences. It is now very scarce and hard to find. Other than this he has no monument except that through his personal courage and determination the deadly interlocking gang of criminals which for so long had things its own way, was dispersed and routed; and for a time at least Illinois, Iowa, and Ohio had relative peace from the ravages of murderers and outlaws.

Bibliography, Evaluated

The literature covering this period and the subject particularly of outlawry, is quite extensive; but much of it is long out of print and available only to the researcher who has the time, interest and facilities which will enable him to examine old and rare volumes, newspapers, and manuscripts. Nevertheless, I will here attempt to list some of the sources which I have found most helpful, with indications of their scope and field.

American Guide Series: *Tennessee, Arkansas, Ohio, Indiana, Illinois, Iowa, Mississippi,* and *Missouri.* Produced by the government Writer's Project, some of these books are fairly good, but others are too patently angled to the chambers of commerce to contain much except material to which those bodies can "point with pride."

Asbury, Herbert, *The French Quarter,* New York, 1946. A specialist in the study of sinful places (*The Barbary Coast, The Gangs of New York,* and others), Asbury does his usual able and entertaining job of describing the bordello sections of New Orleans. His book contains some brief mention of outlaws up the river, but is chiefly concerned with the heyday of vice in New Orleans, including sketches of a number of the more famous *filles de joie.*

Audubon, John James, *Delineations of American Scenery and Character,* edited by Francis H. Herrick, New York, 1922. A collection of the great naturalist-adventurer's writings describing the frontier life and the peoples he knew so well.

Beadle, J. H., *Polygamy, or the Mysteries and Crimes of Mormonism,* Philadelphia, 1904. In spite of the sensational title and the author's frank anti-Mormonism, this book is fairly accurate concerning events in the Nauvoo era. Of value is a statement contained, given by Governor Thomas Ford, from the viewpoint of a much harried chief executive in the State of Illinois during the troublous period.

Birney, Hoffman, and Kelly, Charles, *Holy Murder,* New York, 1934. A closely studied biography of the greatest (or worst) of the Mormon Danites, Porter Rockwell; describing also the bloody activities of other members of that body, including Bill Hickman and Return Jackson Redden; and mentioning Bonney's role in running down the murderers of Miller, Leicy, and Colonel Davenport.

Bogart, W. H., *Daniel Boone and the Hunters of America,* Philadelphia, 1876. History of the early "long hunters" containing some interesting and little-known episodes.

Bonney, Edward, *The Banditti of the Prairies,* Chicago, 1850. Not well written, since the author was an amateur in letters, it nevertheless is a full account of Bonney's adventures and experiences in running to earth the chief members of the gang that at one time terrorized the upper Mississippi valley. Contains also the trial jury's resolutions concerning his good efforts and a certificate of high character and gratitude for his services, signed by Governor Thomas Ford.

Brazeale, J. W. M., *Life As It Is,* Knoxville, Tennessee, 1842. Account of early Kentucky, including the activities of the Harpes and other outlaws, by a man who was in the country and knew the circumstances.

Burroughs, Stephen, *Memoirs of Stephen Burroughs,* New York, 1942 (republication). Recollections of a scamp who continually got into trouble and was exceedingly sorry for himself. Notable as a record of brutal treatment in prisons at the early part of the nineteenth century.

Cannon, George Q., *The Life of Joseph Smith, the Martyr,* Salt Lake City, 1888. A Mormon version of the career of that strange man.

Cartwright, Peter, *Autobiography of a Backwoods Preacher,* edited by William Strickland, New York, 1856. Story of one of the most famous, fearless, cantankerous, and powerful revivalists of the early frontier.

Clark, Janice, articles concerning John A. Murrell, published in the Crossett, Arkansas, *News-Reporter.*

Clark, Thomas D., *The Rampaging Frontier,* Indianapolis, 1939. Highly interesting and well-documented general survey of the forest frontier, including some of its humor, its customs, and descriptions of its rough life.

Coates, Robert M., *The Outlaw Years,* New York, 1930. Coates levies freely on tradition, and does not deal with some of the outlaws of the era. But his is beyond comparison the best-written book on the subject of those river and land pirates with whom he concerns himself.

Collins, Lewis, *Historical Sketches of Kentucky,* Cincinnati, 1847. Episodic, but with some interesting details of the Harpes, including one of the most connected versions of the Stegall murders and the final pursuit and death of Micajah Harpe.

Connelly, W. E., and Coulter, E. M., *History of Kentucky,* five volumes, Chicago, 1922. A rather standard history of the state.

Croswell, Colonel Ken and Mrs. Daphne, manuscript and source materials on the Murrell legends, particularly in Arkansas.

Daniels, Jonathan, *The Devil's Backbone*, New York, 1962. Well-done volume in the American Trails Series, concerned particularly with Natchez and the Natchez Trace.

Devens, R. M., *Our First Century, Great and Memorable Events*, Chicago, 1877. A curious and interesting volume reciting events considered outstanding from 1776 to 1876, ranging all the way from a "dark day" which frightened the superstitious, and the appearance of a "sea serpent," to great battles and one of the best descriptions of the terrible earthquake of 1811. It includes an account of the Mormon faith and some of the vicissitudes the sect encountered.

Dictionary of American History, edited by James Truslow Adams, five volumes and index, New York, 1940. A convenient reference for events in American history, arranged alphabetically, and written by authorities on their various topics.

Doty, Silas, *The Life of Sile Doty*, Toledo, 1888. Adventures of a thief and murderer, who had connections with several criminal rings, including the great one established by Murrell.

Dowdey, Clifford, *The Land They Fought For*, New York, 1955. A volume in the celebrated Mainstream of America Series, this book describes the Civil War from the standpoint of the Southern Confederacy. Of interest is the account it gives of the Nat Turner slave revolt of 1831, showing why there was deep fear of further uprisings of Negroes, such as that planned by Murrell.

Dunbar, Seymour, *A History of Travel in America*, four volumes, Indianapolis, 1915. It would be difficult to overstate the value of this work to the student of travel in America up to the advent of air transportation. Types of vehicles, water craft, rivers, canals, roads, manners and modes of the people, public houses, and natural and man-made obstacles, all are dealt with by a very thorough researcher and historian. This book, now unfortunately out of print, richly deserves republication.

Finley, Alexander C., *History of Russellville and Logan County*, pamphlet form, Russellville, Kentucky, 1878. Local history of interest but without documentation. Nevertheless, this account fills some gaps in the careers of the early outlaws.

Gard, Wayne, *Frontier Justice*, Norman, Oklahoma, 1949. Thoroughly studied and eminently readable account of the events, causes, and public feeling behind extralegal law-enforcement by vigilantes and regulators, written by a highly respected historian.

Hackett, W. M., Little Rock, Arkansas, correspondence, locating the area of Murrell's "Garden of Eden," and other valuable details concerning that bandit chief.

Hall, Judge James, *Letters from the West*, London, 1829; also

Story of the Harpes, in *Port Folio,* a magazine, Philadelphia, 1824 and 1825. These writings by Judge Hall represent his personal observations and best beliefs concerning the Harpes, their deeds and deaths.

Hollinshead, Margaret B., Nashville, Tennessee, correspondence establishing the place of Murrell's burial and circumstances of his last days.

Howard, H. R., *The History of Virgil A. Stewart, and His Adventures in Exposing the Great "Western Land Pirate,"* New York, 1836. An amplification of Stewart's original published account of his experiences in exposing the Murrell conspiracy, both before and after the arrest of the arch-bandit. Particularly valuable because it contains affidavits and sworn statements by many persons verifying the truth of Stewart's extraordinary account; and including a history, not in Stewart's original story, of the attempt, fortunately defeated, by leaders of Murrell's outlaws to carry out his plan in spite of his incarceration, documented with public records, correspondence, and newspaper articles at the time.

Kane, Harnett, *Natchez on the Mississippi,* New York, 1947. Always eminently worth reading, Kane here gives a delightful history of Natchez, its great families chiefly, but including some discursions along the Natchez Trace and a look at its dangerous freebooters including the Harpes, Mason and Murrell.

Keating, J. M., *History of the City of Memphis and Shelby County,* Syracuse, New York, 1888. Recollections of the early history of eastern Tennessee by the famous editor of the Memphis *Appeal,* with perhaps a shade of cynicism permissible in an old journalist.

Lowry, Robert, and McCardle, William H., *History of Mississippi,* Jackson, Mississippi, 1891. Pedestrian but fairly thorough history of the state up to 1890.

Marshall, Paul, *John A. Murrell and Daniel Crenshaw,* article in *Tennessee Historical Magazine,* April, 1920.

McKnight, Charles, *Our Western Border,* Philadelphia, 1879. Contains many adventures along the river ways, including two of John James Audubon's, and relates Samuel Mason's early brave services in the Revolutionary army against the Indians, together with descriptions of boating life and overland travel to the forest frontier.

Monette, John W., *History of the Discovery and Settlement of the Valley of the Mississippi,* New York, 1848. Considerable attention is paid to the careers and deaths of Samuel Mason and other outlaws in this book written when recollections of these episodes were still fairly fresh.

New Doane Book, The, publication of the Bucks County Historical

Society, Doylestown, Pennsylvania, 1952. Interesting because it describes the origin of counterfeiting on a large scale as a war measure by the British during the American Revolution, and also the activities of a family of Tories, turned bandit, during and after that conflict.

O'Callaghan, Sean, *The Slave Trade Today*, New York, 1961. If anyone thinks that slavery has been abolished all over the world he is due for some blood-chilling revelations in this book concerning *contemporary* slavery in certain African countries, such as Abyssinia, the Congo, Egypt, and the Sudan, and certain Arabic countries such as Yemen and Saudi Arabia.

Palmer, Frederick, *Clark of the Ohio*, New York, 1929. Mention of Samuel Mason and his brothers, and also John Duff, in connection with the Vincennes expedition of 1778, though with no specific description of Mason's activities during that campaign.

Patton, Dr. James W., Director Southern Historical Collection, Chapel Hill, North Carolina, letter concerning final days and death of Murrell after his release from the penitentiary.

Phares, Ross, *Reverend Devil*, New Orleans, 1941. A worthwhile book-length biography of John A. Murrell, including the account of the abortive effort by the Mystic Clan in Mississippi after the leader's imprisonment, together with interesting legends of hidden treasure believed to have been left by Murrell and perhaps others.

Rascoe, Burton, *Belle Starr, the Bandit Queen*, New York, 1941. Some mention of Murrell, but attempts to discredit his story as an "invention" of the *National Police Gazette*—which it assuredly was not.

Robison, Dr. Dan M., Tennessee State Librarian and Archivist, Nashville, Tennessee, letter concerning final disposition of Murrell's body, and citing valuable sources.

Rothert, Otto A., *The Outlaws of Cave-in-Rock*, Cleveland, 1924. This book, carefully and thoroughly researched, is by far the most valuable reference work on the river outlaws up to, but not including, the Murrell days or thereafter. Connects the Ford's Ferry gang as a possible link with the Murrell Clan through the person of Henry C. Shouse, James Ford's lieutenant, who visited the Murrell headquarters in Arkansas, and prior to his execution for murder, left a list of accomplices, which however was destroyed without being published.

Russell, Charles Edward, *A-Rafting on the Mississip'*, New York, 1928. Interesting account of the loggers who floated their rafts of lumber down the river. Contains a version of Bonney's adventures in capturing the murderers of Colonel George Davenport and the slayers of Miller and Leicy.

Smith, T. Marshall, *Legends of the War of Independence*, Louisville, 1855. Romantic and with its chronology badly scrambled, it nevertheless has some accounts concerning the Harpes that have the ring of truth—so much so that as careful a historian as Otto A. Rothert has quoted it. The author claims to have interviewed the Harpe women personally after they were captured.

Sonnichsen, Dr. C. L., *Ten Texas Feuds*, Albuquerque, New Mexico, 1957. A careful historian directly connects the rise in outlawry on the eastern Texas border with the breakup of the Murrell conspiracy in 1834–35, and the resultant flight of many outlaws to the Sabine region.

Thorp, Raymond W., *Bowie Knife*, Albuquerque, New Mexico, 1948. A collector and expert on bowie knives, gives a concise but well-studied biography of James Bowie, including a full account of his duel with Bloody Jack Sturdevant.

Twain, Mark, *Life on the Mississippi*, 1883. One of America's most beloved authors comments on Murrell in a way which reflects the manner in which the memory of that great outlaw remained green fifty years after his career ended.

Wellman, Manly Wade, Chapel Hill, North Carolina, correspondence, research, many valuable contributions to this book.

Index

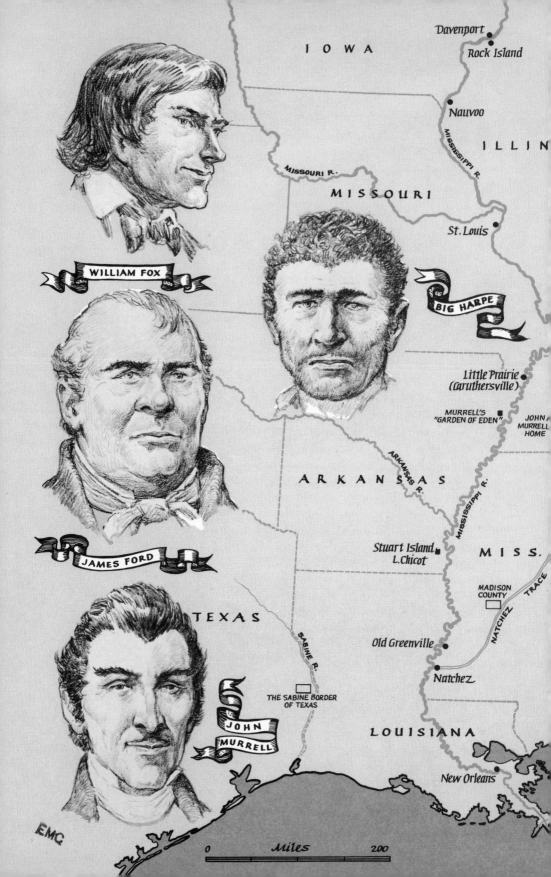

IOWA

Davenport

Rock Island

Nauvoo

MISSISSIPPI R.

ILLIN

MISSOURI R.

MISSOURI

St. Louis

WILLIAM FOX

BIG HARPE

Little Prairie
(Caruthersville)

MURRELL'S
"GARDEN OF EDEN"

JOHN
MURRELL
HOME

ARKANSAS R.

ARKANSAS

MISSISSIPPI R.

JAMES FORD

Stuart Island
L. Chicot

MISS.

MADISON
COUNTY

NATCHEZ
TRACE

TEXAS

SABINE R.

Old Greenville

Natchez

THE SABINE BORDER
OF TEXAS

JOHN
MURRELL

LOUISIANA

New Orleans

EMG

0   Miles   200